GAVIN FARINGDON –
PORTRAIT OF A REBEL PEER

GAVIN FARINGDON – PORTRAIT OF A REBEL PEER

Roger Vlitos

First published in 2022 by Libri Publishing

The right of Roger Vlitos to be identified as the author of this work has been asserted in accordance with the Copyright, Designs and Patents Act, 1988.

Hardback ISBN: 978-1-911450-46-7

Paperback ISBN: 978-1-911450-45-0

A CIP catalogue record for this book is available from The British Library

Design by Carnegie Book Production

Printed in the UK by Halstan

Libri Publishing
Brunel House
Volunteer Way
Faringdon
Oxfordshire
SN7 7YR

Tel: +44 (0)845 873 3837

www.libripublishing.co.uk

Contents

Foreword

*"I think that on the whole it is better to wash one's dirty linen in public.
It shows that when one's linen is dirty one is prepared to wash it,
and that seems to me really the important thing. It is all
the difference between a democratic country
and the totalitarian countries."*

the 2nd Lord Faringdon. Hansard Vol 118: 5th March 1941.

Introduction

Some years ago, my employer, the 3rd Lord Faringdon, asked me if I could find time to do him a favour. This was to go up to a room on the top floor of the Georgian mansion where I worked as his curator and delve through the stack of boxes filled with papers belonging to his late uncle, the 2nd Lord Faringdon. Mine was a relatively new appointment, but I had already found that it was part of my employer's customary charm to *ask* if I would *find* time to do this, rather than *tell* me – to *make* time to do it. I was keen take on this unexpected task – especially as it would allow me to browse through mysterious boxes in a room that few ever entered. On the way up there, he suggested that I stop addressing him by his title and use his first name instead.

Charles Faringdon accompanied me to the room and showed how he had started sorting the papers into a modern filing system. As everything had to be read and identified he set me up with a desk and chair before leaving. Then he returned with a fine old lamp, which proved useful once he had rewired it himself. While doing this he warned me that I would get a bit dusty doing the work. This turned out to be because the papers lay in stratum, each with a thin layer of dust dating back to the decade it had been placed in its box. When I came down a few hours later Lady Faringdon drew me aside and explained that she was glad I was to take on this task because whenever her husband went up there it meant he would disappear for hours and return dusty. The same was to happen with me – it was difficult to leave that "jigsaw puzzle" upstairs in pieces.

He was interested in papers relating to his uncle's "Setting the Thames on Fire" in the 1927; a Rolls-Royce driven to the Republican front during the Spanish Civil War in 1937 (this had been converted into an ambulance and driven back riddled with shrapnel and bullet holes); his pacifist uncle's service as a fire-fighter during the London Blitz in WW2; and finally, to find out about a Renaissance palace his uncle was rumoured to have purchased in Malta. No one could have made all this up. I had other work to do but returned to my new task when I could, and gradually uncovered significant details about these subjects. Then I wrote up my findings and went through them with him. After a while, these research notes began to look like the building blocks of a biography. This seemed likely to be of interest to readers of novels by Nancy Mitford or Evelyn Waugh – for the 2nd Lord Faringdon had been part of their circle. It also looked like it would appeal to people interested in colonial history, as he had spent much time on the subcontinent where he stayed with Lord Irwin at the Viceroy's palace in New Delhi, met Nawabs, Indian princes, princesses and politicians, and had interviewed Mahatma Gandhi. What was buried in those boxes were stories of a life lived more fully than most.

The Honourable Gavin Henderson, the 2nd Lord Faringdon from 1934, had been born into a privileged echelon of Edwardian England and become one of the wealthiest young men of his generation. As a boy he was seen as bright but lazy. His family and tutors attributed his frequent periods of apathy to recurrent health problems. Still, he was a good student and got into Oxford in the early 1920s – one of the most legendary times to be there for frivolity and fun. After a bibulous phase as one of the "Bright Young Things", he suddenly developed passionate political beliefs. Now he was seen as rebellious, idealistic and headstrong. Perhaps the circumstances of his childhood had suppressed a latent personality. Whatever the reason, he developed into a fervent pacifist and socialist. After he came into his inheritance, he began to give much of it away in the hope of making the world a better place. A journalist friend, who thought this might be a phase, wrote that he was had "turned from purple to pink". Less friendly political hacks, and some of his mother's cohorts, were to claim that he was a "Red" and a "traitor to his class". He was highly cultured and a fine orator, but some whispered that he was "not as other men". This may have been not a compliment but a reference to his homosexuality – which remained a criminal offence for most of his lifetime. Prejudice against this and his left-wing views resulted in his being denigrated in print. "Mud sticks", as they say, and it is surprising how much still clings when his name appears today on internet sources. However, my research revealed him to be a private man with a public face – indeed, someone whose many contradictions formed a unique character. Perhaps the simplest way to describe him is as someone for whom a kind heart meant more than a coronet. As his nephew put it, "He always thought with his heart and not his head."

Over the years I found myself referring to him as Gavin – as his friends had. I did not know much about him when I started, apart from the fact that he had been a close friend of the travel writer Robert Byron. So, it seemed like serendipity when the first letter I came across was from 'Robert'. That envelope included a letter Byron had been asked to pass on to Gavin from an intrepid woman who described her trek to Tibet in 1930. This was Thyra Weir, wife of Lt.-Col Weir, the Resident of Sikkim. Research revealed that she was Joanna Lumley's grandmother. That tale was anecdotal but well written and worth passing on. Similarly, other connections worth reading about were disclosed in letters from General Dwight D. Eisenhower, Leon Trotsky, John and Penelope Betjeman, Cyril Connolly, W. Somerset Maughan, E. M. Forster, Peter Rodd, Bryan and Diana Guinness, Evelyn Waugh and Nancy Cunard. In addition, in those boxes there were facts about the refugees from fascist Europe Gavin had supported. To this could be added information gleaned from the stacks of newspaper clippings his secretary had compiled, as well as significant details from Gavin's diaries. A personal landscape of sorts could be glimpsed in the first editions of books by his friends and influencers on the shelves in Buscot Park's library. This growing sense of his time was enhanced by signatures in the visitors' books and detailed entries in the housekeeper's accounts. Another room at Buscot Park was lined with copies of Hansard where one could find a complete record of all Gavin's speeches, questions and contributions to debates in the Upper House. I extracted what seemed relevant and compiled it all into chapters for Charles Faringdon to read. He did so, made corrections and comments, and then returned them to me. Happily, he always ended with the remark: "Well done. Keep going."

Over the years I converted some of this material into public lectures. These proved popular in the theatre at Buscot Park, with the University of the 3rd Age, Marlborough College Summer School, and the Wantage Literary festival. But some subjects were too complex to be condensed into a lecture, and others begged questions. For example, an enigmatic letter and covert photographs of a military parade in Red Square sent to Gavin by a former butler during Stalin's "great terror". This resists interpretation as it belongs to the ambiguous looking-glass world of pre-war espionage. More revealing were Gavin's letters from Military chiefs and Whitehall mandarins during WW2. These concerned losses of RAF crew flying obsolete aircraft; incarceration of refugees as 'Enemy Aliens'; persecution of conscientious objectors; recognition of combat fatigue in servicemen; improved pensions for war widows; and the execution of Allied servicemen under martial law. Whilst all these issues were prompted by social conscience, they came during wartime when the orthodox belief was that everyone should stick together. Socratic questions, however well intentioned, exposed weakness and were widely perceived to be "bad for morale". Gavin's tenaciousness was admirable, but it lost him vital support in parliament and resulted in his being side-lined by Attlee's Labour government in 1945. In spite of this setback, Gavin had the moral courage to raise humanitarian issues that challenged the Colonial Office. For example, corporal punishment by flogging of African soldiers carried out by European officers – he regarded this as barbaric, shameful, and hushed up. It was largely thanks to his dogged persistence that this subject was aired and then abolished.

I would like to thank the historian Dr Alison McClean of Bristol University for her invaluable assistance over the years. She started by helping to interpret the artist Viscount "Jack" Hastings' frescoes at Buscot Park; went on to help explain Gavin's activity during the Spanish Civil War; and then advised about Gavin's relations with the major Labour Party figures who came to stay with him at Buscot Park. Her understanding was such that once, when we were going though newspaper reports of Gavin's political speeches, she leapt up and punched the air crying, "What a man!" Alison and I shared a fascination with Gavin's closest female friend, someone who (perhaps unfairly) remains an unsung feminist heroine, Lady Ankaret Cecilia Howard Jackson. Known as "Susu" to her friends and family, she was the first woman barrister in England, a writer and broadcaster, and like Gavin, a free-spirited, one-off, upper-class rebel. The daughter of Rhoda, Countess of Carlisle (L'Estrange), the nickname Susu came from her inability as a child to pronounce her middle names Cecilia Caroline. She wore trousers in public long before Marlene Dietrich made them fashionable. She had an "open" marriage, three children, smoked a pipe, and was one of the first Bright Young Things to get bored with the round of drunken all-night parties. Her letters give hilarious accounts of aristocratic country houses where some of what she called "the old firm" came for the weekend. At one, she and her bosom friend Rosa Lewis (aka "The Duchess of Duke St"), escaped to hunt in local antique shops for curios that Rosa used to decorate her eccentric Cavendish Hotel in Piccadilly. Susu loved fell-walking and horses. She died after a riding accident in Cumbria. Gavin's world seems to have grown smaller and less round without her. I am grateful to Tarn Bailey – Gavin's god-daughter – for generously sharing information about Susu, her mother.

Finally, as everything that appears here has been shared by my employer, Charles Faringdon, I want to say how grateful I am for the privilege and experience; and to apologise in advance for anything I may have misconstrued. I imagine that his uncle Gavin would have laughed that off or ignored it. He was good at that, as you will see.

Roger Vlitos
March 2021

Gavin Faringdon – Portrait of a Rebel Peer

A biography of Gavin Henderson, the 2nd Baron Faringdon.

Based on the unpublished diaries, letters and documents in his former home Buscot Park, by its curator and archivist Roger Vlitos.

CHAPTER 1

"An Unusual Boy"

In 1954 Gavin Henderson, the 2nd Lord Faringdon, a wealthy, unmarried, Labour Party activist, art connoisseur and pacifist, received a letter from someone he had not seen for over forty years:

> "This does not require an answer, but I think you will be amused to know that I have some green ornaments with penguins painted on their sides which you gave me after you had made up your mind to marry me. When I told you that your father would probably not approve, you asked him about it at bedtime."

Gavin's father was Captain, the Hon. H.G. Henderson, adjutant of the Berkshire Yeomanry, an MP as well as heir apparent of the financier Lord Faringdon. Gavin's mother was Lady Violet Dalzell, daughter of the Earl of Carnwath. This fortune-favoured couple probably had their own ideas about who might be a suitable match for their first-born son. As his former nursery maid knew, she would never be one such. But it is surprising to read that Captain Henderson replied

> "Yes Sonny, you certainly can marry Margaret when you grow up and I shall be quite willing."

And so, her letter went on

> "After your father had expressed his approval of this unsuitable match you began to buy things for 'our home',

*but your pocket money would only allow of an occasional
purchase. Still, you did your best. One was a glass butter
dish with cover, which you said would do for salad, and
several more things which were lost in my travels, but the two
ornaments have come safely through."*

Harold Henderson's response might have been just one of a father
indulging his son's whim – a pragmatic move taken to get a child
off to sleep. But as one seldom reads of Edwardian fathers visiting
their offspring in nurseries, it suggests a special bond between them.
This was probably due to the fact that both had suffered debili-
tating health problems. Over the years to come, in spite of their very
different characters, this father often displayed affection for a son he
called "unusual".

As a child, Gavin's weak constitution had consequences frequently
mentioned in school reports. At the age of 12, his Eton housemaster
described him as

*"Capable and sound in all subjects but much handicapped
by absence…Indisposition has hindered his work…If you
take into account the various disabilities under which he has
laboured, I think that you will agree that his marks in his
trials are much to his credit…"*

This pattern of behavior was repeated over the years. The boy was
clever but had bouts of "lethargy" which led some to call him "lazy".
However, a more perspicacious view of him came in a school report
written when he was 14 years old:

*"I do not suppose that he finds any of the work makes much
demands on his powers. His lack of energy is as much
physical as mental. He is a gentle, intelligent boy, with plenty
to say for himself, and a wide range of interest."*

By then it was clear that being excused from games had led Gavin to
read more widely than most of his contemporaries. A private tutor

reported that Gavin devoured books on the Classical, Renaissance, Baroque and Rococo periods, before becoming keen on writers and artists of the aesthetic movement. The latter, this tutor suggested, may have led him to pose as aloof and impeccably bored. Which helps explain why during his teenaged years he was also prone to "play the fool in class".

In contrast, Gavin's father had robust health as a boy, and never lapsed into torpidity like his son. Harold became a cadet in the militia at the age of 16 and a Lieutenant in the Household Cavalry at 18. He prospered in the Life Guards until he led a squadron in the Boer War from 1889-1900. There, months of arduous campaigning resulted in the loss of four cavalry chargers due to overwork. He wrote home asking his father to keep his "eyes open for long-tailed black horses" – the kind used by the Household Cavalry – "as I fear ours will not be gone after this war". Patrols and picketing reduced his belt's girth by "6 holes". Bouts of gastroenteritis and dysentery weakened him until, as he described it in a letter to his sister, "I have entirely lost the use of my right leg, it has all swollen up and they tell me I shan't be able to walk for some weeks." This was diagnosed in the field as phlebitis – inflammation of a vein due to repetitive strain. Harold's physical condition, weakened by campaigning in the field, had exacerbated a condition commonly known as "Housemaid's knee". Clotted veins in his leg burst and the internal haemorrhaging was severe, so the ward sister wrote his letters home for him. Then he collapsed into a coma and his doctors expected he would "soon go skywards". After being bed-ridden for "45 days with no prospect of walking" he was able to report an improvement as "veins less swollen, the boils gradually come to head". But he was to remain in hospital for eleven months, after which time photographs of him show a gaunt man who had lost six stone in weight, carrying a walking stick.

Harold was invalided home and recuperated. Promoted to Captain, he returned to active duty at Knightsbridge and Windsor barracks. But few knew that the straight-backed guardsman astride a big black horse was hiding constant pain. He confided this to his future wife, writing that sometimes his leg swelled so large that it was difficult for him to get out of his uniform at the end of a day. By the time he retired in 1902 brother officers had nicknamed him "Hoppy". He was to have further physical collapses before he died in 1922 twelve years before his own father.

In spite of this common ground of shaky health, there were clear differences of outlook between father and son from an early age. These can be seen in photographs taken when each was aged around 12. For example, Harold appears as the youngest member of a shooting party at Lord Faringdon's country seat, Buscot Park. His head is barely chest-level with his father, uncles and other guests, but he holds a shotgun upright and looks as eager to get going as the retrieving dogs crouching nearby. Gavin, on the other hand, posed on his grandfather's grouse moor at Glenalmond, Perthshire, looks like he would have been happier indoors. Lord Faringdon stands like a jaunty sportsman in a tweed cap and plus-fours, his jacket collar turned up against the wind. Below him Gavin lounges on a bed of heather. He wears a mackintosh over his tweed plus-four suit and his leather cartridge bag has been left far to his right and his shotgun lies well to his left – as though he was mentally and physically detached from them. He was never to fully engage in field sports, which the rest of his family saw as a social event; and after he inherited Buscot Park he banned hunting in 1936, only to reinstate it after wartime rationing made game an essential food resource.

Soon after their marriage, Captain Harold and Lady Violet moved to what promised to be a rural idyll in Berkshire. Their new home was situated conveniently seven miles from Lord Faringdon's Buscot Park estate, one and a half miles from Faringdon town, six from Wantage, and twelve from Abingdon, where Harold became a Liberal and Unionist MP like his father. It had everything a country gentleman could desire – apart from a river to fish in. However, Lord Faringdon owned a long stretch of land with a boathouse (previously lent to William Morris) beside the upper Thames nine miles away at

Kelmscott. An estate agent in Mayfair gave the particulars of their new home as:

> "The Kitemore and Shellingford Estate comprising The
> Modern Elizabethan Mansion with 19 bed and dressing
> rooms, and a fine suite of reception rooms. Electric light.
> Up-to-date Sanitation. Good water supply. Southern aspect.
> Inexpensive pretty gardens, enjoying magnificent Views across
> the Vale to the Downs in the distance. Home Farmery and
> Stabling with about 180 acres or including a fine farm of 207
> acres."

With the above came six farms ranging in size from 322 to 205 acres (over 1,700 acres of prime grassland) and:

> "Virtually the whole of Shellingford Village and Parish is
> included in the sale, which comprises 22 cottages, the majority of
> which are of modern stone construction, after the Tudor style."

The couple settled in and produced four children over the next 12 years – Gavin, Margaret, Michael and Roderic. Here they and their growing family were immersed in country pursuits, bred horses, livestock and pedigree dogs. Apart from Gavin, everyone in the family rode or hunted as their estate lay in the most favoured area of the Old Berks Hunt and within easy reach of the best meets of the Vale of the White Horse. Harold was promoted to Lt.-Colonel of the Berkshire Yeomanry, a respected regiment in the territorial army. Its officers were largely drawn from the hunting fraternity. Kitemore's visitors' book shows signatures of the country gentry from the big houses and estates around local towns around, such as Wantage, Fairford and Abingdon. Scions of notable families, such as the Pleydon-Bouveries from Coleshill near Buscot appear. Friends from further afield came to stay, such as Harold MacMillan, the future Conservative Prime Minister. From time to time, pages were devoted to the officer staff of the Berkshire Yeomanry on training exercises. Several are headed with the signature of its commander Brig-General William

Pakenham, 5th Earl Lord Longford. He was the father of the Labour Party peer and social reformer "Frank" Longford, and grandfather of historian Lady Antonia Fraser. Three of Harold's younger brothers were Yeomanry captains, as was their brother-in-law "Jack" Wigan, who outshone them all by being awarded a V.C. in WW1. Lady Violet kept photos of many of these officers astride splendid chargers with regimental "jowl plumes" hanging from their bridles. She and her sons might well have seen them as reincarnations of the knights of old, ready to fight for God, King, Country and Empire.

Gavin would meet them all at Kitemore; the grandees, officers, their wives and children. If he had been a socialist then, as he became after WW1, he might have viewed Edwardian Kitemore as a microcosm of outdated feudal society. For the officers' presence reflected their privileged positions and wealth; and they invariably brought the most robust estate staff into the regiment as troopers. For example, Buscot Park's estate manager and his son were stalwart members of the regiment. Officers were expected have at least two chargers, and these might cost up to 150 guineas apiece. Troopers were provided with Yeomanry mounts and tack, which some might never have been able to afford. And so humble estate workers rose in status – at least as high as their seats in gleaming saddles. They all trained as dragoons – to charge into a conflict, sabre in hand, and then dismount, unsling their carbines and fire them on foot. There was a great sense of camaraderie in Yeomanry regiments, reinforced by local pride when they paraded through the towns, displayed their military manoeuvres at fetes, or ceremonially guarded visiting dignitaries.

Whatever he might think as a socialist later in life, Gavin clearly felt close to these men in August 1915. For after his father was made their Lt.-Colonel and marched the regiment off to fight in the Dardanelles campaign, 12-year-old Gavin spent all the money in his savings account on a patriotic purchase – £5 of War Bonds.

Soon after the regiment arrived in Egypt, they were dismounted, ordered to hand in their sabres, saddles and carbines, and rapidly re-trained as infantry. Their nine-day crash-course included entrenching and barbed wire cutting, using Enfield rifles (longer and more accurate than cavalry carbines) and bayonets. They exchanged their caps for pith helmets. These made them look more imperial when they embarked to form part of the 40,000 men sent to reinforce the troops pinned down on the landing beaches by Turks defending the Gallipoli peninsular. There they joined other Yeomanry regiments, as well as troops from Australia and New Zealand. There were also Gurkhas and units from the Indian army. The Berkshire Yeomanry landed and spent two days digging-in and road-making under frequent Turkish shelling. Their orders were to remain under cover until the main infantry advance began, and then move forward to the brush-covered promontory called "Chocolate Hill".

Photographs in Harold's files show the regiment throughout this period. In several he leans on a walking stick or is shown lying down in a dog tent. In these photos one sees the regiment training on sand between palm trees, queuing up to board transport ships, crowded aboard, disembarking under shell fire, and huddled below cliffs under the baking sun of an August afternoon. The Turks – advised by officers of the Imperial German Army – had barbed-wired the beaches to the water's edge, zoned in their artillery, dug deep trenches and had machine guns covering all approaches inland. The invasion force would face a lethal cross-fire in the "horse-shoe"-shaped landing zone. Harold and his brother officers were informed of this and told to expect 50% casualties. But the British generals thought the defenders were outnumbered and would crumble under a sustained assault. They were to discover that "Johnny Turk" had the advantage of a charismatic commander – the blonde and blue-eyed Mustafa Kemal Atatürk, who was to become a national hero and first president of his country.

The Berkshire Yeomanry Journal of 21st August 2015 recorded the Berkshire Yeomanry's first attack in plain words that convey the shock of the survivors:

"The Regiment went into action with 9 officers and 312 men,
of these five officers and 165 other ranks are reported killed,
wounded, and missing".

It mentions that Harold had led his men into the attack, only to collapse while trying to ascend the sandy hillside under fire and have to be "admitted to a field ambulance". The next most senior officer, Major E.S Gooch, assumed command until he was wounded. Then Captain J.B. Hurndall took over. Later, he wrote to Lady Violet:

"I know so well what a hard time he had in the Gallipoli
op, struggling along with a game leg when he ought to have
been in hospital long before he went."

The attack had been led by its overall commander Lord Longford. His last words were "Don't bother ducking, the men don't like it and it won't do any good." His body was never recovered due to a brush fire ignited by shelling that engulfed Chocolate Hill. Many wounded men were trapped and consumed by it. One trooper won a V.C. after managing to rescue a comrade from the flames. Talk of these things became the stuff of legend amongst the survivors, many of whom Gavin would have met after his father and his younger brother Alex were invalided home. There, Lady Violet had converted Kitemore into a Red Cross Auxiliary convalescent hospital to help deal with the causalities. Its list of admissions and treatments shows 105 patients. Doctors came regularly, professional female nurses and male orderlies dealt with the bed-ridden. VAD's (Voluntary Aid Detachment) – women auxiliary volunteers from the wealthier families – helped wherever needed. All staff were managed by a Red Cross registered matron. Double-paged spreads in Kitemore's visitors' book were headed "Troops". Here 85 men signed their names and expressed thanks for treatment between Sept 1915 and July 1916. These were all from the lower ranks of Yeomanry regiments and others – who identified themselves as privates, corporals, riflemen and troopers. One calling himself a drummer may have been a boy. Another was an ambulance man. And there was a motorcycle despatch rider from the Indian Army.

They came from 42 different military units. Returning home from boarding school, through these casualties from right across Britain, Gavin would have seen how the war was affecting the entire country. Lady Violet's collection of photographs show all those not bed-ridden wearing "Hospital Blues" (sometimes called "Invalid" or "Convalescent" uniform). These were single-breasted suits with a white lining, always worn with red ties and white shirts. Some wore regimental caps and displayed medals on the left breast. Men appear on crutches or being perambulated in wheelchairs by friends, or nurses or orderlies in white uniforms. Some played croquet on the lawn. Baden Powell, who Harold had met at the relief of Kimberley in the Boer War, arranged for a Boy Scout band to come and play for them. The Henderson family's dogs became part of the therapy. Soldiers were photographed with Lady Violet's elkhound puppies, the hunt terriers; and a bearded collie, that appeared in photos with Gavin's arm around it, now lounges with the men.

One or two soldiers may have been suffering from "shell-shock" as photos of them show that blank "thousand-yard stare" which characterises the condition. Seeing them may have had a dramatic effect on Gavin, for in the 1930s he was to pay fortnightly visits to hospital wards catering for such cases, and some of his first speeches in the Lords concerned this touchy subject. The military authorities conflated "shell-shock" with cowardice, which led to many sufferers from extreme post-traumatic stress disorder – such as these men – to be abandoned by their families, who did not receive pensions. Elsewhere at the convalescent hospital at Kitemore he would have seen women who had come as guests before the war who were serving as nurses. Some, like Violet Wroughton and Olive Orr-Ewing, had lost brothers at Gallipoli. There were also examples of courage and resilience in the convalescents who returned to active service – as their letters and postcards to Lady Violet tell. For Gavin, it must have been a great time of learning. Later that year his Eton report card read:

> "He is in many ways, old for his years, and yet, at the same time, he is not always as ready as he should be to do what he is told."

In the meantime, his father Harold's cavalry training seems to have advised him that the best thing to do after a fall was to get back into the saddle. Within three months he found work as Parliamentary Secretary to Lord Derby then Director of Recruiting, subsequently Deputy Assistant Adjutant General at the War Office. Harold's "do or die" approach earned him respect in Whitehall. Word spread and six months later he was asked by the Duke of Devonshire, the newly appointed Governor General of Canada, to become his Military Secretary there. This appointment may also have been prompted by the fact that both belonged to Liberal-Unionist party. They set out to counter the widespread disenchantment with the conduct of the war which had arisen due to heavy Canadian causalities. Harold's main task was to raise morale and further recruitment. So, he resigned his position at the War Office and as M.P for Abingdon. Lady Violet arranged for Kitemore's Red Cross Auxiliary hospital to be relocated to the Pump House in Faringdon's market square. Lord Faringdon bought that building and granted it to the town at a peppercorn rent. This arrangement still stands and it is currently used as the town's Council Offices. On the ground floor is a tourist information centre and a permanent exhibition on the WW1 Red Cross hospital.

In May 1916 Harold and Lady Violet sailed to Canada, where they became the first occupants of Rideau Cottage. This well-proportioned Georgian Revival brick building with a large bay window and elegant pediment over its door still stands close by Government House. It was their home for five years, and then became the official residence of Canadian Prime Ministers. In Ottawa Lady Violet resumed her "War Work" with the Ministry of Pensions on behalf of Veterans and their families. Harold soon began to accompany the Governor General on official outings and long tours of the country. Gavin remained in England. A photograph shows him looking miserable in a black Eton uniform with its distinctive high collar. In another, he wears a dark lounge suit. He was meant to be studying hard so that he could transfer to McGill University in Montreal as soon as possible. But in April 1916 his parents received a report card that may have caused them to worry. Not about his intelligence – that was never an issue – but about his health and attitude:

> "He really is quite able enough to get a first class, but
> at present he is not inclined. He dreams far too much,
> & constantly needs spurring on. If he were a little more
> ambitious and methodical, he would do a great deal better.
>
> The little escapade – about which I wrote to you not long
> ago – was a symptom of a certain lack of readiness to obey
> laws: on various occasions there have been signs of this in
> various directions. Such behaviour does not make me feel that
> I can trust him a much as I should like to be able to do, and I
> hope that we shall not have any more of this kind of thing. He
> read a couple of books about Indian History in the 16th and
> 17th centuries with great interest, and seems to have a great
> taste for general information, which should be useful to him.
> He must, at some time, learn the value of steady application
> to his ordinary work, and show himself less anxious to loosen
> the bounds of discipline."

Later that year the housemaster wrote again after Gavin had been ill:

> "It is unfortunate that Gavin was unable to sit his Trials, for
> I think that he would have done well.
>
> I cannot say that he is definitely more ready to take trouble
> about his ordinary everyday work. He prefers to loiter on the
> way. He has good wits, when he chooses to use them, and I
> do not suppose that he finds any of the work makes much
> demands on his powers. I suppose that his lack of energy is as
> much physical as mental.
>
> He is a gentle, intelligent boy. With plenty to say for himself,
> and a wide range of interest. He will, no doubt, get stronger
> and more vigorous as he grows older."

Gavin continued his studies at Eton until September 1918 when he was transferred to Ashbury College, in Ottawa. This was a single-sex school for 115 boys, 48 of who were boarders. The headmaster promised he would keep strictly to the rule of "no going home except on Saturdays and then only after at least 60% of the week's work has been obtained", He added that Gavin would have "a small room to himself". A year later, aged 17, he was accepted at McGill University in Montreal. He did so well there that in December 1920 his father wrote to the Dean of Admissions at Oxford asking for Gavin to be admitted in the following year:

> *"My eldest boy who after being at Eton for five years, owing to indifferent health, came out to Canada & last year entered Mc Gill passing nearly top of the list for matriculation, & I am anxious he should if possible complete his second year here & then go to Christ Church. This would be in the autumn of 1921. May I ask you to be good enough to put him on your list? He is considered very clever, he wrote the "Brinkman" at Eton & was fourth for the Rosebury history for Lower boys. He has passed all his examinations since he went to McGill with honours".*

In October 1919 the Adjutant of the Life Guards wrote to Harold.

> *Dear Hoppy,*
>
> *Haven't you a son about right to come into the Regiment & if so might I put his name down for it? We are badly in need of some good boys….*

Harold replied:

> *"My boy is 17 and a half and unfortunately has been pretty delicate all his life. In the ordinary course of events he would have gone to Kingston* (Note: the Royal Military College of Canada) *this year, but his chest measurement is not sufficient*

*to warrant his doing so, and he is at present at McGill. He
is a curious boy, exceptionally clever, having passed into the
University at the top of the list despite the fact that he has
been too unwell to do anything like the normal amount of
work. Much as I would like him to soldier I am not quite
sure it would suit his temperament. He is devoted to politics,
philosophy and kindred knowledge, in which I find myself
very little sympathy. If a year or two at McGill and Oxford
can possibly reduce him to a more normal state, nothing I
should like better than that he should go into the Regiment,
but as I say he is for the present somewhat delicate and I
cannot contemplate it. It looks to me as though his role will
be the Diplomatic Service or the Bar."'*

After Gavin prospered at Ashbury and McGill, Harold arranged for
him to take an extra Greek exam in order to ease his transfer to
Oxford. So, he came home to study at their home in Ottawa that
summer. Harold wrote to his parents that they were pleased with
how he had done, but that he was withdrawn and uncommunicative.
This may have been normal behaviour for an 18-year-old, but there
could have been another reason – something brewing in his personal
life which emerges in some letters he kept from that time. These
came from a man called Arthur, and several suggest that he had –
or hoped for – an intimate relationship with Gavin. If they did, it
did not last long, as ten of the twelve letters Arthur wrote complain
about Gavin's rejection of his advances, so their affair may only have
existed in Arthur's imagination. However, the letters were written at
a time when sexual relations between men were a criminal offence.
In malicious hands they could have been construed as incriminating evidence; or used to expose Gavin to scandal or blackmail.
Arthur comes across as older and far worldlier than Gavin, though
he constantly demands emotional support. These letters reveal that
he was a law student who was to fail his Bar Exams three times. Still,
Gavin kept his letters, tied in a faded blue ribbon, with the envelopes
they came in addressed to: Gavin Henderson Esq, Rideau Cottage.
Government House. Ottawa, Qub.

Arthur's letters may have expressed sincere feelings, but they seem histrionic.

One of the earliest reads:

> *"Must I reiterate the thousand and one reasons why I should not come to Ottawa – O silly coaxer!... So many things I have to tell you – O delicately carved figure of Ivory! In my little temple of Love I've given you a very respectable position, Oh! Quite near the little figures of gold (of those, none are pure: too much alloy is fused with them). Then there are the figures of silver, the figures of onyx and jasper and the figures of wood, of iron and stone. You're the only figure of Ivory I possess – and quite my favourite."*

Another letter in his characteristic "purple prose" blends argument and seduction:

> *"How now – sweet Gavin?*
>
> *Should I protest my love, since you have questioned it – or rather, it was "friendship" that you wrote or spoke, or Thought of – or is it sympathy, or kindly feeling and sweet to embrace – suffer both your virtue and your ills (?)- I'd have you by my side to feel your pulse, to probe your heart, to un-mask your mind – and discover what you have, thus! And flatter myself – or you -which is it? Where are you – where am I?*
>
> *My love you have: (have I yours?) – my friendship – 'that is the question….!"...The word is abused so much, I've lost its meaning. Will you find it for me? …Since I've searched the books and find the Masters disagreeing as to the colour of its cloak….*
>
> *Tell me of your plans for the summer when your people are arrived and draw them up. Yet you will keep a week,*

or fortnight for me – with us at our shooting box in the
Mountains, during the latter half of August, or in September.
And love me ever as I love you- (which is another version
I construe, for "Your love as mine to you') – if for ever – if
forever – still for ever, fare thee well affectionately."

Apparently, Gavin did not agree to spend time alone with Arthur in a remote Canadian mountain cabin. Instead, he returned to Montreal to visit some other friends, one of whom told Arthur. The result was a furious note scrawled with a thick blue crayon on a page torn from a notebook: *"The deception 'now it can be told' is amazing. It has been a real disappointment to me".* Then he signed off theatrically with the words *"My blasted love".*

In another letter Arthur vents his frustration:

"Your occasional bursts of tactlessness and deliberate lack of
discretion – or feeling for other's feelings – can become very
nasty, if not positively rude. Lady Violet, I'm sure, knows this
better than me and perhaps, now, rues the day she "spared
the rod" to your present misfortune and unhappiness. Don't
I know it too well? Even now I should have you thrashed.
Though you can be such a dear at times."

Later, resigned to being what he calls 'relegated to the shelf of dim memories', he struck a tragic pose and wrote

"Being the slave of circumstances as I am, and unable to
shake myself free from (Mis-) fortune's hold, desire rarely
takes the shape of Reality. For I have doomed myself to the
practice of Law, in search of Justice! My university career at
McGill came to an end about two months ago when I received
a Bachelor of Law. The next stage is to go to the Bar Council
Examinations. This I did last week in Quebec without
success…"

In December Arthur sent another short but pretentious note:

> *"Joking aside – dear Henderson, I am deeply stirred -that in the throes of Life, in Ottawa's small big-world – you should have given me a thought. As a rule I consider Christmas cards as so many arrows of irony from the one great bow – illusion."*

In 1920, after Gavin had returned to England and entertained a mutual female friend at Buscot, Arthur wrote to say that it was kind of him and Lady Violet, signing off:

> *"I am sorry to hear that your father has suffered so much, and do hope that he convalesces speedily.*
>
> *Gavin my dear, I would utter words of undying affection, etc, etc, – and pray that you might return even the smallest fraction of it too – Arthur."*

Arthur's mention of Gavin's father's health reveals that Gavin is concerned about it. After the war his father's mission as a goodwill ambassador continued as he organised Edward, the Prince of Wales' grand tour of Canada from August to October 1919. For this Harold had to arrange scheduled events as well as "tacks and bunting" as he put it, in 55 towns where the royal train and entourage were to stop. He had to liaise with local politicians, committees and dignitaries; arrange for accommodation, etc. As Harold put it in a letter to the adjutant of the Life Guards he had been:

> *"...very busy with His Royal Highness's tour across the Continent, which I have travelled twice in the last three months, and am just now having a few days respite before resuming my duties with H.R.H. His tour in this country has been a phenomenal success, and he has in my opinion done more to cement imperial unity than anything that has taken place in our life-time. It is particularly fortunate that the*

heir to the Throne has the extraordinary charm that H.R.H
possesses and he can make himself beloved by everybody who
has seen him, and I do not think I am exaggerating when
I say that be the place large or small at least 70% of the
populace have turned out to see him in every case."

A month after the tour ended Sir Joseph Pope, Under-Secretary of State for External Affairs, sent Harold a handwritten letter. This mentioned that he was "sincerely sorry" to hear of Harold's "indisposition in Halifax" and hoped that he was "on the way alright again". He went on to say that Harold had been awarded the C.V.O. These initials stood for a Commander of the Royal Victorian Order – a knighthood established by Queen Victoria to recognise distinguished personal service to the crown. Pope described this

> *"a fitting recognition of all your hard work in the most*
> *successful Royal tour. There is a personal touch about the*
> *Victoria Order which is especially gratifying to its possessor. I*
> *hope this is a prelude to greater distinctions."*

The medal could not compensate for the collapse of Harold's health. The demands of the tour had proved too great and resulted in the return of his old complaint. He soldiered on, and then suffered a relapse. In early January 1920 he had recovered enough to write to his mother:

> *"…doing so much better that the doctor is allowing me to get*
> *up and go for a sleigh drive tomorrow. He is quite pleased*
> *with me and says that if I am careful I ought to be alright… I*
> *really think that if I stop here much longer I should go off my*
> *'rocker'… I do so hate being shut up in one room for a long*
> *time."*

By the end of the month, he was able to write "up and abroad again, I can't say I feel very robust" …In February he confided, "feeling better now, but am not free of this silly pain in the heart region when I walk or otherwise exert myself". It would seem that what he called "a silly pain" may have been evidence of an undiagnosed congenital heart problem, which might well have contributed to his health problems. Harold's mother was to die of heart failure in 1921; and four of her five sons were to pass away before Lord Faringdon died in 1934 at the age of 84. These were Harold (aged 46 in 1922), Frank (aged 47 in 1924) Alec (aged 55 in 1931) and Arnold (aged 50 in 1933). However, by June 1920 Harold had recovered enough to write a revealing letter to the Dean of Admissions at Oxford:

> *"You will remember my boy Gavin who was in your Division during the short time he was at Eton, and of whom I see very pleasant reports written by yourself. He has put in a year at McGill and I had intended that he should put in a second, but circumstances have arisen which necessitate my return to England at the end of this year, when I shall send him to Christchurch, Oxford. He is a curious boy and very clever in many ways. His health is good, but he is far from being robust. As you wrote me about him at the time he was at Eton 'he is by no means orthodox' and therefore difficult to manage in a school like Eton, but he may find his level at Oxford."*

Gavin and his siblings returned to England with the servants on the *SS Victoriana* in August. Lady Violet had telegrammed Mrs Crosland, wife of the Estate Manager at Buscot Park, asking her to look after them there "until their schools open". In October 1920 Harold, Lady Violet and her maid, as well as Miss Orr-Ewing (who had served as a VAD at Kitemore) boarded the prestigious *SS Mauritania* to return home. Shortly after their arrival they moved into Buscot Park, which had been given to them by Lord Faringdon after his wife died. Landowners plant trees for their descendants to enjoy, and a newly timbered area named "Canada Wood" commemorated their return. Today one finds an avenue of mature plane trees lining the lane up to a three-arch bridge designed by Harold Peto in 1913 across Buscot Park's "Big Lake".

The family moved into his father's former home and were soon pillars of their community. Harold served as Justice of the Peace, and supported the Old Berkshire Hunt. Photographs in the family album show them gathering on the front lawn with their hounds. He became a progressive agriculturalist, investing in a herd of award-winning Jersey cows, Shire horses, as well as Black Berkshire pigs. Lady Violet served on the Conservative & Unionist Party's election committee, helped rehabilitate war veterans, was a leading figure in the Women's Institute, and was active with the hunt, as well as point-to-points and show-jumping trials. She also bred pedigree horses and dogs.

One of Harold's last letters was written to his mother from Buscot Park on 25th March 1921:

> "Gavin is home, working for an exam next term, quite unnecessarily I believe, but as all the ordinary forms of recreation & exercise are abhorrent to him, he may as well fill in his time as suits him best. I do not understand the boy, he is abnormal. Perhaps it will work out all right & one must hope for the best."

A snapshot of Gavin from these times shows him holding up a lap-dog – possibly one of his mother's pedigree pugs, by a fountain in the grounds. He wears a three-piece suit and large floppy hat. He does not look like the son of a military man; his pose was distinctly "aesthetic".

A photo of his father at this time shows a tall gaunt man leaning heavily on a stick, almost a shadow of his former self when compared to earlier photographs. During this period doctors and nurses kept records of his decline. The family's happiness in their beautiful home was to be short lived. He had another relapse in the summer of 1922. Notebooks logged "the Colonel's" numerous symptoms: a "tight band" feeling across his chest, cramps in his arms and legs, copious perspiration, insomnia, restlessness, difficulty breathing, coughing, retching, vomiting, "gripey pains" in his stomach, indigestion, flatulence, diarrhoea. One night-nurse resuscitated him when she found him "comatose and pulseless". From Sept to Oct his pulse rate moved from slow to high.

His treatments included regular small doses of strychnine – a poison whose convulsant effects were thought beneficial. He was given camphor – in milk or on sugar – as a pain killer and to help him sleep; bicarbonate of soda to aid his digestion; and cascara – a herbal laxative. They burnt stramonium or misted his room with ether to help his breathing. He had to have oxygen regularly. As his condition worsened his daily doses of heroin were increased in strength. The notebook column headed "Nourishment" listed chicken jelly, poached egg, rice pudding, blackcurrant tea, barley water, rusks in milk. On occasions he had fish, oysters, custard, junket, lemon pudding, and a glass of champagne. His diet during his final days was brandy, milk and heroin. He died on 1st November 1922.

His funeral took place five days later at St. Mary's Church, Buscot. This was a private service which Gavin attended with Lord Faringdon and their family. A telegram sent from Buckingham Palace to Lady Violet Henderson arrived in advance. This read:

> *"Please accept my sincere sympathy in the loss of your husband, whose help and guidance during my visit to Canada I will never forget.*
>
> *Edward P."*

After the private funeral Lady Violet commissioned Sir Edwin Lutyens, who had designed Whitehall's Cenotaph monument in 1919, to create a memorial for Harold in the graveyard of St. Mary's Buscot. Five months later Harold's remains were moved into Lutyens' elegant Portland Stone sarcophagus set on a plinth. The monument was placed in an enclosure lined by a privet hedge with plaques of Maltese crosses set in the ground around it. A public memorial ceremony was held and the congregation included Lord Faringdon and Lady Violet's family, the deceased friends from military and civilian life, as well as many locals. Newspapers covered the ceremony and one thought fair to add that Lt.-Col Henderson's son and heir had not attended. Whether this was true or not, the controversial nature that became a feature of Gavin's public life had appeared.

CHAPTER 2

"Delighted to Defy Officialdom"

Whatever the reason for Gavin's not attending his father's memorial service – illness, emotional exhaustion, or university commitments – he was seen as a rebel at Oxford. As the 20-year-old Robert Byron – who became one of his closest friends – wrote: *"Gavin came home to Oxford... delighted to defy officialdom."* Byron also gives us what is perhaps an overly optimistic view of Gavin's lethargic episodes: *"a kind of supernatural vigour is his outstanding natural characteristic. He is lazy, partly because this exhausts him. But whatever he does becomes in itself remarkable."*

Like many of his contemporaries in the aftermath of WW1, Gavin felt rebellious of the "old order" due to the loss of a generation fighting for God, King, Country and Empire. His library shelves show books from this time by pacifists such as Siegfried Sassoon, Aldous Huxley and H.G. Wells – all of whom he had met. However, like many of his generation at Oxford, he learned to practise the art of doing nothing gracefully. One of his best friends there was the writer Patrick Balfour, a man who was caricatured in *Tatler* magazine holding a cocktail shaker. As he put it, *"In Oxford we wasted time and money but we did so with a glorious and reckless abandon. We had a horror of turning serious."* While this was going on, Arthur was reaching out to him:

> *"...the fragrance of a letter coming from Oxford, from you, dearest Gavin – undergraduate at Christ Church...I had no idea the entrance was so simple.... Whatever the course*

you are following at Oxford may be – I haven't the slightest
inkling; you have never told me what it was leading to."

Between 1922 and 1924 Gavin was to sit and pass exams in Holy
Scripture, Modern History, Greek History and Literature. However,
he sent Arthur a book that shows how he was reading around these
subjects. Arthur's reply was characteristically self-absorbed:

> *"Your little book is sheer delight to my heart; what is there*
> *that interests me more than the Italian Renaissance? You*
> *have chosen well…. As the season advances, I miss you the*
> *more; many times, I pass down Metcalfe St. to wonder at*
> *your absence. Perhaps, only now, do I fully appreciate how*
> *much you filled my life, a year ago…like a fair dream broken*
> *at its very birth…and all the other sentimentalities, keenly*
> *felt, nevertheless! In your new existence! Your weekends are*
> *pleasant and pleasantly retold – and "fun" is at its pitch…*
> *I would rather learn something of the people you meet – not*
> *as to their heraldry (please), and the woman whom you have*
> *chosen for your wife."*

Arthur's mention of a potential wife suggests that Gavin may have
aroused his jealousy by mentioning a woman friend. In spite of his
previous criticisms of Gavin's tactlessness, he went on to suggest a
career in the corps diplomatic as he was well set-up with

> *"…connections and money! Birth and rank. You have (or*
> *will) all these qualifications – and it would in time become*
> *infinitely more interesting to your complexion than sordid*
> *jollities at home. You will be moving from one Court and*
> *Embassy to another: you will need a secretary, a Valet, a sort*
> *of Boswell – and for this job may I apply now?"*

In 1922 he wrote to thank Gavin for a copy of *The Oxford Verse of 1921*
which Arthur felt *"smacked too much of a conscious attempt to impress"*.
Then he asked if Gavin knew its editor, Sir Arthur Quiller-Couch, as

Arthur wanted to send him some of his own poems. His final line is revealing:

> *"Would you imagine it; I have now enlisted in that inglorious army of the unemployed. I am looking for a job. Can you advise anything?"*

The first time Arthur asked for employment was as a *"Valet, or sort of Boswell"* and might have been meant as a joke. Still, only Arthur could have imagined himself backing into Gavin's limelight as his literary amanuensis. His latest request, however, was more serious. By then Arthur had informed Gavin of his having failed his bar exams for the third time. The only thing positive in his life came when he joined an amateur theatre group in Montreal and performed Hamlet in French. The irony of his playing a brooding prince never occurred to him. He had always been emotionally needy, but importuning for work was new. Gavin did not offer him a job in his entourage and this was his last letter.

Gavin's new friends were a group who became known in the press as the "Bright Young People" or "Bright Young Things". The writer Lytton Strachey described some he knew as

> *"Delightful, but with just a few feathers where their brains ought to be."*

They were a wide range of individuals who delighted in causing a stir. For the most part, they simply wanted society to climb down off its high horse, and their antics were a reaction against the dullness of social life exemplified by dowagers and debutante balls. Of course, the press was always keen to express outrage on behalf of its starchier readers, for the BYPs drank to excess; cocktails – an American import that came in with the Charleston dance craze and syncopated Jazz – had become their daily ritual. The BYPs delighted in antics that let them shriek with laughter. Much was just undergraduate japes, such as a Chloroform party in the Royal Hospital Road or a Fancy Undress party. A *Daily Express* gossip columnist laughed with them one week and in the next deplored the loss of masculinity in the men in the next, calling them "anaemic, dolled up like girls, resembling silken-coated lapdogs". Elsewhere they were seen as amusing modern successors of the 18th-century "Fops", or Regency "Bucks". Perhaps fear of being sued for libel led one columnist to criticise an aristocratic young man as "effeminate" and then write "it is not suggested that he is sexually depraved". Basically, the BYPs were a gift to bored journalists who regularly encouraged them.

Some of these BYPs matured into Gavin's circle of close friends over the next decade. Among these were Patrick Balfour (who worked as *The Daily Sketch*'s society columnist "Mr Gossip" before inheriting the title Lord Kinross and becoming a respected historian); John Betjeman (architectural heritage campaigner, broadcaster and future Poet Laureate), Bryan Guinness (a sensitive poet and heir to a brewing fortune who married Diana Mitford, who left him for Sir Oswald Mosley); Peter Rodd (who proposed to three debs at one party in the hope of finding a wealthy wife so that he would not have to suffer the indignity of working for a living); Robert Byron (travel writer photographer and artist); Harold Acton (an aesthete famous for reciting his poems through a megaphone to Oxford undergraduates); Tom Driberg (promiscuous gay journalist and future Labour Peer); and Anthony Powell (author of *A Dance to the Music of Time* – a series of 15 novels about his generation). Many of these Oxford contemporaries were morphed into characters in Evelyn Waugh's novels. In fact, his first novel was dedicated to Harold Acton, who remained close to Gavin. But Gavin's relationship with Waugh was not friendly; and the signatures of all the above appear in the Buscot Park visitors' book many times – but not Evelyn Waugh's.

Waugh had arrived in Oxford on a scholarship in 1922. He enjoyed a whirlwind social life and did just enough work to pass his final examinations in the summer of 1924. But a third-class degree prevented him from returning to complete the nine terms' residence necessary before his degree could be awarded – so he left without one to work as a tutor in a provincial private boarding school for boys. This experience embittered him and, as Gavin's closest friend Robert Byron, who was his "best man" at Waugh's first wedding, wrote to Gavin, *"I fear that Evelyn's envy and malice are making him enemies".* Waugh was certainly one of the most talented writers of his era, and some of his artful envy or malice went into making people he had known at Oxford appear disreputable. Foremost of these was Basil Seal, based on Basil Murray – son of the scholar Gilbert Murray and Lady Mary Howard, daughter of the 9th Earl of Carlisle. Basil's alcohol-fuelled pranks formed half of the character that featured in *Black Mischief* and *Put Out More Flags*. The other half was inspired by the roguish and irrepressible Hon. Peter Rennell Rodd, son of the British Ambassador to Rome, and future husband of the novelist Nancy Mitford. Like Gavin, Basil and Peter became anti-fascists in the 1930s. Waugh – ever the contrarian – supported Franco and Mussolini. Waugh went on to combine two quick-witted friends, Brian Howard and Harold Acton into the camp aesthete Anthony Blanche in *Brideshead Revisited*. He was to caricature Gavin cruelly too – as we shall see.

Gavin's time at Oxford offered him fun and personal freedom. Little correspondence survives, apart from a few scrawls to say he would be offering cocktails in his rooms or accepting an invitation for them. These suggest that like his contemporary Bob Boothby wrote "there were far too many other things to do at Oxford than attend lectures". There was, for an example, the Hypocrites' Club whose members took a pledge to forsake alcohol and then got drunk in public. According to John Betjeman, Gavin was a pillar of The Railway Club. Its members donned evening dress and boarded trains to drink and dine. Then they would clamber out onto station platforms to deliver speeches as they made their way across the country. Some of these outings took place on Gavin's grandfather's Great Central Railway. The Railway Club was conceived by the future film producer John Sutro. Unlike the BYPs, most of its members were awaiting their hereditary seats in the House of Lords. These included Edward Fox-Strangeways (future Earl of Ilchester), Henry Weymouth (future Marquis of Bath),

Michael Rosse (future Earl of Rosse), Bryan Guinness (future Lord Moyne), Patrick Balfour (future Lord Kinross). There were other colourful and convivial members, such as the Hon. Hugh Lygon (destined to become the tragic anti-hero of Evelyn Waugh's novel Brideshead Revisited); Roy Harrod (future Economics Don); Henry Greene (future novelist); and Brian Howard (a decadent exhibitionist poet).

In spite of a bibulous social life, Gavin managed to pass his exams. And so, as a treat, in March 1924 he travelled by ship to Spain with his mother and grandfather. This journey offered a different kind of education when they then boarded a train in Gibraltar to travel first class on the railway that his grandfather had built in the 1890s. The line spanned the deep Ronda gorge on a three-arched viaduct his great-uncle had designed – a great feat of engineering at the time. Near the port of Algeciras, they lodged in the Reina Cristina, a superlative hotel his grandfather had built. This had an Anglican chapel decorated with stained glass windows designed by Sir Edward Burne-Jones and made by William Morris & Co. The hotel was so well-appointed and glamorous that 70 years later it featured in the James Bond film *Thunderball*. After staying there with his mother and grandfather, Gavin headed off on his own across Europe before returning to sit his final examination in Modern History.

Gavin's studies were interrupted two months later when he contracted mumps. This started with a low fever and inflammation of the salivary glands. The swelling spread to his cheeks, jaw and neck, and was followed over the next few weeks by high fever accompanied by nausea and vomiting. Then the virus developed into Orchitis – swelling in the scrotum – which produced severe testicular pain. Mumps in a 22-year-old like Gavin can result in gonadal atrophy. This appears to have been the case as friends reported that afterwards he spoke with a higher register. This may have been what Evelyn Waugh was referring to when he wrote that a character based on Gavin spoke in "a shrill and emasculated voice". Whatever the result, Gavin sat his final exams later that term and in January 1925 was awarded a BA in History (Fourth Class). It was generally assumed that his low university grades were not a true measure of the man and his potential.

In December 1924 Gavin went to live with his grandfather in Arlington Street, notable for its buildings designed by Robert Adam and Sir John Soane. There were so many high-ranking politicians living there that it was nicknamed "Ministerial Street". Lord Faringdon's home, 18 Arlington St., had been built between 1756 and 1769 by the architect Stiff Leadbetter for the widow of the Earl of Pomfret, Countess Mary Wortley Montagu, and was called Pomfret Castle. It was the only "Strawberry Hill Gothick" house in London, an ornate but elegant style promoted by the aesthete Horace Walpole. Number 18 had a gatehouse on the street, a private forecourt, beyond which lay the three-storied mansion overlooking St. James's Park. Pomfret Castle was within walking distance of Piccadilly and Green Park. Photographs show that its hall was a tall wedding cake of moulded plaster in the Perpendicular style. The doors were 3-inch thick mahogany with fluted panelling; the windows all had stone mullions carved into elaborate tracery. Each room was filled with period furniture. Lord Faringdon was an art connoisseur and his collection, that one can view in museums today, included works by Millais, Watts and Burne-Jones. When Gavin stayed there this costly "high art" was for the family's exclusive enjoyment.

A letter from Gavin to Patrick Balfour, then working as the gossip writer for *The Sketch*, gives an insight into Gavin's feelings while living and working with his grandfather:

"18. Arlington St. SW

4.12.24

(Written from the premise of the British Trade Corporation)
& that is the reason I have not been in Oxford for some time!
Yes Balf' – I've become one of the workers – my mornings

start with me making a hectic & always unavailing effort to reach Austin Friars by 9.30."

Gavin had rooms in Pomfret Castle and worked at the British Trade Corporation at Austin Friars in the City of London. This had been set up by his grandfather and housed his London offices. Austin Friars was originally a medieval priory. It was dissolved in Henry VIII's reign and became the home of Sir Thomas Cromwell and his administrative offices. All the Henderson family's investment companies were based there, and as Austin Friars stood close by the Stock Exchange, the place was a home from home for his grandfather. Here Gavin's real education was set to begin; for he was being groomed as his grandfather's heir, and initiated into the secrets of global finance at its London hub.

After sixteen months at the British Trade Board, Gavin started to work at one of his grandfather's affiliate companies, the London Associated Assurance Corporation of No 1 King William Street in the City of London. This supported his grandfather's free-trade interests within the Empire and, whenever possible, breaking new commercial ground beyond, as was his wont. But working with clerks, brokers, accountants and businessmen in the city did not grab Gavin's attention. He still had a strong desire for fresh fields and pastures new. So, he took a couple of months off in the summer of 1925 to drive his stylish new Talbot Sunbeam roadster across Europe with two former Eton and Oxford chums. One of these was Robert Byron, a budding travel writer who shared his tastes in art and politics. But unlike Gavin, Robert got into Eton and Oxford thanks to scholarships. He came from a middle-class background and rented a dilapidated stable block of a burnt-down Georgian mansion in Savernake Forest, romantically called 'The Ruins'. The other traveller in that chic cabriolet was Arthur Duggan, stepson of Lord Curzon, the former Viceroy of India (then Secretary of State for Foreign Affairs). Their contemporaries at Oxford, Evelyn Waugh, described Alfred as "living flamboyantly for pleasure" and the future literary critic Peter Quennell, likened him to a "dashing, Restoration rake". However, this letter from Alfred to Gavin shows him morphing into quite the opposite.

"Worcester College, Oxford, Tuesday, Midnight, 5ᵗʰ-6ᵗʰ July /25.

My dear Gavin,

Thank you ever so much for the extremely kind invitation, It is awfully good of you, but really, I'm not fit for 'polite society' – having neither clothes not manners. And honestly, with my very violent, revolutionary socialist class-war ideas – which, however much one may laugh at them, I hold with the greatest sincerity – it is really better that I should not stay with people, as, since I feel so strongly about things, my attitude being quite reprehensible, I would rather not risk giving offence to others, or – to be frank, for this is probably the more powerful and egotistical motive – feel myself in an awkward position. I hope you'll understand I'm absolutely refusing all parties or even to have anything to do with any 'Capitalist' society whatsoever, except in so far as seeing my family and my friends at Oxford (apart from their families) & my literary and journalistic work are concerned...."

Alfred studied history and emerged as a committed communist. For a few years afterwards, he suffered from an alcohol addiction that nearly killed him. Each of the three travellers had an escapist streak. They set out for Constantinople via France, Italy and Greece – before returning via a different route, visiting Salzburg, Innsbruck, Verona, Bologna, Florence, Rome and Naples. After the car broke down in Athens they returned home by rail. In 1926 they extended their "grand tour" to France, Spain, Hungary, and Germany in Gavin's new Bentley. The result was Robert Byron's first book: *Europe in the Looking-Glass*. Whilst the trip had begun as a "lark" it opened their eyes along the way to the perils of fascism, which was spreading across the continent.

The first leg started in Grimsby – a port partly owned by Gavin's grandfather. They nicknamed the open-topped Sunbeam tourer "Diana". All three men crammed into the front bench seat with their luggage lashed behind them into the rumble seat. Gavin refused to let anyone else take the wheel. Robert Byron, the plumpest, always sat in the middle as Alfred's map reading was better and he demanded the seat beside the window. Robert wrote their travelogue when he was a 21-year-old undergraduate. Whilst uneven the book remains a highly entertaining and informative period piece. One amusing aspect about the author came to light afterwards when Waugh was putting together a posthumous biographical sketch of Byron in 1961. Waugh wrote to Duggan asking if he had a copy of the book he could borrow to read and refresh his memory of Byron's style. Duggan replied that he no longer had a copy as his had been stolen by the author. Apparently, Byron had wanted to suppress it due to some juvenile passages that he regretted having written. Duggan complained to Waugh that the only place he could find a copy to re-read himself was at the British Library. However, Gavin had managed to preserve a first edition at Buscot Park by hiding it on the low shelf of his study where Robert did not find it, as all his other books by the author were stored at waist height in the library. *Europe in the Looking-Glass* presents Gavin under the pseudonym David Henniker, who lives in a country mansion at Highworth (a town five miles from Buscot). In it, Byron gives a character sketch of his 23-year-old friend:

> *"...totally devoid of even a decent sense of embarrassment*
> *and can make inexhaustible conversation to any living*
> *creature that understands a single word of French, German*
> *or English. He also has a knowledge of history, but his chief*
> *interests are decoration and architecture..."*

More importantly, in view of Gavin's future development, was that he

> *"...possessed more than a superficial familiarity with Europe,*
> *her countries and their inhabitants. He knew France...*

33

Germany after the war. And in 1924 he had motored to the Russian frontier, spent six weeks in Poland, and then taken Prague, Vienna and Rome in his stride home. This had been a most remarkable tour, which only his initiative could have carried through. It is his outstanding ambition, in fact, to make the acquaintance of the whole earth and the races with which it is peopled."

A memento of his trip now hangs in a corridor between the first-floor bedrooms at Buscot Park. It is one of the few surviving paintings by Robert Byron, whose work was admired by Paul Nash and exhibited several times in London galleries. The painting records the time after they had met some "blackshirts" in a café who told them that they deplored the way English people came to paint the pleasing decay of Rome. The fascists assured them that picturesque sights were part of a decadent past, which was soon to be expunged by Mussolini. Afterwards, Byron went upstairs and painted the rooftop view from the Hotel de Russie (still an exclusive hotel today) and this passage from his book tells us why:

"The charm of Rome is a hackneyed subject: but one aspect of it that writers usually fail to mention is the colour with which so many of the buildings are coated. It is difficult to describe this particular shade. The effect is as though a kind of dull burnt orange had been covered with a roseate wash, yet at the same time the whole is flat and restful. Our rooms at the Russie – a hotel which the others affected to dislike as I had recommended it – gave out on to a large, leaded expanse of roof, surrounded on three sides by walls of this colour... The fascisti, impelled by a secret hankering after skyscrapers and municipal Gothic, hold that this colour is incompatible with the dignity of a great capital, and have given orders that it should be used no more. It is only natural that they prefer that Italy should live in the present rather than the past. But there is something a little grotesque about the hysterical

modernity that has inspired such edicts as this, and the
threatened prohibition of the gondolas in Venice."

On his return to London at the start of 1925, Gavin gave up living
and working with his grandfather. Pomfret Castle in the 1st Lord
Faringdon's time was as much a private museum as his home. Here
Alexander Henderson and his grandson could enjoy many of the fine
things he had accumulated in a lifetime of hard work. But Gavin
seems to have been more interested in the accumulation of pleasures.
He wanted his own home and so purchased a Georgian town house
in fashionable North Street, Westminster. This, like Pomfret Castle,
was within strolling distance of Piccadilly and St. James's Park.
Then he started work with the decorators W. Turner, Lord & Co in
Mount Street. This firm had commissioned Harold Peto to design
the first-class interiors for Cunard liners. These were the height of
elegance and his parents would have enjoyed them when they sailed
home from Canada a few years earlier. Whilst Lord Faringdon and
Lady Violet may not have approved of him spending time with a
firm of interior decorators, they were friendly with two key people
linked to the company. One was the society hostess Lady Emerald
Cunard and the other Harold Peto himself. Lady Cunard was the
American-born heiress to the company that owned the ocean liners
bearing her surname; and Lord Faringdon had employed Peto to
design the forecourt of Buscot Park and its famous water gardens.
Although now elderly, Peto was still working as a consultant with W.
Turner, Lord & Co.

While Gavin was to spend only four months with W. Turner, Lord
& Co it was an experience that would serve him well in the future.
When he went to work there, "Emerald" Cunard was an influential
society hostess in London. However, the former British Prime
Minister David Lloyd George had called her "a most dangerous
woman", because of the way she meddled in politics. And Lord
Berners, Gavin's friend and neighbour in Oxfordshire, joked that
she was such a social climber that when she came to stay, she had
kept him awake one night as he could hear her scrambling up the

walls. When "Emerald" learned that Gavin was planning to travel to India, the Middle East and Somalia on a fact-finding tour she wrote to him:

> *"Don't go abroad, and if you must, don't stay away for*
> *so long. Please join the League for Africa before you go.*
> *Please send me anything if only £2. 2. 10. which makes you*
> *a member. Perhaps Lord Faringdon would like the same.*
> *It all helps and he must get his money's worth. Ask Lord*
> *Faringdon to send this please."*

Gavin's grandfather would certainly have been aware the "League for Africa" as it lobbied for changes that would directly affect his family's commercial interests – but neither he nor Gavin appear to have joined. Lord Faringdon had his own way of dealing with investments in Africa. Always in favour of international trade, that year he had successfully encouraged the Government to relax immigration regulations in Tanganyika, thus permitting the return of German settlers to their former colony in order to increase its prosperity. He had also encouraged Britain to cede a strip of territory along the Juba River in Somaliland to Italy and promised to aid Italian development of Ethiopia in return for support of British plans to build a dam at Lake Tsana. These projects were to improve the water supplies of a number of other countries and open the way for the pipelines, canals and bridges that his engineering companies would supply. Lord Faringdon's brother was Chairman of the Royal Institute of Civil Engineers, and when plans were drawn up for Gavin's fact-finding tour, both his grandfather and great-uncle had urged him to visit these places. The Henderson family were surprisingly far-seeing and had many connections and companies in South America as well.

Emerald Cunard's beautiful but troubled daughter Nancy was six years older than Gavin. However, he admired her independent streak and they had a close relationship that lasted for several decades until her death. After her father passed away, she inherited a large fortune and fled to Paris to be free of her dominating mother, with whom her relationship had always been difficult. Paris in 1925 was at its creative peak. Nancy became a writer, publisher and muse for many writers and artists. These included Aldous Huxley, Louis Aragon, Ernest Hemingway, James Joyce and Constantin Brancusi. She spent her inheritance supporting artists and publishing wonderfully crafted editions of modern writers until the Spanish Civil War when, like Gavin, she went to assist Republican relief efforts near the front lines. Exhaustion forced her to return to Paris where she published and distributed pamphlets of anti-war poetry, which included the work of W. H. Auden, Brian Howard, Tristan Tzara and Pablo Neruda. Her much publicised sexual relationship with an African-American jazz musician resulted in a total break with her mother. Nancy became a selfless civil rights activist and set up an anti-fascist forum in the major newspapers. This antagonised Lady Cunard even further as she was a staunch supporter of the Government and its policy of appeasement. In fact, Lady Cunard was a friend of Joachim von Ribbentrop, the Nazi Foreign Minister, and supported his view that the former King Edward should be restored with Wallace Simpson as his Queen.

In June 1926, Honor Chedworth Philipps was introduced to Gavin at Buscot Park. He was 24 years old and she had turned 18 four months earlier. Apart from attending a girls' boarding school, Honor had not spent much time in the world outside her parents' home in rural Pembrokeshire. What brought her to Buscot Park was their mothers. Four years had passed since Gavin's father had died and people expected his son and heir to marry. Gavin had many female friends and acquaintances, but he had not been linked romantically with any. As he had not made any attempts to find a suitable bride, Lady Violet arranged for a potential bride to meet her son in what would be their future home. She was too young to have "come out" as a debutante, which left her innocent, trusting and no threat. Unlike some of the girls Gavin had met at BYP parties, she was not wild, beautiful, sophisticated or glamorous. Honor was bright, genial, and straightforward – people such as Evelyn Waugh, who met her ready to sneer, found her delightfully unaffected. Her mother and older sisters were all remarkably tall and thin, but *Tatler* magazine had cruelly caricatured Honor as "short and pie-faced". Still, her father was one of the world's largest shipping tycoons, director of the Royal Mail Steam Packet Company with interests in over 40 other companies that included port development, shipbuilding and oil refining. Her mother, Lady Kylsant, was domineering and used to getting her own way.

Most of Gavin's male friends might have been called "not as other men" – a 1920s euphemism for gay. The author Beverley Nichols was one of these and wrote that the word homosexual was rarely used outside of psychology books. Most people referred to gays as "effeminate" or "pansies". Some upper-class mothers keen to get their sons married took them to a Harley St. consultant who maintained that they were "circumstantial homosexuals" – the result of having been sent to single-sex boarding schools from puberty. It was widely believed that grown men could be cured by marrying, settling down, and having children. Other "cures" were attributed to sessions with the Mayfair courtesan Viscountess Castlerosse. She was widely quoted as saying *"There are no impotent men – only inexperienced women"*. Her attentions certainly helped Cecil Beaton to conquer his fear of women.

The courtship was slightly unconventional. In November 1926, six months after their first meeting, Honor came to stay at Buscot Park for ten nights. A few days after this sojourn their mothers announced that the couple were engaged to be married. Honor was so grateful to Gavin for being gentle to her that she fell head over heels in love with him. Once Lady Kylsant sensed that things were moving in the right direction she began to press Honor to get Gavin to propose. She wanted them to marry as soon as possible. Perhaps she knew that Lord Kylsant had financial troubles. Certainly, not even the astute Lord Faringdon suspected how bad things were or he would have done something to prevent the marriage. Whatever their motives, Lady Violet and Lady Kylsant were a forceful alliance. The young couple were caught in a maternal pincer movement from which there seemed to be no escape. Gavin kept letters from Honor which paint a vivid picture of her side of the predicament:

"Dear Gavin,

I'm ashamed of writing this letter before I begin, & by the time it's posted I shall be cursing myself, but I just have to it. It isn't me truly, it's that beastly mother; she's being just so <u>*foul*</u>*. I've been travelling 12 hours today and have got a splitting head – & when I arrived I found a* <u>*12-page*</u> *snarl from her – so I thought I'd just write & get it over. Gavin, for the last week I've been getting* <u>*hateful*</u> *letters from her. She says that I have seen too much of you; and that we are getting talked about; she just blatantly asks if you mean to marry me or not; she says that if not I've got to drop you, & not see you again. Of course, all this is* <u>*covered*</u> *with a heavy sprinkling of "darlings", "my pet" "beloved child's "and other decietful-nesses (sic). Gavin, if she's going on like this for months. I can't* <u>*bear*</u> *it. She knows just how to nag so that it hurts.*

Couldn't you be kind & tell me if you <u>*do*</u> *mean to drop me, or if you might want to get engaged to me in about a year? Please don't loathe me for asking this frightful question, but I* **<u>can't</u>** *face many more letters from that woman. If you're bored with me I could understand, & I'd rather know now that I can go on loving you for a year – If you're not, might I hope that you might be wanting me when you come home from Persia? Please don't think I'm not ashamed of my forwardness, because I am.*

You will be honest, won't you? You understand how mother bates me? I loathe her even more than I ever have in my life for having more or less forced me to write this. You know if it hadn't been for <u>*her*</u> *I'd have waited years & never let you know I minded. It's all very shaming for me. Even if you do write & say you are sick of me, you won't be very angry, will you? Because I'm unhappy now. I'm so tired tonight. Please forgive me for being awful.'*

Love from <u>Honor</u>"

Gavin clearly did as Honor asked and a subsequent letter from her shows that the marriage began to move inexorably closer,

"Tuesday,

Chelsea House,

Cadogan Place. W1.

My dear – would you do something for me? If you can spare half an hour Thursday or Friday will you come& see father? He seems to want to be told that we are going to get married some time. You probably won't but of you could come in Thursday evening about 6 he'd be awfully grateful, he really is an old dear, isn't he? I can't help his being so atrociously "proper". I can merely apologize – He has some old-fashioned idea that you should tell your grandfather. I am sorry to bother you, but I really can't help the sort of things he thinks!

Robert Byron is a Love!

I remain Yrs. truly,

Honor Philipps."

Gavin confided to his friends that he felt his life would never be his own again. Whilst he had seemed buoyant and optimistic to his friends up to this time, he began to suffer from anxiety and depression. There had been a decline in his health and outlook when Robert Byron wrote to him from Athens in August 1926. Gavin was to have joined him and a group of Oxford graduates to visit Mt Athos – the Orthodox monks' republic from which "women and beardless boys have been banned since the ninth century". Lady Violet had probably heard that what an Oxford don called "the unmentionable vice of the Greeks" still existed in the monastic cloisters of Mt Athos, just as it had at Eton, McGill and Oxford. She sent Gavin to Dr Rawle, a Harley St. specialist, who advised that Gavin was too fragile to travel to Mt Athos. So, Byron wrote to console his friend and propose an even greater escape.

> *"I do hope you will turn out all right. I am sure you are*
> *doing the best thing. But for a year now your nerves have*
> *been bad. Perhaps this – whatever "this" is – will turn them*
> *too. You ought never to set foot in London again. Why not*
> *go to Thibet? When my publishers think sufficiently of me*
> *to advance money as £1,000 instead of £100, we can make a*
> *joint expedition..."*

On 20th November 1926. *The Times* announced that Gavin and Honor's *"marriage has been arranged"* and he left for Australia the very next day. Before going, Gavin agreed to let Peter Rodd, who had been sent down from Oxford, have stay in his London house while he was away in India. Peter was soon to write to Gavin in Calcutta:

> *"Honor asks often about your absence but I am going to try*
> *and send her out to Rome to stay with my family in January.*
> *So I shall delegate my duties as consoler to my Mama."*

Six days later Peter wrote again to say:

> *"How are you? Honor says you ought to come home, but*
> *on the whole seems to be bearing up...It might amuse you*
> *to know your engagement was announced in no less than 9*
> *papers not I believe excluding the Daily Herald. I don't know*
> *who did it. Lady K I suppose."*

Peter Rodd's information that the engagement had been announced in seven more papers than was usual for a society wedding would probably have added to Gavin's fears for his future. Circumstances were conspiring to change his life forever after the wedding in seven and a half months' time. In the meantime, as his health was causing concern, he managed to get away. Word spread that this was a long-planned "voyage of discovery" to aid Gavin's study of peoples, infrastructure and politics in foreign countries, which his grandfather Lord Faringdon thought desirable. He and Lady Violet believed this would lead to a significant career in the colonial administration.

Freed of the pressure at home, Gavin replied to Byron, addressing him facetiously as *"Robert, My Poppet"* while on board the Orient Line's *S.S. Orama*. This passenger ship had been launched two years earlier to cater to the needs of well-heeled travellers. It had everything on board to help him enjoy a relaxing voyage to Australia via Spain, Africa, Arabia and India. But in spite of these diversions Gavin's only comments were that he was *"between Port Said and Colombo"* and that the *"sea remains unfailingly calm"*, giving the impression of having shrunk into his shell. *"I may as well confess that I have not kept a diary & if I had there would still be nothing in it"*.

Interestingly, that letter from Gavin included a sketch of a ship passing through the Suez Canal beneath a Cubist rendering of Port Said. His sketch shows how the canal banks were lined with large B.P. and Socony (Mobil Oil) storage tanks, as well as coal and sand bunkers. This was the sort of commercial information his grandfather would have appreciated. Soon afterwards, Byron sent a letter about Lord Faringdon, relaying a potentially scandalous tale penned by a French conspiracy theorist.

> *"My dear Gavin,*
>
> *Have you ever seen a book called 'Les Démons de l'Espionnage Anglais I bought it in Constantinople & looking through it found some delicious passages about your grandfather."*

Byron copied out and sent two foolscap pages in French, which claimed that in 1915 Sir Alexander Henderson – Gavin's grandfather – was at the centre of a conspiracy to bankrupt the French and

German governments. The author suggests this was so blatant that *"even a child of five could see through"*; and here Byron marked the phrase margin with four broad pen strokes and three exclamation marks in the margin. The author went on to allege that Gavin's grandfather's reward was to be created Lord Faringdon by his fellow conspirators, Lord Grey, the British Foreign Secretary, and Sir Robert Cecil, the Minister of Blockade, who had been responsible for devising procedures to bring economic pressure against Germany. The anonymous author adds that Alexander Henderson's guilt was so great that if his family knew, they would suffer insomnia for the rest of their lives. Robert marked this with a broad pen stroke and the words *"I hope it hasn't"*. Byron ended with the lines

> *"Isn't this wonderful? I will give you the book sometime – not just yet as it contains similar details of Zaharoff's private life. He also says that the intelligence service has its headquarters on the 2nd floor of Downing St!"*

Byron told Gavin that he bought the book because of its tales about Sir Basil Zaharoff – an arms dealer who had become notorious for selling British machine guns and munitions to the Boers and Turks. Gavin's grandfather had invested in a ship-building firm which was commissioned to provide some battleships for the Turkish Navy – but they were never delivered due to the outbreak of WW1. So, the connection with Zaharoff, if there was one, may have been tenuous. The story seems to have been over-cooked by the French journalist. Byron clearly thought that it was absurd and would amuse rather than alarm his downcast friend.

When Gavin returned in April 1927, after four months abroad, he found that Honor had been to stay with his mother at Buscot Park on three separate occasions – in fact, for a total of 14 nights. Lady Violet had given regular reports of his travels to the *Daily Mail*; such as on January 27th, *"My son is still in Australia"*; on April 9th, *"He has been staying with the British Legation in Athens and is due back in Britain within the next few days"*. Soon after his return on the 16th the *Daily*

Mail reported that the Conservative MP Bob Boothby attended the coming-of-age party of Lady "Nina" Seafield at Castle Grant in Morayshire. She owned the house adjacent to Gavin's in North St., W1 and had invited her cousin Mark Ogilvie-Grant and a group of his amusing friends for the weekend. The guests included Robert Byron, Oliver Messell, Tom Driberg, Patrick Balfour and John Betjeman. These men were more interested in each other than any of the female guests. Nancy Mitford was there, hopelessly chasing the man she called her fiancé, Hamish St. Clair Erskine, who set his hair in curlers and dressed as a girl for the weekend. Honor was not invited to this largely *BYP* gathering.

Two weeks later the *Daily Mail* reported that Gavin and Lord Rosse, Harold Acton, Patrick Balfour and Mark Ogilvie-Grant attended a party hosted by Mrs Francis Howard (mother of the outrageously camp Brian Howard) at her home in Bryanston Square. Again, Honor was not among the amusing guests. Clearly, Gavin had not been eager to spend a weekend with his fiancée. His anxiety about marrying had not been quelled by his trip abroad. This probably accounts for some rebellious incidents leading up to the wedding. The first was when an evening out with Gavin's best man, Bob Boothby MP, at the fashionable Night Light club ended badly. According to Robert Byron, they got drunk and disorderly. Luckily, all mention of this was kept out of the press.

However, five nights later, when some people expected to see a firework display over the river due to Gavin's bachelor party being held at an up-market club in Henley-On-Thames, passers-by witnessed illuminations of a different sort – "a conflagration", "flames of terrifying dimensions", etc. This time, the influential MP was very involved and not able to hush it up.

CHAPTER 3

"Setting the Thames on Fire"

On 1ˢᵗ June 1927, the eve of Gavin and Honor's marriage, thirty of his friends drove to the exclusive riverside Phyllis Court Club, Henley-on-Thames, for his bachelor night dinner. Most of his guests were titled, and some were commoners who would become household names; such as John Betjeman, the future Poet Laureate; and Beverley Nichols, the journalist and author (who advertised Jellymeat Whiskas cat food on television in the 1960s and 70s). Another untitled guest at the time was Tom Driberg (later Baron Bradwell) who had been one of Gavin's contemporaries at Oxford. Driberg was working at the *Daily Express* and described the events that night as an *"attempt to literally set the Thames on fire"*. His eyewitness report was recycled and expanded by rival newspapers. Four days after the event the following appeared in the *Daily Mail:*

> "BACHELOR REVELS. SETTING THE THAMES
> ON FIRE."

> *"Mr Gavin Henderson, who was married to Lord Kylsant's daughter on Thursday, gave a bachelor party to about 30 friends at the Phyllis Court Club here on Wednesday night. The young men arrived in motorcars and before dinner ordered 20 gallons of petrol "in buckets". After dinner they pinned on the walls bills bearing the inscription "This garage does not stock motor spirit derived from plundered Russian oil."...*

> *The petrol was poured into the river and matches were*
> *thrown into it. The petrol caught fire and the flames leapt up*
> *the Cromwellian wall, burning off the roses for which it is*
> *famous, scorching the lawn, and burning the chestnut trees,*
> *which stand in the grounds...When the fire had died down*
> *the young men returned to their cars and went back to town."*

A few days later the *Daily Mail* added:

> *"Phyllis Court Club issued a writ for damage to the*
> *rose-covered Cromwellian wall which overlooks the Thames*
> *at the winning post of the Henley boat races is said to have*
> *been badly damaged by fire...and the legal advisors of the*
> *Thames Conservancy Board are considering this matter and*
> *legal proceedings against Mr Henderson are likely ...."*

On 8th June – over a month after the incident had taken place – *The Western Daily Press* quoted Gavin stating that he *"had absolutely nothing to do with the incident"*. The paper speculated that the madcap event must have been just the latest Bright Young People's prank. Then they brought the *"staggering costs of the evening"* to their readers' attention with: *"The bill for the dinner, including the item for the petrol, was a hundred guineas"*. This would have seemed profligate to most people in 1927 as it amounted to roughly £5,000 in today's money. The Hon. Patrick Balfour (the future historian Lord Kinross) was one of Gavin's closest friends. Writing as *Mr Gossip* for the *Daily Sketch* he tried to shift the blame to unnamed others: *"It was the BYP who set the Thames afire at Henley"*. He tried to take some of the heat out of the subject by pointing out that it was clearly a joke that got out of hand, and that until now *"'setting the Thames on fire' has been regarded as the epitome of all that is dashing and picturesque"*. Patrick tactfully omitted that the travel writer Robert Byron had written the remark about plundered Russian oil and that he and the Hon. Peter Rodd had cooked up more mischief to make Gavin's wedding memorable. This was not quite a scandal but interest was sufficient for the story to be stretched in the *Daily Mail* a week later:

> *"Phyllis Court Club, Henley, has issued a writ for damages against Mr. Gavin Henderson, the club member who on the evening of June 1ˢᵗ, the eve of his marriage to Lord Kylsant's daughter, gave a bachelor party there to about 30 of his friends. On the same evening it is alleged, petrol was poured on the river and set on fire. The legal advisers of the Thames Conservancy are considering this matter.*
>
> *Mr Henderson's wedding, it will be recalled, was the occasion of a practical joke, a large number of people receiving bogus invitations to the ceremony. Despite the efforts of Scotland Yard, the authors of the hoax have not been found.*
>
> *The suggestion has been made that this particular "joke" was a reprisal for a "joke" for which Mr Henderson was alleged to have been responsible some time ago when the moat of a country house in Berkshire was set on fire by the use of petrol."*

Then the *Sunday Post* added some vivid details:

> *"A witness, describing the scene, said there was a sheet of flame of really appalling dimensions. It hid the trees on the other side of the river. Some of the guests threw heavy garden seats into the river."*

It was now late July, the midsummer "silly season" for news stories. Increasingly, Gavin appeared in a poor light as the latest articles were written to appeal to the morally indignant readers of tabloid papers. Unsurprisingly, Gavin received this anonymous letter:

> *"Who were the 30 young cads you entertained at Henley? If you do not disassociate yourself from such riff-raff you will be judged as one of them – You must not think that because you may be a Lord some day you can afford to avoid being a good*

> *example, for Lords are nothing nowadays or any ass can be*
> *one. At present you are associating with time wasters.*
>
> *A well-wisher.*
>
> *There are plenty of good objects which deserve money instead*
> *of your wasting it."*

The writer had put his finger on a pulse of disapproval and feeling that retribution was due. For all that, there was also a sense of envy in some others, as Robert Byron discovered when sailing home from Greece:

> *"I am terribly worried over Gavin's case – as it might have*
> *vile repercussions. Its fame has spread to this boat. I heard*
> *an old bearded man saying: 'What I want to do is to set the*
> *Thames on fire like those young chaps…'"*

Things were still rumbling on two months later. *The Western Daily Press* reported:

> *"Mr Henderson accepted full responsibility… but on July*
> *22nd his lawyer wrote that he denied taking any part in the*
> *incident….an employee at the club said that he was <u>not</u> one*
> *of the gentlemen at the party that night who came to him*
> *about petrol…"*

Finally, on August 5th 1927 Gavin appeared before the Henley Borough Bench of Magistrates charged that:

> *"He with others did unlawfully do an act injuriously*
> *affecting safety of the Thames, to wit by burning petrol…*
> *and of causing oil to pass into the Thames near Henley and*
> *procuring persons unknown to set fire to it."*

Many witnesses gave testimony and it became clear that Gavin was not one of the men who collected and poured the petrol onto the

Thames. The fire had demolished a 40-foot-long line of rose bushes growing along a wall that Oliver Cromwell's forces had constructed during the English Civil war. Its flames had scorched the leaves off some chestnut trees and threatened to engulf a pavilion built for the regatta. Some of the guests had got together to lift heavy iron benches from the lawn and tumble them into the river. Gavin was certainly there. But he had repeatedly assured worried staff members that the petrol and any damages would be paid for. In this promise he was as good as his word and paid promptly. The *Evening Standard* covered the trial at length and recorded the following enigmatic exchange between the prosecutor, Mr Gerald Dobson, and a defence witness, Mr Charles Emmott. The latter was a guest at the bachelor night dinner party who described himself as a member of the Bar.

> When asked who poured the petrol on the water the following exchange ensued:
>
> *"I don't think I can say."*
>
> *"Do you mean you do not know the name of the person?"*
>
> *"No. I do know the name."*
>
> *"Was he a person of reasonable reputation?"*
>
> *"Oh, certainly".*
>
> *"Do you know why this man should not come forward and say 'It was I who did this thing and Mr Gavin Henderson is being wrongly accused?'"*
>
> *"No – I can offer no explanation."*

Then the magistrates retired for five minutes and on returning the Chairman announced the charges would be dismissed. Mr Henderson was congratulated by many friends outside the court.

The culprit's name was never divulged. Gavin paid 100 guineas for the dinner, petrol and ancillary costs to the club. On top of that, he paid £228 for legal services. Altogether, that one evening's entertainment had cost him **£340** at a time when the average wage for a male agricultural worker was £1. 11s. 8d. per week (Hansard, December 1927). It would seem that he took that to heart, for he never did anything as frivolous again. Newspaper reports of misbehaviour by privileged men were frequent in 1927. After further pranks were reported at his wedding reception on the following day, the impression grew that Gavin was more involved that he claimed. This was exacerbated by several papers reporting that the groom arrived at St. Margaret's, Westminster – the most fashionable of society marriage venues – *"over twenty minutes late"*. Amongst those kept waiting inside were Princess Alice, the Countess of Athlone, Princess Marie Louise, nine bridesmaids, and members of the couple's extended families. In addition, there were six hundred guests – many of them titled – as a long list in *The Times* showed. The officiating clergy were the Archbishop of Wales, the Bishop of St. David's, accompanied by two reverend fathers. Outside the church a crowd of press photographers and spectators were awaiting the arrival of the bride and her father. That group buzzed with rumours as Lord Kylsant's limousine drew up several times – only to move on after ushers rushed up to inform the occupants that the groom had not yet arrived. When Honor eventually descended the onlookers were able to see

> *"a dress of ivory satin on medieval lines with a girdle of diamante and pearls along with pearl tassels falling to the hem of the trailing skirt. Her Court train of ivory satin was bordered with silver embroidered applique on silver net, and over it fell the long tulle veil held in place by a pointed coronet of diamonds and pearls outlined with small orange buds. She carried a sheaf of white orchids tied with silver".* The nine bridesmaids wore *"dresses of ibis pink chiffon with draped skirts in two tiers, and short capes hanging from the shoulders. Their bandeaux of silver embroidered tulle were*

outlined with miniature rosebuds, and they carried sheaves of shaded blue delphiniums."

At the end of this paragraph *The Times* mentioned

"The best man was Mr Robert Boothby MP and Lady Kylsant held a reception afterwards at Chelsea House, Cadogan Place."

Why didn't Bob Boothby MP get the groom to the church on time? Gavin's friend Peter Rodd sent a jocular note to Gavin a few days after the wedding hinting at the reason:

"I am becoming a wedding expert and have made up a list of contingencies and steps that must be taken when they arise.

Circumstances: Bridegroom drunk at Wellington Barracks at 1 a.m. on wedding day.

Cure: Obtain permit from Colonel to introduce into mess room the Lady K.

N.B. This cure is believed to be infallible."

Reports of his misbehaviour affected Bob Boothby's position as Parliamentary Private Secretary to the Chancellor of the Exchequer Winston Churchill, as he lost his job eventually. This was due to what he referred to as his *"little red devil"* who could be *"great fun"*. A contributing factor may have been that a police sergeant investigating the fire at Phyllis Court Club noticed that bills bearing the words *"This garage does not stock motor spirit derived from plundered Russian oil."* – identical to the one stuck up in the garage – lay on the back seat of a car parked inside. It emerged that this vehicle belonged to a member of parliament, and that Boothby had been one of a group of four MPs who visited Russia in an attempt to get the communist government to restore stocks of oil it had confiscated from former British owners. He had continued to campaign against

Russian exports afterwards, which made him a prime suspect for one of the guests who had taken petrol from the garage. Notwithstanding this revelation and setback, Boothby went on to rise again in political circles and became famous (or infamous) for his extramural love life and louche friendships.

The *Times* piece was written by its special correspondent Jock Murdocke, who Robert Byron described *as "a magnificent example of a successful journalist…also writing for American papers".* Two days after the wedding, Murdocke was astonished to receive a letter from Gavin. It had been written in his honeymoon suite at the Villa Serbelloni Hotel, beside Lake Como. That letter did not survive but Gavin kept Murdocke's reply which reads:

"28a Albemarle St,

Piccadilly.

10th June 1927.

My dear Gavin,

Your letter this morning was certainly a surprise…I was not quite prepared for a letter from the happy bridegroom. All the cuttings are being collected from the Daily Mail, Daily Express, Evening News and Evening Standard, of the 2nd, 3rd., and 4th. and are being sent to the address you give. I do hope you receive them. You might let me know.

With this letter I am sending only possible photograph I could get of you both. I think your race down the aisle was the most amazing piece of matrimonial hurriedness that the world has ever experienced. I had photographers stationed at every door, and alas for my expectations.

I did not know you were flying across. How marvellous to have out-Lindenberghed Lindenberg (sic).

You never introduced me to your wife. I felt such a fool.
Honestly Gavin, but then I expect your head was turned with
all the excitement and you quite forgot."

The reference to Lindbergh was topical as the pioneer airman had made his famous non-stop flight from New York to Paris a month earlier. The newlyweds had been driven to Croydon airport and flown to France before motoring to their honeymoon hotel beside Lake Como. Murdocke was to pass on newspaper clippings and a second letter full of delicious gossip:

"I have not seen the noble Robert since, but ran into one of
your ushers Prince Lexel Hochberg from Poland. We had
roars of laughter over your wedding. The scream it all was!
Who do you think sat behind me, dressed all in black save
for a gorgeous rope of pearls, with a wide brimmed hat
that completely hid her face? The Divine Doris Delevingne,
unattended, for my Lord Castlerosse was busy writing
scandal…Gavin, your wedding made me roar, but my
sincerest wishes for both your happiness, for after all that is
what matters in life. If there is anything else I can do let me
know but do write clearly. I had to consult the good advice of
Ferraro of the Berkeley to figure out the name of your hotel at
Bellagio.

Yours,

Jock

J.A. Murdocke."

A brief look at the guests Murdocke mentions gives us an impression of Gavin's milieu. Count Lexel Hochberg, the Prince of Pless, was a bisexual Silesian and Polish nobleman who had a fleeting affair with Robert Byron before he had another with Hamish St. Clair-Erskine, the promiscuous gay whom Nancy Mitford forlornly hoped would marry her. Robert Byron wrote to Gavin that he feared she would be hurt when she saw them together at the wedding. He was greatly relieved when Nancy dealt with the awkward incident smoothly. The Prince of Pless soon began an affair with Jock Murdocke; and Jock was mentioned in Byron's letters as having had a fling with both him and the Hon. Hugh Lygon. The latter was the model for Sebastian Flyte in Evelyn Waugh's *Brideshead Revisited.* Hugh's father, Lord Beauchamp, had fled Britain to avoid prosecution for homosexual acts in 1924. So three years later, five of Gavin's close friends could have been found guilty of that same crime. Nancy Mitford habitually referred to these men (most of whom were close friends) as "pansies". As her brother was one as well it would seem that the term did not imply any negative judgement. Beverley Nichols, another discreetly gay man in that wide circle of friends claimed that the word "homosexual" was rarely used in those days outside of books written by psychiatrists.

In addition to this "gay" element, Gavin invited Doris Delevingne, the Countess of Castlerosse. She was a strikingly beautiful woman, certain to be noticed. Her physical attractiveness can be gauged today by glancing at her great niece the model Cara Delevingne, although the latter cannot claim to have the long legs that people of her aunt's day praised. The National Portrait Gallery has several images of Doris wearing her signature white shorts – and she was painted in these several times by Winston Churchill as well as John Lavery R.A. Both claimed to have had affairs with her, as did Randolph Churchill, Winston's son. Doris was the daughter of a butter merchant from Beckenham and had worked as a model in Mayfair until a succession of "Sugar Daddies" began to pay for the pleasure of her companionship. The result was that she was now well known as a modern courtesan and owned a Georgian house near the Grosvenor House hotel. Stunning jewellery, furs, and haut-couture gowns all came as gifts from her admirers. Whilst she would auction off gowns and lingerie for charity – having worn them once – she was proud to maintain that she never sold an item of jewellery. Doris described herself as *"simply a magnet for men"* and signed into the visitors' book at Faringdon House as a *Poule de Luxe* (the French euphemism for a rich man's plaything). Her wit became legendary after she quipped that *"An Englishwoman's bed is her castle"*. She had many society friends, and aristocratic mothers were rumoured to have asked Doris to "convert" their gay sons, who had emerged from the best British public schools without having met many young women. Doris was said to have also tutored women the arts of love, for as she put it, *"There is no such thing as an impotent man, only inexperienced women"*. Her presence would have set tongues wagging.

Doris had met Gavin and her husband Valentine Castlerosse at a BYT late-night playground, the Cavendish Hotel on the corners of Duke and Jermyn Streets near Piccadilly. Its proprietor Rosa Lewis, knew everyone's secrets and joked that Doris's autobiography should be called: *Around the World in 80 Beds*. Lord Castlerosse was deep in debt when they met there. He was also drinking heavily, vastly overweight and working as a society columnist for the *Sunday Express*. Still, his *"Londoner's Log"* was immensely popular, and he was due to inherit a castle and estates in Ireland when his father, the Earl of Kenmare, passed away. Doris married him two weeks after they met and he soon complained of her *"shameless infidelity"* as she continued to entertain wealthy men in private because, as she put it, they *"needed the money"*. **They were separated after only six weeks together and he felt humiliated and jealous.** For years afterwards she refused to grant him a divorce as she wanted to keep her title.

Those who attended the wedding found it memorable for unusual reasons. There was no stately walk down the aisle onto the green outside St. Margaret's Westminster; no bouquet thrown to shrieking bridesmaids; and the press only managed to get one shot of the newlyweds – with their faces down as they rushed out of the church into a waiting limousine. A small album of photographs survived in Gavin's files showing unidentified guests leaving the church. The women shown are all fashionably flat-chested and men stiff in formal attire with top hats and gloves. The reception was held at the Kylsants' home of Chelsea House, Cadogan Place. Here further surprises lay in store. To entertain his friends – and presumably to annoy his mother and Lady Kylsant – Gavin had invited the jazz singer Florence Mills, an entertainer who had recently been billed as the "Dark Star of the London Pavillion". "The Blackbirds", her dance troupe from Harlem, New York, consisted of nubile black women in skimpy skirts and blouses. At Gavin and Honor's wedding they performed their hit song *"The black-bottom"* and mingled with the other wedding guests.

A few days later Jock Murdocke sent Gavin some newspaper clippings about the "Setting the Thames on Fire" incident. One from the *Sunday Post* read:

> *"It was discovered that 'Bogus' invitations had been sent out. Scotland Yard were called to investigate on the request of Lord Kylsant and found that excellent copies of the originals had been sent to members of the theatrical professions, the Japanese and Russian Embassies, and others who were unknown to Lord and Lady Kylsant…Most of the forgeries bore an East End postmark. This was suspected to have been another practical joke by one of the 'Bright Young Things'."*

A few days later *The Times* reported that "*it is feared that a powerful gang was responsible and had eluded Scotland Yard*". On the following day the *Daily Mail* claimed to have found the culprit, a *"well-known young man avenging a practical joke played on him two years earlier"*. However, Beverley Nichols wrote that *"the Hon. Peter Rodd had sent out the false invitations"*. According to him, Gavin was *"in on the joke and enjoyed it immensely"*. The story carried on growing in fits and starts. For example, in the following week the *Daily Express* added:

> *"Detective officers have not overlooked that many of the bogus invitations found their way to famous theatrical stars, including Mr Billy Merson".*

The latter was a music hall star, famous for his risqué songs and cockney banter. He was reported to have taken the joke in good part and wished the bride and groom well. Another fake went to an

Asian politician married to a Mr Shapurji Saklatvala, Communist MP for North Battersea. The *Sunday Post* claimed that he told them that several Russian Embassy staff were disappointed and annoyed at having been duped. Other fake invitations had gone to the German and Japanese embassies, as well as to British civil servants. The *Daily Mail* estimated that hundreds of well-printed versions of the real invitations had been sent out but, as many had arrived just days before the wedding, not everyone had been duped.

Afterwards, Lord Faringdon and Lady Violet appeared to believe that Gavin had been the innocent butt of all these practical jokes. They felt that it was to his credit he had taken responsibility and paid the costs out of his own pocket. However, some of Gavin's Bachelor Night guests thought that he had initiated and enjoyed the rumpus. Some speculated that he had wanted to get back at his mother and Lady Kylsant for having trapped him and Honor in a marriage. Both felt that they had been locked into a commercial union that suited these matriarchs. Clearly, not enough thought was given to the consequences. The result was that Gavin resolved to let them work to erase memory of his pranks.

To achieve this Lady Violet, the daughter of an Earl and widow of a Lieutenant-Colonel, pulled strings like few could – and all to help her son fulfil his potential for the family. She was friendly with Lord Rothermere, proprietor of the mass circulation tabloid, the *Daily Mail*. It had been the first to mention Gavin's *"Bachelor Night Revels"*, but soon after the wedding it began reporting details about Gavin and Honor in the best of lights. For example, society people tended to leave London between August and October, and normally, during this period the gossip columnists reported on who was in Monaco, Capri or Biarritz. But two months after their June wedding, the *Daily Mail* gossip column reported that Honor went to a nightclub with Lady Phyllis Allen and The Hon. David Plunkett Greene, a prominent member of the "Bright Young Things" who had been in the Oxford Railway Club with Gavin. In the same month the *Daily Mail* announced that Gavin and Honor had entertained a dozen guests, *"including Lady Massereene"* at *"a popular west end restaurant"*. In September the paper reported that the couple went to a nightclub with "Babe" Plunkett Greene – another prominent "Bright Young Thing" – who was about to divorce her husband.

On 16th November 1927 the *Daily Mail* announced that Gavin attended a dinner in honour of the Belgian Ambassador at Claridge's. Then on the 14th December 1927 that he and Honor left London the day before because *"Mrs Henderson is not very well and has gone down to her parents' place in Wales. Her husband has gone on a visit to Brussels. Before they went, they gave a farewell cocktail party in their house in Westminster"*. In late December the *Daily Mail* informed its readers that Gavin had just returned from Brussels by air and that the landing had been adventurous:

> *"We ran into a dense fog over the Channel and had to turn*
> *back and circle round twice before getting across at a height*
> *of 50 ft, with the spray from the sea almost wetting the under-*
> *carriage. It was quite palpitating. Finally, when we did reach*
> *England, we made a forced landing at Littlestone with the*
> *wireless catching in a hedge"*.

On the 1st December 1927 the *Daily Mail* announced that Gavin and Honor's neighbours in North Street, Westminster, were Lady Seafield and Commander Locker-Lampson. Then it reported that Lady Seafield had hosted a party where the guests included Gavin and Bryan Guinness, before going on to say:

> *"Mr Henderson is now seriously contemplating politics. He*
> *is one of the quickest brains of any young man I know – with*
> *the possible exception of his friend, Mr Peter Rodd"*.

Later that month the *Daily Mail* mentioned that Nina, the Countess of Seafield, had hosted another party – this time at a *"popular west end restaurant"*. Again, her neighbours Gavin and Honor had attended. And so, slowly and steadily, the newlyweds were established as a feature of London society.

In June 1928 the *Daily Mail* reported an important announcement by Lady Violet. She informed them that Gavin and Honor had "*just returned from abroad and that Mr Henderson was now seriously contemplating a political career*". An unkind caricature of the couple aboard ship appeared in *The Tatler* that month. Gavin was depicted as little more than a large thin nose with hands and feet; Honor as a pie-faced homunculus. Three weeks afterwards Lady Violet announced Gavin's intention to enter the political arena as a conservative. But a few days later the *Daily Mail* told its readers that

> "*Mr Henderson has temporarily abandoned his intention of going into politics*", and quoted him as saying, "*I had hoped to be adopted as the Conservative candidate for Southampton but, as you may have seen it announced, Lord Thirlestone was nominated in my place. So I am now going off to Athens to collect my motor-car which I left there not long ago.*"

The paper soon added that Gavin had "*arrived in Athens*", where he met up with Robert Byron and Mark Ogilvie-Grant to visit the male-only monastic preserve of Mt Athos. They neglected to report that he had spent most of his time in the company of unmarried young men – many unlikely to marry – before his return via Austria. The newlywed Gavin was back in England for only two weeks before setting off to drive to Spain. His companion was Robert Byron, who gave a vivid account of the journey. It took place in Gavin's new Rolls-Royce Phantom cabriolet tourer, which was painted "Faringdon Green", the same colour as the steam locomotives named after his grandfather. According to Byron, Gavin refused to let anyone else touch the wheel, and drove "*574 miles (923 kms) from Le Havre to San Sebastian at 70 m.p.h. most of the way – only slowing down to 50 m.p.h. to swig from a bottle of Vouvray*". They made it in two days – an unofficial record for the time. Then Gavin drove 1,000 miles further "*like a man possessed, on to Toledo and Madrid to view the El Greco paintings*". Then he drove back to London. On their return, Byron recorded that his friend threw a cocktail party where 60–70 people came and *"Gavin made cocktails from 5.30 – 8.30 in 2 shakers until all the drink was exhausted"*. There was no mention of his wife Honor here but a photo of her appeared on the Society page of *The Sketch* on Feb 28th 1928 with the following paragraph:

> *"CREDIT for having given the most amusing party during the last few weeks belongs to Mr. and Mrs. Gavin Henderson. Pressure on the space of their small house in North-street was so great at the party in question that every room, up to the attics, was thrown open to guests, some of whom overflowed into the streets and were received in the house of a neighbour who had obligingly lent much of his crockery for the occasion."*

Around this time, Nancy Mitford met the newlyweds at one of Nina Seafield's parties in North St. Nancy had known Gavin for years, but this was her first chance to have an intimate conversation with Honor. Afterwards, she wrote to Evelyn Waugh that she had learned Honor had no idea about gay men before she married. Nancy implied that everyone else knew that Gavin would never be the orthodox husband that Honor had expected. Waugh wrote back mentioning that he had been to a party when *"Gavin was there with his wife, whom tho' it sounds absurd, I rather liked"*. Why he should it have been absurd for him to like Honor was never explained, but it was probably linked to Evelyn's resentment of Gavin's relationship with Robert Byron. When Waugh married "She-Evelyn" Gardner, Byron had been his best man. The newlyweds were so strapped for cash that they spent part of their honeymoon in Robert's small London flat. Since then, while Waugh struggled to keep himself afloat, Gavin had been paying the costs of Robert's trips abroad and then provided Robert with an interest-free loan to help him become a travel writer. Evelyn had hoped that travel writing would provide the income to sustain him during the periods when he was writing novels. But Gavin had made their mutual friend a rival talent, and the ambitious writer – destined to be one of the finest of his generation – resented it bitterly.

The extent of his animosity revealed itself in October 1928 when Waugh's novel *Decline and Fall* came out. The book was well-received, particularly after Arnold Bennett, literary reviewer of the *Evening Standard*, praised it as *"an uncompromising and brilliantly malicious satire"*. One of the first to read the manuscript had been the budding novelist Anthony Powell, then working as an editor at Duckworth's. Powell got the firm to agree to publish on the proviso that anything likely to cause offence be removed. Waugh said he would prefer not to change anything and managed to get Chapman & Hall, where his father was a director, to take it. But they too asked for cuts. Waugh made as few as possible in order to keep – as he put it in the book's preface – *"the light, bright, tone of what was meant to be funny"*. However, Cyril Connolly, another Oxford contemporary, thought these cuts would not be enough when he reviewed it for the *New Statesman*. Connolly felt he should make clear that

> *"it is not a satire, but a farce... the humour throughout is of that subtly metallic kind which more than anything else seems a product of this generation."*

Cyril Connolly was right to refer to its "Bright Young Thing" style of heartless humour as one character was named "The Hon. Kevin Sanderson". Connolly saw this as a swipe at The Hon. Gavin Henderson. So did Robert Byron. Waugh's diary says he rang *"very cross to complain"*. This was because the name Kevin Sanderson was so close to Gavin Henderson, and linked the latter with Sanderson and Sons, the Victorian company with the Royal Warrant as Purveyors of Wallpapers to the King. Robert saw this as a barbed reference to the time Gavin had spent with the elderly Harold Peto at W. Turner, Lord & Co. That company's domestic clients were certainly upper class, while Sanderson and Sons were middle class. Robert felt that Evelyn's snobbishness was malicious. The author agreed to change the name in order to placate Byron, but 2,000 copies of the first edition had been sold before the 2nd impression arrived at the booksellers. Then it was found that Kevin Sanderson had been changed to Lord Parakeet, a self-centred, bird-brained, toffee-nosed, spendthrift:

"At half-past three Lord Parakeet arrived, slightly drunk and in evening clothes, having just 'escaped less than one second ago' from Alastair Trumpington's twenty-first birthday party in London.

'Alastair was with me some of the way,' he said, 'but I think he must have fallen out.'

The party, or some of it reassembled in pajamas to welcome him. Lord Parakeet walked around bird-like and gay, pointing his thin white nose and making rude little jokes at everyone in turn in a shrill, emasculate voice."

Byron was furious. He thought that the words "shrill" and "emasculate" would be conflated to mean "effeminate". In addition, those words were unkind, as the pitch of Gavin's voice had risen after he had suffered from mumps a few years earlier. This seemed caricature, not satire or farce. However, Waugh argued that as Gavin was not a Lord any connection was tenuous. Lord Parakeet is largely a reincarnation of an 18th-century fop – only his evident wealthiness singles him out as different. For after playing a *"hand of cards"* with a fellow guest *"Parakeet lost thirty pounds, and opening his pocket-book, paid him in ten-pound notes."* This was perhaps the root for Waugh's dislike of Gavin – envy of his abundant wealth and ability to pay for his follies at a moment's notice.

At the same time, a very different artist, saw Gavin as someone witty, unconventional and amusing. This was Simon Elwes R.A. who painted Gavin's portrait in 1928. He depicted Gavin in a dark brown suit lounging on a yellow armchair in a room lined with green wallpaper. Something self-assured, rebellious and yet playful comes across. Again, it is a portrait of a modern man of a particular set in his own times. Gavin appears to Elwes as he did to others: clever, cultured, defiant and amusing. The freelance journalist Jock Murdocke in the *Times* gave an insight into how the painting was created:

> *"Mr Henderson thrives on repartee, and Mr Elwes told me*
> *that when he was painting him all he had to do was fling*
> *some insult at him from time to time to get just the right*
> *expression: and Mr Henderson enjoyed the sitting immensely.*
> *Afterwards Mr Elwes told me 'I cabled him to ask if I might*
> *exhibit the portrait at the Royal Academy show that summer,*
> *and had a reply from Bangkok, in these three ambiguous*
> *words: 'Hang my Picture.''"*

During this period a very influential young man had made his way –
almost unnoticed – into Gavin's background. This was the remarkable
Irishman Brendan Bracken, soon to become his neighbour in North
St., Westminster. The Buscot Park visitors' book shows that over the
next few years no one came to stay more regularly. Only a year older
than Gavin, Bracken was a highly successful businessman. He had a
controlling hand in seven of the most influential financial papers: *The*
Banker, The Financial News, The Economist, The Investors Chronicle,
The Practitioner, and *The Liverpool Journal of Commerce.* Lord
Faringdon and Lord Kylsant were amongst the many Conservatives
who admired his *laissez-faire* approach to commerce. Furthermore,
at the age of only 23 Bracken knew his way around the corridors of
power. He was a close supporter of Sir Winston Churchill – who
was then serving as Chancellor of the Exchequer in the Conservative
Prime Minister Stanley Baldwin's cabinet. Some even claimed that
he was so close to Churchill that he must have been his illegitimate
son, much to the chagrin of Churchill's son Randolph.

Brendan Bracken was someone who could be counted on to get
things done behind the scenes. Whilst his background in Ireland
was obscure, his prestige and influence in England was clear. For
example, after he moved into the fashionable town house two doors
down from Gavin's in Westminster, he got North Street renamed
Lord North Street. Between 1927 and 1929 he came to stay at Buscot
Park on five separate occasions for two nights, as well as twice for four
nights over Christmas. On top of this close contact, it is certain that
Gavin met Bracken at numerous cocktail parties and society dinners

in London. During this time, it seems likely that Bracken was behind Lady Violet's declaration that her son would stand as a Conservative MP for Southampton in 1927 – only for Gavin to announce shortly afterwards that he would not. Gavin did have an interest in politics – but in the anti-colonialist and separatist movements of India since his 1926 visit there. After the Wall Street Crash in 1929, Bracken's financial reputation helped to get him elected as a Conservative MP In parliament he supported Churchill (dedicated to keeping the Empire intact) and staunchly resisted any move towards Indian self-government. This coincided with Gavin's decision to distance from any political preferments in the UK.

Bracken was a larger-than-life character whose reputation was distorted in fiction. His busy social life brought him to the attention of Evelyn Waugh, who based a memorable character in *Brideshead Revisited* on Bracken. This was the Canadian (an outsider like the Irishman Bracken) Rex Mottram; a social-climbing, fast-talking, businessman with fingers in every pie. Rex had somehow come to know everyone and thought he could fix anything because of his right-wing friends. Another caricature of Brendan Bracken was published in the same year, 1945. This followed his time as Sir Winston Churchill's wartime Minister for Information where civil servants referred to him as "B.B." due to his habit of signing memos with his initials. Orwell had worked at the BBC's India desk during WW2. After Gandhi declared that a Japanese invasion of India would simply lead to an exchange of Imperial rulers, Bracken tightened censorship. Orwell saw this as an attempt to stifle the truth and suppress free speech. The result was that "B.B." was morphed in Orwell's novel *1984* into the despotic "Big Brother" and the Ministry of Information was satirised as the "Ministry of Truth".

Interesting glimpses of the secretive side of Bracken's personality emerge in notes to Gavin from Whitehall signed "B.B."; but more particularly in a short letter addressed to his mother: "Lady Violet Henderson, Barnsley Park, Cirencester" (her home during WW2). This was typed on a sheet of notepaper headed: MINISTRY OF

INFORMATION, MALET STREET., W.C.1. and dated 27th October, 1942.

(Handwritten:)

"My dear Violet,

(Typed:)

Everything you say about the gentleman in question is wholly accurate. I think, however, that your criticisms of him are an understatement. I am asking the fuel people to look into his petrol allowance.

(Signed)

Brendan Bracken"

Gavin was not at Buscot Park when B.B. came to stay with Lady Violet in June 1929. By then he had left on *"a fact-finding tour of the sub-continent"*. Honor, as usual, was simply left in England while Gavin travelled with his friends. This tour was set to take in Ceylon, India, Tibet and southern Persia. His objective seemed to be to start to make his way in the world abroad – very much in the Henderson family mould pioneered by Lord Faringdon and his four enterprising brothers. One presumes that his family thought this might work if he stuck to it. The one thing certain was that Gavin would not agree to stay in England and follow the safe paths prescribed by others. The result was that when Brendan Bracken arrived at Buscot Park in his chauffeur-driven Hispano-Suiza, Gavin was not there. The prodigal son was already on board a boat to India. When he returned two years later it would be as a supporter of Indian separate development, colonial independence, and worse still, as far as his mother B.B. and Winston Churchill were concerned, he was a budding socialist.

While Gavin was taking control of his own life what was to become of his wife Honor? Whilst she had the means and freedom to do as she pleased, she seemed to have been cut loose. Decades later, one of the couple's mutual friends, Alan Pryce-Jones passed on an anecdote she had confided in him. This partially explains how things were when they were together:

> *"Honor had been one of the daughters of Lady Kylsant,*
> *who demanded that her daughters make fine marriages,*
> *and chose for Honor Gavin Henderson, a lively and even at*
> *times dazzling figure, but not by temperament marriageable.*
> *She told me once that after a miserable year or two she had*
> *woken in their North St. home to hear a rhythmic knocking*
> *sound, and concluded that Gavin had hanged himself on*
> *the bathroom door. Should she cut him down? Should she*
> *stop the tap of his heels? She decided, no; then woke up*
> *thoroughly, with a start of remorse, to find that the tap was*
> *simply that of two heavy dressing gown cords in a draft."*

Clearly, the marriage had given Gavin such bouts of depression that she sometimes feared he would take his own life. Travelling frenetically with his friends had provided him with much-needed relief. When he returned to India this time, she was uncertain how much time she would be spending on her own in London. So, they agreed to leave North St., Westminster in the care of Peter Rodd, who was, as ever, at a loose end between jobs. A few days after Gavin left, Peter wrote to him saying, *"Honor is doing as well as expected"*. A month later, in July, Peter mentioned that she had gone to stay with family or friends. Then in January Rodd wrote, *"Honor I have not seen since Xmas when I heard she was OK."*

Whilst the marriage was effectively over, neither party would be free without a divorce or annulment. At the time, divorces involved lengthy public procedures after which they could only be granted by an Act of Parliament. The advantage of an annulment was that the marriage could be considered invalid retrospectively. As the couple had married in an Anglican ceremony, the Church might nullify it but could not grant a financial settlement. That could only be granted under English law and the best way to proceed would be via an annulment if it could be claimed that the marriage had never been consummated. If both parties agreed on this, a petition for annulment could be applied for. Both parties would have to sign the necessary papers in a court of law. This appears to be what happened before Gavin left for India, as an annulment took up to eight months to process. He was abroad when it was announced, and from that time on he provided her with an annuity. Happily, for them both, this was the sad end of a stressful time – for they were to develop a remarkable friendship afterwards.

In spite of the stress involved with the end of his marriage, Gavin appears to have found something inspiring and consoling. This was a dream of a new world order far away from B.B.'s sphere of influence. It was an ideology that took root when he read *The Open Conspiracy: Blue Prints for a World Revolution* written by H.G. Wells in 1928. This promised that *"universal peace, welfare and happy activity"* would result in the establishment of a *"world commonwealth"*. Wells warned against *"false loyalties, false standards of honour, false religious associations"* that are *"vestiges of the ancient order"*. Wells urged his readers to expect hardship and martyrdom, if need be, in order to attain *"a world at peace and liberated for an unending growth of knowledge and power."* The author came to stay for five nights at Buscot Park and would have discussed his ideas with Gavin. Wells wanted to change the structure of society forever. Since the early 1920s Wells had been not only a novelist but an outspoken socialist and pacifist. He had co-authored two books with Viscount Grey on the need to set up the "League of Nations". Gavin acquired a complete set of Wells' books, including extra copies of the political titles (presumably to give away to friends) many of which still survive in Buscot Park's library. Reading these had awakened Gavin's political awareness. Later, he was to serve with Wells as a committee member of the Fabian Society, and National Council for Civil Liberties (now known as Liberty).

In the meantime, what Wells was preaching could be seen in the struggle for Indian independence. Whilst progress was painfully slow, the Viceroy, Lord Irwin and the India Office had been encouraged by Prime Minister Stanley Baldwin to start on the long road that might lead to Indian self-government. The aim was to achieve this with as little strife and bloodshed as possible, which was largely what came to pass. This would not have been possible under a Conservative government headed by Sir Winston Churchill – who was staunchly opposed to any break-up of the British Empire. And so, Gavin left a failed marriage, his disappointed mother, and Brendan Bracken, behind him when he set off for India. He had set the Thames on fire. Was he aiming to be an arsonist in Calcutta?

CHAPTER 4

Ceylon, India, Persia, Tibet, Sikkim, Somalia

Two years after Gavin's wedding, his grandfather hoped that since his heir showed little interest in the financial whirl of the City, he might find a position in the diplomatic or colonial service. Lady Violet Henderson, Gavin's well-connected mother, had set her sights even higher – hoping that he might become Viceroy of India. Whilst Gavin had *"blotted his copy book"* they hoped he had matured, rehabilitated, and that his interest in the Empire and colonies would sow the seeds of his future success. This may have seemed the case over the next few years as Gavin traversed the sub-continent several times, then went as far north as Persia, Tibet and Sikkim; and south to Ceylon and Somaliland. He was welcomed everywhere; introduced to officials and enterprising people in commerce and engineering –many of whom his grandfather would approve. His mother would have been pleased to hear that he had met prominent figures in the Raj at the stately Government Houses of Calcutta, Madras and Darjeeling. He had even been invited to stay with Lord Irwin, the Viceroy, in New Delhi. He explored India's diverse cultural aspects by visiting Hindu, Muslim and Sikh maharajas. He stayed with princes and their families in Jodhpur (Rajasthan), Cooch Behar (West Bengal), Kollam (Kerala), Barandari (Punjab), as well the Khas Bagh (Rampur). He was there during a period of political turmoil when all the rulers faced challenges to their traditional roles and alliances on the country's path to self-government. What Gavin's family did not expect was that he hoped to attach himself to the rising stars of the new Indian order and to work for the anti-colonial movement. Gavin was determined not to be part of the past; however grand the Raj had been. He idealistically expected a brilliant new India, prosperity for all its constituent parts. It was a beautiful dream.

In July 1929 he set up a home from home at Flat 9, No 4 Elysium Row in Calcutta with his friend Robert Byron. Robert, of course, had no money apart from what he made as a freelance writer. He lived in fairly sumptuous surroundings thanks to Gavin's largesse. Their home was an elegant Georgian building that had been built in the East India Company quarter. It was a peaceful residential area inhabited by colonial administrators and foreign merchants. The two-storey house they inhabited was painted white. Neat lawns and a picket fence separated it from a tree-lined avenue that ran between well-spaced houses and gardens. A veranda ran around the ground floor, shaded from the baking sun by an over-hanging roof. The floor above had tall windows fitted with long awnings to keep the interior cool. A balcony with neo-classical columns was on the south side. The rooms inside had high ceilings and were arranged into two self-contained flats. In a letter to Patrick Balfour, he gave an idea of how he was living almost incognito there – as he had not come for the social life:

> *"There is no one I want to see, so I have made the exhaustion*
> *of my cards an excuse for not calling – a formality that is still*
> *rigidly observed here. But it had its own rules; outside on the*
> *gatepost of my part of the house is a little box (rather like*
> *the nests that children hang on trees to tempt tits or wrens),*
> *which I have labelled 'Mr Smith is not at Home'. Into this*
> *the jeunesse dorée, the dancing tribe of Calcutta, drop their*
> *cards."*

Gavin had sailed from Southampton to Calcutta via Algiers. Malta, Port Said, Aden and Columbo. He was fresh and ready for action. Robert, on the other hand, had arrived dishevelled and exhausted, for he had been commissioned by Lord Beaverbrook to write an account of the first Imperial Airways Mail flight to India for the *Daily Express*. His journey had consisted of a series of aerial hops to the sub-continent. It had taken 12 days to make his way with the mails via France, Italy, Spain, Greece, Egypt, Palestine and Iraq to Calcutta. For much of his career Byron would try to earn his keep as a freelance writer and photographer. Although his output was published in Beaverbrook's newspapers as well as *Country Life* and *The Times* and *Vogue*, he was often without sufficient means. This commission was paying for his journey to what he called "Thibet" with Gavin and some his other friends. Contrary to appearances, Gavin had not turned his back on the Bright Young People set who his family thought had led him astray. Some were hoping to join to him in India. Gavin's friend from Oxford, Tom Driberg, who was now working as a journalist for the *London Evening Standard*, served as an unofficial publicist for them when he wrote:

"A Lofty Enterprise

> *In view of recent criticisms of the manner in which the Bright Young People of London amuse themselves, it is refreshing to learn that there are at least four young members of Mayfair Society who are not satisfied with the novel entertainments lately introduced. Even the diversion of dressing up as babies does not appeal to them as sufficiently exciting. They yearn for excitement of a higher kind than anything they hitherto found in London, and no one can accuse them of failing to aim high when their aim is the Himalayas. Nor must it be rashly assumed that that they expect to find higher excitement in Himalayan hill-stations. Were they to come to India in that belief their quest would be in vain. It is no reflection on the ingenuity of hill-station entertainers to say that they could hardly hope to satisfy the cravings of these blasé young Londoners. The fact is that the Four are not so much in search of excitement as of adventure and they hope to find excitement in the exploration of the Himalayas, in the high adventure of climbing mountain peaks and*

*crossing glaciers. By doing so they will not only confound the
critics who imagine that our Bright Young People generally
are incapable of anything but banal and childish diversions,
but will give a salutary lesson to the writers who waste space
in complaining that their generation is lacking in the spirit of
adventure..."*

Gavin and Robert arrived in Calcutta just before Gandhi came,
defying the Police Commissioner's order not to light a bonfire of
foreign cloth in a Mirzapur park. The significance of this action
was that before British rule Calcutta had been the city that led the
world in exporting cloth; now it was an importer of cotton goods
manufactured in Manchester. Gandhi was arrested after excited
onlookers threw brickbats at the police holding back the crowds. He
was only detained for a few hours before being tried and released
on bail of just one shilling and discovered to his consternation
that someone had paid this without his consent. Gandhi hoped
to prompt Indian politicians to declare independence and start a
non-violent revolt intended to render British rule in India inoperable.
His visit to Calcutta had sparked widespread civil disobedience.
After spending several of the hottest summer months in Calcutta
attending speeches, meeting the activists and witnessing riots, Gavin
and Robert met up with David Fyse, one of their contemporaries at
Oxford. Together they set off to explore India's ancient culture and
architecture.

After graduating, David Fyse had found a job with the Burmah-Shell
Oil Storage and Distributing Company of India Ltd. This had been
set up in 1928 to import and market Persian refined kerosene to
Indian towns and remote villages. Lord Faringdon had urged his
grandson to discover what he could about commercial enterprises
abroad. This enterprising company must have appealed to him as it
had diversified to build roads that linked remote areas. Within a few
years Burmah-Shell was doing more than supplying canned petrol
for motorcars in established commercial outlets – it was building its
own service stations. David Fyse had progressed from salesman to

marketing executive and he was able to offer his old friends salaried jobs. But in spite of the opportunity "to get in on the ground floor", fuel distribution held little appeal for Gavin. His main interest was historic architecture, and so they visited Travancore in Kerala and the ancient Dravidian temples of Madras. At the time these were seen as the "lost" temples of southern India because they were so different in character from the Islamic style complexes such as the Taj Mahal. The travellers' first stop was the Black Pagoda four hundred miles south of Calcutta. Here Byron was able to start production on a fine photo-essay, which he sent to John Betjeman, another old Oxford chum, who had found work as the assistant editor of *The Architectural Review*. This was well received at home and a hardbound copy of it survives in Buscot Park's library.

In late summer Michael, the Earl of Rosse, joined Gavin and Robert back in Calcutta. The urbane Michael – who gossip writers had dubbed "the Adonis of the Peerage" – soon got the trio invited to stay with Lord and Lady Irwin and to stay at the Viceroy's imperial palace in New Delhi. This had been designed by Sir Edwin Lutyens and recently used to host a forum on Indian independence, which had included Mahatma Gandhi, Nehru, Jenna, along with the major Indian independence movement leaders. Here Gavin was able to learn more about the prospects for political change in India. Robert Byron, on the other hand, was given permission to start writing and photographing a photo-essay on Lutyens' architectural achievements in the Imperial palace, and how the work of this "greatest living architect" was being received in India. This was mischievously called "Lady Irwin's Bathroom"; and so, Lord and Lady Irwin were not being regarded with the sort of respect they would normally receive in the Raj. On their return to Calcutta, the trio began detailed preparations for their expedition to Tibet. During these weeks Gavin featured in the correspondence between Evelyn Waugh and Nancy Mitford back in England. Both of these very English writers – surely amongst the best of their generation – wanted to come out to India to write a film-script for John Sutro – a mutual friend of Gavin's, Robert's and John Betjeman's. This idea had taken root as the result of a remark in a letter from Robert Byron, who wrote (in Waugh's words) *"Gavin has plenty of money and nothing to do".* Unfortunately, Gavin did not agree with Waugh's assumption, and the film project (which for some reason required two expenses-paid writers) never got off the ground. This incident may well have contributed to the falling out between Evelyn and Robert (Waugh's former "best man"). In addition, Waugh mentioned in a letter to their mutual friend, the novelist Henry Green that *"Robert Byron has beaten us all by going to India in an aeroplane".*

Competition and jealousy of writers aside, proof that newspapers were as inaccurate as the rumour mill came when *The Singapore Free Press and Mercantile Advertiser* reported the travellers – already arrived – had just departed from England, and misspelt David Fyse 's surname:

> *"Earl of Rosse to visit India.*
>
> *Four young members of Mayfair Society – the Earl of Rosse, who is described as the "Adonis of the Peerage," the Hon. A. Gavin Henderson, who, when he succeeds Lord Faringdon, will be one of the richest men in England, and Messrs' David Fyfe and Robert Byron – are at present on their way to India. They hope to find Himalayan exploration more exciting than life in London."*

Actually, preparations for their expedition to Tibet had begun long before, when Gavin met Sir Charles Alfred Bell who had served as Political Officer in Sikkim, Bhutan and Tibet from 1908–20. Due to his close relationship with the 13th Dalai Lama, Bell became known as "British India's ambassador to Tibet". He had retired to Oxford in 1921 where he was writing books on the language, history, culture and religion of Tibet. Bell's signature appears several times in the Buscot Park visitors' book, and he was to write letters of introduction to influential figures in India and Tibet, as well as a couple in Sikkim who Sir Charles Bell described in print as

"Lieutenant–Colonel Weir, who visited Lhasa twice, mainly
I think, in connection with the Chinese threats against the
eastern frontier of Tibet. From Tibetan sources I gather that
the British Government made representations to China, and
thus the Chinese advance was stopped…

Lt.-Col Weir held the Political Officer's post from 1928 to
about 1933, visiting Lhasa in 1930 and in 1932, for two or
three months each time. His genial, kindly disposition helped
him to establish relations of personal friendliness with the
Tibetans, especially as he aided them in their troubles with
the Chinese. The Tibetan Government's biography records
one of his visits. And Dor-je Pa-mo, the holiest lady in Tibet,
regarded him as a real friend."

Bell explained that British political officers stationed on what was
called "the roof of the world" could only achieve success if they
understood the local culture. For example, he pointed out that one
of the most influential people was a woman the called Tibetans the
Dorje Phagmo ("Thunderbolt Sow") as she was the reincarnation of
Tara, consort of Buddha Chenrezig, the Bodhisattva of Compassion.
Colonel Weir's closeness to her indicated great acceptance, which
resulted in his far-reaching influence. Bell's description of Colonel
Weir's wife Thyra was equally impressive as she was:

"the first Englishwoman to visit Lhasa… Mrs Weir had a
conversation with the Dalai Lama. Wishing to make him
appreciate the achievements of her sex, she told him how
Amy Johnson had flown from England to Australia at such
speed that she held the record for men as well as women. The
Dalai Lama pondered over the story a few seconds, and then
remarked, with some surprise, 'And why was she in such a
hurry?' Typical indeed of timeless Tibet, which sees no merit
in a 'record' as such."

Lesley and Thyra Weir were to become better known decades later as the maternal grandparents of the actress Joanna Lumley, whose BBC documentary *In Granny's Footsteps* recorded her journey to Bhutan. Joanna, her sister Aelene, and her cousin Maybe Jehu helped interpret the significance of some of the details that were to come up in their grandmother's letters to Gavin which follow below.

Before Gavin's group set out for India, they applied for permission to enter Tibet from its administrative centre in Lhasa. This produced the usual delay and prevarication. Tibetan policy was to maintain their autonomy by not antagonising the ever-watchful Chinese, whose claims to large parts of the country as former provinces had been halted for thirty years by a token British presence in Gyantse, a small town on the road to Lhasa. The India Office told the travellers that numerous arrangements would have to be made with local officials in the remote areas where the travellers would need to be provided for. But they were to discover that this was only part of the problems they would encounter. The fact was that the Tibetans were not keen on English visitors after the last one had written a patronising article published in *The Illustrated London News*. The result was that the officials in capital city of Lhasa had advised the India Office for any travellers wishing to come to "the forbidden land" to try again in a few years' time. Undeterred by this oriental protocol, Gavin wrote to the Foreign Secretary who advised them to make a fresh approach through Colonel Weir, who held the post of Resident of Sikkim *"which, though outwardly insignificant, carries with it the highly important duty of liaison between Lhasa and Delh".*

Gavin wrote to Lt.-Col Weir who replied that he would agree to arrange for the party to get to Lhasa with the Foreign Office in Delhi's permission to enter Tibet on the strict understanding that they go no further than Gyantse, half way to Lhasa; and that for diplomacy's sake they must agree to comply with the strict ban on hunting and fishing while in that obsessively pious Buddhist country. Having agreed to all this, Weir agreed to reserve accommodation for the party as British officers stationed in Gyantse were due to be replaced around the time the group proposed to travel. Captain Blood, his colourfully named assistant, booked their stays in the Bungalow Daks along the routes. Captain Blood also arranged for mounts, guides, porters and pack mules.

In October 1929 David Fyse left them in Darjeeling due to the demands of his work for Burmah-Shell India Ltd. Gavin's group now consisted of Michael Rosse and Robert Byron, who made their way to Darjeeling in September. Here they had a memorable stay with the Governor of Bengal, and his Lady wife at their official residence. This started with all the stiff formality one might expect of the Raj, and developed into hilarious chaos after everyone had gone to bed. According to Robert Byron, their hostess burst into their room *"naked"* in the small hours shouting that the house was on fire. The travellers rushed outside to find her husband Sir Henry, standing under an umbrella in a cloud of smoke complaining, *"I keep blowing my whistle but nobody comes"*. Then the fire department rang to ask if Government House really was on fire. While they were waiting for the tender to arrive, Gavin emptied a fire extinguisher up the blazing chimney in Lady Jackson's bedroom *"to see what it would do"*. Twenty minutes later a siren and bell announced the arrival of the fire-fighters. Wearing brass-buttoned uniforms, gleaming helmets and heavy boots they entered the house to find that the fire had gone out. The three travellers were in the hallway tittering about what had gone on when they noticed Sir Henry glaring at them. Byron was to write about the events that night several times. His accounts showed this outpost of the Raj in a poor light. In this he felt he was expressing the idea that change was due. Evidently, the editors at *Country Life* and *The Times*, who published these accounts, clearly believed that their readers would agree.

In Darjeeling, on the recommendation of Sir Charles Alfred Bell, they met up with Mr Macdonald, the retired British Trade Agent to Tibet. He advised them on Tibetan etiquette, such as which officials to approach, who was to receive the essential gifts of white silk scarves, as well as what other presents were suitable. They were then asked to take a wedding present for the son of Rajah Tehring and his new wife Mary Tsarong. The importance of this connection only dawned on them weeks later when the Rajah's son, whose name was Jigmed (meaning Dreadnought), came to meet them after they crossed the border. He had wonderful manners and fluent English. When shown Sir Charles Bell's latest book *People of Tibet* which had a frontispiece of a family group with a caption saying that two living Buddhas appeared in the photograph, Jigmed pointed to one of them and exclaimed, *"That's my sister!"*

The trio left Darjeeling mounted on small but sturdy Himalayan ponies, with a pack train of sure-footed mules to carry "essentials" they had argued over. These included cases of rum, whisky, tinned sardines, soups and sausages, jars of pickled beetroot, as well as packets of Fortnum & Mason's ginger biscuits. Winter had arrived a month early and they wore woollen caps with earflaps, thick coats and jodhpurs made of carpet felt to fend off the icy winds. The highest point of their journey was the 15,300-foot Tang-La pass, and they suffered from altitude sickness (nausea, headaches and breathing difficulties) as they made their way to Gyantse. A few miles from there they visited the home of Rajah Tehring, half-brother to the Maharajah of Sikkim. He had left his homeland when the British arrived *"to protect it from Chinese invasion"*. After marrying a highborn Tibetan wife Rajah Tehring had acquired vast estates in Tibet. His son Jigmed – who was serving as their guide – was Sikkim's heir apparent – the Rajah Kumar.

In this company they learned that Buddhist Tibet was not the fabled land of peace but one split by warring political factions. Tsarong's family ranked higher than anyone apart from the Dalai Lama and his chief ministers. This resulted in high-ranking Tibetan officials viewing them as arch-rivals. Tsarong was Commander in Chief of the Tibetan army and friendly with the British who were so worried about upsetting the Chinese that they supplied military weapons – but not ammunition. Chinese merchants and spies were everywhere, bribing whomever possible and creating factions. In addition, many conservative monks loathed Tsarong's family as "modernisers", partly because he had his children educated in India. Tsarong's daughter was known as Mary to the British because her real name, Tromsa, meant "mother of God" in Tibetan. She and his son Jigmed spoke perfect English and offered to take the travellers on a pilgrimage to the most revered of all Buddhist sacred sites in Binar, where a temple, lotus pond and a descendant of the legendary Bodhi tree under which the Buddha attained enlightenment was still said to exist. They all agreed to come. However, after their return to India only Robert and Michael went with them. By then Gavin had grown tired of ancient religious traditions and wanted to concentrate on contemporary Indian politics.

After ten days of trekking, they had reached their destination – the garrison town of Gyantse, which lay below an impressive medieval hill fort, which the Tibetans called a *Jong*. From an observation post on top, they saw a vast panorama spread out below. There were only a few staging posts visible, each connected by dirt roads to other *Jongs* or to monasteries perched on high points in the far distance. The latter were inhabited by thousands of monks, and the travellers were warned that some would be fiercely unwelcoming. Each religious contingent governed a windswept plain around it, and sometimes fought the other for control of the roads. The monasteries were spaced out across a vast plateau hemmed in on the horizon by shimmering snow-covered mountains. It was a spectacular scene, but having seen it from a safe distance, Gavin's party were keen to leave.

Soon after they set off, their caravan was swept by a snowstorm so dense they could not see more than the tail of the pony in front. Then they were lashed by icy rains and winds. In between these, the sun came out and burnt them sore. The journey back was arduous and used up all their reserves of inner strength. Michael complained that the experience would never be worth the suffering. Protective face creams from the Army & Navy store in London proved useless. The conditions reduced their faces to a mess of sores. Then scabs formed that clung to their stubbly beards. Happily, they had taken Captain

Blood's advice and bought Tibetan felt masks. Wearing them saved what was left of their faces from frostbite. It was impossible to wash, and their bodies ached day and night. They all suffered from nausea due to altitude sickness. Like their Tibetan porters, they survived on warm tea laced with butter. The trio were disappointed to find that the whisky they had with them tasted disgusting. But Gavin claimed to have made one outstanding discovery for future travellers – that rum remained palatable and was a valuable restorative! The trio were exhausted when they reached the Residency in Sikkim. But they were soon cheered up by Mrs Weir, who arranged for each of them to have their first hot bath in a month, after which they lay down to sleep in beds made up with linen sheets. Here they lay happily for several days.

Afterwards, Thyra Weir corresponded with all three of her former guests. Her letter to Gavin of November 1931 was written from their camp in Lhasa two years later. Its breezy and colourful commentary suggests friendship. She did not rub in the fact that Lt. Colonel Weir's expedition had a far more arduous journey over twice the length of his.

> *"My Dear Gavin,*
>
> *I must write you a few lines from here even though I have lost your address & haven't the faintest idea if you are in England or not. Robert Byron wrote after hearing our arrival here broadcasted in England & said you had gone off somewhere into the blue again but that you may be in Calcutta again this winter. I hope this is so.*
>
> *We had a wonderful journey up here (though perilous & very uncomfortable at times). Reception like a scene from a play-pageant and brass bands playing 'Tipperary'. Thousands of people from Lhasa (to see me I'm afraid. I was nearly mobbed) given a long house, but Leslie is apparently so important – he ranks as a Prime Minister here (next to*

King!) that we can't move about without at least twelve
attendants in their best clothes all mounted on fiery chargers
(having about 12 hands/accompanying us.

This fierce importance I find rather irksome, as I love creeping
away to sketch. We are being entertained like royalty.
Mercifully, our doctor tends us after each banquet otherwise
we should have succumbed before now. The ladies are
gloriously decked up in thousands of pounds worth of pearls
and jewels & brocades – the women are dirty & unattractive
– & the poor people terribly pitiable – disease rampant
everywhere. I had the great honour of a private interview
with His Holiness the Dalai Lama. The only conversation
audience ever given to any female whatsoever. He has merely
blessed other females, they lying prostrate before him. I
found him rather delightful & very dignified – superbly
'caparisoned' & terribly well staged. I had the audacity to
make him laugh, so I shall never be forgotten.

He asked to see my sketches & asked me to do one of the
Potala for him which I shall do & present to him. I have
made about twelve rough sketches of it – it is the loveliest
thing in the world. Lhasa is lovely – but the journey down is
going to be awful. Snow early this year.

We go via Shigatse (another forbidden city) & cross one pass
nearly 17,000 on the way, avoiding the second 17,000 one. We
shall probably sleep in monasteries where we can – canvas is
no fun at these heights. We are due in Gagtok about Nov 3rd
just about the time you arrived last year. It is 170 miles from
here to Shigatse & another 60 to Syantse. Don't you wish you
were here?

I could write miles of letters but am surrounded by servants
packing and people shouting, we leave tomorrow. The social
business here is terrific. We have fed hundreds of souls & been

*fed by more than I care to recount. Result we are terrifically
soft and unfit for our artic near future. No doubt a few days
simple life will harden us up.*

*I hope you are going to Calcutta. We pass through about 20th
Nov and go to Delhi where Leslie has to report our mission.
We then tour Bhutan for two months. What a life! How are
you? I should love to hear all about everything.*

Yours ever,

Thyra Weir.

*P.S. I have a cinema and am keeping as many notes as I can
so hope to be allowed to use the results of my efforts someday
if Foreign don't cut out all the nicest bits."*

This letter had been sent to Byron's address in Savernake Forest.
He corresponded with Thyra Weir at least seven times after their
time in Sikkim, and both he and Gavin saw the Weirs when they
visited England. She was a very fine amateur artist and some of her
paintings of Lhasa still exist, rightly treasured by her granddaughters
Joanna (Lumley), Aelene and Maybe Jehu.

Another letter from Thyra Weir to Gavin confided that the Secretary
of the Royal Asian Society had warned her that Robert Byron was
a *"young man who spent most of his life travelling, wrote well, but is
one of those young things very scornful of us"*. By then his articles on
the fire at Government House in Darjeeling had come out, as well
as a piece he had written on New Delhi for *Country Life* entitled
"Lady Irwin's Bathroom". Thyra Weir reported that the title had
shocked the Viceroy's wife, who found the subject *"quite inappropriate"*. Still, Byron managed to get the article re-published by *The
Times*. The piece was polemical, poking fun at those in the Raj who
openly disapproved Sir Edwin Lutyens' new architecture at New
Delhi. Byron wrote that this was *"a prejudice that revealed the most*

ungenerous qualities of the English mind, its complete lack of taste and its animal suspicion of novelty". In spite of difficulties this may have caused, Thyra Weir wrote that she would be *"overjoyed"* to have them come to stay again. In the meantime, Gavin and Robert Byron returned to their flat in Calcutta, and Lady Jackson, the *"pukka"* wife of the Governor of West Bengal, wrote a short note to them: *"I hope you are enjoying the riots".*

In January 1929 Peter Rodd, the roguish friend who was occupying Gavin's London home, sent a long letter. Many people regarded Peter as a great raconteur. Nancy Mitford, who married him in 1933, wrote that at times he would be so keen to tell all he knew about a subject that he would drone on like a fly circling a spot without landing. To a certain extent this is what he did in this gossipy letter. Evelyn Waugh described him as *"highly cosmopolitan, but without any taste for conventional high society"*; and someone who *"rejoiced, always, in the spectacle of women at a disadvantage".* Readers of Waugh's novels will recognise him as part inspiration for the well-born buccaneering character Basil Seal. Rodd was to play leading roles in key events in Gavin's life for decades to come. Handsome, clever and charming, he was a complex character who could be well informed, misguided, amusing, exasperating, duplicitous, driven, lazy, and piratical – these sides of him seems to be evident here:

> *"Mr dear Gavin,*
>
> *I am glad that you are happy. What exactly are you doing in Calcutta? Can you get away from it all to do sight-seeing in the rest of the 'Empire'?"*

Peter goes on to say there is *"little gossip as everyone has been away"* but then proceeds to fill four pages with snippets of exactly that, such as

> *"The Duggan is not over sound, one hears".*

This brief sentence touched superficially on the crisis that Alfred Duggan was in. He was the stepson of Viscount Curzon, former Viceroy of India, and Secretary of State for Foreign Affairs when Alfred appeared with Gavin in Robert Byron's book *Europe in the Looking Glass*. Alfred had attended Eton and Oxford with these two, only to emerge as a devout atheist and Marxist. At the time he is mentioned here other friends feared that he was about to drink himself to death. Happily, he managed to turn his life around. He then became a successful archaeologist, and author of a dozen historical novels, first editions of which Gavin was to keep in his library.

Gavin had many lesbian and bisexual friends, and so it is interesting to find that he knew the ground-breaking lesbian author Marguerite Radclyffe Hall well. This is revealed by the way that Peter mentions some changes in her love life. In 1928 her autobiographical novel *The Well of Loneliness* caused a sensation in some quarters and raised praise in others. It concerns the life of an upper-class woman whose *"congenital sexual inversion"* was apparent from an early age. The novel portrayed lesbianism as natural and pleaded for *"the right to our existence"*.

Hall's companion for many years had been Una Vincenzo, Lady Troubridge, a talented sculptor. This did not prevent Radclyffe from having several affairs. A female admirer – a translator nicknamed "Sparky" – had just discovered that Radclyffe was going to travel abroad with another woman (unnamed). According to Peter Rodd, this had resulted in a highly emotional parting:

> *"Rad appears to be mad, and has gone (in tears) to South Africa with a 'companion'. Sparky has gone rather further afield to Java. I was made to camp Sparky and dine en tete a tete several times before the farewells in the hope that by spreading sufficient 'well of loneliness' stuff about her rival she would let off going. But it was all of no avail perhaps I was a little too ambitious for Sparky…"*

Empathy for women's emotional problems never featured high amongst Peter's skill sets. For example, in the same letter he made a passing mention of the sad death of someone from a famous banking family:

> "Kitty Hambro drowned herself in a bath a week or two ago. The inquest said accidental death but one suspects suicide..."

Nor was he the least bit compassionate when he passed on scurrilous gossip about a Maharani who Gavin had visited at her family home, the Victor Jubilee Palace in Cooch Behar City. This had been modelled on Buckingham Palace – but was slightly larger:

> "The Cooch Behar has been sent home to India by the I.O. for pawning family jewels to pay her debts".

Indira Devi, Maharani of Cooch Behar, was known for her beauty, wealth and social life. She had five children with the Maharaja before he died of alcoholism after ten years of marriage. Indira became regent during the minority of her elder son. However, as a widow, members of her extended family expected her to retire from active life and let the court bureaucrats manage things. But the Maharani had been a princess of Baroda in her own right before her marriage, and ignored those advocating Purdah – the tradition of female seclusion. Despite her best efforts as regent, she came in for sustained criticism from her husband's family. Hoping to enjoy a social life she spent long periods of time in Europe. Trouble often brewed in her absence and, as Peter mentions, the I.O. (the India Office) may have been prompted to act after some high-caste Indians were shocked after they learned that Indira had appeared unveiled on the cover of *Vogue*. The photograph by Cecil Beaton showed her wearing a silk sari unbuttoned at her neck to reveal two strings of pearls. However, ten months later Gavin included this news of her in a letter to Patrick Balfour, then working as the gossip columnist for *The Sketch*:

> *"Cooch has gone home. The police here assert that she*
> *poisoned her secretary in January, but that is just slander and*
> *gossip".*

Four months later Michael, the Earl of Rosse, wrote to Gavin from Paris to express his concern about her. As a BYP he was known to have had a carefree social life, so he was probably not being priggish when he wrote disapprovingly of two socialites associated with "Cooch" in the newspapers. The first mentioned was the American wife of a British baronet. This was a lady whom the poet Dame Edith Sitwell disliked so much that she described her as *"a cheap little slut"* and nicknamed her *"Bitch-Balls"*. The other socialite Diana Fitzherbert, was rumoured to be one of Armand de la Rochefoucald's many high-born mistresses. He was a French Marquis and playboy son of the 14th Duc de la Rochefoucald. Clearly, Michael Rosse was worried that Cooch was in bad company with this libertine and his cronies.

> *"I want news of Cooch please if there have been any recent*
> *developments. Everyone here is asking after her doings, &*
> *I find it difficult to very kind about them. But then after all*
> *why should I? People say that Diana Fitzherbert may have*
> *had a certain unsettling effect, but the general opinion seems*
> *to be that Armand de la Rochefoucauld is chiefly to blame".*

However, in spite of all the rumours and disapproval Maharani Indira Devi continued appear on magazine covers abroad as a celebrity. When she eventually returned home, she became a powerful advocate for the Indian women's liberation movement.

Peter's letter went on to make a prophetic observation:

> *"Bryan Guinness marries in a fortnight. Personally, I think he*
> *picked the wrong sister."*

Bryan (the future Lord Moyne), one of Gavin's closest friends, was about to marry the Hon. Diana Mitford. Gavin knew her as a near neighbour since her hunting-mad family lived in Swinbrook – only twelve miles from Kitemore – and both families were very much part of the country sports set. Peter was right to suspect that the beautiful but headstrong Diana would not make a perfect partner for Bryan. This heir to the brewing fortune of Guinness was also the author of slim volumes of sensitive poetry. He had fallen head over heels in love with her, proposed and was accepted, but her family made him agree to wait a year for her to marry at the age of 21. This he did but three years after the wedding Diana left him and their two sons. She had fallen head over heels with the British Union of Fascists leader Sir Oswald Mosley, and the couple were married in a private ceremony at Joseph Goebbels' Berlin home in 1936.

The six sisters Peter Rodd was referring to were the Mitfords: Nancy, Pamela, Diana, Unity, Jessica, and Deborah. Each developed in a different way as shown by someone who referred to them in the manner used to describe Henry VIII's wives: *"Author, Countrywoman, Fascist, Nazi, Communist, and Duchess"*. Perhaps the Mitford sister Peter had in mind for Bryan would have been his own future wife, Nancy. She agreed to marry Peter at a party in 1932, after he had drunkenly proposed to three other women and been rejected by them. Peter's final comment below reveals his opportunistic approach to debutantes:

> *"The Debs have just appeared. The old ones are getting old 'Counting the fly buttons before they are undone' as the saying is.*
>
> *Goodbye.*
>
> *I will write again when I have any more news."*

In March 1930 Michael Rosse wrote to Gavin at 4 Elysium Row, Calcutta. Michael passed on the news that *"The seeds have arrived &*

are safely installed at Kew, where I will go & sort them". These had been collected on their expedition to Tibet and added a scientific aspect to their otherwise recreational jaunt. Michael ended his letter with the words *"Give my best to David and Robert"*. By then, both were working in the marketing department of Mobil-Shell. Gavin went on his own to the Princely states and stayed with some of their owners. Perhaps the most notable of these was the Muslim Nawab Sayyid Hamid Ali Khan Bahadur of Rampur. His Khas Bagh palace in Uttar Pradesh was set in a 300-acre compound. Designed to impress, its 200-rooms blended Islamic and British architecture and housed a vast collection of Islamic miniatures spread amongst apartments, offices and music rooms. It had a cinema as well as an imported Italian marble staircase, adorned with Belgium chandeliers and carved teak fittings. But this opulence did not impress Gavin. Afterwards, he met up with Robert Byron and David Fyse to travel as far as Persia. Then he left for Somaliland, where he was to spend a month meeting the people involved with the roads, railway and infrastructure around a dam that his grandfather and uncles' companies had built there.

In October he received a breezy letter from "Susu", Lady Ankaret Jackson, an extraordinary character who was a novelist, broadcaster and the first woman barrister in England. Her Christian name derived from the Welsh Angharad, but she preferred her nickname "Susu". The latter came from her inability as a child to pronounce her middle names Cecilia Caroline. Her father was Charles Howard, the 10th Earl of Carlisle, a Liberal – and the family had a home in Eaton Place. She had done the usual round of debutante balls before marrying a friend of Gavin's the future baronet Sir William Jackson in 1927, three months before Gavin's wedding. She attended that with her mother Rhoda, Countess of Carlisle. In 1928 Susu had become Britain's first woman barrister after she passed her Bar exams while pregnant. Unconventional would not be a strong enough word to describe her. Susu habitually smoked a briar pipe and wore men's trousers – a combination that had once led her to be attacked by an outraged stranger in a Dublin street. Her love of horse-riding led her cousin Nancy Mitford to put an in-joke about Susu in her novel

Wigs on the Green. Here a character rides a mettlesome hunter called *"Jackson",* who she explains *"simply loves jumping fences".* The same could be said about Susu. The Buscot Park visitors' book shows that she came to visit Gavin with her husband five times, then sixteen times on her own. She also visited Gavin (without her husband) abroad – in India and in Corsica. Her daughter believed that her parents *"were both very naughty"* but all this is not in itself evidence of an affair. They were clearly very close friends, and she ended one letter with the words *"I love you".* Susu's first letter to Gavin in India began in great style with:

> *"Gavin my sweet,*
>
> *I was miserable to hear that you had gone straight to India as I had hoped you were coming back after Somaliland before your final departure for the most unpleasant place you could have elected to live in. However, I still live in hopes of your expulsion.*
>
> *I think that I shall still have you as godfather but I shall have to get a proxy for the christening and shall make a point of choosing someone you particularly dislike."*

In this letter she gave him a taste of home with an account of what happened when she went to stay at Sir Osbert Sitwell's family home of Renishaw in Derbyshire, where his eccentric father Sir George – a notoriously short-tempered red-haired man nicknamed "Ginger"– ruled the roost:

> *"Have you ever been to Renishaw? It is lovely, & was so hot Osbert & I bathed 5 times a day in the lake. The only blot on an otherwise perfect visit was that he would tell Ginger that my subjects were Polar expeditions & medieval church vestments, it was difficult to be intelligent or amusing. However I could get by just listening as he expounded on both topics, and was having such a success with the old*

*man that he gave me a signed copy of his book on gardens.
Anyhow I was more of a success than Christabel McLaren
who turned to him at dinner & asked, 'Is there much incest
about here Sir George?' to which he replied 'Not as much as
you might think'."*

The story is probably true as Sir Oswald Sitwell's younger brother
Sacheverell wrote *"When Lady Ankaret Jackson, born a Howard, came
to stay with her husband William, Ginger was unwise enough to enquire
of Osbert: 'What are Lady Ankaret's interests? I should like to draw her
out on her own topics.' 'Polar explorations' was his misleading answer".*
Their other female guest that day was the more glamorous Christabel
McLaren, who became Lady Aberconway of Bodnant. She found
Ginger's comments that day so outrageous that she quoted the ones
above in her autobiography.

Susu wrote far more amusingly and it is worth knowing who the
people mentioned were. David was her cousin David Tennant (son of
Lord Glenconner) who had created the fashionable private members'
Gargoyle nightclub in Soho. He had decorated this with several large
Matisse paintings and a mirrored ceiling designed by the same artist.
Rosa owned the Cavendish Hotel on Jermyn St., near Piccadilly. This
was a popular after-hours rendezvous for the "Bright Young People"
and ageing boulevardiers. It had recently featured in Evelyn's Waugh's
1930 novel *Vile Bodies* as The Shepheard's Hotel. In the extract below,
William is Susu's husband, Sir William Jackson. Alistair was Alistair
Graham, Evelyn Waugh's lover at Oxford; Evan was Evan Morgan,
the eccentric Lord Tredegar, and Igor was Igor Vinogradoff, the son
of a brilliant Oxford don in the Bloomsbury set.

*"Since my return on Sunday, to what I expected would be
a cloistered existence I have been in a constant whirl of
cocktail parties & others. Last night we went to Gargoyle &
went down stairs to see David's new room but he had a cold
& was crosser than usual so we repaired to Rosa's but I am
thankful to say that she was on her way to bed as I felt like*

bed myself by then. Only William penetrated the portals of the Cavendish & his conversation with Rosa (who was in her dressing gown) re-echoed from end to end of Jermyn St.

Apparently, William has used Cavendish as a home from home during my absence & we have got to go to a party there tonight. It is a farewell party for Alistair Graham, whom I don't like. Apparently, there have been the usual scenes there as Igor Vinogradoff, tiring of his history chair in Edinburgh wants to live there, knocked poor Evan down & followed that up by buying a horse whip to beat Basil Murray as the latter has turned him out of his house in Burford for being pretty tight. When he got back down there Basil very wisely kept out of the way & he was persuaded to return to Cavendish where Rosa locked him up & sent for his sister. She arrived got hold of his whip & took it back to Fortnum's where she got 30/ on it, now Rosa has added it to the bill.

The final scene was at Euston when Rosa & Igor's sister had put him onto the night train for Edinburgh. Rosa had gone to the waiting room to get him a whisky & soda, and collar & tie but he jumped onto the platform minus these in a final bid for freedom.

I don't know when I have written such a long letter to anyone!

Best Love from

Susu."

The farewell party for Alastair Graham took place before he returned to Cairo where he was working as honorary attaché at the British Legation. Gavin had stayed with him and his lover Mark Ogilvie–Grant when they worked at the British Legation in Athens. Alistair was a hard-drinking practical joker who Susu mentions that she disliked in several letters. Her favourite cousin Basil Murray was described in Evelyn Waugh's biography as *"a satanic young man, strange offspring of puritan parents"*. Later, Susu wrote another letter to tell Gavin about what he had missed at The Glen, a neo-gothic castle in Peeblesshire, which was the Tennant family's country seat. Other guests there included Susu's mother Rhoda, the Countess of Carlisle, Sir Osbert Sitwell, Lady Emerald Cunard, Susu's husband Sir William Jackson, and Peter Rodd – who misbehaved true to form, as described here.

> *"I have been attending a lot of works parties lately – one at the Tennants in the country was a party in the good old-fashioned North Street style excepting that I was fearfully sober, when we got down the next morning the sitting room was full of men who had been too tight to leave…. Rosa Lewis arrived before I had succeeded in getting my mother and Mrs Jackson home. Rhoda was quite green with jealousy because Osbert had eyes for no one but Rosa, however she consoled herself with Emerald. Rosa was very shocked to discover that William was not my son – I pointed out that incest has always been a feature of the Howard family. I don't know how I survived in any way without a losing an eye as Peter, in his usual way, let off a lot of rockets in his hand. They exploded all over me, William and himself, however I am glad to say that Peter got the worst of it."*

A month later she was pleased to write:

> *"I am so glad to hear I am going to be home in the spring my sweet lovely Gavin*
>
> *I wrote to you at length the other day & don't suppose you will get this one for ages as you are starting another tour of India from what I can make out."*

Susu was well informed. Gavin did return to England in May 1930 to face the fact that his marriage to Honor had been annulled. This seems to have been as amicable as possible in the circumstances as he paid the legal costs as well as a cash settlement to her of £250 – the equivalent of £11,424.86 today. An annuity of £200 p.a. followed, in spite of the fact that she came from a wealthy family. The amount of this annuity was raised several times, even after she remarried in 1936. It is feature of Gavin's diaries that he met with Honor before and after all the main events in his life, as though they were still married in spirit.

CHAPTER 5

"An Unpredictable Pendulum"

When Gavin came back to England in the spring of 1930 some of the Bright Young Things were still burning their candles at both ends. In was still stylish to be light-hearted; anyone "turning serious" was called a "bore" or "bogus". Frivolity was the heart and soul of this party-world where drinking and dancing were seen as the prerequisites of personal freedom. The novelist Nancy Mitford claimed *"We hardly ever saw the light of day, except at dawn"*. Noel Coward's 1928 hit song Dance, *dance, little lady dance* warned that whatever went up too high would come crashing down – just like the stock market had that year. But Gavin's closest female friend Lady Ankaret Jackson "Susu" confided in a letter to him:

> *"I rather dread getting involved in the round of parties which*
> *will begin soon & which for some unknown reason one goes*
> *to, however little one wants to."*

Gavin had come home from India rejuvenated with the belief that change for a better world was in the offing. He was still weighing the pacifist-socialist ideology of H.G. Wells against Gandhi's solution – a gradual approach in which progress would come by awakening social conscience in the world. In Britain the divisions of wealth, race and class were widening and deepening due to the worldwide economic depression. Politicians had responded by re-grouping to form a "National Government", consisting of shifting alliances between Conservatives, Liberals and Labourites. The nation's foremost orators Sir Winston Churchill and Sir Oswald Mosley had both lost their seats in parliament. They stood on the side-lines bellowing like *"ancestral voices prophesising war"*. Everyone proposed radical solutions and Gavin sought to fit in somehow. After all, as his friend Patrick Balfour pointed out in his book *Society Racket – A Critical Survey of Modern Social Life*, theirs was a decade when

"Peers had become socialists and socialists peers".

In May Susu and her fun-loving stock-broker husband, Sir William Jackson were Gavin's first guests when Gavin returned to Buscot Park. A day later they were joined by the rollicking Peter Rodd, whose signature was always larger and more flamboyant than anyone else's in the visitors' book. Susu may have advised Gavin in India on the best way to end his marriage, but – that dealt with – events in the subcontinent were calling him back. At the closing session of the Round Table Conference in January 1931, the new British Prime Minister, Ramsay MacDonald, expressed the view that further talks would not progress without the presence of Gandhi and the Congress Party. This prompted the Viceroy, Lord Irwin, to order the unconditional release of Gandhi and all members of the Congress Working Committee. Tens of thousands of Indian prisoners (including the future Indian prime minister Jawaharlal Nehru) were freed, and Gandhi responded by agreeing to meet for talks. This marked the end of civil disobedience against British rule. Gavin returned to Calcutta and was there when delegates were coming for preliminary talks. Susu wrote another facetious (possibly flirtatious) letter to him there. Having just visited Spain, she urged him to return with her:

> *"I went to Ronda which I thought lovely, particularly your grandfather's hotel – we should create a scandal by going and staying there together.*
>
> *As usual I miss you very much & wish you would come back before June, you are the only person I know who has the sense to go abroad for no particular reason. But I love you.*
>
> *Susu."*

A letter from Gavin to Patrick Balfour crossed paths with the one above. This told that Gavin had met and been disappointed by a *Nabob* invited to the talks:

> *"One of the conference delegates I know is Durbhanjan, and his appointment is surprising as he is an awfully gauche young man without any knowledge or experience. Of course, he is not a prince but only a grandson (the grandpa is said to be worth 77 lakhs p.a. which his father has said to have doubled here); but he is very orthodox and the head of a Brahmin caste".*

In spite of the difficulties getting all Indian princes and politicians to agree on a way forward, the talks went well and the "Gandhi-Irwin Pact" was signed in March 1931. This led to the second Round Table Conference in London and Gavin returned home where he began to make closer contact with the Labour Party, which had developed radical pacifist-socialist and anti-colonial factions. Gavin took in their heady ideas but he refrained from making any public commitments.

He must have felt relieved at becoming single again when in July one of the major scandals of the decade emerged. Lord Kylsant, his former father-in-law, was accused of publishing fraudulent balance sheets with intent to deceive investors. For over twenty years this colossally successful shipping tycoon had been director of the Royal Mail Steam Packet Company. During this time, he had acquired a controlling interest in over twenty other companies, including the prestigious Union-Castle Line, the Pacific Steam Navigation Company, and the White Star line. The latter had built the *Titanic* at Belfast's Harland and Wolff shipyards, which Lord Kylsant acquired in 1924. Kylsant liked to manage this vast portfolio himself and seldom took the time to consult other board members. The complex share structure of his companies had allowed him to hide his trading losses by moving cash funds between them to suit his expanding needs.

Lord Kylsant was referred to in the press as *"The man who wrote a £5 million cheque"*. The scandal started after his own brother accused him of falsifying a prospectus while seeking sole rights to distribute the Royal Mail. The 68-year-old peer was committed for trial at the Old Bailey where he was charged with larceny. The legal proceedings lasted nine days, after which he was found guilty and sentenced to a stretch of twelve months imprisonment. After spending one night behind bars Lord Kylsant was released on bail, pending what was to be a costly appeal. This was heard in November 1931 and when it was dismissed Kylsant was sent to Wormwood Scrubs prison to serve his full sentence. This must have been a very stressful time for the disgraced peer and his family. It says a lot about Honor and Gavin's relationship that she felt able to come and stay with him at Buscot Park for the first time since her annulment on the night her father went to prison, and again, a few days before he finished his sentence and was released.

Earlier that year in July, light relief arrived in a letter from Rosa Lewis, proprietor of the Cavendish Hotel in Jermyn St., near Piccadilly. She was a friend of Susu and Sir William Jackson. Evelyn Waugh had portrayed Rosa in his novel 1930 novel *Vile Bodies* as the tipsy hostess, Lottie Crump of Shepheard's Hotel. That name probably relates to the way she had decorated her establishment to resemble a shabby-chic Edwardian country house. In Waugh's book he implies that she was in the habit of handing large bills out at random for her guests to pay. This actually happened to Cyril Connolly, Evelyn and Gavin's Oxford contemporary, but when he pleaded poverty Rosa relented and gave him a free bottle of champagne. The novelist Anthony Powell, another of their Oxford contemporaries, claimed that she moved as if in a dream, getting past and present mixed up, and often arranging for bills to be paid by whoever she considered to be the most affluent person present. Rosa's letter to Gavin resulted from his refusal to pay such a bill. Here she apologises grandiloquently and claims the bill was sent in error by a feckless member of staff. In truth, this was an upper-class woman who the kind-hearted Rosa gave a job to as she was penniless after leaving her husband.

"Dear Gavin,

I do not know what I shall do with that vile Diana Campbell Carter, with her pinks and blues, tips and toes. Imagine them trying to charge you for the magnums of champagne I gave you and Peter. I am glad you did not pay your bill. Never pay without coming to me. Do you and little Bartlett come to Cowes, if only for Sunday night. I will have a speed boat for you.

Gavin you are my real sprig of Aristocracy, and you will be the heir to all the millions I leave. You are Champagne in itself. Do come to Cowes and a million thanks for the way you cheered me up over the weekend.

All my love,

Yours always gratefully,

Rosa Lewis.

P.S. Give my love to Lady Jackson and tell her I will give her a real Party."

"Little Bartlett" was Vernon Bartlett, a diminutive but dynamic journalist who had been sacked by Lord Rothermere's mass-circulation newspaper the *Daily Mail* for being too left-wing. In spite of this setback, Vernon Bartlett soon managed to become a foreign correspondent for *The Times* and on *BBC* radio, which was expanding its coverage. Then he became a director of the London office of the League of Nations. This came about because of shared values with one of its founders, Viscount Edward Grey – a friend of Gavin's grandfather – as well as the pacifist author H.G. Wells. That night the rise of fascism in Europe would have been the main topic of discussion. Bartlett was keeping a close eye on the erosion of freedoms in European democracies. Gavin and Vernon were to find much in common after Bartlett became the left-wing *News Chronicle's* diplomatic correspondent on the Spanish Civil War; and in 1938 after Vernon was elected as the "Anti-Appeasement" MP for Bridgewater in Somerset.

"Peter" was Gavin's friend Peter Rodd, who was still looking for work. He had been living eventfully as ever and earlier that year had lost a job in the City after a disagreement with his employers over what they called *"the importance of time-keeping"*. A sojourn in Brazil followed, but Peter had to be rescued from penury (and perhaps prison) there by his elder brother. He then managed to find work as a journalist in Germany – but soon lost that position for failing to meet deadlines. None of these setbacks dented his confidence for long and he was soon able to persuade Susu's stock-broker husband that he could help to drum up business in Germany. Having enjoyed the freedoms offered by William Jackson's expense account for a few weeks – and gaining no new clients – that venture ended when William returned to London. Peter had written to Gavin to try to persuade him to come over to Germany – casually mentioning in passing that he was flat broke. Gavin, in India, declined the invitation and suggested that Peter try to make his way as a freelance journalist. He did, but editors were not keen on his windy – somewhat fantastical – contributions. The example below shows why. Here, a week before the elections that brought Hitler to power, Peter sent Gavin a nine-page hand-written report on the candidates and his in-depth view of the likely outcome. As Nancy Mitford had complained, Peter liked to show off his erudition which led him to drone on and miss the obvious:

> *"Unlikely to win is the Nazi group with Hitler as figurehead*
> *– a feminine and rather hysterical figure with a strong sense*
> *of vocation – with Goering, a blonde Napoleon who takes*
> *drugs and is the real iron hand in the movement. They have*
> *no political ideas but lots of enthusiasm and a vast number of*
> *people to whom they have promised jobs. They have a perfect*
> *party organization are decidedly proletarian and an army of*
> *about half a million the S.A. & S.S. rather a wild army. The*

Nazis' only contribution so far has been to sack all officials and replace them with their own followers".

Peter's mountain of facts did not add up to a molehill of truth. The menacing nature of fascism only dawned on him a few years later. And that was after he and Nancy Mitford had joined the British Fascist Party. By then her nickname for him had become "Prod" – a fusion of his name the Hon. Peter Rodd with his reputation as a virile and promiscuous man-about-town. She was probably only joking when she wrote that they joined because *"Prod looked very pretty in a black shirt".* The manic-aggressive nature of British Union of Fascist members, coupled with their anti-Semitism – soon dashed any hopes they may have got from Mosley that his organisation could help British society. The couple left within a year and she was to lampoon her sisters' hero-worship of fascist leaders in her novel *Wigs on the Green.*

The couple had begun their married life began in December 1933 at Rose Cottage, Strand-on-the- Green, Hammersmith, which had been rented to them by her cousin "Susu". Baron Rennell, Peter Rodd's father, had limited his errant son's allowance to *"just enough for bread and butter – he will have to find the money for jam himself".* Soon after the marriage Peter lost another job and as his monthly allowance was quickly spent, they were living off what little income Nancy earned from her writing. So, she had to set about picking up second-hand furniture from sale-rooms, e.g.: a large sofa for £2 and a carved mantlepiece for £1. Gavin's wedding present to the couple seems to have been well-chosen. A bill for it dated 25th January 1934 reads:

Invoice A. G. Henderson Esq from Howard & Sons, Ltd of Berners St., London.

Cabinet manufacturers by appointment

A Grafton East Chair, siege de Duvet £13. 10s.

A Clayton East Chair £13. 5s

Total + £26. 15s.

Sent to The Honble Peter Rodd, Rose Cottage, Strand on
the Green, Chiswick

Paid by cheque.

Gavin had spent the equivalent of £1,774.40 in today's money on his
gift – a pair of His and Hers armchairs in designs noted for their style
and comfort. Howard & Sons had the Royal Warrant and supplied
several of the Royal residences. Their "siege de duvet" cushions were
designed with pockets that prevented the filling moving within. The
company's furniture had been exhibited at the Great Exhibition
of 1851 and all the subsequent shows at Crystal Palace, as well as
in America and France. However, Peter had continued to frequent
nightclubs even when he was unemployed. Nancy confided to friends
that the bailiffs called frequently to deal with the debts he ran up. As
she was proud of the frugal way she had decorated their home, it is
likely that she never got to enjoy Gavin's generous wedding presents
before Peter sold them.

In 1933 the world seemed to start spinning faster. In February that
year Gavin attended the Oxford Union Debate when the pacifist
motion: *"This House will under no circumstances fight for its King
and country"*, was carried. He went with the writer and translator
Humphrey Hare – who Gavin, Nancy Mitford and "Prod" would
work with on behalf of Spanish Republican refugees a few years
later. Their characters were being reformed by a new sense of social
conscience, and people were deciding to make firm breaks with the
past they had inherited as their probable futures. For example, it was
clear to Gavin that his escape to Tibet had not been the life-changing
spiritual event predicted by *"seekers after truth"*. While visiting what
such romantics called *"the island in the sky"* he had not encountered
anything like the timeless Shangri-La that John Conway, the peace

campaigner in James Hilton's book *Lost Horizon*, had in that year's best-selling novel. Gavin came away from Tibet appalled by its backward feudal society. He could not ignore the sight of peasants living in poverty, the tales of violent Buddhist monks and their dharma wars. To him the religious traditions of Tibet were stifling its people and any progress; especially as so much in that society was based on the belief of a better life after death. Neither he nor Robert Byron had any faith in this concept. Robert outlined these concerns in his book *From Russia to Tibet*, which came out a few months after Evelyn Waugh had converted to Roman Catholicism. Reviewing his old friend Robert Byron's book, the zealous new convert called it *"marred by atheism"*. Gavin phoned Robert to console him. Robert's considered response came in a letter to Gavin:

> *"Yes – Evelyn. Silly fool – as you say this religious mania*
> *could destroy his writing. But he does not really believe in*
> *Christ and it is only the Church that attracts him – so there*
> *may be hope still He is at present attending the coronation*
> *of the Emperor of Abyssinia, which is just as well, as he has*
> *made so many enemies by his malice that one doesn't hear a*
> *good word for him from any one."*

This was followed by a life-changing decision from Gavin:

> *"My dear Robert*
>
> *As I told you today I have appointed you an executor under*
> *my will.*
>
> *I have directed that I do not wish my body to be buried in*
> *consecrated ground not to have any religious funeral service*
> *committed over it. I hope that you will see that my wishes are*
> *carried out – cremate me if you like*
> *Yrs,*
>
> *Gavin Henderson."*

This was another step on Gavin's path to becoming his own man. His family were religious by convention rather than deep conviction. Both they and the church held inherited rank in society and with that came responsibilities and privileges. Denying any form of divinity was close to dismantling the system. Gavin was severing this connection. When his mother came to know about it she was appalled. It is likely that his 82-year-old grandfather was never told. Illness had caused him to spend much more time at 18 Arlington St. (also known as Pomfret Castle) rather than in the stock exchange, which seemed to him to be his real home. Gavin visited his grandfather for tea and lunch from time to time, and started to prepare himself for his succession to the title by studying law before he inherited his estates and took his seat in the House of Lords. His mother still regarded Buscot Park as *her* home, though they tended not to be there together unless it was to host the traditional shooting weekends in the winter months.

In the meantime, Gavin's close female friend Nancy Cunard was rebelling against society in her own inimitable way. She had moved to Paris where she became a muse to some of the 20th century's most distinguished writers and artists. Nancy was wealthy, well-dressed and striking enough for Cecil Beaton to photograph and feature her with the most glamourous women of the early 1930s in his *Book of Beauty*. At the time she was gaining fame for publishing weird and wonderful Surrealist poetry. Amongst her succession of lovers there was a black American Jazz musician, as well as an Indian socialist leader – both living there in exile from the home countries. But then, she produced and distributed a little bomb of a book. Whilst this contained only eleven pages, Gavin and Nancy's mutual friend Beverly Nichols claimed *"there was enough in them to make society rubs its eyes. Even the title made people sit up... BLACK MAN AND WHITE LADYSHIP"*. Here Nancy announced that a black man was a *"very close friend"* who had often accompanied her to London. She introduced her mother as *"Her Ladyship"* and explains that they were on distant terms. Nancy explained what had led her to have nothing to do with her mother's salon in her home at 7 Grosvenor Square. An example of why she found it repellent was that when Margot Asquith, Lady Oxford, heard that Nancy had a male black friend, this widow of the Liberal Prime Minister burst into a lunch party to ask:

"Hello Emerald – what is it now…drink, drugs and niggers?"

Whilst Emerald Cunard was keen to have Gavin attend her salon at Grosvenor Square, he, like Nancy sedulously avoided it. Still, he continued to enjoy social life in London where his appointments diary shows nearly twice as many entries reading *"Cocktails"* than lunch or dinner. Lunch dates were generally at the Savoy (with Susu on Jan 14th and Feb 22nd; Peter Rodd on Jan 22nd and ex-wife Honor on Oct 24th); the Carlton (with Jock Murdoch of the *Times*), the Garret (with Bryan Guinness and prominent Bright Young Person Eddie Gathorne-Hardy). Dinner was at the Ritz or Quaglino's. The latter was then very fashionable, with the black singer and pianist "Hutch" performing regularly. He was another black man said to have had affairs with white Ladyships as well as the composer Cole Porter. But Gavin's interest was mainly in classical music at the time.

Gavin's diary shows weekly visits to concerts and operas. In June he went to the ballet with Honor on one night and on the following night with Robert Byron. Amongst these entertainments, two political engagements stand out. One with the Jewish Labour Party MP George Strauss, and the other with the Sikh writer, Randhir Singh, who had come to Britain after being released from a lifetime prison sentence for sedition in India. It is worth noting that many would have found it radical for a man of Gavin's class to meet with a Jew and a Sikh.

Weekends at Buscot Park in 1932 included one where Honor came to stay for two nights along with his gay friends Mark Ogilvie-Grant, as well as Harold Acton and Brian Howard, aspects of whom would be blended by Evelyn Waugh into his camp character Anthony Blanche in the 1945 novel *Brideshead Revisited*. With them were Alfred Duggan, Bob Boothby, David Fyse, Patrick Balfour and Michael

Rosse. On another weekend the married couple Bryan and Diana Guinness came – just a year before she would leave him to become one of Sir Oswald Mosley's lovers. Gavin's ex-wife Honor came again in July, with their former neighbour in Lord North Street, Nina, the Countess of Seafield. They were joined by Robert Byron and David Fyse, together with Nancy Cunard and Allanah Harper – both publishing up-market poetry books in Paris. After these social breaks Gavin would return to London and devote himself to studying law at Lincoln's Inn. He attended lectures from Monday to Friday and dutifully met with his tutors every Tuesday and Wednesday. The result was that by the end of the year he had passed his examinations in Criminal Law and Procedure; followed by Law of Contract and Law of Tort. He celebrated his success at lunch with Susu at the Temple, before giving himself a special treat – one word scrawled across a page in his diary, *"Corsica!"* He left to spend Christmas and New Year on the island, returning several times in 1933.

In May that year, while Gavin was in Corsica, a memorable letter from Diana Guinness arrived in England. Diana had left Gavin's close friend Bryan (and their two children) for the British fascist leader Sir Oswald Mosley. Oswald's wife "Cimmie", who had served as a Labour Party MP, was a friend who had recently written him long letters about her travel and political aspirations, so Gavin's loyalties were challenged. His appointments diary shows that Diana came to see him on her own soon after it had begun. Presumably this was to discuss that she wanted a divorce, which would have had to be a very public matter in the time, requiring someone to admit fault in a civil court before it could be granted, and then, as Bryan was Lord Moyne, there would have to be a second hearing in the Upper House. Annulment was out of the question as they had two children and up until then the couple had been known as leaders of London's artistic and social scene, with Evelyn Waugh dedicating his second novel *Vile Bodies* to them. Now Diana had fallen under the charismatic leader's thrall and was determined to *"nail her colours to the mast"*, as she put it. Diana publicly declared that she had left Bryan and then went to Germany with her younger sister Unity.

Diana's letter reveals her anger at Gavin's refusal to come and witness what she considered the exciting new developments there. Diana wrote from Hanover, where anti-semitic rallies and attacks had become frequent in what was then a city with one of Germany's largest Jewish communities. Jewish staff were being fired from department stores. Jewish-owned businesses, legal and medical practices closed down. Gavin's reasons for not coming to visit Germany may well have been this open persecution of Jews, as well as gays and left-wingers who were being arrested and detained in concentration camps without trial. Nevertheless, Diana wrote:

"*Hanover, 14th May 1933*

*Dear Gavin, thanks for your recent note. I am sorry that
you have changed your plans and decided, not to come to
Germany. You ought to study the conditions in Germany on
the spot. The papers abroad are full of lies. I am sure you
would rectify your views about present-day Germany quite
a lot, as many have done, who have had an opportunity
to see Germany during the last few months. I am afraid
England does not like us at present moment. We are going to
build up another Empire with the youth of Germany. I quite
understand, that the other nations resent the awakening of
the German people, but the whole world cannot prevent,
that the Germans recover their self-consciousness. We are
determined to create the 'Dritte Reich'.*

*I too have become a member of the national-socialist's party.
I shall probably join the brown army of Hitler in the next few
days as a horseman.*

*Of course, small minorities may have to suffer. There will be
perhaps less understanding and sympathy for them under the
new government, than under the democratic system. It may
be, that they suppress minorities, but it cannot be helped as
long as it serves the country.*

I have got a personal request. I would ask you, to open a bank account for me in London, since I want to deposit a little money abroad, so as to be on the safe side. One never knows what happens and a few pounds may be very useful one day. I would send you a draft on London for about £100/-/-, which is to be paid in on my behalf. I cannot arrange this transaction from this end for certain reasons and I hope therefore, that you will help me and take the trouble, to serve as my banker. Please let me know whether I may send you the draft.

The weather is still terribly bad in this northern part of Germany, but I shall have to remain in this cold country.

Always yours,

Diana."

Diana's zeal for the Nazis shows as she refers to them as *"We"* and mentions their efforts to create a new Germany six times. Her younger sister Unity was equally if not more fervent – they were photographed in that same year by Gavin's neighbour Gerald Berners giving Nazi salutes while standing on a mountaintop in the *"fatherland"*. The sisters loved horse-riding, but it was a girlish fantasy for Diana to think she could join the brown-shirt cavalry. This did not exist outside of a few ceremonial outriders in the parades and rallies she had seen that year. Mosley's long-suffering wife Lady Cynthia "Cimmie" was to die of peritonitis later that year. The phrase "long-suffering" seems apt as Sir Oswald had enjoyed other affairs during their marriage – including ones with Cimmie's younger sister and their step-mother. Two years after this letter was written Sir Oswald married Diana in Berlin. The secular ceremony took place in the home of Joseph Goebbels, the Nazi Minister of Public Enlightenment and Propaganda. Their guest of honour was Adolf Hitler. As far as Diana's request for a bank account goes, there is no record of Gavin having acceded to this request.

When Gavin did return to England it was to find that the gap between his mother and himself had widened. This started after Gavin commissioned an architect, Geddes Hislop, to start on the restoration of Buscot Park as a "Palladian" building. All Victorian and Edwardian additions were to be removed. Lady Violet did not see the need for this and expected it would cost a fortune. She also preferred not to have to mingle with visiting socialists, so in March 1934 she took as lease on "Beckett", a house a few miles away and moved there. This was a large, crenellated building in the Scottish Baronial style, surrounded by formal gardens with ornamental lakes and parkland. She and her son would never share life under the same roof again. Ironically, Beckett survives today at the centre of a modern complex called "The Defence Academy of the United Kingdom".

In the same month the 1st Lord Faringdon passed away and Gavin inherited the title all the contents of 18 Arlington Street. Newspapers reported:

"FAMOUS PEER DEAD

The death was announced yesterday of Lord Faringdon of Buscot Park, Faringdon, Berks, and Glenalmond House, Perthshire.

Lord Faringdon, who was born in 1850, was a former Chairman of the Great Central Railway, and a member of the Tariff Commission,1904.

A member of the Stock Exchange for more than sixty-one years, he was one of the few amongst the oldest members "Father of the Stock Exchange" who kept daily contact with the City.

His heir is his grandson, Mr A.G. Henderson, of Buscot Park, Faringdon, Berks."

A clipping from the *Investor's Chronicle* gave detailed financial information:

> £1,021,696 Will of Lord Faringdon. £394,349 Paid *in Estate Duty*
>
> *Lord Faringdon of 18 Arlington-street, W., a member of the Stock Exchange for 61 years, who died on March 17th, aged 83, has left a fortune of the gross value of £1,021,696, with net personality £986,076, on which £394,349 in estate duty has been paid.*
>
> *His furniture at 18, Arlington-street is left to his grandson, Alexander Gavin Henderson, and all his property is to be divided into nine parts – one to each of his children, Philip, Arnold, Eric, and Margaret; one between his grandchildren, Michael Thomas Henderson, Roderick Dalzell Henderson and Margaret Violet Henderson, and one between his grandchildren, Susan Violet Henderson, Rosemary Gladys Henderson, and Adrian Donald Henderson.*
>
> *Among bequests is that to the National Gallery of "The Harvest Moon," by Mason, while his pictures by Rembrandt and Sir Joshua Reynolds are to be held as heirlooms.*
>
> *Lord Faringdon was the second son of Mr. George Henderson, Langholm, Dumphries, was created a baronet in 1902, and elevated to the peerage in 1916.*
>
> *He was M.P. for West Staffordshire (1898-1906) and for St. George's, Hanover square (1913-1916). He was at one time chairman of the Great Central Railway.*

Archival photographs of Pomfret Castle show its interiors covered with decorative plasterwork. The ceilings of the hall and principal rooms were fan-vaulted (with Gothic pendentives similar to those in King's College Chapel, Gloucester Cathedral or Westminster Abbey).

It was built on an opulent scale and difficult to maintain in good order. Lady Violet told her grandson, the current Lord Faringdon, that *"the copper bath tubs were so huge that the maids had to get into them in stockinged feet to clean them and it took days to get them gleaming".* The family felt that it should be sold, and as Gavin had plans for architectural renovation of Buscot, he agreed to an offer from a property developer. Pomfret Castle was torn down and replaced with a block of modern "mansion flats". Gavin regretted this a few years later when he saw how much Georgian architecture was going the same way and he became a founder member of the Georgian Group with Robert Byron, James Lees-Milne, John Betjeman and others. Arlington Street lost neo-classical facades by Robert Adam and Sir John Soane to further redevelopment and bombing during WW2. These losses were keenly felt and guided Gavin when he became Chairman of the G.L.C.'s Historic Building Committee.

In June 1934, Sotheby's auctioned all the furniture and some of the paintings, raising £10,405. In July 1934 Sotheby's held a second auction, this time of the first Lord Faringdon's collection of silverware, enamels and Jacobite relics. *The Times* noted that some works of paintings sold fetched far less than the first Lord Faringdon had paid for them. This was probably because most were by Pre-Raphaelites, who were very much out of fashion at the time. The sums raised went towards paying death duties, which were mercifully less than after Gavin's father died. In 1922 the Government had sought to offset the cost of WW1 by imposing the highest death duties of all time – 90% of the value of an estate.

Whilst paintings were sold for less than their purchase prices, Fortune's wheel has turned again since those days. Some now hang in major collections: Sir Edward Burne-Jones: *Cupid Delivering Psyche* and *The Baleful Head* are both now in London's Victoria & Albert Museum. Other Burne-Jones' sold were *Spes (Hope)* and *Fides (Faith)*, which Morris & Company had adapted into stained glass memorial windows at St. Mary's Buscot, as well as for Lord Faringdon's chapel at the Reina Cristina Hotel in Algeciras. Two paintings by J.W.

Waterhouse sold were *The Lady Clare* and *Nymphs Finding the Head of Orpheus* and are now owned by Sir Andrew Lloyd-Webber. *Esther* by John Everett Millais is in another private collection. Here the model had been draped in a yellow cloak with Chinese embroideries that had belonged to General Gordon (popularly called *"Chinese Gordon – the saviour of Peking"*). One of the finest paintings to be sold was *Choosing* by George Frederick Watts. This shows the 17-year-old actress Ellen Terry's profile between symbolic flowers: luscious camellias, with little scent, and humble sweet-smelling violets. The choice had a personal significance for the artist and sitter as in 1864 Terry gave up the stage to marry Watts, 30 years her senior. The marriage did not last a year before she left him "choosing" to return to the stage. Some regard *Choosing* as one of his best paintings and it now hangs in the National Portrait Gallery. Other paintings sold were far less arresting, such as Thomas Armstrong's *An Aesthetic Interior* and *Girl Watching a Tortoise*; both were very large and had been left in situ when Alexander Henderson bought 18 Arlington St. from its former owner.

In October Lady Violet, a long-time Conservative party supporter, was shocked to learn that her son Gavin had thrown his weight behind a Labour Party candidate in the local elections. This was Dr Christopher Addison who was seeking to regain the seat he had lost three years earlier to the Conservatives. The press reported that Gavin's chauffeur-driven Rolls-Royce was being used to fetch constituents to rallies where Gavin had delivered speeches in support of Dr Addison. Press photos showed Gavin smiling alongside Dr Addison outside venues, and the right-wing *Daily Mail* reported:

> *"Conservatives had a fleet of about 250 motor-cars at their disposal, while the socialists mustered about 30, headed by Lord Faringdon's car."*

The political divide between Gavin and his mother widened further when he refused to renew a lease of a townhouse in Abingdon to the Conservative Party. His father Lt.-Col Harold Greenwood

Henderson MP had arranged for his party to have this at a peppercorn rent when he resigned his seat in 1916. But Gavin wanted to install the Labour Party there instead. He refused several offers to increase the rent, as well as bids to purchase the building outright by wealthy Conservatives. However, as there were few Labour voters in Abingdon, Gavin had to arrange for one of his own employees at Buscot to stand as the Labour candidate. This was Frank W. Bourne, a Labour party activist and socialist, who was Gavin's poultry farm manager as well as part-time secretary. Gavin paid all the election expenses for Bourne's unsuccessful campaign.

Word of the rebellious new Labour peer had spread by the time that Gavin gave his maiden speech to the House of Lords in November 1934. Here he rose to support pacifism and the freedom to possess anti-fascist literature. This was during the debate on the Disaffection Bill, which would have made both criminal offences. Conservative peers heckled him and the Speaker of the House had to remind them that this was in breach of the tradition of no interruptions during a peer's maiden speech. Soon afterwards, Gavin joined the National Council of Civil Liberties (NCCL), now known as Liberty. Its president at the time was the author E. M. Forster, and committee members included the writers H.G. Wells, Aldous Huxley and J.B. Priestley; the philosopher Bertrand Russell; the psychologist Havelock Ellis; and the Labour MPs Clem Attlee and Aneurin Bevan. In his second speech that month Gavin criticised Government policies in the debate on Indian reform. He was to do so again in December, protesting at *"the treatment of the Indians as a backward race".*

This year saw Gavin's emergence as the second Lord Faringdon as well as a left-winger. Some journalists called him a class-traitor while others praised his convictions. As usual with Gavin, when he set himself a course of action, he went at it full-tilt for a period of time – then lapsed into a state of apparent indolence. Over the next few years, he would retreat repeatedly to a mountaintop on a remote Mediterranean island. But before he went there, he was a whirlwind of activity. For example, in one month he drove to six British towns to deliver campaign speeches on behalf of the Labour party. Letters of thanks from candidates and party supporters prove that his passionate oratory cut through class divisions. A mark of his effectiveness was that right-wing journalists began to refer to him as *"The Red Peer"*. Gavin remained, as always, controversial. And as his Oxford contemporary Harold Acton commented: *"His pendulum might swing in unforeseen directions"*.

CHAPTER 6

The Corsican Interlude

Gavin spent Christmas 1931 on the Mediterranean island of Corsica. He went back to England in January and then returned to Corsica for a month that summer. He spent a further five weeks on the island in 1932. By then he had moved into an old farmhouse in a remote spot in the hills above a romantic coast. He left deposits with local builders and they executed his plans for renovation. He returned and invited friends to stay in 1933 – spending ten weeks there altogether that year. In 1934 he passed another ten weeks on the island with more friends. In 1935, he stayed ten weeks and had many guests. In 1936 he passed eleven weeks there and after that he never returned. Perhaps he meant to go back because he continued to pay relatively large sums to someone who lived there until her death in the early 1970s. Who was that? What was his attachment to this remote place?

Perhaps he was attracted initially by Corsica's reputation as a refuge for outlaws. Locals of Italian extraction claimed they had rebelled against their French overlords. Local legend and folklore had Corsican "Robin Hoods" lurking in the densely wooded mountains. Many of the upland villages had tales of bandits robbing the rich French and protecting the poor. Gavin was drawn to mountain fastnesses near the rugged northern coast. He may have fallen under the spell cast in the fictional works of Guy de Maupassant as there were a number of editions in French on his bookshelves. In these tales Corsica is an elemental place, where people are free and not ruled by bourgeois values. For example, in a short story called *Happiness*, a beautiful French aristocrat abandons her privileged life in Paris to become the wife of a desperately poor hill farmer. In de Maupassant's novel *A Life*, the main character's memories of a honeymoon in the wilds of Corsica sustain her throughout a long sterile married life afterwards. Another inspiration may have come from Edward Lear's illustrated book *A Landscape Painter in Corsica*. Gavin owned a watercolour by him, as well as an edition of his *Nonsense Verse*, in which one can find the following limerick:

> "There was a young lady of Corsica,
> Who purchased a little brown saucy-cur;
> Which she fed upon ham
> And hot raspberry jam,
> That expensive young lady of Corsica."

In more modern times, the painter Henri Matisse had visited and painted in Corsica. Whilst Gavin did not own any paintings by him, his friends David Tennant, Peter Watson, Edward James and Gerald Berners had all purchased Matisse paintings. The artist was inspired by its intense colours and described Corsica as a place where:

> "Everything glistens, everything is colour, everything is light."

Gavin chose a remote spot near the mountain village of Lumio (the name means "the place of light" in the Corsican dialect). His retreat was a two-storey stone farmhouse of a type known in the Mediterranean as a *Mas*, a vernacular style with a flattish roof of interlocking terracotta tiles. It was a long building – possibly built on what had once been a longhouse where people lived on one end and animals in the others in a barn. It was perched on the crest of a hill and there were no windows on the South side – for that was where the Sirocco wind and fiercest sun came from. From the west side one could see the village church's tall campanile (bell tower). From the east side of the house there were views across mountains to the Tyrrhenian Sea between Corsica and Italy. A short walk below the *mas* – which probably had around six bedrooms once he had renovated it – was a sandy cove where he and his guests could swim and sun-bathe. The shore down there was lined by large rocks and there were shady places under Corsican pines that resembled giant parasols. Elsewhere the landscape was covered with olive, citrus, pomegranate and cork-oaks, with prickly pear, cacti and arbutus scrub in between. It was quiet, apart from the electric buzz of cicadas, droning insects and the wind swishing through the pines.

Lumio lies in the *"Haut Corse"*, a mountainous area popular today with the prosperous modern holiday villa owners. Gavin came when Corsica had begun to attract those keen to bypass the more popular resorts of the Cote d'Azur. Some were ex-patriots who had chosen to live in Italy and France, mainly because the laws governing homosexuality there were less strict than in Britain. They found greater freedom here as penalties were limited to a charge of indecency for sexual relations in public; and this did not apply between consulting males in private. Access to Corsica was by ferries from Marseilles, Nice or Toulon to L' Île-Rousse (the port nearest Lumio); or to the other Corsican ports of Ajaccio, Bastia, Porto-Vecchio and Propriano. Gavin may have seen an exhibition in London by M.C. Esher of Corsican scenes in 1931. He came first came in the following year when he was aged 30. He travelled on a new passport where he left the section labelled "Wife" blank. He must have known someone on the island as he arrived on December 20th and stayed over the Xmas and New Year holiday period, leaving after spending an entire month on the island. On Jan 24th 1933 he boarded a ship bound for Nice with someone named in his diary as "Juan". This is the usual southern French (and Corsican) variant of the name Jean, as in as in St. Juan des Pins. The name pronounced with two syllables as *"Ju-whan"*. Gavin's appointments diary of 1935 shows a Juan arriving in Southampton three weeks before Gavin left to spend the weeks around Christmas and January 1936 in Corsica. This man seems to have been very much on his mind as the name J. Giudicelli appears in pencil on his diary's text block (page's edge). A few years later the name "Juan Giudicelli of Lumio, Corsica" was added to Gavin's will. It would seem that for at least four years Juan was involved whenever Gavin visited Corsica. The earliest evidence of a close relationship comes in an invoice dated 4th April 1933 from Thos. Cook & Son, Ltd, which reads:

> To: Reservation of cabin 102 in favour of yourself and
> Mr. Giudicelli for the cruise of the "MONTE ROSA"
> leaving Venice on
>
> Aril 24th @ £30. 10. 0 each.
>
> Supplements for gratuities on board @ 15/ each.
>
> Two tickets for shore excursion No 26. @ 10/6d each.
>
> Continental Travel tickets as per separate account attached.

The bill for this came to roughly £6,500.00 in today's money. Gavin's diary shows a meeting with a Captain Johannesen of the *SS Monte Rosa* in Venice on April 13th 1933. It is interesting to note that the *SS Monte Rosa* was a German cruise ship launched in 1930. During WW2 she was converted into a troopship, fell into the hands of the Royal Navy, and was renamed the *Empire Windrush*. As such, she is famous today for bringing 492 passengers from Jamaica to London in 1948. Over the next month the *Monte Rosa* cruised through the Gulf of Venice, Ionian, Adriatic and Tyrrhenian seas to visit Corfu, Delphi, Athens and Constantinople, Naples, Capri and Genoa. On Tuesday May 16th Gavin wrote these words excitedly in his diary: *"To Corsica!"*. He was to stay on the island for another ten days. Presumably, most of this time, like that spent sharing a cabin with his companion, he was in close proximity with Juan Giudicelli.

Once he was established in Lumio, Gavin invited friends to visit. Later that year his diary records that on August 1st Susu came with Jack and John. Whilst Susu is clearly Lady Ankaret Howard Jackson, there is no clue who the other two were. He wrote that these men, who arrived on the ferry from L' Ile Rousse, stayed for three weeks, and they were joined by Axel (Dr Axel Munthe, who lived on Capri) for two nights. After these guests left, Gavin played host to a well-known pioneer aviator of the time whose name appears in the diary as Charlie Chichester. He was planning to circumnavigate the world but his hopes were dashed when his aeroplane crashed in a snowstorm in Russia. However, the same man went on to become famous as the round-the-world-solo yachtsman Sir Francis Chichester in the 1960s. Few of Gavin's other guests that year at Lumio can be identified as he seldom wrote names in full. One wonders who Tuffu and Sotaris were, as they came and stayed repeatedly for long periods. Still, Gavin enjoyed a private life there far from the prying eyes until early October 1933.

In June of the following year, he invited Robert Byron, who was in Persia researching *The Road to Oxiana* along with Christopher Sykes – a mutual friend from their Oxford days.

> *"My dear Robert,*
>
> *It was good to hear from you & I envy your Oriental junket trip. Are you preparing another book? ...I suppose so. From what point of view architectural, political, geographical or racial?*
>
> *Don't go directly home. You must pass by Marseille so stop off & come to see me in Corsica. There is a boat that leaves Toulon for Calvi on the same day that the P.O. reaches M. An easy connection – or you can go Nice – the Rosse just sent me a wire to HENDERSON (incog in Corsica!) LUMIO & come & stay just as long as you like. Very quiet but lovely scenery & bathing & possibly, this year, some sanitation!*
>
> *Love to Christopher.*
>
> *Do come and bring him too.*
>
> *Gavin."*

At Eton College 1916.

An Oxford undergraduate 1922.

The 2nd Baron Faringdon 1936.

An Auxiliary Fireman 1941.

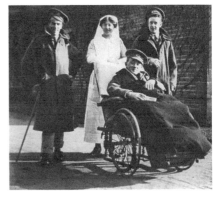

Top: His mother Lady Violet, riding side-saddle, and father Lt.-Col. H.G. Henderson MP, Adjutant of the Berkshire Yeomanry mounted on a charger called "Granite".Middle: Kitemore, their family home and estate in Shellingford, West Berkshire. Below: Inmates in the Red Cross convalescent hospital at Kitemore during WW1.

Christopher Sykes was a Persian scholar and writer who travelled with Robert in Central Asia during 1933–34 when most Westerners regarded the region as unexplored. Sykes and Byron got along well enough to write a novel together under the pseudonym Richard Waughburton, *Innocence and Design*, which was published in 1935. People found it a clever but forgettable book. A copy of this was sent to Gavin and remains in his library.

Gavin also invited Harold Acton, his friend from Eton and Oxford, who replied on headed notepaper from the British Legation in Peking. Harold wrote that he was living *"within a stone's throw of the forbidden city"*. At Oxford, Harold impressed everyone with his sophisticated blend of Renaissance style and modernist panache. A drawing by Evelyn Waugh that appeared in Isis shows Harold holding the megaphone though which he recited poetry to students passing in the quad below his balcony, who he described as *"new born babies cooked in wine"*. In 1932 he went to China to immerse himself in Oriental Art, poetry and music. Harold's letter mentions that he was glad to hear that Gavin's *"crise"* had passed. He went on to write that *"I should love to hear your news if you are not too engrossed in politics or at the Bar"*. These comments show that he was aware of the latest developments – some of which had probably been passed on by Robert Byron, who had visited him in Peking. There he found Harold living with Desmond Parsons, the younger brother of Gavin's travelling companion to Tibet, Michael, the earl of Rosse. Desmond was Byron's great unrequited love. News about him emerged later. Other information may have come from another mutual friend:

> *"I have happy memories of coming to Corsica with Patrick Balfour...both of us gave full attention to the elementary appetites available at Calvi or L' Île-Rousse. I preferred Calvi as a setting. It was full of Russians and extraordinary women who seemed to have migrated from Capri."*

Corsica's picturesque coastal towns dated back to Roman times and had been re-developed by Genoan and Venetian traders in the 16th to

18th centuries. During the Bonapartist era French Empire style added to the architectural mix. What *"elementary appetites"* Acton and Balfour enjoyed there were unexplained. Both men were bisexual. With a few carefully chosen words Acton made Corsica sound louche. One of the *"extraordinary women"* they met was Camille de Buisseret, the estranged wife of a Belgian baron. She was a bisexual living in Ajaccio who became very friendly with Gavin.

Travel posters of the early 1930s depicted Corsica with fashionable motorcars sweeping uphill on coastal roads lined with pine trees. Motoring had long been a passion of Gavin's. He had driven through Belgium, Holland, France, Italy, Spain, Greece, Romania, Turkey, Czechoslovakia, Austria, Hungary, Poland and Germany. He wanted to drive in Corsica, so on one of his earliest trips he had come to Marseilles in his Rolls-Royce "Tickford" Cabriolet, which had been winched onto the deck of the *Ile de Beaute.* The ship's name translated from French means *"Island of Beauty"* – another name for Corsica. After berthing at Calvi, Gavin's Rolls-Royce was winched off the deck and onto the pier. From there he drove slowly to Lumio as the Rolls was too long to negotiate the switchback bends of the winding mountain roads smoothly. In the following year Gavin bought himself a smaller car to use on the island. This was the latest Fiat 522 with a "torpedo" chassis, equipped with a 6-cylinder engine and four-speed all-synchromesh gearbox; very technically advanced for the time. Gavin paid Fiat's main dealer in Nice to customise it with cushioned leather seats as well as curtains. The *Ile de Beaute,* carried it to Corsica where Gavin was waiting to zoom it up to Lumio. This purchase in 1935 showed his commitment to Corsica the year after he became the 2nd Lord Faringdon. By then the house had been supplied with electricity, new plumbing, a modern kitchen and some en-suite bathrooms. Outside, a patio and tennis court had been added; and a gardener had been at work cutting back maquis, and tending the old olive, fig and lemon trees. In August that summer two of his servants from Buscot were sent out to prepare everything for his arrival. Soon afterwards, there were the usual plethora of guests for two months until Gavin left in mid- October.

Cyril Connolly's novel *The Rock Pool* (a first edition exists in Buscot Park's library) was set on a Mediterranean island where a group of ex-patriot decadents have gathered to enjoy the heat and each other's favours. The book was said to have been inspired by Connolly's visits to nearby Capri – but photographs show that he came to Lumio with "Susu" and a group of friends before he wrote it. A number of British writers had settled in Capri. These included several Gavin knew, such as Somerset Maugham, Compton Mackenzie and Norman Douglas. The latter was notorious as a former diplomat who stayed one step ahead of the British Police, who were seeking to interview him over allegations of pederasty. Another with a louche reputation was Peter Watson, who took a lease on one of Capri's oldest villas, the splendid 600-square-metre Villa Cercola. Gavin and Peter knew each other from their time at Eton and Oxford. Since then, an enormous inheritance had helped turn Peter into a millionaire art-collector with a reputation as a gay playboy.

While Peter's debonair manner and looks got him adored by Cecil Beaton and the Mitford sisters, Gavin's friend and neighbour Lord Berners called him *"Frog-Face"* and made Peter into a lead character in his comic novel *The Girls of Radcliff Hall* in which Berners deliberately misspelt the lesbian writer's name as the book's title to tease her, and used it as the name for a girls' boarding school. In this spoof Peter's character (Lizzie Johnson) uses her wealth to win friends and impress others, which sets off jealous spats between pubescent girls whose names hint at well-known people. According to Cyril Connolly, the character Cecily Seymour – an artistic girl – was a caricature of Cecil Beaton, and the melodramatic "Little Olive Mason" was the theatre designer Oliver Messel. The notorious Mayfair courtesan Doris Castlerosse (a memorable guest at Gavin's wedding) appears as Vivian Dorrick – a dancing master *"skilled in the arts of love"*. As Berners was poking fun at Peter Watson's love of gossip and private life dramas, we should not take everything that he wrote in the letter below at face value. Watson may well have been *"stirring"* with this account of what went on at his villa in Capri when he suggests that Gavin's ex-wife, Honor, was involved in several *ménages à trois* there.

"Tuesday, 26 August.

Mr Dear Gavin,

I'm writing out of a sense of shame, because I've left it so long. The main thing you wanted to know, anyway, I told you: Honor's well enough. She's as well as anyone ever is, more or less. Only she's Over-Strung, to my mind, and I suppose she may well be: that <u>ass</u> Spiro brought out an unmentionable little bounder called Peter Reed-Davis, and the three of them lived in the villa together, like three cats in a bag. Thank god the Reed-Davis has gone now, and Honor and Spiro have got on better since he went. But yesterday there arrived a Tony Rumbold, and the wretched girl is already seeing herself the remoter corner of yet another triangle. Probably quite without any grounds.

I can't imagine anyone wanting to sleep with either of them, but then one can never imagine these things, and there's forever happening for all that. Oh god – this is turning into a nice gossipy letter, which is the last thing you want to read – or to write. But its all so idiotic and sapless and eunuch. Spiro's not a bad creature, I think, but a born eunuch; Honor's off her head to want to marry him. And what's more she never will. I'd bet on that. I wish she'd get over it, for the atmosphere here is becoming unbreatheable; naturally they're not the only ones with troubles; there's never a party now without someone's face slapped; there are <u>too many women</u> here, that's what's the matter. Is Corsica full of women? Is there any place that isn't?

I suppose they are going to confiscate my house in a few weeks time and so I may just possibly come your way…. I believe those blithering idiots are really going to go to war with all takers; and my chief concern is going to be to keep quite out of it. I'm not going to fight for or against anyone. I'm going to sulk. And you?

Yours ever,

Peter

P.S. I'm told Brussels is <u>indescribable</u>."

The last paragraph of this letter suggests that Watson is about to leave Capri because of fascist threats – and he did move to Paris in 1935. Mussolini had issued a warning that foreigners living in Italy who did not support his government could have their property confiscated. For an Art collector like Peter, that was a terrible threat and fascism spread after Mussolini's invasion of Ethiopia (Abyssinia) that year, which was heralded as the beginning of his re-colonisation of Africa. The postscript at the end of his letter confirms this year as the date in which the letter was written as it is more than likely that he was referring to the *Exposition Universelle et Internationale Bruxelles* held in Brussels between April and November 1935. This included pavilions designed by the modern architect Le Corbusier and an exhibition of paintings by the Belgian artist Rene Magritte – who Peter Watson collected. However, Peter gives us what appears to be some scurrilous information elsewhere. Tony Rumbold's time at Eton and Oxford overlapped with Peter and Gavin's. He went on to have a highly distinguished career in the diplomatic service. He may have been bisexual, but that was not a side of his character mentioned outside of this letter. Whilst the best man at Rumbold's wedding in 1937 was his friend and fellow diplomat Donald Maclean – a member of the Cambridge ring of homosexual spies – nothing has ever been made of this connection. As regards that *"unmentionable little bounder called Peter Reed-Davis"* he seems to have vanished without trace. *"Spiro"* who Peter refers to as *"a born eunuch"*, may have been a nickname for Prince Paul of Greece, who the scurrilous Lord

Tredegar alleged had some gay liaisons before he married Princess Frederika of Hanover in 1938.

Peter Watson did not mention, but must have known about, someone who had a louche influence on Honor. This was Evan, Lord Tredegar – who mentioned her as a house guest in a letter he wrote to Gavin from Capri in 1935. Tredegar was a notoriously eccentric Welsh peer, a bisexual poet who spent a month each year as chamberlain to Popes Benedict XV and Pius XI. After a day's work at the Vatican, Evan claimed to like to go to sit by the grave of the poet Shelley to communicate with his spirit. The occultist Aleister Crowley described Evan Tredegar as his *"perfect adept"*. Others claimed that his secret presence at a satanic mass was revealed by his exceptionally long red nose poking out from under his black cowl. Tredegar's weekend house parties attracted a wide variety of guests, who included Aldous Huxley, H.G. Wells, and Augustus John. There he would amuse his quests with his blue Macaw and by staging boxing matches with his pet kangaroo. Vere Pilkington, a director at Sotheby's auction house, chose Lord Tredegar to be his best man when he married Gavin's ex-wife Honor on Feb 5th February 1936. Perhaps the presence of Evan Tredegar explains why her parents did not attend the wedding, and why Evan sent this doggerel about them to Gavin:

> *"Said my Lord to Lady Kylsant*
> *I very much fear that I shan't*
> *Be able to tonight,*
> *Oh, I think that I might*
> *Hold on, I see that I can't."*

Perhaps a better indication of what went on at Gavin's summer retreat survives in Susu's photo albums, which now belong to her daughter Tarn Bailey, to whom the atheist Gavin eventually consented to serve as godfather. His gifts to her include Venetian candelabras but no encouraging words on religion or the afterlife. Still, he gave her a sense of style and grace she never forgot. The albums show the villa in Lumio where she stayed with Gavin and some of their mutual friends. They also show the sights worth seeing in the *"Haut Corse"*, which remain much the same today while the overall quality of life for the locals has changed enormously. For example, Susu's albums have snapshots of the campanile of Santa Reparata in Monosaglia, a village to the northwest; and the mountainous and forested landscape, with hamlets scattered along ridges – still famous for its scenic views. Of equal importance are the local people appearing with their donkeys, old ladies carrying bundles of kindling or bunches of herbs gathered from the maquis; and one of a strong peasant woman carrying a large galvanised bucket on her head on a lane between vegetable gardens.

One man stands out in the album as the most photographed. He appears to have been a handsome Corsican with a dark complexion and thick, black hair that flopped over one half of his forehead. He was often captured smiling warmly at the camera, and sometimes posing with locals and their donkeys. But this smiling man's clothes and demeanour set him out as more sophisticated than the locals he stopped and got to pose for the camera. For example, he appears wearing a long, loosely tied bandana, a striped yachtsman's jersey and loose white trousers – very modish at the time. He was physically fit and posed bare-chested with a shy flirtatious smile when holding a phallic prickly pear fruit up for the camera. In another photograph, he sits bare-chested beside Gavin who was dressed in khaki shorts and a black singlet. Elsewhere these two appear sitting close together by the sea – both wearing only towels around their waists. In another photograph, the Corsican man sits beside Gavin and is looking back as if to check that anyone was watching. Then two other men joined them by the seashore, and these have all thrown their arms around Gavin to give him a three-man hug.

Elsewhere in Susu's album another unidentified man appears. This one is slim, athletic and wears a black woollen skull cap in spite of the heat. He and Susu sit on rocks by the shore in the bright sunshine – both in black bathing outfits – and here he still wears his woollen cap. In another photo he stands holding a mirror to reflect light up into his face; and in a third, sits on a wall wearing his cap and a black singlet, talking to Basil Murray. One assumes that Susu took most of these photos, as it was her album. However, as her husband William does not appear in any of the photos, he may have been the cameraman. Basil Murray, Susu's cousin, appears several times more. He had become a major force in anti-fascist politics by heckling Oswald Mosley during a speech at the Oxford Union in 1936. Mosley's supporters attacked him and Basil was arrested, accused of inciting a riot, tried and convicted of causing a breach of the peace. The philosopher Isaiah Berlin described that legal decision as a *"disastrous miscarriage of Justice"*. Basil became notorious as an *enfant terrible* after Evelyn Waugh used aspects of his personality to create his anarchic character Basil Seal. The real Basil showed considerable courage when he became a journalist during the Spanish Civil War and made regular radio broadcasts from the Republican front lines in Valencia until, in 1938, he was reported to have died of pneumonia in Spain. Later, a fellow journalist Claude Cockburn claimed that he had bled to death after being bitten by his pet monkey while lying in a drunken stupor on his hotel bed. Whatever the truth, Basil had a rakish smile on his face in Susu's photographs of him. In one photograph a dapper man sits beside him while Cyril Connolly, wearing a white yachting cap and striped jersey, lies at their feet like a playful cat. The dapper man may have been the millionaire art-collector and publisher Peter Watson who sponsored Connolly's magazine *Encounter*. Whoever this group of men were, they seem very gay in both senses of that word.

Susu's albums give us a good idea of what the villa looked like from various angles. However, it was never her intention to record the look of it in the landscape. For that we have to trust two snapshots that were found stuck into a 1933 book on the Indian Independence movement (*India What Now? A Study of the Realities of Indian Problems* by N. Gangulee C.I.E., Ph.D. Author of *Problems of Rural India, Notes on Indian Constitutional Reform*. London. George Allen & Unwin Ltd.) which Gavin might well have been reading at the time as he spoke repeatedly in the Lords debates on India in 1934. These photographs show a Mediterranean *mas* with rendered walls and tall wooden shutters. There is a shady arcade on one side and a tennis court can be seen behind. Gavin's mother's papers show that she and Gavin's younger brother Roddy visited in 1936. Her collection of photographs shows the Corsican villa from other angles. In one of these photos Roddy stands in the shady arcade below the house holding a pug – a variety of lapdog Lady Violet bred.

Evidence that Gavin had invested in this holiday home comes from Buscot Park's account books. These show that in May 1936 Mr Savage, 2nd footman at Buscot Park, was given £4 travelling expenses to Corsica. There is a receipt for a British Airways return flight to Marseilles, and the Buscot Park account book shows that expenditure on postage to Corsica was £8. In the following year (1937) the 3rd footman, Mr Booth, travelled to Corsica. It is clear that Gavin and his guests were not "roughing it". Whatever the villa was like before the war, things had changed greatly when Cyril Connolly visited it again afterwards. Corsica had been occupied by the Italians and Germans when there was a strong resistance faction on the island – as one might have expected. Corsica had been liberated and occupied by Allied troops before Connolly returned in October 1946 and wrote:

> *"Dear Gavin,*
>
> *I saw your villa while in Corsica and promised to deliver this letter. It has been used as a children's Holiday Home and appears considerably the worse for wear, but the writer of this letter spoke warmly and regretfully of you.*
>
> *Yours ever,*
>
> *Cyril Connolly."*

The "letter" that Connolly delivered was simply an envelope with two pages of printed blue notepaper headed *"Lumio, Corse"*. Who the occupant was and just why "*the writer of this letter spoke warmly and regretfully"* is not fully revealed in a poem on a folded page inside. This is inscribed on the outside:

"To dear Gavin,

With best wishes for his comfort.

Jules."

His poem gives us an intimate view of events at the villa at a time when Juan suddenly left the villa, Gavin felt rejected but turned to Camille (de Buisseret?) for physical consolation:

"When Pussy's out, or so they say
The little mice come out to play
And so, it seems but just and right
That when Juan vanished in the night
Dear Gavin (with the longest face)
Deserted his accustomed place
(Which as you doubtless knew before
Was in the corner by the door)
And with an air distrait, though free,
Retired beneath an olive tree
If not alone: then with Camille
And had a most delightful *feel*
For though, of course it's very nice
To burn your life's experienced bright
There really isn't any harm
In holding to a friendly arm
And surely, when your life is free
T'will do no harm to press a knee.
In fact, and should you take the Torse
T'will help you forget the Corse."

The O.E.D. gives *"Torse"* as a noun for a heraldic wreath, derived from the obsolete French and Latin words *"torta".* Jules probably intended this word to have a sexual symbolism, although the outcome seems just to have been *"a delightful feel"*.

Another envelope marked "Lumio" contained two medium-format photographic negatives. When printed these showed the handsome man with the floppy hair – presumably Juan Giudicelli. Yet another envelope contained a snapshot showing him sitting on a parapet next to Gavin and Susu. In this all three are wearing the same clothes as they do in Susu's album. Elsewhere amongst his papers from this time were four pencil sketches of the same man. These show his left and right profiles, his face straight on, and a sketch from below-left. They are not highly accomplished, but nonetheless are good likenesses. As they resemble pencil drawings in Gavin's sketchbooks it would seem that he drew them. They may have served as studies for an artist who did not meet the subject face-to face to paint his portrait. This might account for why an oil portrait hanging in a bedroom at Buscot looks very much like the photographs and sketches of Juan Giudicelli. Untitled and undated, this painting is called *A Corsican Man* (F.C 219) and has a "flat" appearance as if painted from a photograph.

Whatever his relationship with Juan may have been, Gavin left the island in 1936 and never returned. From that time on the Corsican spell seems to have been broken. His last guests there that summer were his ex-wife Honor and her new husband Vere Pilkington. They came with Dr Christopher Addison – the Labour MP for Swindon. On his return to England that year Gavin threw himself into campaigning for the Republican side in the Spanish Civil War. He threw himself into fundraising campaigns for the Republicans and into countering fascist propaganda about Spain. Two years later in September 1938 he officially ended his affair with Corsica when he had a legal document drawn up stating that a Mademoiselle Eugenie Giudecelli was to be paid £4. 3s. 4d. (£290.00 in today's money) annually *"for the rest of his or her life – whichever was the shorter"*. On his copy of this unusual document, he was to add notes in pencil that he paid her an additional £28. 1s. 0d. in October 1938; £21. 10s. 0d., in October 1939; and £32. 10s. 0d., in March 1940. All these amounted to an extra £3,330.00 in today's money. Gavin's income and expenditure account of 1940 shows that he was paying her £50 p.a. (£2,775 today) on top of these sums. This looks like a mortgage on the villa in Lumio, but it may have been a sentimental goodwill gesture. All payments to her ceased in the mid-1960s, and so one wonders if she had passed away.

Corsica provided an important chapter in Gavin's life but one has to leave it with a lot of unanswered questions. Was Eugenie Giudecelli Juan's sister, wife, mother or relative? Could *"Camille"* with whom he had *"a delightful feel"* have been a nickname for one of these women or a man? Who was the occupant of the house in Lumio who sent their *"regrets"* to Gavin in 1946 via Cyril Connolly? Perhaps these questions will be answered in the future. Until then it is interesting to note that the legal document made out to Mademoiselle Eugenie Giudecelli was folded neatly four times and that Gavin wrote the word *Guidicelli* (the alternative spelling) in pencil on the uppermost side. In his will of 1972, he left a legacy of £1,000 to Jean Giudicelli of Lumio, Corsica. A few years later he added a codicil amending that sum to £10,000. If this proves anything it can only be that he still thought fondly of him. A final touch perhaps is that Gavin arranged to have some Corsican shrubs (arbutus) planted around the urn he bought and placed for his ashes in the garden at Buscot Park.

CHAPTER 7

A Busy Idle Man

Gavin was 33 years old in 1935 when an important new political friendship began. This was with Lord Snell, the Under-Secretary of State for India, Labour's leader in the Upper House and Vice Chairman of the British Council. Snell was a man very much involved in Foreign Affairs, he had left the Liberal Party for Labour and passed on his seat in the lower house to a prominent member of the TUC before being elevated to the peerage. Gavin had written to this 70-year-old elder statesman to thank him for his support in the chamber. Lord Snell's handwritten reply showed appreciation and encouragement – as well as criticism – after Gavin's first 18 months in the Upper House.

"PRIVATE.

5th Dec 1935

My dear Faringdon,

I thought that I might have thanked you verbally for your kind note to me, but in case you are not present in the House today I just write this line.

I have not been very happy about your attitude to your own work and life and while I must avoid trying to play the role of aged and heavy father, I should like either to persuade or bully you into a more eager outlook for your future.

*I am sure that if you yourself know, you could do well in the
House and for the Labour Party or whatever other activity
you took up. Is it not worthwhile for you make a real effort
to make your own contribution to the solution of the many
problems of our time? You have the advantages of youth
and education, and if you were always careful to prepare
your speeches, I am sure that you would do well, and you
would also receive the rewards of self-satisfaction – the most
precious of all.*

*I do hope that you will put away all idea about your
incapacity or 'idleness'. The first of these barriers does not
exist, and the second, if it is really so, can easily be overcome.*

Yours sincerely,

Snell."

Gavin's family and friends had all commented on his apparent
"idleness". Snell had noticed it as well and claimed it would be *"easily
overcome"*. One wonders if he was referring to the months Gavin had
been spending in Corsica in the early 1930s. But all that was about to
change due to the economic crisis and the rise of fascism in Europe. In
the meantime, should Lord Snell and others consider him "idle" that
can only have been because he did not broadcast what he was doing
for others in his own time. Several of Gavin's diaries show regular
entries each and every week of the year – in effect – unshakeable
commitments. These were the names of psychiatric hospitals in the
greater London area, which he aimed to visit weekly, or at least every
fortnight. Colney Hatch Mental Hospital had been renamed Friern
in 1937 in order to avoid association with the derogatory term "Booby
Hatch". Cane Hill's asylum held 40 shell-shocked WW1 soldiers,
who had been disowned by their families after the First World War,
and at least 26 were buried in its grounds in unmarked graves. Baxley
pioneered in electro-convulsive therapy for severe nervous disorders.
Since WW1 cases of "shell shock" were seldom discussed. By and

large the military declared that these former soldiers were simply cowards. However, by 1937 over 100,000 ex-servicemen had received awards for psychiatric disability. This amounted to around 15% of all those in receipt of disability pensions. In most cases there was no doubt that patients were suffering as a result of enemy action during their patriotic service. However, there was a widespread suspicion that some were cowards or fakers. Gavin had experience as a regular hospital visitor before he spoke in support of the patients and what was called "The Cripples Bill".

In spite of such weighty concerns, Gavin's social conscience did not prevent him from throwing a party at Buscot Park in the spring of 1936. This resulted in a delightfully equivocal thank you note from a guest – one of the most popular and highest-paid authors of the 1930s, W. Somerset Maugham:

> "I was under the impression that the lake party was given because Mr Fortnum was at last going to make an honest woman of Mrs Mason, but now I learn that Fortnum was a butler & Mason a footman & it all sounds worse & worse to me."

At the time, "Willie" (as his close friends called him) was taking pains to hide his preference for male partners. He had been married for 13 years to Syrie Wellcombe – a top British interior decorator of the 20s and 30s best known for popularising entirely white rooms). They had divorced in 1931 and the writer was living in his Mediterranean villa on the Cote d'Azur with a male companion. This jocular mention of Gavin's staff prompts the question of how many there were in his nominally socialist household. Buscot Park's accounts book lists them that year as: Mrs Goodall – the Housekeeper, Mrs Long – the Assistant Housekeeper, Mr Buck – the Butler, Mr Leslie – 1st Footman, Mr Savage – 2nd Footman, Mr Thomas – Oddman, "Ciggie" – Chauffeur, Mrs Wildman – Cook; and then were various staff who came and went as Kitchen maid, Scullery maid, Head Housemaid, 2nd Housemaid and 3rd Housemaid. In addition, there was "Captain

Francis" – Secretary); plus, under "Extra Help", Mrs Reynolds and a "Chauffeur-Valet" for special occasions. Others who came and went were Mr Booles, Mr Gladstone and Mr Allingham in his London home. So up to 15 staff at times and probably as many working on the estate and in the dairy, stables and on the poultry farm.

This was a conventional number of staff for a mansion, but Gavin had made some innovations that were socialistic in that he paid Employer's Liability Insurance for 13 staff at Buscot plus two London Servants. Their wages in 1936 included a 10% bonus in compensation of his having abolished tips. It had been normal for guests to leave cash sums for the staff who attended them, but in Gavin's households guests were asked not to do that, but contribute to a staff box. Every December the contents were divided equally and topped up with a Christmas bonus if necessary. In addition to their pay, staff received 3s 6d per week to cover their laundry expenses. Mr Buck, the butler, received extra payments for his pantry; luxury items such as jars of truffles, quails' eggs in aspic and tins of Turkish cigarettes. Motorcars were very much Gavin's province, and he insisted on dealing with all the bills personally. His chauffeur was given cash for the "2nd Rolls-Royce" which was used for ferrying Labour voters to campaign meetings and polling booths in the local and general elections. Proof of how "Ciggie" spent his expenses came in a file of receipts for trips to Westbury; Wells; Plymouth, Romford; Ashton Under Lyme, Stalybridge, Maidenhead and Swindon.

In March 1936 *The Times* reported that Gavin had sent a transcript of an interview he had conducted with Mahatma Gandhi concerning the All-India Village Industries Association. This was described as Gandhi's proposal *"to turn waste into wealth"* in village India. Gandhi was quoted as saying that this initiative was meant to encourage basic hygiene in spite of the endemic social problem of *"untouchability"* in India. He was urging villagers to keep their water tanks, wells and streets clean in order to end the Western notion that India consisted of a series of rural *"dung heaps"*. This perception, he suggested, was caused by the centralised Imperial government and he wanted *"to return to the villagers what has been cruelly and thoughtlessly snatched away from them".* Better clothing and a balanced diet were to be created with a volunteer army of self-effacing workers. Gavin's release of his interview was timed to have maximum effect during the talks leading up to the long-awaited India Bill.

In August 1935 Gavin was supported by Gandhi in a press statement (see page 484, *The Complete Works of Mahatma Gandhi, Vol 66*) on Indian self-government. This was an issue that was anathema to Conservative colonialists like Winston Churchill. To them Gavin appeared dangerously deluded. In spite of criticism by powerful forces in parliament Gavin complained that the Government had made *"concessions to its more reactionary followers"* in the India Bill, and *"so entrenched the representatives of wealth and property that the people might not be able to make their demands effectively heard".* In order to emphasise this, he revealed that the Home Office had refused to grant a passport to Mr M.R. Masani, a member of the All India Congress Socialist Party, thus preventing an important delegate from attending the "Round Table" talks in London. The official reason was that Masani was suspected of having communist links as he had stated that he wanted to investigate Russian's rural regeneration programme. Gavin took up the case with the Home Office and Masani was issued a passport (valid for one year only). In thanks, "Minoo" Masani sent him a signed first edition of his book *Our India*, with 100 woodcut illustrations by Indian artists. It was printed on handmade Indian paper and published by the Oxford University Press. Whilst this did not sell widely, it showed that others in Britain had faith in homegrown solutions for Indians. Ironically, Mr Masani's book states that he felt that *"British adminis-trators would be preferable to Communist commissars, but India does not need either to progress".*

Throughout his time in Britain during 1936 Gavin contributed to debates from an increasingly socialist standpoint. He criticised the Government's proposed measures for the Special Areas Bill – places where poverty and unemployment were worst – calling them *"half-hearted"*. He raised hackles in the Upper House by suggesting that better results would come from reducing the retirement age and *"nationalising the mines to make more work available for the unemployed"*. A few weeks later he called the Government's proposals for rearmament *"damnable"*, adding that the money would be better spent on slum clearances. In a second debate on the Special Areas Bill, he called the Conservative Government's proposals *"fiddling little measures"* and *"eyewash"*. In July, Gavin, who was no longer a practising Christian, described a proposal to increase tithe charges as *"morally obsolete"*. So, it was not altogether surprising that the right-wing *Daily Mail* dubbed him the *"Red Peer"* and implied that he lived a life of double-standards by mentioning that he was wont

> *"...to arrive at Westminster in a green chauffeur-driven Rolls-Royce...and then, after railing against the government would return to his country mansion recently renovated at great cost."*

In 1936, the last year in which he was to spend two and a half months away in Corsica, his name was seldom out of the press. The main reason was his having nailed his colours to the mast in support of the apparently contradictory issues – pacifism and rearmament. For example, in early September 1936 the *Manchester Guardian* reported that he was amongst the signatories of *"A Manifesto for Peace and Disarmament"*. In late September 1936 *The Times* reported that he had participated in the Committee of Enquiry into Alleged Breaches of the Non-Intervention Treaty in Spain, and the publication of its interim report which stated *"that breaches of the non-intervention agreement relating to the Spanish Civil War, enabling the rebels to obtain arms denied to the Government, have placed the loyalists in a disadvantageous military position"*. A few days later the *Manchester Sunday Chronicle* reported that he was among those forming a pacifist group within the Labour Party to oppose rearmament. Within a week the *Oxford Mail* reported that he was about to host two Labour Schools at Buscot, and was intending to bear the entire costs himself. In the following week the *News Chronicle* reported on the Labour Party

Conference and noted that Gavin was one of the signatories to a memo demanding that the arms embargo on the Spanish Republic be lifted immediately.

Early in 1936 he had signed a cross-party pacifist group's Manifesto for Peace and Disarmament, which was delivered to Downing St. Later in the year he had called on the Government to allow Spain to be armed as it was a country where democracy was being threatened. This blatant contradiction had arisen after he had served on the Committee of Enquiry into breaches of the Non-Intervention Treaty. During a visit to Spain, he had witnessed multiple cases of military aggression by German and Italian fascist troops. The facts were undeniable. However, the governments of Britain and France believed that any assistance they gave would be certain to escalate the conflict and the result would be another world war. This belief was widespread, and led many politicians to refuse to address the problem unfolding behind their backs. Some voices were crying in the wilderness that this was not simply a civil war, but a violent rehearsal for a war the fascists planned against democratic countries that refused to defend themselves. Whilst liberals and left-wingers volunteered to serve in the poorly equipped Spanish Republican militias and the International Brigade, only two countries sided with them – Mexico and the Soviet Union. Theirs was a lost cause being slowly crushed. In spite of this Gavin used whatever platforms he could to speak repeatedly on *"the crisis for democracy"* in Spain. Eventually, a hesitant Labour leadership announced support for non-intervention, and Gavin managed to get two Spanish Republicans to address the Labour Party conference. Their speeches were so moving that the Labour leadership were persuaded to petition the Prime Minister for a change in policy.

Standing together to fight fascism was not something that most people in Britain understood the need for, and far less welcomed. Gavin was one of the first to see that the fascists were directly antagonistic to democracies, especially weakly defended ones as Britain had become. And so, in spite of disapproval of both the Labour and

Conservative parties, Gavin joined the Labour MPs Ellen Wilkinson and Sir Stafford Cripps in the Council for the Friends of the Spanish Republic, to publish an illustrated monthly journal. Ellen Wilkinson was a mental health campaigner and famous as the co-organiser of the Jarrow march (or crusade) for jobs. H.G. Wells mentioned her in his futuristic novel *The Shape of Things to Come* where he predicted a Second World War in which Britain would try to effect a peaceful compromise using her *"brilliant pacific speeches"* which would *"echo throughout Europe"*. Sir Stafford Cripps lived at Filkins, seven miles from Buscot Park. He had set up the Socialist League with anti-appeasement Liberals, Conservatives and Labour Party members. Their stance was humanitarian and anti-appeasement. Gavin kept a few copies of their publications in his files, with the signatures of the contributors to them proudly added to each of the title pages.

Whilst the Government's non-intervention stance on Spain prevented progress, Gavin attended rallies across country in which pacifists pleaded for arms with which Spanish Republicans could defend themselves. To this end he hosted fundraisers at Buscot Park, before returning to the Lords to demand the lifting of the arms embargo. His increasingly passionate speeches aimed to persuade others that the British and French governments were appeasing the German and Italian fascists. He was one of twenty Labour MPs and Peers to sign a letter to Adolf Hitler protesting against death sentences on left-wing activists. Even at a small Labour Party rally in Faringdon, Gavin's main topic was the necessity of fighting fascism. Things came to head when he was persuaded by the Labour Party to stand as their candidate for the London County Council elections. Using the considerable funds at his disposal, he bought and took up residence at 36 Barrington Road, Brixton. Here he installed two servants and set out to woo the electorate by hosting tea parties and fund-raisers. Going by newspapers reports of 1936 it would have been possible to suppose that he had become solely focused on a local politics. However, readers of *The Times* might have noticed that he was elected as a Fellow of the Royal Society of Arts in December. And then it became clear that an aspect of his character hadn't changed as on January 1ˢᵗ 1937, the *Evening Standard* reported that Gavin had been fined 20 shillings for speeding in St. James Park on New Year's Eve. An entry in the Buscot Park Accounts books that year shows he paid that promptly: *"Jan 5ᵗʰ fine remitted to Bow Street £1.00"*.

Gavin was not an entirely reformed character – there were still sparks of recklessness hidden under that cloak of respectability. For example, he had given up his elegant town house in North St., Westminster, and bought a much larger and less fashionable one in Brixton. However, this was given over to socialists and Labour Party operatives, and he did not spend every evening or night there. Receipts and debits in his bank books show that between 1935 and 1937 he spent £540 on 50 nights spent at The Bachelors' Club at 106 Piccadilly (seven miles from Brixton and thus a short cab ride from home). The Bachelors' had a younger and livelier membership than other gentleman's clubs in St. James. It was the model for P.G. Wodehouse's fictional *"Drones Club"* in the 1920s – a home from home for *"chinless wonders"* who had never grown up. During the 1930s there were persistent rumours that many members of the Bachelors' Club were men who were happier in the company of other men. Apart from staying at the Bachelors' on 50 separate nights, he passed 30 nights at the Ritz Hotel (at a cost of £325); and eight nights at the Argentine Club (which cost him another £140). He stayed once at the Park Lane Hotel, which charged him £10, and once at Rosa Lewis' Cavendish Hotel – the cheapest at £7. 7s. od for the night. As he regularly dined at the Savoy Grill or Quaglino's it is fair to say that Gavin's private life was not a trudge down the dank path of self-denial.

Over the first part of 1937 months Gavin attended numerous Brixton Divisional Labour Party functions, such as annual dinners and tea parties, before standing as a candidate in the ward. The Labour MP Herbert Morrison came to address Gavin's London County Council election campaign meeting. Morrison had been a conscientious objector during WW1 and they shared pacifist views, which many others in the Labour Party strongly opposed. In February, Gavin's address to the SMAC meeting in Colchester was quoted in *The Times*. In it he stated that fascism was *"present in England"* and that *"Spain has been chosen by the fascist forces as the battleground: Spain, I believe, is saving us all, and I think every party in England ought to resist fascism, for its defeat is a cause which should appeal to all"*. These were not the views of a strict pacifist and it is clear that he, like many, had begun to see a war in Europe as an inevitable moral imperative. This explains why he wrote to Sir Philip Sassoon in January. This multi-millionaire art collector was famous for entertaining celebrity guests such as Sir Winston Churchill and T.E. Lawrence (aka "Lawrence of Arabia") at his home at Port Lympne in Kent – where the decor included *trompe l'oeil* murals by Rex Whistler and surpassed anything Gavin might have dreamed of for Buscot Park. Sassoon had served in the Air Ministry and as a Privy Councillor before becoming the Chairman of the Trustees of the National Gallery. He had since been appointed First Commissioner of Works – a cabinet-level position. Most people at the time believed what H.G. Wells had predicted in his book *The Shape of Things to Come*; namely that aerial bombing would decide the outcome of any war almost immediately. And so, Gavin had written soon after hearing of Sassoon's appointment to make an extraordinary offer of Buscot Park as a wartime repository for the national art collection. Sassoon replied promptly:

"6th Feb 1937.

My dear Lord Faringdon,

Thank you for your letter of 2nd February about the proposal to store pictures at Buscot Park. We have recently been discussing the question of evacuating the pictures with the National Gallery, and we came to the tentative conclusion that it would probably not be necessary to trouble you with them. I had been going to suggest that you might be agreeable to keeping the house on a reserve list against unforeseen demands from the Museums and Galleries, but if you are considering placing accommodation at the disposal of the

*Evacuation authorities and would prefer to do this, I do not
think that I ought to ask you to hold it back.*

*May I say how much I appreciated your public-spirited
action in offering to help in an emergency in this way.*

Yrs Sincerely.

Philip Sassoon."

In February 1937 the *Ipswich Evening Star* gave a paragraph in their
report of Gavin's address at a SMAC meeting in Colchester:

*"Fascism he said, was not a German or Italian thing, but
was universal and was present in England to a greater or less
extent. In helping the Spaniards, they were helping themselves
to avoid the same thing. Here, the fascists for the moment
were only a joke, but he reminded the audience that about
five years ago the Nazis of Germany were also a joke. Spain
has been chosen by the fascist forces as the battleground:
Spain, I believe, is saving us all, and I think every party in
England ought to resist fascism, for its defeat is a cause which
should appeal to all."*

Gavin's calendar of events in 1937 continued to unfold in the newspapers
– and by now he was employing a secretary, Frank W. Bourne, to keep
albums of press clippings. In March Gavin came third in the LCC
elections. His confidence, however, was undented as he was soon
addressing SMAC meetings at Kingston and Poplar. Then he hosted
a third week-long Labour School at Buscot and went on to defy the
Labour Party leadership by speaking out against non-intervention
in the House of Lords in April. In May he appealed again against
non-intervention in Spain and denounced the Government's failure
to respond to Italian actions in Mallorca. He described the Spanish
General Quiepo de Llano as *"a drunken sadist"* after it emerged that
he had ordered Republican supporters to be executed in public
and their bodies to be left for several days afterwards. Then Gavin

appeared in numerous newspaper articles after he warned in the Upper House that the fascist forces had deployed heavy artillery around the Straits of Gibraltar. This alarming story was taken up by nearly every major newspaper. The *Daily Mail* included a picture of a deeply worried looking Lord Faringdon staring out at readers over the lines:

> *"The mystery of the guns alleged to menace Gibraltar deepened in the House of Lords last night, when Lord Faringdon challenged the Government to say what steps it was proposing to take with regard to the 'recent' fortifications on both sides of the straits."*

On the following day Lord Faringdon expressed further concern in an article headed:

Calibres, Numbers and Emplacements.

> *Then he gave details which, he said he had received from "authoritative and reliable sources" about batteries erected on both sides of the Straits of Gibraltar. Lord Faringdon read out calibres, numbers and geographical details, and said that some of the guns were of German origin.*

> *He wanted to know why, when a civil war was going on in Spain, all these activities were going on so far away from the battlefields.*

> *It was sinister, he said, that at a time when it might be supposed that all the fascist forces in Spain would be concentrating on the battlefront, "somebody" acting for them should be taking so much pains to fortify the approaches to Gibraltar.*

The *Times* recorded Gavin's detailed description of new German fortifications, both in Southern Spain and in Spanish Morocco:

"On the Cape Tes Forcas, there are several 35-centimeter cannon of German origin, which have been mounted on the Punta del Atlalayon; on the heights of the hills of the naval base, anti-aircraft of 7.5-centimeter bore have been mounted, and it is believed that others of long range also exist.

In Benzo, hidden in a small oak wood situated just above the town, there is a battery of 5.5-centimeter guns, and almost in a straight line with this to the right of the town toward Ceuta (in Spanish Morocco). About 330 meters away on the coast, three big German guns of 12-inch caliber have been mounted.

There are six very large guns in Yebel Sidi: of the renovation of the old fort between El Hacho and Ceuta, with new German armament; of 22—centimeter guns in Galdeagua and La Bracha, and a series of new artillery emplacements between Tetuan and the international zone of Tangier in Morocco, besides numerous other details of fortification unrelated to the necessities of the Spanish war itself."

Some in government claimed this was unproved and an official at the War Office speculated that the armament may have been added by the Spanish government to defend the straits. The story attracted much attention for a few weeks until it faded away – replaced by the excitement due to the coronation of George VI and his wife Elizabeth as King and Queen of the British Empire and its Commonwealth at Westminster Abbey.

Gavin attended this historic event, and on the following day met with the Spanish Medical Aid Committee in Westminster. He then returned to his routine visiting of mental hospitals in North London and Kent. Having done all that he lunched with Honor. Meetings with his ex-wife – now one of his closest friends – can be said to have bracketed all the major events in their lives. In the following month (June 1937), he contributed to a debate on the Marriage Bill by arguing against the five-year waiting period it proposed prior to a divorce being granted. In July, this owner of three houses with around 15 servants, was reported in *The Times* to be concerned with workers' conditions in an amendment to the Factories Bill. Here he was demanding an end to night work in bakehouses due to the unsociable hours. And in September, *The Times* referred to him as a prominent member of the Parliamentary Pacifists Group. With scarcely a week without Gavin's activities attracting comment by journalists surely no one could accuse him anymore of being *"idle"*.

Gavin's name was in the press so often that it was not surprising that it attracted a few opportunistic hangers-on. In November 1937 a story emerged about events at a weekend house party at Buscot. This was said to have been gate-crashed by a couple of rebellious upper-class communists, whose life was being chronicled by a teenaged follower – the budding writer Philip Toynbee. Jessica Mitford, nicknamed "Decca" by her sisters, was the sixth daughter of Baron Redesdale. She had little formal education, her older sisters Diana and Unity hero-worshipped Hitler, and her father was described as *"one of nature's fascists"*. Decca rebelled and declared herself a communist, after which her eldest sister Nancy Mitford christened her *"the Red Sheep of the family"*. At the age of 17, Decca eloped with her 19-year-old communist cousin, Esmond Romilly, a nephew of Sir Winston Churchill. The couple moved to the East End of London where they lived hand-to-mouth, one step ahead of debt-collectors. Decca had led such a sheltered life that she was surprised to learn that people had to pay rent and for the electricity and gas that they used. A decade later their friend Philip Toynbee wrote a highly imaginative account of their visit to Buscot Park, claiming that they had arrived in Oxford and persuaded a socialist don (Frank Pakenham – later Lord Longford) to take them to Buscot where a group of left-wingers had gathered for the weekend. According to Toynbee, Esmond Romilly introduced himself and was soon pouring drinks and dispensing snacks to the boring guests. Toynbee wrote that he put a hand on Gavin's shoulder and confided that Jessica was pregnant before asking to stay the night. When this was agreed they took advantage of his hospitality and left at dawn without saying thanks and goodbye. Philip Toynbee claimed that they arrived at his flat in Oxford later and:

> *"When Decca opened her bag Balkan Sobranie cigarettes cascaded to the floor of my room, and it was clear that the barbarians had not come away without their spoils. They had gone late, it seemed, to their handsome bedroom, where a switchboard of electric bells had tempted them to experiment with each in turn. Three different servants had appeared, and to each they had made a different and increasingly preposterous request. Sandwich, tea, rum and cigars had all been brought to their room while the Romillys lay like royalty against the pillows. In the morning Esmond had checked Decca as her scissors were poised above the curtains - which would, she had felt, have made an elegant addition to the furnishings at their flat. They had driven away from the house before anybody else was up."*

This was pure fiction. Years later Decca admitted that she and Esmond used to invent adventures to impress their friends. Buscot Park's visitors' book shows that there was no party of left-wingers staying that weekend. Toynbee's tale of fleeing at dawn with their loot does not ring true as guests signed into a country house visitors' book when they left – and that is what Decca and Esmond Romilly did. They stayed for two nights: Sat 13th and Sun 14th November. Immediately below their signatures are those of Nancy and Peter Rodd – Decca's sister and brother-in-law. This older couple's stay over-lapped the younger's: Sun 14th to Tues 16th. In the previous year Decca and Nancy had argued and avoided each other. Newspapers reported that Nancy and Peter Rodd had followed the young couple to Spain and done their best to get them to return home as she was pregnant. Since then, Decca had given birth to a child that sickened and died in their cold London flat. Toynbee wrote that Esmond Romilly said she was pregnant again – but no one else made that claim. The estranged sisters had met up in the comfort of Buscot Park – 14 miles or half an hour's drive from their parents' home at

Swinbrook. Philip Toynbee's account of the Romillys' visit is still circulated on the internet.

On the Friday before the *enfants terribles* Romillys arrived, the Labour MP Sir Stafford Cripps wrote to invite his neighbour Gavin to an Aid Spain Rally at the Royal Albert Hall. In this letter he asked outright for him to provide *"a really big cheque, which could be handed up for the collection"*. Whilst this was a propaganda stunt it had the desired effect of encouraging donations from the crowd who came to hear the celebrity speakers. Foremost among these was the Black American actor, singer and civil rights activist Paul Robeson. Others were the writers Cecil Day-Lewis, Rebecca West, H.G. Wells and Virginia Woolf; as well as the poets W.H. Auden and Stephen Spender, just back from Spain. Soon afterwards on December 10th a photograph of Gavin appeared in *The Times* and also in *The Daily Worker* showing him standing next to a Rolls-Royce Silver Ghost with a report that he was about to drive it to the front in Spain. *The Times* published the following:

> *"LORD FARINGDON GIVES AMBULANCE TO SPAIN*
>
> *Lord Faringdon, a member of the Spanish Medical Aid Committee, has had his car converted into an ambulance and will, driving it himself, leave for Spain today. To present it to the Government. This will be the fifty-fifth ambulance sent by the committee since August, 1936."*

Then the *Evening Standard* reported a few weeks later:

> *"ANOTHER AMBULANCE.*
>
> *Lord Faringdon, a member of the Central Spanish Medical Aid Committee, went off to Spain just before Christmas. He drove his own Rolls-Royce car which has been converted into an ambulance and which he will present to the Spanish*

Government. It was filled to overflowing with cigarettes,
chocolate and cans of condensed milk for the wounded."

A fortnight later newspapers mentioned that Gavin had delivered it
to a hospital in Barcelona. Then reports arrived saying that it was
being driven by a pair of British aid workers and helped to evacuate
Republican wounded in the Battle of Teruel. In the meantime, Gavin
had visited field hospitals on the Aragon and Madrid fronts where he
volunteered as a stretcher-bearer. On February 1st 1938

The Daily Mail's foreign correspondent reported:

> **"Barcelona searches for Bomb Victims.**
>
> *When the final toll of Barcelona's dead is made, it is expected*
> *that 500 people have been killed and 2,000 wounded during*
> *two terrible raids made by Franco's bombers yesterday. The*
> *raid made by 15 warplanes and lasting together for only*
> *11 minutes were not on military objectives, as the fascist*
> *communique issued today from Salamanca tries to make out.*
> *It was made on the densely populated, roof to roof working-*
> *class quarter of the city. Not a single military building was*
> *hit.*
>
> **Rescue Work**
>
> *As I write the rescue work is still going on. By the light of*
> *torches and of fires. Armed with picks and shovels, some*
> *using only their bare hands, Barcelona's more fortunate*
> *civilians, hastily formed into auxiliary rescue squads, are*
> *searching the debris.*
>
> **CHILDREN KILLED**
>
> *One of the buildings which was destroyed utterly was a home*
> *where 170 Basque children, refugees from Franco in the north,*
> *had hoped to escape further terrors of the war. But today out*

*of that 170 only 25 were alive. Partially destroyed also was
the motor ambulance which Lord Faringdon presented to the
Spanish Government. This ambulance, which was converted
from Lord Faringdon's private car, had been doing excellent
work on the Teruel front."*

Still more news about the ambulance appeared in the *Evening
Standard*.

"From the Ashes.

*A few days ago I referred to Lord Faringdon's Rolls-Royce
ambulance and its destruction in Spain. I now learn that the
ambulance has risen like a Phoenix from the Spanish ashes.*

*After it had been hit by a bomb in Valencia, it appeared to
be irreparable. But by an extraordinary chance, its chauffeur
found the abandoned remains of a Rolls-Royce, of the same
model, on a car dump. He was thus able to replace every part
of the ambulance which had been destroyed and it returned
once more into service. Its running costs, however, proved too
high, and the ambulance is now touring England with its
chauffeur, collecting money for Spanish medical aid."*

Three months later, after the Rolls-Royce had been patched up, and
still riddled with bullet and shrapnel holes, it was driven back to
Britain where it was displayed to delegates at the TUC conference,
and toured to raise funds for the SMAC (Spanish Medical Aid
Committee). After Gavin became the Treasurer of Voluntary
Industrial Aid for Spain, (VIA) – which encouraged factory workers
to contribute hours of their labour in exchange for ambulances,
bandages, mattresses, blankets and other non-military essentials
– the war-damaged Rolls-Royce was toured to raise funds again.
However, it was typical that whilst the Voluntary Industrial Aid
for Spain was set up to promote humanitarian aid, it was regarded

warily by both the Labour and Conservative parties as a front for communist cadres.

A partial summary of Gavin's life in the 1930s came from his Oxford contemporary Beverley Nichols, who had a long-running weekly column in the *Sunday Chronicle*. He had written dozens of novels and plays; some best-selling books on gardening illustrated by Rex Whistler; and produced a polemical book on pacifism entitled *Cry Havoc*. Nichols had come to stay at Buscot Park regularly and wrote about his old friend:

> *"Occasionally the socialist ferment, acting on a mind that is sensitive and alert, produced a gay and bubbling figure like Lord Faringdon. He is one of the party's most energetic hosts: he has drunk many a champagne cocktail to the downfall of the upper classes, and though the red flag does not actually fly over the ramparts of his house at Buscot – a stately home, if ever there was one – the sentiments that echo through that imposing pile, on the week-ends when he is entertaining his buddies of the extreme left, are decidedly revolutionary.*
>
> *One cannot help liking Gavin Faringdon; he has a well-stored brain; it is pretty certain that he believes what he says; and he had shown considerable courage in espousing causes which would have brought him the concentrated abuse of the ruling classes to which, by right, he belongs. If it would not be true to say that he was born to the purple, he was at least born to a fairly vigorous shade of mauve, and during his early years he showed every sign of living life in terms of this colour. He was one of the brightest of the bright in the 'Dance, Dance, Dance Little Lady' period: as an undergraduate he was of the breed that climbs statues in order to place on their heads objects which are usually reserved for the shadows of the bed chamber; as a bridegroom he literally set the Thames on fire – pouring immense quantities of petrol on the river in its*

upper reaches at Maidenhead, the night before his wedding.
So, something – as they say – was to be expected of him.

But what has actually occurred is not at all what I,
personally, should have expected.... one has the strange
prospect of Gavin, still very much the lord of the manor, still
very much the connoisseur of good claret, and still fully, and
to my mind, rightly, appreciative of the good things of this
world, playing host to people whose main object in life – (if
one is to believe their own statements) – is to strangle lords of
the manor in the nearest ditch."

At the end of December 1937 Gavin gave £14. 10s. 0d as "*Xmas presents*" to the staff of fifteen at Buscot Park. To this was added "*Tip money from 76 guests £8 distributed*". As Gavin did not allow tipping this £8 was probably change that guests traditionally left on dressing tables. Gavin contributed 2s/6d for every name that had appeared in the visitors' book. This would have amounted to the equivalent of £862.52 as his Xmas bonus plus £492 left in change, and so a £90.00 payment for each member of staff. In addition, he paid for their health insurance and medical attention. The result was that his staff did not show any signs of wanting to start a revolution.

CHAPTER 8

Spain, Refugees and Reputation

A newspaper clipping in Gavin's files from *The Times* dated April 28th 1937 reads:

> *"The most ancient town of the Basques and the centre of their cultural tradition, was completely destroyed yesterday afternoon by insurgent air raiders. The bombardment of this open town far behind the lines occupied precisely three hours and a quarter, during which a powerful fleet of aero planes consisting of three German types, Junkers and Heinkel bombers, did not cease unloading on the town bombs weighing from 1,000 lbs. downwards and, it is calculated, more than 3,000 two-pounder aluminium incendiary projectiles. The fighters, meanwhile, plunged low from above the centre of the town to machine-gun those of the civilian population who had taken refuge in the fields."*

The bombing of Guernica shocked the world and is still seen as a landmark atrocity of modern warfare. The Labour MP Leah Manning was in the Basque region and led the relief effort at the blockaded Basque port of Bilbao where thousands had gathered hoping to be evacuated. She helped to create the National Joint Committee for Spanish Relief (NJCSR) with the TUC, the Society of Friends (Quakers), Save the Children, Spanish Medical Aid and numerous Church groups. Gavin soon became a very active supporter and fundraiser, campaigning for the Government to abandon its *"non-intervention"* policy. The Basque Government declared that it wanted to evacuate 150,000 *Niños de la Guerra* (Children of the War). However, only 33,000 were embarked from their ports. Of these 20,000 went to France, 5,000 to Belgium, 4,000 to the Soviet Union and Mexico (the only countries to support the Spanish Republican governments), and 4,000 *Niños de la Guerra* came to Britain. Some 45 of those were to find a haven of refuge at Buscot Park.

A year after the bombing of Guernica, he was closely involved with the SMAC and helping to administer its "Milk for Spain" scheme. Here tins of condensed milk purchased from the Co-op were shipped to the Republican side to help avert malnutrition in the civilian population. But as the ports were being blockaded by fascist forces fewer ships were available to bring in food and essentials such as blankets. This prompted another well-publicised visit to Spain by Gavin. On his return he told a reporter that the fascist forces had gathered to fortify the straits of Gibraltar. When a Conservative MP called this *"fiction"*, Gavin called him a *"fascist representative at Westminster"*. His remarks were swiftly taken up by the press and circulated – inflated and distorted – throughout the Empire. For example, this appeared in the *Natal Advertiser*, Durban, S.A.

> *"There were cries of "order" when Lord Faringdon said*
> *the trouble about Spain was that the British Government*
> *had no foreign policy, and as such was run by a prominent*
> *reactionary in the Foreign Office…. He alleged that the*
> *Italians were now masters of the Balearic Islands…and*
> *that 40,000 troops were preparing to attack Barcelona and*
> *Valencia on the Spanish mainland."*

Gavin was portrayed as a modern Cassandra in conservative papers abroad. For some reason his reputation in South Africa was particularly bad. The following appeared in the for example in the *Cape Argus*, Cape Town 27th November 1936:

"The Comfortable Socialist

I see that young Lord Faringdon (short, pale, dapper in a portly way, and a rapid talker) has been making a fuss in the House of Lords over the suspected occupation of Majorca by the Italians. (you see the cause of British fears? An Italian submarine and aeroplane base at Majorca would threaten Gibraltar naval harbour.)

A peculiar person is Gavin Faringdon, Though he is one of the most violent and outspoken of the socialist peers, he is at the same time one of the richest and most luxury loving of Englishmen.

After he finished debating the plight of the Welsh miners or the gross unfairness of the Means Test, for example, he will drive down, in a most magnificent green Rolls-Royce, to his country estate Buscot Park, in Berkshire.

Red of Reds

And this 34-year-old socialist, a Red of Reds, owns one of the best houses in England. Every room in the building has its own private telephone, and every guest is more or less allotted his own Conservative party servant; yet another wing has just been added, and recently the young owner, who is concerned with the welfare of England's unemployed, completed building two squash court and a swimming pool.

He attacks Mussolini

And this is the Lord Faringdon who denounces capitalism and in the same breath that he orders a table for dinner at the Ritz; who refuses to set foot inside Germany because it is a fascist country, and who only recently became reconciled to the regime in Italy. Still, it seems he is not allowing the opportunity of attacking Mussolini to pass."

On the same day, Nov 27th 1936, the following appeared in the *Brixton Free Press:*

> *"Lord Faringdon, who contested the recent L.C.C. election in Brixton in the Labour interest, has been co-Opted a member of the L.C.C. Mental Hospitals Committee."*

Widespread ridicule of Gavin in the right-wing newspapers continued, but Gavin carried on regardless. Soon after the above appeared he appeared as a principal speaker alongside other so-called "Reds" at the SMAC's "Save Spain, Save Britain, Save Peace" rally in Hyde Park. Here the Duchess of Atholl, who was the first woman to serve in a Conservative cabinet, took the stage and addressed a crowd of 120,000. The press dubbed her "The Red Duchess" due to her opposition to the policy of non-intervention. Few realised that she and Gavin (the "Red of Reds") were distant relatives. Another prominent speaker that day was Sir Harold Nicolson, a retired Diplomat, newspaper columnist and husband of Vita Sackville-West. They were joined by Lady Violet Bonham-Carter (a Liberal MP), Clement Attlee (the Labour Party leader), Eleanor Rathbone (a left-wing Independent MP), Ellen Wilkinson (the Labour MP for Jarrow), Victor Gollancz (the left-wing publisher), and J.B.S. Haldane (the Marxist scientist). Gavin raised cheers when he called the Government's policy *"fascist"*. In the following month he raised more controversy when he was quoted as saying, *"the majority of Conservative members of Parliament are undoubtedly fascist in sympathy"*, and went on to call the Prime Minister, Neville Chamberlain's foreign policy *"distinctly fascist"*.

Gavin's views drew the attention of a non-aligned activists who were equally uncompromising. Poppy and Chloë Vulliamy were sisters raised by Quaker parents who had been active in helping prisoners of war and conscientious objectors during WW1. The sisters had run a hotel in Barcelona where they had been radicalised by some of their guests after the start of the Spanish Civil War. Two of these had been the poets W.H. Auden and Stephen Spender. They had gone on to become volunteer workers with the Basque Children's

Committee. After they came to Buscot Park they were depicted as demure grey- haired women in "Jack" Hastings' frescoes there. Their involvement with Gavin began after the Conservative government had agreed that Spanish child refugees could come to Britain, but insisted that they had to be found homes within 30 days of their arrival. Failing that, the *Niños de la Guerra (Children of the War)* were to be repatriated. In an interview with the *East Anglia Daily Times* in 1985 Poppy recalled that the 4,000 child refugees she and her sister saw in Southampton *"were in a terrible state. They'd been eating rats, seagulls, anything they could catch. The camp was very dirty and I caught scabies. All the refugees had head lice".* She remembered that when Lord Baden Powell, founder of the Boy Scout movement, visited with some of his followers in uniform, refugees thought they were *"some kind of fascist group".*

Poppy and Chloë Vulliamy were given charge of *"fifty-five big, bad boys".* In effect, this was the camp borstal consisting of the roughest, toughest and most traumatised. She remembered that they fought amongst themselves but *"never deliberately hit me although I did get a punch while trying to split two of them up".* She felt that the bombing and having to leave their country had made them emotionally volatile. For example, when news came that Bilbao had fallen to the fascists some of the teenagers broke out of their camp at Brechfa in Carmarthenshire in a forlorn attempt to get home to see if their families had survived. Others had become so highly politicised that they cheered whenever a traffic light turned red. Unsympathetic press reports of *"unruly"* behaviour deterred potential foster parents, but the Vulliamy sisters found homes wherever they could. Poppy managed to place one boy with the composer Benjamin Britten. Sadly, he had to be returned *"because he did not speak a word of English and cried all the time. When they found someone to translate for him, he said that he just wanted to be with the other refugees".* The writer Adrian Bell was a volunteer helper working with the Vulliamy sisters. His book *Only Three Months*, recorded that 40 to 60 Basque boys were camping in tents donated by Boy Scouts on a farmer's field and being fed in a village hall when Poppy said

"I wrote to the Labour Peer, Lord Faringdon, and told him
that as a socialist he should not be living alone in such a big
house, and suggested that he should let us all live there with
him".

Gavin's experience of hosting three Labour Party summer schools
at Eaton Hastings had given him an insight into having groups of
children under one roof. He did not invite the 60 potentially unruly
boys to share his home, but offered something more manageable:
the use of a lodge on his estate. This seemed ideal as it lay within
a few hundred yards of a sports ground. There was a lake at the
bottom of their garden, and the boys would have woods and fields to
roam in. The lodge was only four miles from the rural market towns
of Faringdon and Lechlade. Poppy immediately accepted the offer
and she and her sister came to stay at Buscot Park in February 1938.
They soon saw that the accommodation would be a bit cramped, and
persuaded Gavin to purchase some pre-fabricated huts to serve as
dormitories for the oldest boys. These pre-fabs had been designed
as garages and sadly, as a former occupant recalled were *"made from*
wood and asbestos; impossible to heat, and very cold in winter". Still, they
were better than spending another winter under canvas in a muddy
field. What from then on was called the *"colony"* of boys arrived in
late April and the lodge was renamed *"Basque House"* in their honour.
This still stands beside the A417 road, a short walk from the hamlet
of Eaton Hastings, where the Labour and socialist summer schools
had been held. Besides free lodging, the *"colonists"* had food, heating,
cleaners and a laundry service provided by Lord Faringdon. He made
a few demands on the Vulliamy sisters – insisting from the start that
they provide a warden, teachers and a cook.

The boys seemed to be settling in well. Then the colony was shaken by
a tragedy when the youngest of two Basque brothers died suddenly.
José Sobrino was by all accounts an extraordinary 14-year-old who –
unlike any of the other Basque boys – had acquired good command
of spoken English during his nine months in England. Gavin was so
impressed by this feat of learning that he offered to send him to a

private school and pay his fees. José, who his elder brother recalled everyone called Iñaki (Ignatius) thanked Gavin but declined saying that he wanted to return to Bilbao as soon as possible to become a steel worker like his father. This reveals the way that the boys had been indoctrinated into wanting to become workers in a socialistic society. After living under canvas for so long Iñaki had respiratory and heart problems. Concern for his health was such that he was moved to the Radcliffe Infirmary in Oxford for observation. Here Iñaki had asked for one of the teachers, Señor Cernuda to visit him. Luis Cernuda was an exiled poet who had worked at the same field hospital as Gavin in Aragon and joined the colony. When he came, all Iñaki said to him was that he felt homesick. Then he asked the poet to recite some verses after saying:

> "Now, please, don't leave but I am going to turn to the wall
> so you can't see me die."

Cernuda and a nurse watched as the boy turned his head, gave a long sigh, and passed away. The poet was so moved that he was unable to return to the colony and the event inspired him to write his *Elegy for a Basque Boy, dead in England*, which became a classic of Spanish Civil War literature:

> "You drank down your death,
> The death they had in store for you,
> In one long single draught,
> Without for an instant looking back,
> Just like a man in close combat.
> A vast indifference came upon you
> Before the earth could close over you."

In May 1938, two months after the Basque colony moved in, Walter Leonard, a German-Jewish refugee became its warden. The Vulliamy sisters had met him in Spain where he had found work as a hotel manager. Years later Walter Leonard wrote a short memoir of his time at Buscot Park:

"Poppy recommended that I should be in charge of the colony at Faringdon, Oxfordshire. It was the home of Lord Faringdon, a Labour peer, and he made available to the Basque boys one of the gatehouses of his country retreat, Buscot Park, at Eaton Hastings, near Faringdon. He provided completely free accommodation, and supplied eggs, milk and other food free of charge from the estate. Near the main house there was a swimming pool and the children were allowed to use it when there were no guests. Lord Faringdon was very ecology conscious and didn't allow hunting on his estate, so he was none too pleased when the boys raided birds' nests for the eggs. Some of the older boys worked on the estate, fruit picking, and painting or on the chicken farm. There was a cook who was an Anarchist and in the evenings he gave the boys political lectures, telling them that Lord Faringdon had plenty of money without having to make the boys work on the farm. So, the next morning, some of the boys refused to work! The cook was subsequently sacked for being a bad influence!"

During the time when the Basque colony was at Eaton Hastings, the Women's Institute and other local groups organised events and excursions for the boys. From time to time, they were able to see films and newsreels in Buscot Park's theatre; and they put on their own play there called *"The Lonely Bull"*, which had an illustrated bilingual programme, a copy of which Gavin kept in his files. In January 1939, ten months after they arrived, the boys moved to Shipton-under-Wychwood, some twenty miles away. This was a less rural setting where it was felt they could be better integrated. Some boys recalled that at a farewell party Gavin expressed his hope that they would return after the defeat of the fascists and rebuild their homeland *"with vigour, and a social consciousness fortified by their stay in England"*.

Sadly, few were able to return for many years to come. Poppy claimed that one joined the RAF. After the Basque boys were relocated, some adult Spanish refugees – mainly Catalans – found a haven at Basque House. Buscot Park's accounts book recorded purchases of *"Stamps and cigarettes for the Spaniards"* 12s (£25.00 in today's values); April 1939 *"Cash to Spaniards"* £2; *150 cigarettes 7s 6d; 300 Turkish cigarettes £12* (roughly £1,000.00 in today's money). The refugees included the poet Domenec Perramón, the journalists Eduardo de Ortañon and Fermín Vergés, as well as an Andalucian poet, Pedro Garfias. Garfias spoke no English and liked to drink to drown his sorrows. A friend wrote that, *"When Garfias was drunk, he spoke like the healthy and honest man that everyone wanted to be"*. Garfias' poem *Primavera en Eaton Hastings* became another classic of exile. A rough translation is:

> *"My sun-bleached Andalucia!*
> *Inevitably, the beautiful blooms around me fade into anger*
> *and grief.*
> *Tonight, while the village sleeps, I'll be crying alone".*

In the summer that followed, Gavin commissioned two artworks from the Artists International Association (AIA), both of which now hang at Buscot Park. This was a left-wing organisation that held a series of group exhibitions entitled Artists Against Fascism and War, and the fees for the works went to the Aid for Spain committee. Gavin commissioned a portrait of his sister-in-law Oonagh Henderson by Mark Gertler, a Jewish artist from the East End of London who had attended the Slade School of Art and been taken up by the Bloomsbury set. Gertler's stylish portrait (FC No. 126) was striking – but the grey lips the artist gave his sitter made her appear cold. The other artwork Gavin commissioned was a watercolour of Buscot House by Eric Ravilious. He was a prolific painter and print-maker who had designed commemorative coronation mugs in pink and gold for Wedgwood. Ravilious stayed for two nights when Penelope Betjeman was a fellow guest. His understated but evocative painting (FC 142) became one of the favourites of many visitors for years afterwards.

Gavin's main concern at the time was to get support for the beleaguered Spanish republicans. One of the ways he did this was by opening a "Spain Shop" in Woking and funding it with a £25 cash donation (£1,600.00 today). All the proceeds from the sales here were destined for the Spanish Republican charities. Then, paradoxically for a pacifist, Gavin appeared on stage at an "Arms for Spain" march in Trafalgar Square, where he addressed the crowd of 10,000 with the words:

> *"Your fight is being fought for you in Spain. It is your duty to see that Spain is not betrayed, and that you yourselves are not betrayed to make a Chamberlain career. Non-intervention is contrary to all interests – even British imperial interests."*

Here he appeared with Jawaharlal Nehru, President of the Indian Congress Party, as well as the Labour MPs Ellen Williamson, Stafford Cripps and Wilfred Roberts. Afterwards, Gavin returned to Buscot to host the annual summer camp for the Labour League of Youth, which the actress Sybil Thorndike supported by giving readings. In August, Gavin hosted the annual fete of the North Berkshire Labour Party; and then opened Buscot House to the public at a sixpence admission charge, promising to donate the proceeds to the SMAC. The accounts book shows that by October 1940 it had 200 paying visitors.

When not devoting himself to the Spanish Republican cause, Gavin was campaigning for civil liberties at home and in the colonies. In September 1938 he signed a letter to Prime Minister from the Anti-Slavery and Aborigines Protection Society, regarding respect for their wishes not to be moved from their tribal lands. This was part of his humanitarian work with the National Council of Civil Liberties (NCCL), which had been formed to oppose the Incitement to Disaffection Bill, more often called "The Sedition Bill". That legislation would have made possession of pacifist literature and anti-war pamphlets a criminal offence. His work with the NCCP also led to his calling for an end to the colour bar in British medical schools, less film censorship, and support for workers' rights. All this criticism of the Government caused some to call the organisation "Red". The NCCL was mainly composed of liberal minded social reformers. Its chairman was the novelist E.M. Forster, and its committee members included H.G. Wells, Clement Attlee and Professor Julian Huxley. None of these wanted bolshevism in the British Empire, but that was the way the press described their goals.

In the same month that the Basque colony moved onto the Buscot Park estate, the *Manchester Guardian* published a series of articles by Gavin's old friend Nancy Cunard. Her passion for the Republican cause matched Gavin's. She had shocked many readers by claiming that 200,000 former fighters, widows, old men and bereft families were trudging towards the French border from defeated parts of Republican Spain. Cunard reported that these refugees were being shot at, shelled, and machine-gunned by fascist aeroplanes. Her articles incited more calls for an end to non-intervention. Nancy Cunard went on to poll British writers on their attitudes towards the conflict and then publish their comments in a booklet, *Authors Take Sides on the Spanish Civil War*. Her words in the preface of this book echoed Gavin's most passionate speeches:

> *"Spain is not politics but life; its immediate future will affect every human who has a sense of what life and its facts mean, who has respect for himself and humanity."*

This slim volume became part of Gavin's library. It shows that less than half of those polled bothered to reply, but of 147 writers who did, 126 supported the Republicans, 16 were neutral, and only five (who included Evelyn Waugh) were pro-Franco and supported the German and Italian fascists. Nancy Cunard left England to serve in the refugee camps until exhaustion forced her to leave and return to Paris and then London. Her mental and physical health declined rapidly during the early war years when she worked as translator for the Free French forces.

Throughout the Spanish Civil War, Gavin was in touch with a number of literary figures who were described as communist *"fellow-travellers"* – a phrase coined to describe those sympathetic with Soviet aims who had not joined the Communist Party. This was because many of them did not approve of the totalitarian state Stalin had imposed on Russia. Some hoped this was a transitional phase – such was Victor Gollancz, whose Left Book Club was the foremost publisher of pacifist and socialist non-fiction. Gavin was a member and his library shelves showed dozens of its orange-clad covers, as the young writer Iris Murdoch noted with approval when she visited Buscot Park in 1939. However, whilst Gollancz called himself an *"Internationalist"*, and had given an advance to George Orwell to write a book on his experiences fighting in Spain, he later refused to publish *Homage to Catalonia* as he feared its exposure of Stalin's agents there would *"harm the fight against fascism"*.

Gavin's friend Rupert Croft-Cooke later translated a book written by a Spanish general which supported this as he claimed that from mid-1937 the Republican Government was under Moscow's control. Gavin's correspondence shows that support for communism was not his objective. For example, the head of the British Communist Party, G.D.H. Cole, consistently championed the cause in his letters, while J.F. Horrabin, a journalist and Labour MP, confessed that he found his loyalties strained by Stalin's duplicity. H.N. Brailsford, the most prolific British left-wing journalist of his day, was consistently critical of the Soviet system in his letters to Gavin, while the critic and author Raymond Mortimer, employed by the BBC, was a strong supporter of the Soviet regime before changing his mind. Gavin had been consistently painted *"Red"* since the time he had joined the Marxist lawyer Geoffrey Bing on the Commission of Inquiry into Alleged Breaches of the Non-Intervention Agreement in Spain. However, he distrusted the communism he had seen in Spain.

The worsening crisis In Spain meant that in January 1939 Gavin attended seven SMAC meetings. With war in Germany looking ever more likely, he met with Robert Byron twice to discuss the writer's latest fact-finding trip there. Byron had hoped to return to Russia but was refused entry – this was probably due to his derogatory comments in a book of his, published eight years earlier. On the 23rd February, Gavin addressed the Lords on the dire conditions in the refugee camps, detailing the shortages of food, water, sanitation and shelter, and the spread of dysentery. He called for immediate support for humanitarian relief efforts, and blamed the Government's non-intervention policy for widespread malnutrition and hunger in the blockaded Republican areas. Lord Halifax, the Foreign Secretary, rose to say that he took the *"strongest exception to any suggestion that the government bore responsibility"*. Unabashed, Gavin gave an interview the next day to the *Manchester Guardian*, which was headlined *"Spanish refugees in France: Peer on 'appalling conditions' in the camps"*. In the meantime, Gavin was expecting war and planning ahead. Proof of this emerged four days later when Sir Philip Sassoon, the Government's *First Commissioner of Works* – charged with safeguarding the nation's historic buildings and artworks – wrote to Gavin again. His letter of Friday 3rd March 1939 was headed

"SECRET.

My dear Lord Faringdon,

Many thanks for your further letter about the use of your house for the Galleries and Museums. I have looked into the situation again, and I do not think I should be right to ask you to reserve any accommodation for the purposes in addition to the space, which you set aside for furniture and valuables.

The possibility of an alternative use of your house for Government purposes in an emergency has, however, occurred to me, and it might appeal to you as preferable to the alternative you mention of making it available for general evacuation purposes.

In connection with certain schemes for which my department

is responsible I have been negotiating with various large
public schools, both girls and boys, which we should have to
take over for national purposes in wartime. These schools are
faced with the problem of finding alternative accommodation
for themselves, and I am wondering whether you would
consider the possibility of the whole or part of Buscot Park
being leased to one of these schools in such circumstances.
The schools would, of course, be allowed compensation by
the Government, but they would be expected to make their
own arrangements with the owners providing them with
accommodation."

In the following week he travelled to Liverpool to address a public meeting on the refugee crisis before returning to attend two SMAC meetings in London and a debate on Spain in the House of Lords. Back at Buscot Park on Sunday 12th March, Nancy Cunard and Robert Byron came to stay and have dinner with Gavin and his neighbour, the normally apolitical Gerald Berners. They may have discussed the catastrophe in Czechoslovakia, which was to be debated in the House of Lords the following day. That country was invaded unopposed by the Nazis three days later, after which Gerald Berners came to dinner again. On the Friday night of that week, Peter and Nancy Rodd arrived to stay for the weekend. Lady Ankaret (Susu) and Sir William Jackson joined them on Saturday. Given the political turmoil in Europe, it can't have been a light-hearted party. Nancy Mitford's lines in *The Pursuit of Love* written a year later might have been partially inspired by this occasion:

> *"Left-wing people are always sad because they mind*
> *dreadfully about their causes, and the causes are always going*
> *so badly".*

In Spain the republican forces were collapsing and the civil war drawing to its close. Franco and his German and Italian fascist allies had all but crushed their opponents. Stalin's promised communist support did not come in sufficient strength or time. Gavin was due to go to Paris that week, but cancelled his appointments. Instead, he worked with Sir George Young of the Foreign Office to commission a ship to take 400 refugees from Alicante to the Algerian port of Oran. On Saturday 25th April the words *"Sail Lézardrieux"* appear scribbled in his pocket diary. This French cargo vessel was filled with refugees and was the last to leave Valencia before it fell to the fascists. Tuesday 28th the word *"Valencia"* appears in Gavin's diary beside a list of meetings. These included the British Consul, the Military and Civilian Governors, the outgoing Political Committee, General Menendez and *"refugees"*. The last two Republican ports, Valencia and Alicante, were thronged with thousands fleeing the fascist advance. Without Spanish Republican navy vessels further evacuations were thought impossible. Up until this moment the French and British governments had refused to assist due to their adherence to the non-intervention treaty. However, Gavin's diary reveals that a few French and Royal Navy vessels were off shore ready to offer assistance to at least some of those wishing to be evacuated.

One of these was the Republican General Menéndez. He was a professional Spanish Army officer promoted a few months earlier who had told the communist controlled government in Madrid that it was impossible to continue the resistance. Menéndez hoped to start peace negotiations, but was prevented from doing so by several communists who had been promoted to the same rank in the final phase of the war. According to Menéndez, communist officers had been appointed to command the last Republican ports, only they vanished when the fascist forces approached. Gavin had arrived in Valencia two days before the fascists occupied it and started to round up the 15,000 Republicans. There were newspaper reports that dozens of former Republican soldiers had committed suicide rather than face incarceration or execution by the fascists. There was panic in the air.

Gavin met the leader of the National Defence Council, Colonel Casado on 29th March, the day after he arrived in Valencia. His diary notes that there were "+5" in his entourage who made their way to the small port of Gandia further south where the *HMS Galatea* was moored. She was a light cruiser that has been active in joint patrols enforcing the Non-Intervention Policy, periodically in co-operation with German and Italian destroyers, throughout the Spanish Civil War. *HMS Galatea* was now hoping to collect Casado's entourage as well as 150 other republicans and contingents of British aid workers. But before the embarkation began, a unit of fascist soldiers arrived to take possession of the port. A Catalonian eyewitness recalled that Gavin behaved with amazing bravado when he *"laid out a Union Jack flag at the dock gates and refused entry to the fascists".* Another version of this event was given in the biography of Isabel Brown, who had worked with Gavin on the Spanish Medical Aid Committee. She recalled that Gavin arrived on a motor bike the British Council in Valencia had lent him to find:

> *"the dock crowded with people who had learnt about the*
> *proposed rescue operation, including a number of British*
> *personnel – Quakers, Save the Children Fund members,*
> *social workers etc. However, time was running short, for the*
> *fascists were already advancing on this port, which had been*
> *built by British capital for the export of oranges. Realising*
> *that the advance guard of the fascist army was nearly upon*
> *them, Lord Faringdon told everyone to go down on the beach*
> *and await the ship that Sir George Young had arranged to*
> *pick up British personnel stranded in Spain. Lord Faringdon*
> *had managed to obtain a large Union Jack, which he draped*
> *around himself, and waited on his own at the gates for the*
> *fascists to come. When a small patrol arrived, he told them*
> *they could not come in, claiming that the docks were British*
> *property. The young lieutenant in charge of the patrol was*
> *so astonished at this effrontery, delivered with the arrogant*
> *confidence of the British upper class, that he was uncertain*
> *as to what steps to take, and decided to go back for further*
> *orders. As the soldiers departed, the British battleship the*
> *Galatea hove into sight. It had been instructed to take on the*
> *British personnel, but the sailors lowered small boats and*
> *rowed to and from the ship, picking up people until there was*

*no-one left standing on the docks. When the fascists returned
the birds had flown".*

Gavin's diary noted the presence of *HMS Sussex* which had just
managed to obtain the release of four British cargo ships that had
been seized by the fascists. Her presence could have been seen as
provocative, but there was no opposition from the Italian navy
offshore. *HMS Sussex* stood by as *HMS Galatea* transferred her
human cargo just outside the harbour to the *HMS Maine*, a hospital
ship. The latter then sailed to the French port of Marseilles along
with a French naval escort.

Gavin found another old friend there, Poppy Vulliamy, one of the
Quaker sisters who had brought the boy refugees to Buscot Park.
Poppy had returned to Spain to work with the Joint Council for
Spanish Refugee Relief. Here she visited schools and helped to
distribute the few supplies that had made it through the blockaded
ports. During that time Poppy claimed that food was so short that
people ate the animals in Barcelona Zoo. She herself had eaten
cats on occasion – which she described as "not too bad as they
tasted like rabbit". When the war drew to its close Poppy was on
"Franco's death list" and fled to Valencia. There she was evacuated
by a British warship and embarked at a French port. Being Poppy,
she accompanied the refugees to a concentration camp. Here she
found that some of the inmates were convicted rapists and murderers
who had been set loose from prisons and forced to join the lines
of emigrants crossing the border. No one had suspected they were
dangerous but soon their characters emerged. Poppy this passed on
to the undercover S.I.S.

Gavin's diary recorded those two Jewish medics, who had been
working with the Republican forces, were evacuated separately
on a British frigate *HMS Lynx*. Reports tell that two other British
merchant ships who had run the blockade, the *Maritime* and *Africa
Trade*, had then slipped out of Alicante without evacuating any
Republicans. A third British ship, the collier *S.S. Stanbrook*, filled

her holds and decks with 2,000 refugees and took them to North Africa – zigzagging all the way for fear of an Italian submarine attack. The French Navy also made an appearance as Gavin's diary notes that his friend, Albert Forcinal, the socialist Deputy of Gisors, left Alicante on Saturday 1ˢᵗ aboard the destroyer *Le Tigre* bound for Toulon. Two days later on 3ʳᵈ April 1939 the *Daily Express* published a photograph of Gavin with Peter Rodd under the headline:

> *"Women flee with babies To England.*
>
> *ONE HUNDRED AND SEVENTY-ONE Spanish left arrived at Marseilles tonight in a special train on their way to England. They arrived this morning on the British Hospital ship Maine. They are going to England under the protection of the Joint Committee for Spanish Relief."*

This reported that Gavin and Peter Rodd were *"in charge of the arrangements"*. The article included an interview with Colonel Casado who described being met by Gavin in Valencia before being evacuated from Gandia. It said that the refugees were due to travel from Marseilles to Dieppe, where they hoped to embark for England. How Gavin got to Marseilles is unclear, he may have been aboard the *HMS Maine* or he might possibly have driven, as his files show that he had the passé partout he would have needed. The SMAC minutes show that in April 1939 he was part of the British Committee for Refugees from Spain (BCRS). This newly formed group that he was to operate with increasingly, had agreed to

> *"...look after the medical cases amongst refugees. No definite arrangements had yet been made regarding the refugee ships to Mexico, but it was suggested to Lord Faringdon that the matter be raised in the press. Lord Faringdon promised to speak privately to Lord Halifax about it, as he considered this a better plan."*

Gavin's diary shows he went on to meet with Lord Halifax, the British Home Secretary, on April 27th. It was his suggestion to speak privately with Halifax, probably because they knew each other, having first met in 1930, when Gavin, the Earl of Rosse and Robert Byron were guests at the Viceroy's palace in New Delhi when Halifax was styled Lord Irwin, Viceroy of India. Since then, he had become Lord Halifax and had chaired the Round Table conferences on India's dominion status (to which Gavin had delivered a letter from Gandhi). Gavin's diary records three more private meetings with Halifax in the Houses of Parliament over the coming months. Clearly, politically sensitive matters concerning Spain were being dealt with outside of the usual diplomatic channels.

Back home in Buscot two months later Gavin prepared for the outbreak of war by selling most of his prize-winning Jersey herd. This was because he expected to have to lose many of his farm staff when war was declared. He continued to cross the country addressing Labour Party meetings before contributing to a parliamentary debate on Army conscription and the status of conscientious objectors in wartime. Here he called for them not to be incarcerated as traitors but given the chance to do useful non-violent work. Then he returned to Paris on Tuesday 21st May for a SMAC meeting before travelling on to Marseilles. Later in June, Leah Manning MP, the SMAC's Honorary Secretary, submitted a report on their clandestine arrangements to get Spanish republican refugees out of the dreadful camps where they were languishing in Perpignan:

> *"The National Joint Committee and the British Committee for Refugees from Spain have been fortunate enough to secure the time charter of the 'Sinaia' at a cost of £11 per head per refugee, and the ship will leave Port Vendres for Mexico on the 17th of this month. The ship carries 1,800 souls. There is one ship's doctor and five sick bays. Miss Pollock, Secretary of the British Committee for Refugees from Spain, approached me at the Committee Meeting in regard to our promise to look after the medical side of the work with refugees, and*

*said that she had been given to understand that included the
provision of doctors and nurses for the ship together with the
furnishing of the sick bays with medical material and drugs."*

The SMAC hoped to get a film unit aboard to help publicise the
evacuation, but what transpired was perhaps better. In July 1939,
Life magazine jointly published with *Paris Match* a *"Photo Diary of
the 1,800 refugees' 20-day voyage to Mexico"* on the voyage of the *S.S.
Sinaia*. Ironically perhaps, the cover bore a full-page photograph of
Lord Halifax at a conference in Geneva. Hamilton Fish Armstrong, a
member of U.S. President Roosevelt's Committee on Foreign Affairs,
wrote the text of this article which began with the headline "The
Spanish 'Army' in France: 350,000 Loyalist Refugees Fill Camps",
and went on to mention that

> *"The port was changed at the last minute to prevent French
> Communists who had nothing to do with the arrangements
> from staging a demonstration and taking the credit…
> One of the most striking discoveries a visitor makes in the
> camps is how disillusioned everyone is about Soviet Russia.
> A few intellectuals and Party leaders have gone to Moscow;
> but, just as with the Jewish refugees from Nazi Germany,
> Soviet Russia has made no move to take in any considerable
> numbers has not helped."*

The photojournalist on board was David Szymin, known as "Chim"
(an abbreviation of his Polish surname) already famous for his
images of the Spanish Civil War. Dozens of his compassionate
photo-essays on Spain had been published previously in magazines.
(Chim was a founder member of the Magnum co-operative with the
photo-journalist Robert Capa.) The communist controversy was not
left behind in France. The undercover S.I.S. agent Donald Darling
mentioned in a letter to Harold Acton

> *"…the communists turned up in the final hours and tried to
> take credit for the embarkation. Then they managed to bring*

a printing press aboard so that they could bore everyone with their propaganda on the voyage."

Despite the publicity of the evacuations to Mexico, there were enormous challenges to provide relief for those still languishing in camps. This caused Gavin to attend an international conference on aid for the refugees in Paris, before returning to join a British all-party parliamentary delegation to inspect the over-stocked camps. Here the MPs found that people were dying of disease and despair behind barbed wire – while hundreds more were arriving each day. Then he returned to England to set sail with Susan Lawrence MP for Mexico City. An interview shortly after their arrival produced the headline *"British Peer Raps Chamberlain for Helping Fascists"* and he was quoted as saying that the British Prime Minister Chamberlain was *"temporising"* with continental dictators. *"He's been letting the fascists know that they can pretty well do what they damned please".* In Mexico City he was photographed with Susan Lawrence on a punt in the floating flower gardens of Xochimilco. Then they were invited to take tea with Leon Trotsky who had rented Frida Kahlo's parents' house. According to the artist Diego Rivera, who used his influence to help get the refugees settled in Mexico, Stalinist NKVD *"sleepers"* had managed to get aboard the *SS Sinaia* in secret. The artist claimed that one of these – a Spanish-born agent Ramon Mercader – hid in Mexico City until he was able to assassinate Trotsky 18 months later.

Much attention was given to the Duchess of Atholl (Katharine Marjory Stewart-Murray, known to friends as 'Kitty') in British newspapers. She had played a vital role in helping to get Basque refugees accepted into the Britain after the bombing of Guernica. She was a Conservative cabinet minister whose conscience had impelled her leave the Government and act. Like Gavin, she visited Spain to observe on compliance with the Non-Intervention Treaty. Arturo Barea, who eventually came to live at Middle Lodge in Buscot Park, described her visiting a front line with him and being fired on by an Italian machine gunner. Her book, *Searchlight on Spain*, sold over 100,000 copies and resulted in the press dubbing her *"The Red*

Duchess". In spite of this nickname she was fervently anti-Soviet and it emerged years later that she had passed information on the communist activists that she had observed in Spain to MI6. At the time of the evacuation to Mexico she chaired the National Joint Committee for Spanish Relief. She wrote to Gavin fifteen years later:

"89 Iverna Court London W8.

September 18ᵗʰ 1955.

Dear Lord Faringdon,

It is a long time since we have met, but I remember you as a friend of the Spanish Republicans, & therefore trouble you with this letter to ask if you went with the boat which took refugees from, I think, Sète in the south of France, to Mexico in 1939?

If so, did they manage to maintain on the boat the wonderfully quiet behaviour they showed when waiting to embark? I think it most striking, seeing all they had to suffer – I was not on the quay from which they went, all through the hours of embarkation but I was there quite long enough to be very impressed by their quietness and patience.

Miss Edith Pye has just lent me her notes on the flight into France. It is even more terrible than I remember hearing at the time. Probably you saw a good deal of the terrible flight from Barcelona?

Yrs sincerely,

Katherine Atholl"

(Note: Edith Pye was a Quaker humanitarian, an English midwife and International Child Relief Organiser, who worked in maternity hospitals for women refugees and became the president of the British

Midwives Institute. She played a heroic role in helping desperate
refugees get into and out of the camps.)

In early August, Gavin returned to Buscot Park where he hosted
the annual "Gala Day" for the North Berkshire Labour Party with
the party's first woman cabinet minister Miss Susan Lawrence. The
columnist Godfrey Winn described her as having *"the serene, gentle
face of a saint in whose eyes the crusading light forever burns"*. But
Beverley Nichols saw her as someone who drew

> *"blood-curdling pictures of British rule in India, and
> prophesying an 'Indian renaissance', complete with lilies,
> lotuses, temples and indoor sanitation, as soon as the last
> British Tommy had been ejected."*

With her was Lady Cristina Hastings, who Nichols described as:

> *"wearing the most delicious clothes, looking as frail as a
> freesia, and hoarsely demanding immediate intervention on
> the side of the Reds in Spain."*

The group included the Labour Party MP Ellen Wilkinson. She had
played a prominent role in the 1936 march of Jarrow's unemployed
to Parliament. Beverley Nichols, wrote that she complained loudly
at Buscot that ignorant people refused to believe *"the 'facts' about
the Russians"*.

Six weeks later on August 29th 1939, the 20-year-old Oxford
undergraduate Iris Murdoch came and recorded her visit to Buscot
Park in her journal. The budding writer had joined a theatrical
troupe called The Magpies on a summer tour where they performed in
aid of the Oxford University Refugee Appeal Fund and the National
Joint Committee for Spanish Relief. It is clear from her journals that
she was greatly impressed by the communist undergraduates at the
time, but the infatuation did not last long. The Magpies arrived the
day after a pact between Hitler and Stalin was signed, leaving the

way open for their invasions of Britain's ally, Poland. Iris noted that Gavin was *"up in London looking after the crisis"* and went on to give her impressions:

> *"Buscot Park is the residence of Lord Faringdon the Labour Peer & ye gods but he has done himself well. Acres & acres of fine parkland we drove thro', up the sweeping drive, flanked by noble trees and commanding a gracious prospect, past the expansive lake & up between the terraces to the magnificent house, a huge 18th century building in good Oxford stone, quiet & well designed. The Theatre is a building in imitation Greek temple style…it had every conceivable gadget for lighting & scenery…*

> *The international situation must be grave indeed. I have not seen a paper for weeks & have not the remotest idea what is happening, except that Germany & Russia have signed a non-aggression pact (over which much unnecessary fuss is being made) & that there is more trouble over Danzig. But all the people we met seem very upset, & it must be a great storm to ripple these placid waters. Moreover, we got a wire this morning asking if we intended to continue the tour. We wire back 'Magpies carry on'. We try not to think too often of it all – and find it amazingly easy. We have so many urgent little problems of our own that it is not possible to look up and see the gathering clouds."*

Gavin's diary of 1939 had no entries that day or the following ones until Thursday August 31st, which says simply *"H of L"*. Then on Friday Sept 1st one word appeared underlined twice *WAR!* This was the day that the Nazis invaded Poland from the west, only a week after Britain had signed a Mutual Assistance Pact with that country. On 3rd September the solitary word *'WAR!'* appears again in Gavin's diary. That was the day that Britain, France, Australia and New Zealand declared hostilities. Two weeks later Russia invaded Poland.

CHAPTER 9

Russia – What Gavin and the Butler Saw

Two years before the outbreak of WW2, on Monday 12ᵗʰ April 1937, Gavin dined with his ex-wife Honor in London on the night before he left for Helsinki. From there he travelled to Stockholm and on to Leningrad, where he and other American and British visitors whose visas had been approved by the Soviet government met their VOKS guides. These were officials from the Intourist agency to whom he paid £58. 14s. od. in cash (the equivalent of £3,976.99 today) on 16ᵗʰ April. VOKS guides closely escorted the visitors around Leningrad, the former Tsarist capital of the Russian Empire. Known as St. Petersburg until 1924, it was now the second largest city in the USSR. This tour included visits to a part of the vast Hermitage complex, a porcelain factory, and the Soviet Children's theatre on the first day; and from then on, the VOKS guides kept them equally busy. On Thurs 22ⁿᵈ April some were surprised that they were taken to see a vast silo filled to the brim with grain. This was to counter widespread reports in the Western press of famine in rural Russia –something Gavin's close friend Robert Byron had witnessed and written about six years earlier. At some point every day they were regaled with patriotic speeches, and often the evenings were spent at a ballet. On Friday they attended a town planning meeting in the monumentally large hall of the Pioneer's Palace, which had been created for sport training and undefined *"extracurricular activities"*. That night they attended what one delegate called *"a long opera based on a short poem Ruslan and Lyudmila. By Pushkin"*. Evidently there was so much to learn about Soviet society, and the VOKS guides were determined that their visitors should not miss out on anything. Unfortunately, as one of his fellow guests put it, they managed this with *"a monotone delivery coupled with officious hospitality".*

Gavin managed to persuade his VOKS guides to take him back to the Hermitage; that vast complex of buildings that included the historic Winter Palace, Small Hermitage, Old Hermitage, New Hermitage and Hermitage Theatre. Here he was shown some of the surviving art collection. Over the previous seven years the Russian authorities had sold over 250 paintings to foreign visitors. Sales had included works by Jan van Eyck, Titian, Rembrandt, Rubens, Raphael, and other important artists. By 1937 twenty-one old master paintings from the former Tsarist collection were hanging in the National Gallery of Art in Washington D.C. Still, there was much to see, and after visiting the Hermitage four days in succession, Gavin left Leningrad for Moscow, which was an overnight train journey of 400 miles. This took around nine hours, during which time the passports of all foreigners were collected and retained for safe-keeping by armed officers.

One of the British party was Lord Strabolgi – Labour's Chief Whip in the Lords. Other Labour Party members, such as Peter Mandelson's grandfather Herbert Morrison, returned to call modern Russia *"the greatest economic experiment of our time".* Another Labour luminary to visit Russia was the future Chancellor of the Exchequer and President of the Board of Trade – Hugh Dalton. He proclaimed Russia *"a most astonishing Industrial Revolution".* Even H.G. Wells had praised Soviet collectivism – but cautioned that that it might *"give a small group of men undreamed-of power and control".* Whilst none of these men advocated Bolshevism, they all shared Strabolgi's views that a better balance of trade would be mutually beneficial:

> *"The Russian market is the greatest potential market for engineering products in the world... Last year we bought from Russia £17,200,000 worth of goods and we sold to Russia in the same period £3,600,000 worth in round*

RIDEAU COTTAGE, ROCKLIFFE, ONT. CANADA

Above: The family's home in the grounds of Government House, Ottawa, now the Canadian Prime Minister's official residence.
Below: Left-right: Roderick, Lt.-Col. H.G. Henderson, Michael, Gavin, Lady Violet and Margaret.

Lord Faringdon's Ambulance

LORD FARINGDON leaves for Spain to-day with the pale green Rolls-Royce car, converted into an ambulance, which he has presented to the Spanish Government.

The car was once put to less Republican uses. As no other car was available at the moment it was used by King George V. for

LORD FARINGDON with his converted car.

a military inspection in the neighbourhood of Faringdon.

Lord Faringdon is a skilful driver, fond of speed. His enthusiasm for the Spanish Government has been keen since the outbreak of the civil war.

Buscot Park, his home near Faringdon, has recently had a private theatre and a swimming pool added, and is to be made available for members of the Socialist

From the Ashes

A FEW days ago I referred to Lord Faringdon's Rolls-Royce ambulance and its destruction in Spain. I now learn that the ambulance has risen like a Phœnix from the Spanish ashes.

After it had been hit by a bomb in Valencia, it appeared to be irreparable. But by an extraordinary chance, its chauffeur found the abandoned remains of a Rolls-Royce, of the same model, on a car dump. He was thus able to replace every part of the ambulance which had been destroyed, and it returned once more into service. Its running costs, however, proved too high, and the ambulance is now tcuring England with its chauffeur, collecting money for Spanish medical aid.

This Rolls-Royce ambulance, presented by Lord Farringdon, has done service for nearly a year in Spain. It was riddled with bullet holes and bomb splinters by Fascist airplanes while carrying out its humanitarian duties.

*figures…This year the Russian Government has taken to
buying large quantities of steel goods—engineering products,
railway material and so on—for cash, and at the end of
January it placed orders for £1,500,000 worth of engineering
goods and it paid cash on the nail for them…the natural
resources—minerals, food-producing resources and timber—
of Siberia only were as great as the natural resources of the
United States and Canada put together. The opening out of
that country has only begun. They need immense quantities of
machinery, railway rolling stock and so on."*

However, Gavin and the others had arrived in the Soviet Union
during one of the most repressive years in its history – now known
as the "Great Terror". For many years afterwards, cautious Russians
referred to it simply as "1937". In that year the Fabian Society
luminaries Sidney and Beatrice Webb published *Soviet Communism:
A New Civilisation?* Historians have since deplored their blindness
to the brutal methods of collectivisation, as well as the ruthless
political purges via show trails, which had created the gulag forced
labour system. Clearly, others took a more objective view than the
Webbs. Gavin received this from W.P. Coates, Chairman of the
Anglo-Russian Parliamentary Committee, dated Feb 1937. The first
page reads:

*"THE MOSCOW TRIALS: BOLSHEVIK 'OLD
GUARDS' OR -?*

*It has been repeatedly stated that the principal accused in
the Moscow trials of August 1936, and January 1937, were
members of the 'Old Guard' of the Bolsheviks and leading
figures in the carrying out of the Soviet revolution. We have
had many inquiries as to the truth of these statements and in
accordance with our usual practice we give the facts, which
are well known throughout the U.S.S.R. and have been
published from time to time by the Soviet Press. Practically*

*every one of them had been, both before and after the
revolution, in open or secret opposition to Lenin."*

Potted biographies of six former key members of the Party followed,
condemning them for their *"anti-Leninist and anti-Soviet activities".*
This tract was tucked into a book of Trotsky's writings published in
France in 1934 at Buscot Park, and suggests that before he visited the
USSR Gavin was aware of Stalin's way of suppressing dissent. He
was seen as the man behind a myriad of plots to unseat Stalin, and
had been formally condemned to death in his absence for writing an
essay entitled "The Revolution Betrayed" in 1935. Trotsky had fled to
France, where Soviet pressure forced the Government to ask him to
leave. He managed to get asylum in Mexico and travelled there in
secret to a suburb of Mexico City. In 1938 he was living there in a villa
belonging to Frida Kahlo's family at Coyoacan. Ironically, Coyoacan
meant "Place of the Wolf'" in the Aztec language. From here he
sent an invitation for Gavin to come to tea. That letter survives at
Buscot Park, along with photographs of Gavin with Susan Lawrence
sitting in a punt at the floating flower markets of the town. By then
George Orwell, who had fought with the anarchist forces in Spain
and then narrowly escaped being executed by Stalinists in Barcelona,
had referred to Stalin's Russia as a *"slave state, or rather slave world".*

The high point of the VOKS guided tour was meant to be visiting
Moscow, which Stalin had turned into a vast construction site for
buildings celebrating Soviet achievements. These were intended to
be a showcase which would influence foreign visitors, providing
proof that Russia was a model society. The new Moscow was meant
to show that the Stalinist state could lead the world to a safe and
prosperous future. Most of the honoured guests were unaware that
the Soviet secret police were scouring the country for anyone Stalin
suspected of being counter-revolutionary. Behind the scenes 1.5
million people were arrested and over 700,000 executions took place
in 1937. These massive purges were meant to remove dissenters and
consolidate Stalin's authority. All potential rivals to his leadership
were being removed, which in effect meant almost the entire

echelon of bureaucrats, professionals and Army officers. Others to disappear were intellectuals, scientists and *kulak* farmers on the most productive lands who were deemed *"too rich to be real peasants"*. The secret police accused most of them, like many others, of being *"fifth columnists"* plotting sabotage.

With all this going in behind the façade of progress, Gavin and the other guests were shown the truly marvellous new underground stations. Then they toured the less wonderful Russian Picture Gallery where propagandist art extolling workers constructing a new state was taking the place of the *"old revolutionary art"* which tended to show Bolsheviks capturing Tsarist palaces. Gavin was taken to exhibitions and lectures on soviet architecture, engineering, collectivism and city planning. The VOKS guides took them to the historic Boyar House – a 16th-century mansion that had belonged to the Romanovs, the wealthy merchant (Boyar) family who became the last Tsars. Evenings were rounded off with visits to the *"the popular theatre"*. An entire day in Moscow was devoted to a study of *"the soviet child and maternity welfare"*. Then Gavin was allowed to attend lunch at the American embassy. On the following days he was taken to visit a kindergarten, the Ethnology Museum, the Museum of the Red Army and to a lecture by the architect constructing "The Palace of the Soviets", which was being built on the site of a demolished cathedral near the Kremlin and was intended to be the world's tallest building. That evening was spent watching the state ballet – an escapist end to another educational day.

And so, it went on. The next day's outing featured the 10th anniversary celebrations of the Bolshevo Commune. Here the communards were former convicts and juvenile delinquents whose civil rights had been restored in return for their participation in a social experiment. For the past seven years their labour had created a town with its own hospital, hostels, apartment blocks, school, shops, cookhouse and refectory, training centre, stadium and steam bath. There were grass verges and flowerbeds which they tended, as well as high fences. Local women and girls from the surrounding area had been encouraged to marry the hard-working communards, and these parents and their children turned out to welcome the foreign guests and journalists. They sang while flags, banners and hands were waved enthusiastically by them for the tourists and film cameras. It was all meant to be a show-case success of communism in the community. But at the end of that year the Bolshevo Commune was closed and all its former convicts returned to prisons or labour camps. In 1937, during the "Great Terror" such things happened. Anyone foolish enough to complain was crushed by the system.

On Friday 30th April Gavin went to view the contents of the Museum of Revolutionary Art, which consisted of Constructivist and Supremacist paintings as well as political posters. This was followed by lectures on the propaganda value of modern Russian film and music. That evening was spent in the more relaxed ambiance of an 18th-century opera house. On May Day Gavin and the other guests were allowed to see the Red Army Review in Red Square. Afterwards, the foreign guests dined at the Park of Culture and Rest. That venue was officially opened as Gorky Park of Culture and Rest in 1937 when 300,000 people were allowed in on the first day. Gavin and the foreign visitors also saw the *Ostankino* – a suburban park meant to host the All-Union Agricultural Exhibition. However, this was only a series of wooden pavilions with impressive façades as Stalin had postponed the opening until 1938. The fact was that the regional authorities failed to deliver proper exhibits, such as modern tractors. Then a commission examined the wooden construction and decided that it was too modest to proceed with. Plans to rebuild it were cancelled in 1941 after the Nazi invasion of Russia.

On leaving Moscow, Gavin travelled roughly 850 kilometres by rail overnight to Kiev, and after a 12-hour journey he was taken on a tour of a collective farm. The next day he toured a dairy, before visiting what are now two of UNESCO's World Heritage sites: the *Pechersk Lavra*, also known as the Kiev Monastery of the Caves. This is an 18th-century Orthodox monastery beside the river Dnieper whose roofline boasts six gilded onion domes. Then he went to the

11th-century Cathedral of St. Sophia, which had been designed to rival Hagia Sophia in Constantinople. On his final day in the USSR, he visited the Derzhprom building in Freedom Square, Kharkiv, seat of the People's Commissioners' Council. Five thousand workers in three shifts had created this, the largest "skyscraper" in the USSR. It was used as a symbol of modernity in films such as Vertov's *Three Songs about Lenin* and Eisenstein's *The General Line*, which were shown at the cinema on his final nights in Russia. He must have been exhausted when he arrived in Warsaw on Friday 7th. There he stayed at the luxurious Hotel Bristol, famous for its Art Nouveau design for one night, in a *"room with bath".* before travelling to Paris. On Monday 9th May he arrived back in London after three weeks abroad.

The Coronation of George VI and his wife Elizabeth as King and Queen of the British Empire and Commonwealth took place at Westminster Abbey, London, on 12th May 1937. Gavin attended and on the following day he went to a meeting of the Spanish Medical Aid Committee before he returned to his established routine of visiting mental hospitals in North London and Kent. On the Friday of the following week, he found time to have lunch with Honor again. Meetings with his former wife, now one of his closest friends, bracketed the most important episodes of his life.

When Gavin visited Moscow on Wednesday 28th April 1937, he wrote the words *"lunch embassy"* in his pocket diary. These words turned out to have a greater significance than the entire plethora of events on his busy VOKS guided tour. He lunched at Spaso House, where someone who he had employed was now working for the American Ambassador, Joseph E. Davies. Within a year that former servant who came to be known as "the English Butler" helped his new employers uncover a Soviet spy operating in the embassy. The details were kept secret for decades and only emerged in the 1970s when the diplomat and foreign policy advisor, George F. Kennan, published his memoirs. Long before then, nine months after his visit to Moscow, "the English Butler" had written to Lord Faringdon and sent him a set of photographs that had been covertly shot on the roof of the American Embassy in Moscow. These survive in the Buscot Park archives, as well as bank receipts which show that Gavin had continued to pay sums of money to his former butler.

Ambassador Joseph E. Davies had taken up his post in Moscow in August 1937. Before moving into his official residence, Spaso House on the border of Red Square, he arranged for the elegant old 18th-century Neo-Classical building to be thoroughly redecorated. After this was done by local construction teams the American embassy staff moved in and discovered that there were some unexpected additions to the embassy's modernisation; namely that microphones had been hidden in the fireplaces, air-vents and wall cavities. It was clear that the Soviet secret police intended to keep the Ambassador, his family, staff and guests under close surveillance. According to George F. Kennan, who was the embassy Security Officer, *"in spite of constant vigilance and regular clean-ups, security within the embassy compound was never satisfactory"*. Kennan advised Ambassador Davies to take the precaution of tapping a spoon on metal or a glass whenever he wished to speak to his staff or visitors on sensitive matters. Guests to the embassy were handed printed cards which warned them that both the buildings and gardens were being monitored by the Soviet secret police, and that their private rooms would probably be searched daily by the cleaning staff.

The most bizarre example of Soviet surveillance came to light in July 1937 when the Ambassador and his wife had gone on holiday and, according to Keenan's memoirs, had gone off *"leaving in the house only the English Butler and one or two other foreign servants"*. During this period, Keenan and a member of the diplomatic staff checked the attic, where they discovered *"that someone was engaged in hollowing out a recess in the brick wall directly over the place where Ambassador Davies had his desk, and that it was intended to use this as a vantage point from which one could eavesdrop on conversations in the Ambassador's study... It was obviously intended that someone should lie in the recess and thrust a fishpole, with a microphone pinned to the end of it. down into the hollow portions of the brick wall adjacent to the Ambassador's desk. We even found later the fishpole with a cloth attached to the end of it – and eventually we found the microphone...".* So, Kennan arranged for the embassy's electrician to rig up a trip wire *"with an alarm bell in the sleeping quarters of the English Butler... later I got a call from him, went to his room, and to my astonishment, sat, on one chair, the residence telephone operator, Sam, and on another chair, covering him with an enormous pistol, was the Ambassador's nephew. The trip-wire had been activated. He and the English Butler had rushed to the attic and found Sam there."*

The culprit refused to confess – but his cigarette butts stained with lipstick were found in the attic. It transpired that Sam, the male telephone operator, for reasons Kennan *"preferred not to inquire into"*, habitually wore the same colour lipstick. On his return Ambassador Davies was informed, but refused to raise the matter with any Soviet officials, saying that his priority was to avoid disrupting diplomatic relations. Keenan tried to persuade him otherwise but Davies was determined. His opinion was at odds with those on his own staff, like Keegan, who had been in the country far longer and strongly disagreed. The result was that Keegan found himself dismissed and sent back to Washington for *"his health's sake"*. The matter lay undiscussed until after Davies was reassigned to Belgium nine months later.

The background to this decision was that Davies had been appointed Ambassador by Franklin D. Roosevelt who admired his skills as a lawyer and as his major fund-raiser as well as his presidential campaign manager. FDR had asked this valued political ally to evaluate the strength of the Soviet Army, government, and industry, as well as find out which side Russia would support in the *"coming war"*. Career diplomats noticed that Davies ignored reports of the disappearance of thousands of innocent citizens during his period serving as U.S. Ambassador. Some complained that Davies glossed over Stalin's brutal authoritarian government and criticised Davies' main concern, which was to praise the USSR's commitment to *"building a new society"*. In a famous memo to Washington Ambassador Davies had written:

> *"Communism holds no serious threat to the United States. Friendly relations in the future may be of great general value."*

Clearly, pragmatism was the Ambassador's guiding principle. Next to this it was felt that the most important activities he performed in Moscow were shopping sprees with his wife, Marjorie Merriweather Post. She was America's wealthiest heiress and an avid collector of Russian Art. Soviet officials arranged for state storerooms to be opened for the couple to visit. Here they had their choice of impounded treasures, and were able to accumulate an unrivalled collection of Russian Art, jewellery, ceramics, textiles and even six exquisite and very rare Fabergé jewelled eggs. Their collection included many icons which had been the pride of Russian Orthodox churches before Stalin's era, and some of the Romanovs' crowns, Imperial porcelain and silverware. The Davies paid in dollars, and export licences were granted promptly as the Soviets needed foreign currency to fund their industrial and agricultural programmes (as well as their military). Photographs of the happy pair appeared on the cover of *Time* magazine and this was not the only periodical to feature their Russian shopping sprees.

Emlen Knight Davies (the Ambassador's second daughter by his first marriage) visited Moscow that summer. Relations with the Soviets must have been very good indeed as a subversive photograph of her was syndicated in American magazines and the Soviets made no complaints. However, this was carefully composed by the photographer to show St. Basil's Cathedral and the Kremlin reflected in her sunglasses. It was strictly forbidden at the time for anything in Red Square to be photographed – especially not by foreigners. Someone in the Ambassador's entourage had taken that photograph, along with others of her looking out from his limousine onto the Kremlin and Red Square. That person on the embassy staff had breached diplomatic etiquette. Actually, the misconduct was far worse than this, as Emlen Knight Davies had been photographed on the roof of Spaso House, watching a military parade in Red Square, and someone had noted down all the details of tanks, transports, etc. on the backs of these photographs. If George F. Keenan was correct in his assertion that Russian staff in the embassy regularly checked the contents of the guests' rooms – the Soviets secret service would have known all about this. But as far as one can tell Emlen Knight Davies' collection of photographs were souvenirs and as such, they were simply pasted into a scrapbook about her travels. This scrapbook was to surface 80 years later in an exhibition held in the USA. Curiously, the majority of these photographs were identical to a set sent to Gavin in 1937 – and that points to them being part of a covert act that Soviet Intelligence – and the great leader Joseph Stalin himself – would have deplored.

Around four months after George Keenan, the Ambassador's nephew, and "the English Butler" had made their discovery of the Russian surveillance in Spaso House, Ambassador Davies was reassigned to Belgium. This was an unexpected decision and so the Ambassador left some staff behind to sort out potentially sensitive papers. There were no immediate plans to hand these over to his replacement. In fact, the embassy was to remain unoccupied for several years. With the cat away the mice began to play. Two months after Ambassador Davies' departure Gavin received a package from Moscow containing a letter and nine photographs. This text was so full of mis-spellings and grammatical errors that it could not have been the work of an embassy secretary. It was signed *Stanly R. Allingham*. This was none other than Lord Faringdon's former servant, who Keenan had called *"the English Butler"*.

"11/1/38

Moscow

Dear Sir,

*I enclose a few snaps that I took on the anniversary (20th)
I thought that you might like them they will be in two
envelopes as one of them might go astray the post here is not
all that it might be*

*These snaps were taken from the roof of the U.S.A. Chancery
and I think that it was the only roof with people on it and the
funny thing there was not a soul on the sidewalks they were
all in the processions and it look most odd. It's raining all the
time and the snaps are quite good considering the weather.*

*I am trying to get statistics on the value of wages and will
let you know later as this will take some time to find out, I
thought I would get you what it cost a man with two children
to live on 500 roubles a month that is about the highest wage
payed here and then 300 and 200.*

*I will be so pleased the day we leave this place I am glad that
I have been here it's a great lesson and a lot of folks I know
ought to be made to come here and live.*

*We have just had News via the Radio that the Ambassador
has been moved to Brussels and I must say I hope that there
is a little more life there than here, you get so tired of walking
the streets but at the same time I have seen a lot that I cannot
put in this letter and was amazed at the way things go on.*

Hoping you are in the best of health.

Yours respectfully,

Stanly. R. Allingham.

P.T.O.

I will print some more different as soon as I get to London in

> *March I hope and send them to you, it will take us six weeks*
> *to pack up here."*

The *"U.S.A. Chancery"* was Spaso House, the American Ambassador's official residence overlooking Red Square. The *"anniversary (20)"* was a celebration to mark the twenty years since the October Revolution of 1917. Fears of surveillance by foreign powers and sabotage by *"fifth columnists"* had led Stalin to decree that it should be delayed, and for the same reasons no bystanders were allowed that day to observe the military parade past the Kremlin in Red Square. It had eventually taken place on the *"7 November 1937"* – the date written on the back of one of the photos Allingham sent. He had typed captions directly onto the back of each of the nine 12 x 9 cm, black and white, glossy photos he sent. These typed captions reveal quite a lot of information the Soviet Secret Service would not have wanted to share:

Photo 1: *Telephoto lens. One of the big tanks that hold six to eight men.*

This appears to be a T35 multi-turret tank with handrails around its top. Only 61 were ever manufactured, and they were only used for parades until 1941. They were too cumbersome and slow for battle.

Photo 2: *Tanks pulling guns off to the Square.*

This shows 33 rows of 3 tanks with one in front – a total 100 tanks – winding around the former Tsar's stables by the Kremlin. Its façade's nine arches each bear a portrait of a revolutionary leader. The largest – in the centre – is Stalin. There are ten red flags arranged in a fan on the portico above.

Photo 3: *Tanks lined up to go by the side of the Tsar's stable now a garage.*

The same building, the Tsar's stables by the Kremlin shown in photo 2 above with 100 tanks.

Photo 4: *Anti air craft guns and searchlights in the back ground.*

Photo 5: *This was taken with a Telephoto lens and you can see Voroshilov addressing the troops in front of Lenin's Tomb.*

This image shows St. Basil's and Red Square with troops and tanks. Kliment Voroshilov was a member of the Politburo from 1926, Commissar for Military Defence from 1932, and from 1935 he was a Marshal of the Soviet Union. He supported Stalin's "Great Purges" by denouncing colleagues; and wrote to exiled former Army officers and diplomats, giving them personal assurances they would not face retribution from authorities if they returned to the Soviet Union. By and large this proved untrue and merely a ruse to get them to return. Voroshilov signed 185 execution lists, the 4th largest after Molotov and Stalin.

Photo 6: *Taken with ordinary lens again Voroshilov talking to the troops. Nov 7th 1937.*

Photo 7: *The Big building is the Moscow Hotel now people are living in it.*

Photo 8: *A part of the Kremlin this house is for the Guard.*

Photo 9: *Horses pulling guns and soldiers in their lorries ready to go there are 12 soldiers in each lorry.*

The photo shows 18 horse-drawn lorries lined up beside a row of 10 tanks with one leader. There are a total of 31 tanks.

Just who was Stanly R. Allingham? Very little has come to light about him, apart from the fact that he seems to have been employed by Lord Faringdon after Gavin stood as the Labour Party candidate for the London County Council elections and leased a residence at 36 Barrington Road, Brixton in August 1936. During his time there the Buscot Park Accounts lists *"Allingham's Wages and Book £18. 3s. 4d."* entered below the first Footman Mr Booth's wages for the same amount. Both men were being used to manage his households away from Buscot Park; Stanly Allingham in Brixton, while entries for Mr Booth show that he was sent to the villa in Corsica several times. Mr Buck, Gavin's butler at Buscot Park until 1945, received £12 per month, whilst Gavin's chef and his secretary got £24.00 and £10.00 per month respectively. Allingham was paid considerably less than these when the last mention of him appears in the ledger of December 1936 as *"monthly salary and book £8. 11s.2d."* However, Gavin's bank book shows that he made another fourteen cash payments to him between 1935 to 1937. These amounted to £520 (= £35,000 today). The last three payments occurred when Allingham was working for the American Ambassador, Joseph E. Davies in Moscow; July 10th – £45; 15th £10; 17th £37. These sums were much higher than Gavin would usually pay to his servants. According to Ambassador Davies, Allingham was employed by him in October 1936 as his *"personal English Butler"* when he stopped in London on this way to take up his post in Russia. This suggests that Allingham accompanied his new employer on a long tour of the continent with the Ambassador's wife, heiress Marjorie Merriweather Post, the wealthiest woman in the United States.

In his letter Stanly R. Allingham says that he has sent another set of *"snaps"* to someone else. These pictures gave a good indication of the quality and quantity of troops and tanks available, as this was a prestigious parade. TASS, the Soviet central news agency, routinely censored images showing military units in and around Red Square, and Soviet Intelligence would have regarded the packet as evidence of espionage and destroyed it – and certainly detained the person who sent it for questioning. Allingham clearly knew this as he says they did not trust the diplomatic bag and had posted two identical packets elsewhere. He promised information on Soviet rates of pay and more photographs after he returned to London. These are not the sorts of promises a butler, however resourceful, would normally make. He must have had accomplices within the embassy. The fact that Gavin did not destroy the packet suggests that he, like those who sent it, was not a committed supporter of Stalin's totalitarian state. But interestingly, Gavin did not pass it on to British Intelligence, he simply left the packet in a box of his letters from that period. Presumably, one of the other packets Allingham mentions reached the right desk in Whitehall. And even if this was not the case, Gavin might well have had ample opportunity to show it to some of the Intelligence operatives who came to Buscot Park before, and during WW2.

Gavin was not alone in having mixed feelings about Russia during this period. These stirrings were developed into a widespread feeling of betrayal after Stalin signed a non-aggression pact with Hitler. Still, many hoped this had been part of a Soviet strategy to buy time before they were invaded by the Nazis. After Germany invaded Britain's ally Poland, Gavin joined a delegation of the "Friends of the USSR" that met with Clement Attlee, the Labour Party leader, in the first months of the Phoney War. They agreed that Britain should seek resolutions without resisting Soviet expansion in Poland and Finland. Some Labour Party members saw this as shameful appeasement. The counter argument was that this was better than war with Russia as Britain was still woefully unprepared for hostilities. In the meantime, the far left sought Gavin's support for a People's Convention formed to rally support from Trades Unionists to promote friendship with the USSR. Prominent communists, such as the barrister D.N. Pritt and Harry Pollitt, wrote to Gavin, as did members of the People's Vigilance Committee. All of these had been expelled from the Labour Party. The People's Convention proposed the abolishment of the ruling class and a "People's Government" rather than the wartime coalition, but this never had any real support and was even disowned by the Communist Party of Great Britain in 1942. Gavin's half-hearted support for them led to his being teased by John Betjeman in a cartoon he drew showing a footballer wearing the People's Convention logo on his puffed-out chest as Nazi bombers fly overhead.

The same disquiet over Russia governed relations between the USA and the Soviet Union after the Molotov-Ribbentrop Non-Aggression Pact. When war broke out Ambassador Davies was recalled to serve as a special assistant to the Secretary of State. However, after Hitler's invasion of Russia in 1941, Roosevelt needed to restore Stalin's reputation before he could fund Russia's war in the east, in order to buy time for the Allied invasion of Western Europe. Davies, who had chaired the president's inaugural committee, claimed that Roosevelt urged him to write a book extolling the virtues of Stalin and the Soviet regime based on his experiences in Russia. What Davies was to call his *"true story"* was written in the first half of 1941, published as *Mission to Moscow* and sold 700,000 copies. The President then asked the former Ambassador to go to Hollywood where Davies was promised script-control on a Warner Brothers production. This was to be directed by Michael Curtiz, who had had brought *The Adventures of Robin Hood* and *The Charge of the light Brigade* starring Errol Flynn to the screen. In 1942 Michael Curtis and Warner Brothers completed two Hollywood *"classics"*. These were *Casablanca* with Humphrey Bogart and Ingrid Bergman, and James Cagney in the extravagantly patriotic *Yankee Doodle Dandy*. Cagney's co-star in the latter, Walter Houston (father of the film director of *The African Queen* and *The Maltese Falcon*) headed the cast of *Mission to Moscow*. Today, that film is remembered as pure propaganda. Former Ambassador Davies appears at the start to tell viewers that what they were about to see was *"a completely true story"*. However, to others the film seemed so biased that after WW2 many involved in its production found themselves investigated by the anti-communist Committee on Un-American Activities. During these hearings a spokesman for Warner Brothers explained that the film was *"An expedient lie for political purposes, glossily covering up important facts with full or partial knowledge of their false presentation".*

When Davies set off for Hollywood Stanly R. Allingham had written another letter to Lord Faringdon.

> *"Dear Sir,*
>
> *I wonder if you would be so kind as to send me a written Reference for the four and a half years I was with you.*
>
> *My employer has gone to Hollywood for 9 months and I am on a retaining fee. I am going next week to try and get a post as Special Constable in the new camp that is being built there and I have to show Refs for 8 years.*
>
> *Trusting that I am not putting you to any trouble. I also hope you are in the best of health.*
>
> *Yours respectfully,*
>
> *Stanly R. Allingham"*

Allingham's claim that he worked for Gavin for *"four and a half years"* seems to be untrue as his name does not appear in any accounts before 1935 or after 1937. One wonders if he meant that he was paid for covert activities or simple stating what he needed in the hope that Gavin might oblige, and thus help him *"get a post as a Special Constable".* Allingham's actions seem to have been low-level espionage – not very helpful to British and American intelligence, but certainly unwelcome to the hyper-sensitive Soviet authorities. He may have been involved in other matters, but there is no evidence of blackmail of his former employer, or payments for works of art smuggled out of Russia. By 1942 over 250 paintings from the Hermitage Museum had been sold to foreign visitors, but these are all well documented.

On 10th January 1945 *The Times* reported that Gavin was among the 10 representatives of the Houses of Parliament taking part in a delegation to Moscow at the invitation of the Soviet Government. This was a *"hands across the seas"* attempt to build trade links after the war. Gavin managed to shock some of his communist hosts by openly criticising Prime Minister Winston Churchill at an official dinner in the Kremlin. However, this was not as unpatriotic as it appeared to have been as they had a long history of disagreements. It could be argued that this showed the strength of British parliamentary democracy as no delegate from the U.S.S.R. would have been so reckless as to criticise Stalin. Nevertheless, some of his fellow delegates were Conservatives and took a dim view of it.

The visit included an audience with Joseph Stalin, and for this great occasion Gavin wore his Nation Fire Service uniform. This was identical to a postman's livery apart from its cloth badge. This plain uniform marked him out for special treatment by *"the great leader"*, for he arranged for Gavin to inspect a brigade of the Moscow Fire Service the next day. Afterwards, Stalin had tea with Gavin from a samovar and gave him some keepsakes. These included a lock of his hair, a tortoise-shell cigar holder, a book of his speeches translated into English, and some Ikat silk from his home state of Georgia. Gavin used this to cover two Regency chairs back at Buscot Park. Years later another gift from Stalin came to light when Gavin mentioned the family's baronial robes deposited at Ede & Ravenscroft, the oldest tailors in London:

> *"Take good care of these as the fur collar was given to me by 'Uncle Joe' and you will be one of the very few peers in the House wearing real ermine".*

Gavin kept a typewritten "REPORT OF THE PALIAMENTARY DELEGATION TO THE U.S.S.R." dated 7/3/45. This tells us that there were eight members besides Lord Faringdon who were:

Colonel Walter Elliott, M.P. M.C. (Scottish Conservative-Unionist)

Mr. Wilfrid Roberts, M.P. (Liberal member for Cumberland North, Secretary of the National Joint Committee for the Relief)

Mr. Tom Frazer, M.P. (Labour member for Hamilton)

Mr P.W. Jewson, M.P. (Liberal member for Great Yarmouth)

Commander Stephen King-Hill, M.P. (Retired Naval commander; Independent member for Ormskirk)

Major R.E. Manningham Buller, M.P. (Conservative member for Kettering)

Mr John Parker. M.P. (Labour member for Sheffield)

Colonel C.E. Ponsonby, M.P. (Conservative Parliamentary Private Secretary to the Foreign Secretary Anthony Eden).

They listed the following *"definite conclusions":*

1. *There is an enormous amount of vigour and determination not only for the war but for future internal development. The recovery of the people from the German invasion is indeed remarkable.*
2. *There is an intense desire for education.*
3. *The atmosphere in the whole of the U.S.S.R. is that of an industrial revolution in full swing and of pride in what has been achieved.*
4. *Throughout there is an inevitable strain due to war and a great unsatisfied desire for consumer goods.*
5. *Finally one would say that in the Soviet Union there is a*

great interest in lands outside its border – or rather in the
people of those lands. The peoples of the Soviet Union are
convinced of their own achievements and want to show them
to others. They also wish to know how others live, to feel
their goodwill, to ensure their co-operation based on mutual
respect and understanding.

The party was in the country for 42 days having traversed the
U.S.S.R. by rail. They spent the first five days and nights in Moscow,
from where they went to Leningrad for two days before returning to
Moscow for an interview with Stalin on the evening of 25th January.
Then the delegation split into parties that visited Siberia, the Ukraine,
the Caspian Sea, the Sea of Aral, Tashkent, Samarkand, Ashgabat,
Bokhara, Stalingrad and Baku.

> *"This long and rapid journey could not, of course, give*
> *anything save a general view of the huge territories traversed.*
> *But the party had many opportunities of free and lengthy*
> *conversations with all sections of the community. Members*
> *of the party would wish to place on record their appreciation*
> *not only of the Russian hospitality but also of the great*
> *trouble which was taken by all concerned to enable them to*
> *go where they wished and see what they wanted".*

Perhaps the best postscript on Gavin's last visit to Russia came in
his *Times* obituary of 29th January 1976, which was written by John
Parker MP the Father of the House of Commons:

> *"I accompanied him on a Parliamentary goodwill mission to*
> *the USSR in January-March, 1945, when we toured around*
> *in one of the Tsar's old trains, a party of eight MPs and two*
> *peers, serviced by members of the Soviet Foreign Office and*
> *the British Embassy.*
>
> *Gavin emphatically stated his views on the Russians at meal*
> *times making clear his disapproval of many of Churchill's*
> *pre-war policies. Our leader Walter Elliot, was informed by*

the senior Soviet Official present that we had a dangerous Trotskyist in our ranks who would certainly be incarcerated if a Soviet citizen. However, in due course, his idiosyncrasies were accepted. He had brought his fire brigade uniform with him and spoke with authority about fire-fighting in the blitz. As a result, he was asked officially to inspect the fire brigades of Moscow, Leningrad and other bombed cities".

CHAPTER 10

"Jack" the Artist and "John B" the Poet

Two of Gavin's most creative friends caricatured him often. For example, there was a contradictory side to Lord Faringdon's character that "Jack" Hastings liked to tease him about. Similarly, John Betjeman who signed his letters "John B" nicknamed Gavin "Gawain" – a reference to an Arthurian knight who undertook seemingly impossible quests.

Gavin always called his schoolboy chum Francis, John, Clarence, Westera, Plantagenet, Hastings "Jack"; styled Viscount Hastings from 1901–39 until Jack became the 16th Earl of Huntingdon after his father died. He and Gavin had been to Eton and Oxford together and then Jack (like Gavin) had rebelled against his family's plans for his future. Jack's father was Lieutenant-Colonel Warner, Francis, John, Plantagenet, Hastings, 15th Earl of Huntingdon. He and his wife the Countess Maud, mainly longed for him to shine on the hunting field to play a traditional role on an Irish estate and to only take his seat in the House of Lords on special occasions. Much against their wishes, Jack had married the bohemian Marchesa Cristina Casati. She was the daughter of Luisa, Casati Stampa di Soncino, a fashionista reputed to have dyed her eyes red with belladonna to match her flame-coloured hair. An artist's muse, she was painted by Augustus John, Giovanni Boldini, Filippo Marinetti, Fortunato Depero, Kees Van Dongen and Giacomo Balla. She was memorably photographed by Man Ray, Edward Weston and Cecil Beaton. Known as one of the most eccentric and nonconformist figures of her era, she declared that she wanted to be remembered as *a living work of art*. The poet and film maker Jean Cocteau claimed that *"her allure was not about beauty but shock value"*. Unsurprisingly, her daughter Cristina had grown up without the usual social constraints. She smoked cigarettes, bobbed her hair, wore short skirts with low necklines, drank cocktails whenever they were available, was generally uninhibited, and held radical political opinions. She encouraged Jack to rebel, and as it was clear that his conventional parents would never accept her, the couple married in secret. Then, to ensure a fresh start, the couple went to live on the remote South Sea Island of Mo'orea (within sight of Tahiti). This was actually the quasi-mythical island of "Bali Hai", and for a while they lived an enchanted life there.

On Mo'orea Jack spent his time painting, writing and playing a ukulele. Cristina was soon pregnant and did her best to become a home-maker. They enjoyed a beach-comber lifestyle and the society of fisher-folk – some of whom claimed to have known Paul Gauguin. They met and entertained occasional well-heeled visitors who arrived on yachts. But they tired of life in a beach house surrounded by mango trees and coconut palms. Dwindling finances and a new-born baby prompted their move to California. Here he met the film star Douglas Fairbanks and fellow ex-patriot Charlie Chaplin, who introduced *"the English Viscount"* to the Marxist muralist Diego Rivera. Jack became his assistant and the couple moved to Mexico where they became part of a circle that included Rivera's wife, the artist Frida Kahlo, and the exiled revolutionary Leon Trotsky. In 1936, soon after the outbreak of the Spanish Civil War the Hastings returned to the UK where fiery Cristina joined Gavin on the Medical Aid for Spain Committee. Jack visited Spain several times on fact-finding trips, but preferred painting to fighting. He worked hard in London and had a couple of exhibitions there. He took up his seat in the House of Lords and made his support of the Republican cause known there.

Jack liked to poke fun at his old friend, as can be seen in the frescoes that Gavin commissioned from him to decorate the arched passageway outside the theatre at Buscot Park. These were painted fitfully between June 1937 and August 1939. By the time they were completed the artist's father had passed away and he had become an earl and his radical wife was being addressed as Lady Cristina, the Countess of Huntingdon. So, notions of social class and privilege cannot be far away in the frescoes at Buscot which show scenes based on real life events there. Above the theatre entrance we can see the 2nd Baron Faringdon sitting down at the head of a table with six guests being served on gilt plates by a butler and three footmen. The irony here is the conspicuous wealth of the socialist and nearby we see Joseph Stalin and Clem Attlee waiting to tee off on a golf course. By the time these were painted Jack had moderated his Marxist views – which were considerably less radical than his wife Cristina's. He had joined the Labour Party and had become Secretary to its leader Clement Attlee.

In another fresco Gavin is shown delivering a speech to an impressive Faringdon Labour Party rally. The joke here is that whilst a Labour rally was held at Faringdon in 1936, attendance was very poor – it would have looked nothing like the grand event Jack painted. And his version is both a celebration of Gavin's endeavours and a tease. For example, Gavin delivers a speech to the faithful from an upturned apple cart, and his fiery oratory frightens two police horses into bucking off their riders. Beside them Gavin's outstretched arm points to a banner reading *"Workers of the World Unite"* – one of the rallying cries from *The Communist Manifesto* (1848) by Karl Marx and Friedrich Engels. Under this banner a handsome young man raises a clenched fist in the anti-fascist salute. He is probably meant to be one of the Basque boy refugees, turning to encourage two grey-haired women – the Vulliamy sisters who brought the Basque boy refugees to Buscot – to join the Labour rally. This consists of soldiers, nurses, sailors, clerics, airmen and workers marching two-by-two. Prominently amongst the leaders is a bearded Sikh in a turban – an Asian Independence leader; and a statuesque woman in tweeds wearing a Tam o' Shanter. This is a caricature of Katherine Marjory Stewart-Murray, the Duchess of Atholl.

Slightly to one side is a roundel similar to where a saint's portrait would appear in a church. In this Jack painted a portrait of a fierce-looking woman wearing owl-like spectacles. This was meant to be Miss Susan Lawrence MP – one of Gavin's most radical political mentors. She was the first woman to be elected onto the Labour Party's National Committee. She wore very thick glasses because she was going blind – but transcribed important socialist texts into Braille before she lost her sight. She travelled to Mexico with Gavin in 1938 after the Spanish Republican from the camps in Perpignan were granted asylum there and Jack's former mentor, Diego Rivera, had welcomed her and Gavin.

Jack's frescoes are filled with anecdotes about the characters who made up that privileged and now vanished world – a world they expected to pass. Indeed, it was a world they wanted to pass. This is evident in the wealth of detail surviving in the luncheon scene that Jack painted. Gavin is shown sitting at the head of a laid table with his butler, Mr Buck, standing placidly behind him. Three footmen dressed in green liveries with brass buttons hover in attendance. According to a memo written by a former footman Mr Little, who appears in the mural on the right, all of Gavin's guests depicted here were titled. They were Gavin's former wife the Hon. Honor Pilkington, his neighbour Lord Berners, The Hon. Wogan Philips, Viscountess Hastings, Jack's sister Lady Anne Cameron; Lady Violet Bonham Carter, and Lady Betjeman. A closer look reveals that the wine glasses are empty and there are no wine bottles on the sideboard for the three footmen to refill the guests' glasses from. The reason for this was that Gavin had reformed since the alcohol-fuelled excesses of the Bright Young Thing era and was now serving his guests only one or two glasses of champagne or wine. No one drank to excess at Buscot Park any longer. Lord Berners' companion Robert Heber-Percy remarked, *"We had to do our drinking before we went to Buscot Park".*

Lady Violet Bonham Carter sits on the lower right-hand corner of the dining table. She was part of Churchill's anti-fascist alliance at the time, and went on to become Chairman of the Liberal Party, and the first woman Governor of the BBC. Lady Violet appears with one hand at her throat as though taken aback. She is looking askance at a gold plate that bears only an apple with a leaf attached. The joke was that she had been a prominent member of the Fabian Society and admired George Bernard Shaw's vegetarianism. Someone had advised that she was a vegetarian as well, which led to her being served an apple when the other guests were given charcuterie. Similarly, Penelope Betjeman never let Gavin forget a meal that she had at Buscot Park. This was when a footman offered her a chop from a salver. Penelope was pregnant and ravenous so she helped herself to two chops and tucked in. Then she looked up to see Gavin eyeing her with nothing on his plate. He had ordered his cook to produce only one chop per person, and rather than order another, he went without. Penelope went on to tease him about this for years afterwards, as a letter from her quoted below shows.

Portraying Gavin as tight-fisted may have been due to another domestic ritual at Buscot. Whilst Gavin happily donated to dozens of left-wing causes and funded a good many destitute refugees, he refused to let his well-heeled guests take advantage of his hospitality. This appears to have been part of the reason for his having installed a telephone exchange in the house. Each bedroom had a telephone extension, and there was even a telephone by the pool. All outgoing phone calls were timed and logged, and before leaving, guests would be presented with a bill. Whilst it was normal for guests in country houses to pay for phone calls by placing some coins on a plate, Gavin was unusual in that he had his housekeeper present itemised bills. Her accounts book reveals that Jack and Cristina made far more phone calls than any other guest. In fact, more than all the other guests combined.

1937:

July 8ᵗʰ Lord Hastings telephone calls £1. 3s. 10d

5th Oct: Lord Hastings phone calls: 10s.

1938

July 12th Lord Hastings phone calls 10s.

August 22nd Lord Hastings Phone calls 10s.

Aug 23rd Lord Hastings Phone calls £1. 10s.

1939

Jan 3rd Lady Hastings Phone calls £1. 14s.
March 31st Lady Hastings for laundry paid £1. 0s. 6d.
May 15th Lady Huntingdon (telephone) 8s.
May 16th Lady Huntingdon (telephone) 8s.
May 22nd Lady Huntingdon (telephone) 8s. 6d.
July 3rd Lady Anne Cameron (Jack's sister) 1s. 6d.
Sept 1st Lord Huntingdon Telephone 15s.
Sept 24th Lord Huntingdon Telephone £3. 3s. od
26th Lady Huntingdon (telephone) 7s.

In modern values, these telephone calls amounted to £700.00 over three years. The Huntingdons might well have claimed that their calls related to political concerns they shared with their host – or that Gavin could afford it – but they paid up.

In recent years some have speculated that Jack's frescoes may have faded because Gavin had skimped on proper materials; used cheaper pigments than Jack would otherwise have employed. However, a letter from another of Diego Rivera's assistants shows this was not the case. Clifford Wright, who had worked with Diego Rivera and Jack in California, came to restore them after WW2. By then Jack was chairman of the Society of Mural Painters and teaching at Camberwell College of Arts, as well as the Central School of Arts & Crafts in London. Clifford Wright sent Jack the following condition report in which he claims to be certain that any problems with the paintings resulted from damp in the walls:

"Much of the colour (including the blue skies & backgrounds)
have flaked off, is just loose powder which falls off at the
slightest touch. I am sure that damp from the inside the walls
was the primary cause of all the trouble. The greens may have
reacted worse to the moisture than some of the other colours,
& the colours put on thickest suffered worse. But there were
areas, even of the green background, where the colour was
fixed as firmly & as perfectly as any colour could be – due in
my opinion to those areas having escaped the water. I think
you were exceedingly unlucky in these frescoes.

I have removed all the green backgrounds. Gavin wants
everything else saved, but apart from repainting the whole
thing, which is out of the question, it will be a difficult &
uncertain business".

Some blamed the deterioration of these frescoes on Jack as he had asked the estate carpenter Mr Darley to mix the plaster and leave it in a barrel ready for his use. If Jack had left the plaster there too long it would have begun to set soon after he spread it before painting his frescoes. This might well have been the reason why the pigments were not fully absorbed. It may be that the plaster used in Britain had more gypsum in it to speed up drying in the damper climate, and this was not what he was used to when making frescoes in Mexico or the USA which have survived intact. But it has to be said that another fresco he made survived well in the Marx Memorial Library.

In spite of their deterioration, much remains to be seen in the frescoes. The quality of the drawing and design shows that they were not just a slap-dash caprice. The artist gave us a slice of social history at Buscot Park with its staff and guests. Black and white photos of the originals show a decorative latticework similar to a Mexican chapel's which has completely disappeared. This made their original appearance similar to the design of a Mexican chapel with a *retablo* where images of saints were reverently hung. On the barrel vault above the main scenes a blazing star, moon and sun were painted

– the same Mexican folk-art motifs that can be seen in some of Rivera's frescoes. The spaces in between these symbols were crossed with writing implements and musical instruments giving the barrel-vault a playful Rococo character. To this Jack added portraits of Gavin's friends in roundels where saints would have appeared if it had been a chapel. Sadly, paint began to fall off soon after they were completed, but in spite of this, Jack and Gavin remained close friends for the rest of their lives.

The future poet laureate John Betjeman met Gavin at Oxford in 1927 and from the early 1930s he called him "Gawain". Betjeman described himself as *"politically agnostic"* and so he could never fully understand Gavin's commitments to the Labour Party, colonial independence, and republican Spain. Betjeman associated these with the challenges that faced *Sir Gawain and the Green Knight*. The eponymous hero of this 14th-century poem is celebrated for his purity, chivalry and bravery. The link between them was made in Betjeman's mind after Gavin became involved with Gandhi and Round Table Conferences on India independence. Shortly before this, Gavin had met John's future wife Penelope in India where her father Field Marshal, Sir Philip Chetwode, was the Commander in Chief of the British Army. Penelope had led a sheltered life and immediately fell in love with Gavin's travelling companion – Robert Byron, and proposed to him in a letter. Robert eluded her with charm and they were to remain life-long friends. She met John Betjeman in England when he was editing Robert Byron's photo-essay about the architect Sir Edwin Lutyens's work in New Delhi. At the time, John claimed to be a Quaker, not something likely to help him appeal to her Brigadier father.

In *Sir Gawain and the Green Knight* the eponymous hero saves King Arthur from a spell cast by the evil enchantress Morgan le Fay. Gawain steps in when King Arthur is challenged to decapitate a magical Green Knight sent to disrupt Christmas celebrations at Camelot. The headless phantom then rises to pick his head up off the floor and command Gawain come and meet him a year later to have his own head chopped off. On the way to fulfil his promise, Gawain is tempted by the beautiful young wife of a nobleman – who throws herself at him three times. But good Gawain's courtly manners help him to resist her fleshy offers. It transpires that this was another test of Gawain's mettle as the young noblewoman was acting under another of Morgan le Fay's spells. And so, Betjeman's nickname Gawain was a tease, touching on Gavin's chastity – possibly his gayness – something which the bisexual Betjeman would have been aware of since their time together in the Bright Young Things. For over 50 years John wrote to "Gawain" every time he wanted Gavin to join in one of his crusades to try and save a portion of Britain's architectural heritage.

A dozen unpublished letters from Sir John Betjeman (he became the Poet Laureate in 1972) survive in the archives of Buscot Park. Four date from WW2 when John was working as the British Press attaché in Ireland, and another came from his wife Penelope, describing their family life in 1942 – the year when their daughter Candida was born. Most of the other letters relate to architectural heritage. These campaigns were seldom as successful as either of them would have liked. In the post-war years they came to think of modernising town planners as almost as destructive as Hitler's Luftwaffe had been. But even though all of these letters were written in anxious times, Betjeman's characteristic humour shines through. Many of the letters were illustrated with his sketches or cartoons, and others written in John's fine calligraphy. There is a spoof political poem, which would have lightened the darkness of Xmas 1944. Theirs was a personal friendship that was not publicly celebrated.

John was apolitical but passionate about architecture. He once commented that he would rather go to church with a woman than sleep with her. In 1937, he and "Gawain" became founder members of The Georgian Group – an offshoot of SPAB; the Society for the Protection of Ancient Buildings, which had been created by William Morris and others in 1877. The Georgian Group campaigned to preserve distinctive 18th-century architecture from destruction. John had begun to see this as vital while he worked at the *Architectural Review* (1930–35). Tactfully, he never complained in print about the destruction of Pomfret Castle in Arlington St., W1 which had been sold to developers shortly after Gavin inherited it. But in his book *Antiquarian Prejudice* (written in 1936 and published the following year by Virginia and Leonard Woolf's Hogarth Press) John complained that *"any scrap of Roman or Medieval building is more highly valued than a whole terrace of 18th century houses"*. He sent a first edition of this to Gavin – and it survived in his library. Later in 1937 their mutual friend Robert Byron wrote a satirical pamphlet published by the Architectural Press called "How We Celebrate The Coronation". This focused on ten sites that had been torn down, or were threatened with destruction. They included Carlton House Terrace, All Hallows Church, Waterloo Bridge, the Adelphi, Sir Joseph Banks's house, and Sir Joshua Reynolds' house. And by the time Byron's pamphlet came out Gavin had engaged the architect Geddes Hyssop to remove all post-Georgian additions to Buscot House in order to restore its original character. Two wings, a front porch and a decorative balustrade below the roof were removed, in spite of their having been designed and added by distinguished Victorian architects. When such things happened elsewhere Betjeman publicly lamented their loss. But if he felt that Buscot's renovation had been too purist – too Palladian – for a country mansion he never mentioned it in print. But a few years later he was one of the founder members of the Victorian Society, which he got Gavin to join and support.

One of the earliest letters from John to Gavin dates from 1939. This was sent after Betjeman was rejected for active war service and found work in the Ministry of Information. Speeches by cabinet ministers were crossing his desk, and he chose to recycle a portion of one of these as if it was his own. This was a subtle way of making it seem absurd as the ideas it contained were totally alien to them and couched in a hackneyed form of political address. Both John and Gavin had probably come to see Sir John Simon as one of the *"Guilty Men"* responsible for the appeasement policy that had led to war. Nevertheless, Simon had become Lord Chancellor in Churchill's coalition cabinet. Betjeman simply lifted a page from one of his speeches and pretended it was a letter by writing *"Dear Gawain"*, at the top and signing *"John Betjeman"* below. Between the two additions the text reads:

> *"I well understand how heavy, under these proposals, will be the weight of Income Tax and Sur-tax which will fall due to be paid next January. Yet it is of vital importance that the proceeds of the tax should reach the Exchequer as soon as possible after that date, I am confident that we can rely on the great army of taxpayers to carry us to success in this part of the field just as we rely confidently on the Armed Forces of the Crown in the grimmer struggle which they have to face."*

This dry humour would have been appreciated by Gavin. It was followed some months later by a wartime Xmas card from John dated 24th December 1940. Again, John chose to recycle some paper that had crossed his desk – this time from the People's Convention. This had been organised by the British Communist Party to rally support from Trades Unions and the Labour Party members. Its aim was to fight for public rights, higher wages, better air-raid precautions and friendship with the USSR. However, some argued that its real intention was to sap the strength of the British war effort. The People's Convention proved to be a damp squib and by 1942 it had ceased to exist. Somehow John got hold of one of its logos, around which he sketched a heroic-looking footballer – converting the People's Convention logo into his team badge. The writing in pencil below reads:

> *"Dear Gavin,*
>
> *Thank you for your card. As I know you want peace not pieces.*
>
> *I send you this with love. Ever, John B. P.T.O."*

The reverse shows his fears for the future. Aeroplanes are dropping bombs on ruined cities and the footballer has been stripped naked to resemble an antique statue which is missing its arms. Behind him a one-legged man rests on crutches in a goalmouth. Sardonically, Betjeman added *"19??"* to this sketch.

Petrified by falling bombs during the blitz, John and Penelope Betjeman moved with their infant son Paul to Ireland, where John was given work as a press attaché. In a letter written in January 1942 from their new home there he wrote with one eye on the Northern Irish Unionists (under Carson) and the other on the Southern Irish separatists, who during the First World War had allied themselves with the Germans. This background seems to have impressed itself on him:

> *"Dear Gawain,*
>
> *I have become very pro-British, Hooray for the Union Jack!*
>
> *I am beginning to think that Ulster started this war. It was Carson's idea. What do you think?*
>
> *The German Press Attaché, my opposite number, is very dim & looks as though he has been dropped by parachute.*
>
> *Have you read a book called The Four Green Fields by George O'Brian (Talbot Press, Dublin 3/6d)? It came out before the war (1936). Do please read it and you will be the only member of the House of Lords who knows about Ireland… I look on you as one of the few people who would see the "issues"…And you might be the only man in the Labour Party on the right lines…I've never been interested in politics before."*

Betjeman went on to mention his pacifist friend's service to the War effort as a volunteer fire-fighter.

"When I was last on – in early December –I took a taxi in
Swindon…the taxi driver said he had driven for you & that
you were a very brave man – that you had gone up to London
firefighting & become a hero in the thick of it."

The taxi driver was correct – Gavin's fire engine log book shows that
in 1941 alone he drove the Faringdon Fire Engine and its team of six
men 121 times.

John's letter from Ireland went on to refer to his wife Penelope and
their son by his nicknames for them:

"Propeller sends her love & so does the Egg & so do I to you
& all our friends. Oh God – to be back in England."

Again, John takes care to sound patriotic. It is significant that all his
letters would have been passed through the Minister of Information.
Its chief was Brendan Bracken, that former Conservative M.P who
was a close friend of his mother's as well as his former next-door
neighbour at North St., Westminster. Later on, it seems that someone
in that office asked John to gather information on Gavin's Labour
Party and TUC connections.

In February 1942 Penelope Betjeman wrote Gavin a letter. This was
the year after they had left England and their daughter Candida was
born. It was also two months after Penelope had called to have tea
with Gavin at Buscot, and so it opened:

"I do not expect you will ever speak to me again after the way
I behaved over the tea. My conscience has been tortured for
several weeks and even months because I have persistently
failed to write and thank-you for it. However, it is not too late
for my heartfelt thanks for your most kind and generous act,
pray do so…. I was deeply touched, especially when I pictured
to myself the noble picture of a pot full of hot muddy water

from your lake being carried up to you in place of early tea
owing to your sacrifice."

Penelope was teasing Gavin over something she never let him forget
– his frugality. But having previously told friends that she preferred
horses to people, she shared softer feelings about her latest baby:

> *"In spite of your theory that no one should no longer bring*
> *children into such a wicked world I have a baby at the bosom*
> *and would like to have a dozen more. I have become very*
> *keen on breeding and am a baby bore and cry out with the*
> *people of Ephesus.*
>
> *'Great is Diana of the Ephesians because she has a hundred*
> *bosoms and can therefore suckle 100 infants at once'.*
>
> *You can't imagine what an agreeable sensation even one is.*
> *Remember that statue in Naples Museum? It is now 10 pm so*
> *I must go and proffer the bosom."*

Diana of the Ephesians was the multi-breasted Greco-Roman fertility
goddess, which as Penelope wrote, they had seen in Naples. It is
interesting to note that the Betjemans had travelled there with Gavin
in spite of the fact that John detested what he called *"abroad"*. Gavin,
on the other hand, loved the continent and most foreign travel. On
that trip to Italy with the Betjemans he had bought a 19th-century
bronze of a life-sized drunken faun copied from a Roman version
in the Naples Museum and had it set up as a fountain in his walled
garden. When Penelope asked why this showed a smiling man
holding a wine-skin leaning backwards John had answered *"Because*
he's pissed".

While Betjeman was stationed in Ireland, he would have been aware
that Gavin, an atheist, had become President of the Friends of the City
Churches. In March 1943 Gavin was quoted in *The Times* pledging
they would rebuild twenty-one London churches which had been

damaged by bombing. After the war twenty-six were restored, but half a dozen had to be abandoned and are today much valued green spaces in the City. This was something they both become deeply involved with and came about unexpectedly after Gavin received the following letter on notepaper from a famous London club:

"Brooks's. St. James St., SW1. 15.12.42.

Dear Lord Faringdon,

A society has been formed, in the City of London, to aim at the repair of Wren's famous churches. The committee of which I am chairman, consisting a number of well-known figures in church and Art circles. The title is 'The Friends of the City Churches' in the same way that cathedrals are 'friends. I would like to mention that the Deans of St. Paul's', Wells, and York are members of the council. The main object of my letter is to as whether you would consent to become President, that is if the idea of churches appeals to you. I am sure the subject offers interest to the public at large but I am not certain that every Bishop deems the churches to be relevant. While it seems that the sites are valuable, they regard the ancient foundations jealously all the plans for regenerating London aim at the preservation of the sites and the towers go further than this and say that in 17 cases rebuilds pertain. Our aims include the repair of the stonework and reroofing. Such things as furnishings and (illegible) can well be left for posterity. Surveys have been made by a competent authority and we have sound reasons for our backing.

If you fall in with the idea you will find willing team of earnest workers. Perhaps you will write to me at Ampthill.

Yours very sincerely,

A.R. Richardson."

Sir Albert Richardson was a leading English architect, teacher and writer about architecture. A Professor of Architecture at UCL, a President of the Royal Academy, editor of *Architects' Journal* and a co-founder with Gavin of the Georgian Group. He lived at 20 Church Street, Ampthill, Bedfordshire, in an 18th-century townhouse in which he refused to install electricity for years, believing that it embodied Georgian standards of living. His sympathy towards Georgian design also helped him in numerous post-war commissions to restore bomb-damaged buildings. Ironically, several of these are now listed buildings regarded as classic milestones of 20th-century design.

"7th Feb 1943.

St. Catherine's College, Cambridge,

Dear Lord Faringdon,

I am sending you a letter which my Council has asked me to write. They were unanimous in accepting your offer and I feel especially grateful to you for consenting to become President. We hope to hold the first meeting in the great Hall of St. Bartholomew's Hospital but this will not take place until late spring or early summer. Do not trouble to answer this letter. We can hand over affairs in a few minutes at the next session of the N.B.R. (National Buildings Record)

With sincere regards.

Yours v. faithfully,

A.R. Richardson."

The National Buildings Record (NBR), was an independent body set up in 1940 *"to meet the dangers of war then threatening many buildings of national importance".* Richardson and Gavin were founder members. Their concern was that whilst works of art could be moved to the relative safety of the countryside, buildings could not be adequately protected. So, they organised the collection of architectural plans, drawings, photographs and other records, and sponsored the extensive photography of buildings at risk from enemy action. Gavin was to raise the N.B.R.'s profile when he spoke in support of the Town and Country Act in the Upper House in 1944. In 1945 the N.B.R. collection had grown to such a size and importance that the Treasury agreed to fund it. After 1947 the NBR had to be informed before any historic building was demolished. All this met with Betjeman's approval, but he would have been especially delighted to know that the N.B.R. collection came to be housed by English Heritage in the former Great Western Railway's Engine House in Swindon. After the collection grew to over twelve million historic photographs, plans, drawings, reports, records and publications covering England's archaeology, architecture, social and local history, it became part of the Royal Commission on the Historical Monuments of England. Tradition was maintained when RCHME's Swindon branch – chaired by Gavin's nephew – was moved to a purpose-built fire-proofed building.

Back in April 1943 John wrote to thank Gavin for tea again. This time the word CONFIDENTIAL was emblazoned in capital letters over the headed notepaper, under which John had crossed out the printed address and written *Dominions Office. Downing Street, SW1.* His return address had changed due to rumours that the IRA had targeted him for assassination, as they felt that he was involved in intelligence work. It emerged after the war that he had been on a hit-list. This may explain his lines:

> *"We hope to be back in September. I handed in my papers…*
> *exhausted by too much war effort and when I get back, I*
> *expect they will put me in a tank to settle my nerves."*

The letter goes on to ask for information about political matters:

> *"I am very anxious to see some T.U.C. people when next I am*

over...
I want your help...fascism is growing here, a kind of Gaelic
speaking Nazism, shamming Catholic. The 100,000 or
however many there are Irish workers must be made T.U.C.
Only about 300,000 are at present."

Betjeman ends the letter by signing his name in Gaelic, which he had been learning along with calligraphy.

Back in England he sent Gavin a spoof poem in a Christmas card. Again, John recycled political material, adapting a grim T.U.C card into an affectionate parody of his friend. The cover is not very seasonal as it shows a stark red and black image of the 1911 General Liverpool General Transport strike. The determined face of a Labour leader appears between a picket line of workers in cloth caps about to be attacked by policemen with guns and truncheons. Below this is printed: No 4: Great Battles of the British Working Class. Liverpool 1911. Handwritten inside is the following:

> *"Here's to Faringdon's Left-Wing Peer*
> *Down with Bourgeoisie, down with Beer*
> *Down with Christmas and down with God*
> *Down with Curtsey, touch'd hat and nod*
> *Down with Greetings, unless they are red*
> *Down with the Church for its damn'd well dead*
> *Up with Progress and up with health*
> *Up with the worker's social wealth*
> *Come Betty Berners join with me*
> *Here's to Buscot till three times three*
> *Come Penelope great the Morn*
> *This is the day that Christ is Bourne*
>
> *Love from*
>
> *John & Penelope"*

As usual, there are in-jokes. Gavin and John Betjeman knew several people called Berners. One *"Betty Berners"* might have been a teasing reference to their friend and neighbour Gerald Hugh Tyrwhitt-Wilson, 14th Baron Berners, whose portrait appears twice in the Buscot Park frescoes. That Berners was co-habiting with a younger man named Robert Heber-Percy. However, *"Betty Berners"* may have been a reference to the wife of Geoffrey Hugh Berners of Little Coxwell Grove. She was a well-known horse breeder, someone friendly with Gavin's mother Lady Violet and John's wife Penelope Betjeman.

The phrase *"Christ is Bourne"* was a witty adaptation of the chorus from the Christmas carol *"Hark the Herald Angel Sings"*. Here Gavin's secretary's surname replaces the word *"born"*. Frank W. Bourne also served as Gavin's poultry farm manager and the Labour Party candidate for the local parliamentary seat. His saint-like portrait appears in a roundel the Buscot Park frescoes painted by Viscount Hastings. Frank had accompanied Gavin to the refugee camps in Perpignan, where Peter Rodd had introduced him as *"Captain Bourne"* in order to *"impress the natives"*. The joke nickname stuck and a few months later Iris Murdoch recorded meeting *"Lord Faringdon's secretary, Captain Bourne"* at Buscot Park. He was relatively unknown in the area until his name appeared in the local newspapers after Gavin proposed him the Labour Party candidate for West Berkshire. Gavin paid all his election expenses to stand for the same seat that his father Harold Greenwood Henderson had held for the Conservative/Unionists before WW1. The colonel had arranged for 27 High Street, Abingdon, to be used as the party headquarters. But when their lease expired in 1938 Gavin refused to renew it. This led to outraged letters in the local papers and a campaign to raise funds resulted in an offer to purchase the building outright. But Gavin refused, explaining that he had already arranged for it to be used by the Labour Party. Elections were suspended during the war and so Frank W. Bourne remained the prospective parliamentary candidate from 1939–1945 when the Conservatives won the seat.

In 1945 *The Times* reported that Gavin chaired a meeting of the Friends of City Churches at Vintners Hall, where John Betjeman was one of the speakers. They were working together at this time to create a list of bombed buildings that could be salvaged. This was the foundation of what we now call the Historic Buildings Register. In the following year Gavin was appointed to the Labour Party's Central Housing Advisory Committee. So, it was entirely in keeping with these shared interests that the next letter from Sir John came on the headed notepaper of the Oxford Preservation Trust, where he was Secretary. Dated 22nd September 1948, the stiff formality of its headed notepaper was lightened by Arts & Crafts style decorations in John's own hand. These include three tall water lilies drawn down the page, curlicues around the text, and the rest in an ornate calligraphic style:

> *"My Dear Gawain*
>
> *'We have had two letters of complaint from people who have been unable to get into Kelmscott Manor House. I have thought of asking the Trustees, some of whom are members of Hebdomadal Council, to authorize me to find out what were the terms of May Morris' will., to which the Manor House was left, I believe to Oxford University. But before taking this step I want to be quite sure that it really is difficult to get into the house, and that the tenants have acted in a way which might be contrary to May Morris' wishes for the future of Kelmscott Manor. You knew her, and, as a neighbour, would you supply me with information?*
>
> *Love and Kisses,*
>
> *JOHN BETJEMAN*
>
> *(Art Letterer & Pewterer)."*

Kelmscott Manor lies four miles as the crow flies from Buscot Park. Some of the farmland on the Buscot Park estate lay across the narrow span of the upper Thames there. Described by William

Morris as *"a haunt of ancient peace"* it was Morris and his family's summer home from 1871 until his death in 1896 (but this was after the departure of his co-tenant Dante Gabriel Rossetti, whose time there was productive but turbulent). Morris' widow Janey continued to rent Kelmscott Manor and stay there with their daughters until she was able to buy it in 1913. The eldest daughter, May, became a famous embroiderer and jeweller, as well as the editor of her father's *Collected Works* in 24 volumes. She also commissioned two houses to be built in the style that he loved in Kelmscott village opposite to where her parents were buried in the churchyard. May had been married, divorced and then lived in Kelmscott Manor with a female companion Miss Lobb until her death in 1939. Betjeman was correct in thinking that Kelmscott Manor with its charming gardens and church-like barns had been left to Oxford University. May Morris' will stipulated that the buildings and their Arts & Crafts contents would be preserved with public access. But a great deal of renovation was necessary to the largely 16th-century structure, and the tenants had denied curious visitors full or instant access. The Hebdomadal Council was the chief executive board of Oxford University. It had insufficient funds to preserve Kelmscott Manor as a living museum and in 1962 passed it on to the Society of Antiquaries. Betjeman and Gavin were to continue to work behind the scenes to create this happy outcome.

For Christmas 1948, the year that the National Health Service was launched, Lord Faringdon was sent a piece of notepaper folded with the words "National Health Greeting Card" written above and below a crown. This unfolded to reveal a sketch of Penelope and a horse's profile on one side, with her dressed as a nurse on the other side holding up a bedpan and a pair of scissors beside the words *"Love for Christmas for you and the Captain from John and Penelope"*. Betjeman appears to have awarded F.W. Bourne the rank of *"Captain"* as an ironic nickname. The title seems to have stuck as others, such as Iris Murdoch, wrote of meeting *"Captain Bourne"* at Buscot Park; and the estate account books list *"150 cigarettes for Captain Francis: 7s 6d"* as well as *"Eggs supplied by F.W. Bourne Esq"*.

The following letter was written in Arts & Crafts style calligraphy with a garbled date in Roman numerals. It appears on Oxford Preservation Trust notepaper, where John was Secretary until 1949.

"XXI.XMLMXLVII

MY DEAR GAWAIN

I THANK YOU WARMLY FOR YOUR MESSAGE
BY TELEPHONE & FOR YOUR LETTER ABOUT
KELMSCOTT. I HAVE NOTIFIED THE UNIVERSITY
CHEST OF THEIR CONTENTS. BY MAY MORRIS'S
WILL THE TENANTS ARE OBLIGED TO SHEW THE
HOUSE TO PERSONS INTERESTED IN MORRIS
& HIS FRIENDS. THE CHEST IS GOING TO TAKE
UP THE MATTER WITH THE TENANTS. IF THE
HOUSE COULD BE OPENED AT STATED HOURS
THAT WOULD SOLVE THE TROUBLE. YOUR
AFFECTIONATE & GRATEFUL OLD CHUM. JOHN B.
ART LETTER & PEWTERER.

The friends collaborated in July 1954 when both *The Times* and *Daily Mail* reported that they were invited to speak at the public enquiry into the planned demolition of The Grange in Fulham. Both were appalled when this historic house near the Thames had been torn down. It had been the home of the writer Samuel Richardson; and then for the family of Sir Edward Burne-Jones. The artist had done many of his most famous paintings in a studio that he had constructed in its garden. A special feature of the place was a narrow gap in the garden wall through which Burne-Jones' large paintings used to be carried out for delivery to galleries. In spite of many protests, the planners approved the developer's proposal to demolish the property and replace the large Victorian house with a block of modern flats.

In 1958 Gavin was delighted to have won a resounding victory in the London County Council elections, gaining the seat of Woolwich

West from the Conservatives with nearly 14,000 votes. In that year Betjeman became a founder member of The Victorian Society, which Gavin soon joined. Soon afterwards, John wrote this letter thanking Gawain for attending a deputation to the Prime Minister, Harold Macmillan.

> *"My dear Gawain,*
>
> *I just wanted to send you very warm thanks indeed from myself and this Society, and I am sure, from all others concerned, for taking part in our Deputation to the Prime Minister on Tuesday.*
>
> *It did seem as though we opened the Prime Minister's eyes to one or two factors of which he had not previously been aware.*
>
> *I wonder what the result will be. With again, many thanks indeed.*

Handwritten below:

> *Penelope is in Spain until Dec 9 & I in Australia till that date. We must save the Rotherhithe houses and the Coal Exchange. Oh God of battles!*
>
> *Yours,*
>
> *John B."*

Gavin retained his place in the Labour Party's shadow cabinet after their disastrous defeat in the 1959 general election. He survived a re-shuffle in 1960 in which Harold Wilson became leader. This was the beginning of an optimistic time for Gavin as soon all the brightest stars in the Labour firmament were coming to stay at Buscot Park to discuss political strategy. Betjeman did not come to join these politically motivated gatherings. But he clearly hoped that Gavin might have more influence over town planners now than before, and his Victorian Society campaigns to save Britain's architectural heritage grew more frequent and important to him:

"4/3/61 The Mead, Wantage, Berks.

My Dear Gawain,

Jolly nice of you to come to Coal Exchange meeting old boy & to speak so eloquently. Its survival to the city is essential. Why not on the river at Hammersmith and so on to the docks?

The Labour Party has been our greatest ally.

Will keep you in touch. Do join the C' Hse if you want to.

Penelope is v well & sunny

Love,

John B

However, Gavin lost his seat in the LCC elections during the following month, and whilst The Victorian Society managed to save one much-loved London landmark – the Albert Bridge – developers were threatening many others, and their list of structures needing to be saved grew steadily longer as a building boom hit British cities.

February 18th 1961; a typed circular with John's handwriting on the top and bottom.

"*Dear Gawain,*

Through the kindness of Antiquaries, a meeting is to be held in their rooms in Burlington House, Piccadilly, on Friday, March 3rd, at 3.00pm. to discuss the future of the Coal Exchange.

*The temporary reprieve given to this notable building by the
Court of Common Council on February 2nd and endorsed
by the Minister of Housing and Local Government in
the following week provides an opportunity for a full and
constructive discussion.*

*We are inviting members of the Corporation of London,
the London County Council, the government departments
concerned, and representatives of societies who might find
use for the building or who are interested in the building on
the grounds of its architectural quality. Provision will be
made for expression of every view, and we are confident that
exchange of opinion and information will be fruitful to all.*

*If you can possibly spare the time to come your attendance
will be invaluable.*

*Sir Mortimer Wheeler has kindly assented to sit as our firm
and fair chairman.*

Yours sincerely,

John Betjeman."

In May 1961 Betjeman visited Buscot in Gavin's absence together
with his daughter Candida as well as the writer Auberon Waugh and
the architectural historian Mark Giroud. Afterwards he wrote:

*"There is a smashing little picture that I had not noticed
before by, I should think Millais in the bedroom full of
Victorian paintings, of a sort of prophet in a desert with a
dark sky and wolf looming enlivened by a vivid white cloud."*

He was partially correct, *The Enemy Sowing Tares* is a biblical scene
inspired by Matthew 13:25 painted by Sir John Everett Millais in 1865,
but it does not show a prophet. It depicts a greedy man sabotaging
his neighbour's fields by sowing weeds while he slept so that his

crops will fail and the miscreant can buy him out. Ironically, this letter mainly concerned the Victorian Society's campaigns to save The London Coal Exchange and Rotherhithe St. The list of campaigners Betjeman gave Gavin here was impressive as they included, Sir Keith Joseph, Tom Driberg, Brian Batsford, Professor Richardson, Tony Armstrong-Jones, and many others. But their efforts were doomed to fail due to mounting pressure for urban development. Betjeman found this very depressing and began to channel his energies into film-making afterwards. They both attended a reception for the Georgian Group at 47 Eaton Square in 1962, but afterwards there were no more letters to Gawain about campaigns to save Britain's architectural heritage.

After the breakdown of his marriage to Penelope, John rented Kelmscott Manor, which made him and Gavin close neighbours. But John said that he couldn't bear being there alone so he sub-let the property. Several of his letters afterwards were sent from 43 Cloth Fair, EC1. This small townhouse in a Georgian terrace faces the 900-year-old St. Bartholomew the Great and became John's home in the City of London from 1954–73. John's last letter to Gawain dates from December 1968, after John had photographed the G.C.R. – Gavin's grandfather's Great Central Railway – parts of which remain in use thanks to Betjeman and a dedicated preservation group. John had been taking photographs of what remained while being filmed for a television programme. A leaflet with some of those pictures survived in Gavin's files. His last letter to his friend mentions Penelope in passing and his beloved Cornwall. The last time they met was in 1983, the year before John passed away:

"My dear Gawain,

Herewith, the honour is mine of photographing G.C.R.

Penelope is abroad till the end of Jan & I am going to Cornwall till then. Back London in Feb and hope to see you then.

Love,

John B."

One charming feature of their friendship is that John sent inscribed copies of most if not all of his books – volumes of poetry as well as architectural studies and guide books to Gavin. These were carefully preserved and can still be found on the Buscot Park library shelves. As he grew older John complained of being bogged down by the correspondence he received each day after being created Poet Laureate – which for him was a blessing and a curse. So, it must have taken a special effort for the 71-year-old to attend a meeting in Gavin's memory held at Chatham House in April 1977, where of course, in deference to Gavin's atheism, there was no mention of any divinity.

CHAPTER 11

The "Phoney War"

The tiny but awesome word *"WAR"* (underlined twice) was scrawled in Gavin's 1939 diary on Friday September 1st – the day the Nazis invaded Poland. The same word appeared a few days later on Sunday 3rd when Britain and France officially declared war on Germany. Gavin's American friend, Mary Louise Breen was in Berlin before the invasion of Poland and wrote to him

> *"I was with a lot of foreign correspondents so it was like*
> *having a box seat at a cyclone where I could see the stage."*

Mary Louise Breen was in Danzig when it fell to the Nazis on 8th September and commented:

> *"Funny thing – the reality that I carried all summer, partly in*
> *my head but mostly in the pit of my stomach, has vanished,*
> *and there is a dreamlike quality about the whole business*
> *that comes from this hinterland's remoteness."*

That feeling of unreality was shared by many and the eight months between the Nazi and Russian invasions of Poland in September 1939 and the fall of France in May 1940 came to be called "The Phoney War". Nancy Mitford, who spent the weekend at Buscot Park between the 29th and 31st August 1939, described her feelings of disquiet with characteristic humour in her novel *Pigeon Pie*:

> *"There was no loud bang, but Mr Chamberlain said on the*

wireless what a bitter blow it had been for him, and then did
his best to relieve the tension by letting off air-raid sirens."

At Buscot Park, preparations for air raids began with a letter from
Captain J.J. College dated 25th August 1939, eight days before the
invasion of Poland, and typed on personal stationery headed *Stallpits,*
Shrivenham, Swindon, with the words "AIR RAID PRECAUTIONS"
in bold capitals.

> *"Dear My Lord,*
>
> *In the event of War, cars will be needed for the distribution of*
> *Equipment from the store in Ferndale St., Faringdon.*
>
> *Please let me know if your car will be available for this*
> *purpose. It would be a help, if it could be accompanied by a*
> *second person, besides the driver.*
>
> *Yours Faithfully,*
>
> *J.J. College. Capt.*
>
> *Transport Officer,*
>
> *Faringdon District."*

During WW2 there was a military supply store in that street and
so it is interesting to see that Captain College was asking for help
with setting it up. Gavin's personal mode of transport in those years
was an elegant Rolls-Royce Phantom II, a cabriolet tourer painted
Faringdon Green – a light shade of green that had been the livery
colour used by the 1st Lord Faringdon for his Great Central Railway.
He also had his grandfather's boxy 1920s Silver Ghost, which had
returned from service as an ambulance in the Spanish Civil War
complete with shrapnel and bullet holes. But the ARP got neither
of these. Instead, he handed over a far more practical vehicle called
"Morris Van WV755". This was a utilitarian vehicle that had been used

to supply his socialist schools and Basque House. Built on a Morris 8 car chassis, the front had that car's distinctive roman-nosed bonnet, but the side windows had been filled in to create a van. There was only a bench seat for the driver and passengers, which left space for cargo that could be loaded and unloaded via double doors at the rear.

There are no records showing that Gavin provided staff to drive the Morris van and help with deliveries as Captain College had asked. However, he did support the ARP by becoming the Staff Officer of the Faringdon Rural District Air Raid Wardens. Four local men (J. Reason, R. Cornley, E.E. Woodward, and W.T. Belcher), who worked and lived on the estate, became wardens with their post in the Eaton Hastings Village Hall. Gavin's contact telephone number was in Buscot House; the wardens shared a telephone in the Eaton Hastings Post Office, part of a dwelling in the cottages that his grandfather had built in 1890. Another indication of preparations for war came a few weeks later when Gavin received a Fuel and Lighting Order notifying him that Buscot Park's coal allowance had been reduced by a third. As roughly a quarter of a mile of Buscot Park's walled garden were under glass the effect of this cut was to stop running the boilers that heated the hothouses that produced his Lordship's peaches, melons, yellow tomatoes and exotic flowers. Heating in the mansion was maintained for the sake of the antique furniture and paintings. One visiting relative wrote to complain that it was so cold that she had to leave early one morning without saying goodbye. But perhaps the real reason was that Gavin had refused to allow her dogs to accompany her into the saloon, sitting and dining rooms. And she found out later that Gavin had asked his staff to make sure that she did not sneak her dogs into her bedroom. She felt it was cruel that they had to spend the night on the kitchen floor.

Gavin's pocket diary records that he spent the week after the declaration of war attending the House of Lords and crisis meetings with the Spanish Medical Aid Committee (SMAC), the British Committee for Refugees from Spain (BCRS), as well as the National Council of Civil Liberties (NCCL). His diary shows that the first part of most weeks during the Phoney War were spent in London, followed by his return to have *"Lunch with Mummy"* on Fridays and to host friends and family at Buscot Park over the weekends before returning to London. He cancelled prior engagements to speak around the country at Labour rallies, and rescheduled meetings with pacifist and refugee groups. In spite of the widespread feeling of betrayal and dread after Stalin signed a non-aggression pact with Hitler, and the invasions by both powers of Britain's ally Poland, Gavin joined a delegation of the Friends of the USSR that met with Clement Attlee, the Labour Party leader, in the first months of the Phoney War. Labour's aim was to seek resolutions to the crisis without resisting Soviet expansion into Poland and Finland, for fear of prompting conflict with Russia. This was a form of appeasement that few could live with and was soon abandoned. It was the beginning of an era when British communists – often the most committed and active in left-wing politics – found their faith in "Uncle Joe" challenged. There was more suspicion of communists and their "fellow travellers" from now on. People were more inclined to support their local interests and less susceptible to internationalist social agendas.

Perhaps this is why, in spite of still being perceived as a "Red Peer", Gavin began to have series of a meetings with the conservative Country Gentleman's Association (CGA). This had been founded in 1893 as a *"society of landowners, land agents, farmers and others interested in the land, numbering many thousands, and residing in all parts of the kingdom"*. Gavin's grandfather and parents had been members, as were many of his neighbours. In the 1930s the CGA published a useful quarterly magazine for farmers and landowners. This provided expert advice on estate management, as well as sales of livestock, timber and produce. It ran a mail-order service for *"all kinds of estate requisites for building, farming, gardening, water supply, fencing, etc"*; and the CGA kept a register of agricultural job vacancies, which Army recruitment had begun to affect. Gavin and the CGA members were concerned that wartime controls of fuel and transport would disrupt the rural economy. In particular, they feared the Government's plans to commandeer land, houses and livestock;

as well as to appoint officials who would decide what they could – and could not grow – on their farms. Gavin had regular meetings with CGA groups in London as well as Faringdon, and was soon to voice their concerns in a series of debates in the Upper House.

Many changes took place in the lives of Gavin's closest friends during the Phoney War. The Hon. Patrick Balfour, for example, had been a gossip columnist at the *Daily Sketch* (he was portrayed in Evelyn Waugh's second novel *Vile Bodies* as "Mr Chatterbox"); and author of *"Society Racket".* Gavin's diary had recorded *"Cocktails with Patrick, London"* often since their time at Oxford and when this old friend came to Buscot Park in the autumn it was after he had just succeeded to his father's title, so he signed the visitors' book as *"Kinross".* He arrived with his stunningly beautiful wife of one year, Angela Culme-Seymour. She had been married previously to Winston Churchill's nephew the artist Johnny Spencer-Churchill. But her second marriage was already *"rocky"* due to Patrick's dislike of Angela's irresistible predilection for casual sex. For example, after meeting a handsome sailor on a train she spent several nights with him in a hotel before returning home. In her defence it could be said that the blackouts, air-raid sirens and threats of paratroopers dropping from the sky made many people feel they should "seize the moment"; or as her friend Daphne, Viscountess Weymouth, quipped, *"We lowered moral standards in order to raise morale".* At Oxford John Betjeman had called Patrick *"a 100 percenter. Meaning totally homosexual".* But his marriage to Angela had changed that until he found himself cuckolded. Patrick joined the RAF and was posted to Cairo, where his knowledge of the Middle East, as well as his facility with languages, earned him the role of Press Councillor and Director of Publicity and eventually First Secretary at the British Embassy. In the meantime, Angela had an extra-marital relationship and gave birth to two sons. This led Patrick to file for divorce in 1942 and the publication five years later of a bitter-sweet novel about their time together called *The Ruthless Innocent*.

Gavin probably found the collapse of Jack and Cristina Hastings' relationship during the Phoney War, more difficult as he continued to regularly see both of them separately. Cristina had always been a free-spirited bohemian and had begun an affair with another old Etonian rebel – the Hon. Wogan Philipps. Wogan had been wounded in the arm by fascist shrapnel while driving an ambulance in Spain, giving him an irresistible romantic appeal to the hot-blooded, half-Italian, Cristina. During this turmoil Jack Huntingdon sought a divorce, but proceedings were drawn out, possibly because the fiercely left-wing Cristina did not want to lose the title Countess of Huntingdonshire, as she continued to write that in Buscot Park's visitors' book, even when the title belonged to Jack's new wife Margaret. Cristina stopped doing that after Wogan succeeded to his father's title and she became the Baroness Milford. Wogan was a competent artist and successful farmer, with the added distinction of being the only communist to sit in the House of Lords and call for its abolition during his maiden speech.

The outbreak of war had an immediate effect on Gavin's most genial and apolitical friend Gerald Berners. Gerald Hugh Tyrwhitt-Wilson, the 14th Baron Berners, was the famously eccentric composer, author and artist, who had been dubbed the "versatile peer" by the press. He had inherited Faringdon House in 1931 and had come to live there with his younger and more extrovert companion, Robert Heber-Percy, who he nicknamed "The Mad Boy". Their home was a magnet for cultured, artistic and amusing characters, many of whom were photographed there by Cecil Beaton. Guests included the Oxford dons David Cecil, A.N. Rouse and Maurice Bowra; artists such as Salvador Dali and Rex Whistler; the writer Nancy Mitford, as well as her sister Diana, who had married the British fascist leader Sir Oswald Mosley. In spite of an age gap of 38 years between Gerald and the bisexual Robert the couple had co-habited happily. But soon after war was declared "The Mad Boy" departed for Arabia to take up an offer of intelligence work in Arabia. Some of Berners' closest friends recalled that he fell into a deep depression. Gavin's diary of 1939 shows that during the first four months of Robert Heber-Percy's absence he arranged to meet with Gerald Berners regularly.

Their first meeting came a few weeks after War was declared on Tuesday 19th Sept, when Gavin wrote: *"Gerald lunch 1.20. William Walton"*. Gavin and Walton had been contemporaries at Christ Church, Oxford, and Gerald had been an inspiration to the young composer. In 1931 Walton dedicated his cantata *Belshazzar's Feast* to Berners. Six years later Walton's *Crown Imperial* march for the coronation of George VI was so popular that he was offered exemption from military service in exchange for composing similar patriotic music. Berners, on the other hand, was best known for his scores for the *Ballets Russes* as well as his avant-garde piano music and his offer to compose as war work was not taken up. The two composers came to Buscot Park for lunch and Gavin returned to London that evening. However, evidence of a somewhat bitchy creative rivalry emerged when William Walton accused Berners of creating a parody of him in a book about an over-ambitious composer called Count Omega. This was a silly thing for Walton to do as attacking Berners was like trying to punish fog. Berners replied that he was thinking of suing Walton for worming his way uninvited into his work of fiction.

On Sunday 15th October, Gerald came to dinner on his own and on the following evening he and Gavin went to the cinema together before having supper afterwards. This was repeated a week later on Monday 21st October: *"Cinema Dine Berners"* and at the end of that week Friday 27th October: *"Cinema. Berners to Dinner"*. One of the films they saw together was the latest Marx Brothers comedy *At the Circus*, which poked fun at those who led countries into war. On Friday December 1st Gerald came to dinner at Buscot Park again; and they had lunch and dinner together on Christmas day, followed by lunch on Boxing Day. As well as these signs of close friendship, the Buscot Park library has first editions of five books he wrote to cheer his friends and himself up during those years. The title page of *Percy Wallington and Mr. Pilger* has an ironic multi-lingual dedication reflecting Gerald's ambivalence about the war:

> *"Gavin, Mit freudichen gross and Mille amities from Gerald.
> November 1941"*

Berners suffered from a depression so deep that friends thought he was suffering a nervous breakdown. Happily, Robert Heber-Percy's career as a spy was short lived and he returned to enlist as an army private in May 1940. Gavin's friend Donald Darling, the MI9 agent, had probably heard of this when he wrote in 1941:

"Are the Berners still with you? Regards if they are."

During the war, Gavin seems to have got along well with his neighbours, especially one with the same initials and surname as Gerald Berners. This was Geoffrey Hugh Berners of Little Coxwell Grove, a major landowner in the area as well as Gavin's "boss" in the ARP Geoffrey Berners and his wife Betty were pillars of the hunting and horse-breeding community, and friendly with Lady Violet as well as Penelope Betjeman. They all came to tea together at Buscot several times in late 1939 and early 1940. Contact with these equestrians may have prompted Gavin to propose a contentious motion in the House of Lords in November 1939:

"To draw the attention of His Majesty's Government to the
ill-considered and inconsiderate commandeering of horses, the
inadequate compensation paid and to the heavy casualties
suffered among the horses so commandeered owing to their
unsuitability for the work and incompetent care of them... I
have been inspired by the sufferings of my neighbours..."

This was strong language for the House of Lords, but Gavin explained that he had

"...found similar cases amongst my neighbours, that can no
longer be maintained...one of my neighbours had a horse
commandeered for which last year she paid £250. For this
she was paid £60. Another of my neighbours was even more
unfortunate. He had two horses commandeered, and was
paid £100 for the pair, after having paid, last year, £300 for
one and £250 for the other. These are the sufferings of private

individuals; but other cases are even more disturbing. One is that of a trainer who had a horse, a thoroughbred, commandeered, which I am informed, not by himself but by those who knew the horse, would be reasonably valued at £1,000. He received £60. Another case is that of a dealer whose stock was decimated by the remount officers. This case and that of the trainer seem to me far more serious than those of private individuals because they represent taking away these particular persons' means of livelihood."

Gavin went on to give detailed case histories of equine misuse and the death of 150 commandeered horses due to mishandling. This received a furious response from Lord Jessel, who had served as Director of Remounts during WW1. Whilst he admitted that mistakes could be made, he cautioned against being misled by *"sentimental ladies"*. Viscount Cobham, the Under Secretary of State for War, claimed that he had investigated the accusations and called them *"utterly unjustified, grossly unjustified"*. However, he then promised to look into the case of £60 being paid for a thoroughbred worth £1,000. He was followed by the Earl of Crawford who condemned Gavin's preamble as *"most offensive"* and expressed his *"emphatic dissent"* to the motion. The only person to speak in Gavin's defence was his parliamentary mentor Lord Snell:

"I think it is the privilege of any noble Lord in this House to move for Papers and to present the best arguments that he has on the best information that he has in support of his case. I resent the censorious attitude adopted by the noble Earl who has just spoken. A noble Lord gets information about this matter and tries to bring it before your Lordships as a matter of public duty. He has to rely upon information that has come to him, and has not all the weight of a Department whose statements we cannot test today. These facts ought not to prevent a Motion so submitted from being received courteously by members of your Lordships' House."

Finally, Earl Stanhope then rose to say that to make charges against *"persons who cannot reply is to set an example which I think ought not to be followed".* And Viscount Cobham, the Under Secretary of State for War, was able to deny the motion being put on this parliamentary technicality.

Six days after the rejection of his motion on the mishandling of requisitioned horses, Gavin met his younger brother Michael for cocktails at the Ritz. This was Lt.-Col. Hon. Michael Thomas Henderson, who had served with the 16th/15th Lancers and was now retired. Their father had been a cavalry officer, to whom the proper care for mounts was sacrosanct. Harold Greenwood Henderson's regiment, the West Berkshire Yeomanry, had trained as dragoons but were dismounted in Egypt before being sent to land as infantry on the Gallipoli peninsula. The survivors were appalled to find how much their chargers had suffered from neglect in their absence. Both Gavin and his brother Michael were worried about the outcome of the debate – but there was nothing further to be done. The brothers must have seen each other regularly during the war years, as Michael became one of the heads of a secret military training centre a few miles from Buscot Park at Coleshill. Here "Auxiliary Units" were trained in clandestine warfare; concealment, camouflage, communications, sabotage and assassination in order to form an underground resistance if Britain was ever successfully invaded.

The winter of 1939 to 1940 was the coldest since 1895. From 27th January to 3rd February most activities came to a halt as the country was lashed by gales and ice and snowstorms, leaving smashed trees, power-lines downed, and 15ft snow drifts in some areas. The Thames froze over and the ice was thick enough to walk over safely for most of its length above London. There were power cuts and transport came to a halt. Many injuries occurred when people ventured onto the icy roads. During this artic period Gavin wrote to Robert Byron,

"31.1.40

My dear Robert,

Yes do propose yourself for any day or days – it wld be really nice to see you. I am rarely away except on Wed. night since I contrive to do most of my business in London on Wed & I hope including two out of 3 working sittings of the House. At present we are without telephone or electricity & the park is a shambles.

It is really heart breaking: not a tree unbroken & the oaks & elms have suffered most. An air raid could not have done more damage.

Do come soon.

Yrs

Gavin."

A few weeks later Gavin wrote to Robert's mother, Margaret, who he had met several times and liked enormously.

"8th February 1940.

Dear Mrs Byron,

Robert has suggested to me that I should write (or rather he suggested that I should telephone) but I expect that you, like ourselves, are without a telephone and with no likelihood of an early reconnection, and ask you about a person called Gorst, who has applied for one of my livings which is now vacant. As he used to live at Savernake, I suppose you will must have known him and will be able to either recommend him or warn me against him

It seems funny to think that the appalling sense of isolation which recent weather has inflicted upon all of us would have

*been quite unnoticed by our grandparents. One wonders once
again whether they were not to be envied.*

Yours,

Gavin"

Wartime measures affecting the British countryside continued to
trouble Gavin. In Feb 1940 he raised questions in the Lords about the
Government's rural housing policy as many farms and cottages had
been commandeered for military use. In February 1940 Gavin pointed
out contradictions where local authorities were being discouraged by
the Ministry of Health from making improvements on the grounds
of lack of supplies while, at the same time, the Government was
offering grants to individuals. Further confusion arose as materials
for agricultural purposes had priority. He was *"convinced that no one
cause – not even low wages – is as responsible for that flow of population
from the land as is the lack of amenities, and, above all, the poor quality
of rural housing."*

He then turned to the growing need for rural housing by urban
evacuees:

> *"I believe, as a result of my own experience, that it will be
> found that the most satisfactory form of such a scheme,
> certainly so far as the children are concerned, is one which
> groups the children in fairly large groups, presumably in
> country houses or in towns…But there is another point
> to which I would draw your Lordships' attention in this
> connection. It is that if, as we all feel, we may within the
> course of the next few months have the bitter experience
> of aerial bombardment, there will be a different kind of
> evacuation, what one may call an involuntary evacuation.
> This evacuation can only be accommodated in the cottages of
> the countryside…"*

He went on to stress that water supplies and sanitation systems must be improved to avoid the spread of disease in the small towns and villages.

In March, *The Times* reported that Gavin acted as the Labour spokesman in a debate on agriculture in the Upper House. The Minister for Food and Agriculture at the time was Robert Hudson, a Conservative, determined to see that farmers and landowners cultivated every acre of soil to help keep the nation from starvation, but Gavin called the measures "*inadequate*". A few weeks afterwards *The Times* reported the sale of his prize-winning Jersey herd. Apparently, this was prompted by Gavin's fear of not having enough staff to tend them or take their produce to market. In early April he returned to the house for another debate on food production and called for more support of the poultry industry, suggesting that maize should be grown as feed so that pullets (hens less than one year old) could be intensively farmed to ensure future supplies. These suggestions came as a result of his experience with the battery chicken farm introduced at Buscot Park five years earlier. Gavin called for more "*backyard growers*", but Ministry officials were focused on delivering higher national quotas in agriculture and forbade growing of chicken feed. The result was shortage of marketable poultry and eggs during the first few years of the war. Later, Buscot Park won several prizes for its eggs. These came from hens fed on maize grown clandestinely by Frank Bourne "*somewhere within Buscot Park*".

Throughout the Phoney War Gavin continued to work on behalf of Spanish refugees languishing in French camps by petitioning for visas to allow such families come to Britain. Sadly, most were to be deported back to fascist Spain, where they were not welcome and did not prosper under the vindictive Franco regime. Sadly, the French government was growing more concerned about the rise of secret communist cells, which they suspected were being organised by some of the refugees. To a certain extent they were right about this, as many of the most resilient and aggressive resistance groups were organised by communist cadres as "*francs tireurs*" (the colloquial

Upper-left: Lady Ankaret Howard was a close friend who leapt social fences when she became Britain's first female barrister. She wore trousers, smoked a pipe, and came to stay with him in India, Buscot and Corsica without her husband Sir William Jackson.

Upper-right: The personable and promiscuous Hon. Peter Rennell Rodd, was nicknamed "Prod" by his wife Nancy Mitford. He inspired Waugh's disreputable character Basil Seal, but did much good rehabilitating refugees from the Spanish Civil War and WW2.

Lower-left: Juan Guidicelli, keeper of Lord Faringdon's house in Corsica, to which he did not return after 1937, but paid the upkeep until his death, leaving Juan a handsome legacy.

LORD FARINGDON poses before a proletarian mural which shows him addressing an outdoor Labor rally. The artist was the Earl of Huntingdon, who is also a Laborite.

BUSCOT PARK is the name of Lord Faringdon's 4,500-acre estate, where his socialist weekend guests are likely to run into white peacocks strutting about the rolling lawns.

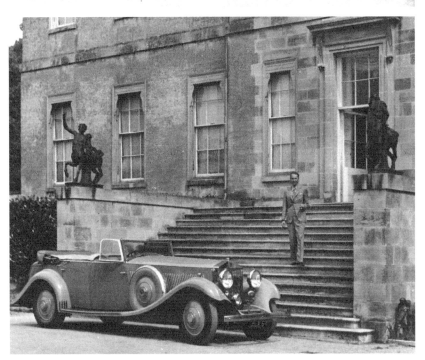

Top: Clipping from *Life* magazine's international edition Feb 1946.
Below: Descending steps at Buscot to his green Rolls-Royce Phantom I1,
the same model and colour as Marlene Dietrich's in Hollywood.

term for assassination squads). Quislings in the Government feared antagonising the Nazi regime in Germany. Hence, Communist Party membership and even its propaganda tracts, became illegal. Thousands of known communists were arrested and detained. Thirty-five communist activists were tried in camera for subversion. *The Times* and other newspapers reported that Gavin was asked to testify on the character and conduct of two of these men known to him, and reported that he said he had seen nothing other than humanitarian actions on their part.

On April 1st 1940 Victor Schiff, the *Daily Herald*'s foreign correspondent reported

> *"Lord Faringdon, treasurer of the British Council for Civil Liberties, gave evidence for the defence at the trial of the 35 Communist ex-deputies here in Paris today. The accused are charged with reforming their banned Party. The appearance of Lord Faringdon created considerable surprise.*
>
> *'I am not a Communist' he said to me later, 'and shall never be, as I am a pacifist…*
>
> *I was asked by counsel to give evidence on the way that Britain treats Communists and other opponents of the war. I had to answer about half a dozen questions put by the defence, none by the prosecution or by the judge.'"*

The *Daily Telegraph, News Chronicle,* and *Birmingham Gazette,* carried the news and pointed out that the number of former deputies being charged had gone up to forty-four. On the 6th April 1940, the *Manchester Guardian* reported:

> *"FRENCH DECREE.*
>
> *Protest by the Council for Civil Liberties.*
>
> *The National Council for Civil Liberties states that it has*

read with dismay the reports that a new French decree
which makes Communist propaganda and the possession of
Communist literature offences punishable with death. The
council, as a non-party body, 'feels that this decree represents
the complete negation of those values for which the present
war is being fought. It is a relapse into the that very form of
savage repression which the Allies have repeatedly announced
is to be ended for ever.

This council urges that every effort should be made to draw
the attention of the French Government to the disastrous
effects of this decree on public opinion in this country, and
to urge that the whole matter be reconsidered and the decree
withdrawn.'

The statement is signed by Henry W. Nevinson, President;
Lord Faringdon, honorary treasurer; and Ronald Kidd,
secretary."

But their fate was sealed when the Nazis invaded and occupied France a few months later in June 1940. Many were sent to concentration camps or forced labour units. Some escaped and crossed the border back into Spain where they formed the backbone of the escape lines and the *Maquis* which was to aid the French Resistance movement. Gavin's friend Donald Darling was involved with these, as we shall see in a later chapter.

On July 19th 1940, with the Battle of Britain raging above the sunny farmlands of southern England, *The Times* and other papers of note reported that Lord Faringdon had been fined *"for failing to plough up land under Defence Regulations on one of his farms"*. Whilst metropolitan papers reported just the bald facts, rural papers went into revealing detail. The fullest account came in the *Swindon Advertiser and Vale of the White Horse Gazette* – a paper that would have been read by most of Gavin's neighbours, some of who were CGA members. The editor devoted 24 column inches of 10pt type to a tale with a depressingly familiar ring. Ministry officials were pursuing quotas officiously in spite of seasonal and geographic variations. There was no defence in law. This was the result of emergency legislation enacted in August 1939, which regulated almost every aspect of everyday life in the country.

"FAILING TO PLOUGH UP LAND

Lord Faringdon Heavily Fined.

Lord Faringdon of Buscot Park, Faringdon, was summoned for failing to comply with a direction made on February 7th, 1940, under Section 62 of the Defence (General) Regulations 1939 made in exercise and by virtue of the Emergency Powers (Defence) Act 1939, directing him to carry out certain works of cultivation, namely ploughing out in respect of certain land in his occupation of the Parish of Buscot and of Great Coxwell respectively. Mr W.B. Franklin defended and entered a plea of 'Guilty'.

Mr A. Richard Ellis, appeared for the prosecution, and outlined the case, stating that the farm in question, Home Farm, had an area of 638 acres, of which 480 were permanent pasture. Defendant was instructed to plough up 144 acres, and he neglected that order. The case was one of no-co-operation and he contended that there had been lost, for the 1940 harvest, about 140 tons of oats worth £14 or £15 per ton."

Going in detail through the correspondence between the Ministry and Gavin's estate manager, Mr Crosland, the prosecutor explained that the issue had begun in September 1939 when representatives of the local Agricultural Committee had visited the farm. In late November they issued a formal order to plough and cultivate 144 acres. This was deemed impossible due to heavy rain, snow and frost throughout December and January. Then in mid-February Ministry officials, in spite of the shortage of tractor contractors throughout the region, insisted the order must be adhered to. Gavin's estate manager, Mr Crosland, informed them that a portion of the farm had been let as previously advised from the traditional date of Lady Day and so he was unable to plough that area. Nevertheless, he was told he had to comply with the original order. He replied that the tenants had a legally binding agreement and their cattle were already on this prime pasture land. The Ministry insisted that the land be ploughed and sown with oats as instructed. Nevertheless, Gavin was fined and his solicitor Mr Franklin reminded the bench that Mr. Crosland had been the agent for Buscot Park estate for 50 years.

"He hoped the Bench realized that in an order of this kind, there was no defence and also no appeal. It was a regulation made for the safety of the country and it had to be put up with. The moment Lord Faringdon got this order, he either had to comply with it or plead 'Guilty' when he was summoned. It seemed to him that the Ministry was not so interested in having the land ploughed as in getting a heavy penalty. The remark that 150 tons of oats was lost was absurd, because if they had been sowed, owing to the bad season there would have been none at all...Mr. Crosland was not the type of man to be obstructive or not helpful, what he did he did in what he considered to be the best interests of the land. He says that when the order was made the Executive Committee knew that the farm scheduled was in the process of being let to a tenant and that in February, it was quite impossible to plough the land, it was like a quagmire. They tried to get tractors but were unable to do so. Mr. Crosland thought that once the firm had taken over the responsibility rested on them. He had been instructed that this land was much better as pasturage. 'What could be sown in May?' he asked. It was quite true, the tractors were offered on April 11th, but the land was then outside his client's control. In his opinion the order should have been made in December instead of February.

The Magistrates considered the case proved and imposed a
fine of £40, plus costs towards the prosecution of £10" (the
equivalent of £2,800 in today's terms).

He suggested that the problem resulted from poor planning as much as the weather. Still, the men from the ministry triumphed. The incident may well have been meant as retaliation to Gavin's claim in the Lords that food production was being mismanaged. He seems to have had a point.

In September 1940 Gavin moved from the comfort of Buscot Park into the roadside lodge, Basque House. This allowed Ancaster House School for Girls to be relocated from Kent to occupy Buscot Park for the duration of the War. The headmistress told her daughter a memorable anecdote about Gavin's handover of his home. Apparently, he placed a large sharp knife in her hands with the instructions that if a fire were ever to break out, she was to use to it cut the canvas of Rembrandt's portrait of Pieter Six out of its frame, and then roll it up and carry it to safety. The Headmistress claimed that he said, *"I can stand losing everything apart from my Rembrandt"*. Sixty girls with fifteen wardens and teachers moved into the house and its lodges. As the school's prospectus put it:

"Ancaster House School, established at Bexhill-on-Sea in
1906 and recognized by the Board of Education as efficient,
has moved temporarily to Buscot Park, Faringdon, the
beautiful home of Lord Faringdon.

It should be an education for the girls to live for a while
in this dignified mansion of fine proportions, studying at
first hand the works of Rembrandt, Van Dyck, Murillo, Sir
Joshua Reynolds, Gainsborough and other great masters, and
learning to appreciate the beauty that is to be found in such
ceilings, mantelpieces and doors as are in Buscot Park.

The Saloon with its Broadway grand piano is used by

the school for music and dancing. On its walls is a chef d'oeuvre of Burne-Jones, the 'Briar Rose' series of paintings, illustrating the story of The Sleeping Beauty. These surrounds should exercise a considerable influence upon the least artistic of girls and be a pure joy to those whose appreciation of beauty is already keenly developed.

The house, built circa 1775, is a product of the exquisitely standardized taste of the 18th century, and the owner set himself in recent years to recover the original style, while installing modern central heating and seventeen bathrooms, one to each large bedroom and another to each dressing room. Two fine Adam-style rooms (without their own beautiful furniture) as well as a delightful library, make spacious classrooms and sitting rooms for the girls. There are schoolrooms in the outbuildings, one of which is used as a laboratory.

In a detached wing, separated from the house by a swimming pool, is a beautifully appointed miniature theatre and a full-sized squash court; while in a corresponding wing at the other end across the courtyard is the Gate House, where most of the Teaching Staff is accommodated".

One former inmate recalled *"We were forbidden to use ink in the house".* This was because Gavin and the headmistress had agreed not to allow ink in case it might spill and stain the 18th-century furniture. So, for all the time the girls were there they only used graphite. Five of them wrote their signatures in pencil under the mantlepiece in a top floor bedroom. These can still be read today as:

S. Armstrong (TOADIE)
A. Stanward (STAN)
B. Hayne (BRAN)
E. Filgate (FILLY),
F. Howard (FANNY)
Spring Term 1943

Photographs of the girls survive and show them playing musical instruments under Murillo's *The Church Triumphant* and Rembrandt's *Portrait of Pieter Six.* Other girls are practising what was called Greek dancing wearing imitation silk shifts (which one former schoolgirl described as *"apricot-coloured and horribly scratchy"*) in the Saloon with Sir Edward Burne -Jones' *Legend of the Briar Rose* on the walls. Girls wearing demure one-piece swimsuits and bathing caps dive into the swimming pool. A photograph of students in the Library shows them reading under Petro da Cortona's *Head of a Woman.* Others show girls outside playing tennis with gusto, cycling along a leafy lane, painting al fresco, collecting butterflies, as well as blissfully rowing on the lake. They appear to have had a good War. Even though some of them must have balked at "Digging for Victory" in the vegetable garden, where they appear wearing land-girl type jodhpurs with tank-top jumpers and turbans.

CHAPTER 12

Fighting Fires and the Home Front

A month after Gavin wrote *"War"* in his 1938 pocket diary he added two words: *"Vauxhall delivered"*. Unlike his other vehicles, this was not purchased to indulge his love of driving as it was a utilitarian van or small truck. BRD 37 was a delivery vehicle, and he was to use it to carry a team of fire-fighters to places where they were needed. How he knew so far in advance that this is what would be required when War came to modern Britain remains unclear. It would seem that someone in Whitehall had a civil defence plan and this was a minuscule part of it. In the next few months, the Vauxhall was converted into Oxfordshire's National Fire Service (NFS) tender No 15. It was garaged in the local town of Faringdon – four miles from Buscot Park. From there it would be driven to support the main fire-fighting crews in Central and Southern England, as well as the Midlands from time to time when that area was hard pressed. Every man in the crew received a postman's blue serge uniform with brass buttons bearing the NFS logo. On the left breast of each man's tunic was a circular red and black badge of wool with NFS 15 in large letters. The crew were volunteers, and had soon nicknamed their driver *"Lordy"*. Evidently, they had a good sense of camaraderie as many kept in touch long after the war.

County Council fire engines of the towns and cities were far larger than this Vauxhall van. They were painted red and were better equipped, with trained crews. Well-equipped tenders with trained crews manned the military fire-fighting vehicles painted "Land Rover green" and nicknamed "Green Goddesses". Then there was a third tier of fire-fighting vehicle – Auxiliary Fire Service (AFS) tenders painted red. These were Ford trucks equipped with water tanks, pumps, hoses and ladders. NFS vehicles, like Faringdon's Vauxhall, were the smallest. They were all painted "battleship grey" as the Royal Navy had paint supplies to spare. In spite of their size, the NHS tenders punched above their weight. They had been meant to provide only local protection, but during the Blitz they were used as a mobile fleet of early response units in bombed towns and cities. This outcome was due to the way that enemy pathfinder aeroplanes scattered incendiaries to create small fires which became beacons for the bombers that followed. Smaller vehicles were better at winding through streets narrowed by bomb craters, fallen rubble and wires, to fight fires caused by these incendiary bombs before their flames could merge to form larger conflagrations. As a result, the NFS tenders gave vital assistance in cities during the bombing Blitz.

Someone in the NFS command may have heard about the 38-year-old 2nd Lord Faringdon's history of driving fast over long distances. Either that, or there was an inspired choice, for Gavin became the dedicated driver. Crews worked a 72-hour-long shift, and it was the driver's responsibility to keep an official logbook. This listed the destination, mileage, fuel and oil consumption involved in each sortie. Only one logbook survived in the Buscot Park archives. This shows that in 1941 alone NFS 15's Vauxhall BRD 37 drove to London 31 times; Oxford 9 times; Reading 5 times; Slough 4 times; as well as to Coventry, Windsor, Bath, Bristol, Beaconsfield, Bracknell, Didcot, Newbury, Wokingham, Maidenhead, Wantage, Witney, High Wycombe, Shrivenham, Bampton, Leamington, Wallingford, Sonning, Wargrave and Henley on other occasions. Gavin was eventually appointed a column officer. He and the Faringdon NFS crew were decorated several times.

Before the war, Winston Churchill had warned of the need to prepare for the devastating effects of incendiary and high-explosive bombs likely to be used in air raids on Britain. The author H.G. Wells had been predicting this for decades. In the 1936 film of Wells' novel *The Shape of Things to Come* waves of bombers appeared with the comment that they would *"always get through"*. That terrifying thought inspired thousands to join the Government's new initiatives The Auxiliary Fire Service (AFS) and the Women's Voluntary Service for Air Raid Precautions (WVSARP).

Volunteers had to be British subjects of good character, mentally and physically fit, between the ages of 20 and 50 on enrolment. Many who Gavin knew volunteered. For example, the poet Stephen Spender (a conscientious objector) joined the AFS; the artist Robert Medley (a pacifist) became an ARP warden; and the author Nancy Rodd (Mitford) became a firewatcher on a Mayfair rooftop. Many of these wartime civil defence roles began as part-time work but developed into full-time commitments. The vast numbers of volunteers and recruits were reflected by increased membership of the Fire Service Union, which rose from 3,000 in 1939 to 70,000 by 1942. Whilst it never got the media attention given to the military, fire service was often front-line work in life-threatening conditions.

At the start of the war women had been kept in administrative roles. By 1943 NFS crews were predominantly women. Gavin joined the Union in 1940 and went on to call in the Upper House for women to have equal pay with men, and, as so many of the male fire-fighters died in action, he called for their widows to have adequate pensions. Two of his former friends, leading lights of the Labour Party's left wing, were on the Fire Service Union committee, Herbert Morrison MP and Ellen Wilkinson MP. But even they were unable to push through Gavin's many requests for better conditions for the fire-fighters and their families. As the war dragged on, Gavin was elected to a key role as Liaison Officer between the heads of the services. He went on to become President of the London Fire Services Association and receive medals from the British, French and Dutch governments.

By 1941 Civil Defence wardens, fire stations, first aid posts and rescue stations ranged across each area of Britain. Whenever an air raid (or "incident" as it was termed) occurred, the warden reported it to the control centre and, if a fire had started, to the fire control centre. The controls ordered out the fire-fighting parties, rescue, ambulance and first aid services. When enemy bombing produced more incidents than local services could handle, a call for reinforcements was sent to the regional headquarters, who passed it on to other areas who might be less heavily attacked. Personnel and appliances were sent from there to "camp" on the fringe of the raided area. There, fire service personnel waited to be sent to where they were needed most. One of the first questions controllers asked about incidents was their size – which was estimated in pumps. Hence, a small incident might be a one-pump fire and a large one a 100-pump fire. As the London Fire Brigade covered 110 square miles and had only 35,000 hydrants, not all of which had the same hose connections, Civil Defence chiefs soon saw the new branches of fire service as a vital component.

NFS 15's logbook indicates that Maidenhead was often a holding point or "camp" outside of Greater London, from which they might be redirected to specific areas such as Paddington. Their destination was often simply listed as "London", and there were times when they attended multiple fires there. A few paintings in the Imperial War Museum show grey painted NFS vehicles such as Gavin's on the way to blazing cities or at work with their hoses and pumps in Parliament Square. The Vauxhall, or "Bedford" as it was often called, was a van that had been adapted for fire service with a bell fitted on its roof and an open back carrying a water tank, hoses, a pump and ladders. These vehicles can be seen working, or on the way to fires, in illustrated wartime booklets and magazines on the fire service.

In September 1940 Gavin had moved into the small lodge on the Buscot Park estate which he called the Basque House. He was still using his Buscot Park notepaper when he wrote to Robert Byron in November 1940, shortly after he had heard the news that a mutual friend David Fyffe had been killed when a bomb had fallen on Sloane Square underground railway station. The ticket hall, escalators and roof over the tracks had all been destroyed. Thirty-seven people died in the initial blast before the flames took more victims when they consumed what was left of the station. David had been with them at Oxford before joining the Burmah-Shell oil company in India. He had travelled with them to visit temples of southern India before they went north to trek into Tibet, without him due to David's work commitments. He was the only one of the group that actually had a job, and he wanted to keep it. Afterwards, David found Robert work in the Mobil Oil advertising department and introduced him to influential people in Persia. David Fyffe had preserved two of Robert's articles on Indian architecture in hard covers with their titles, the author's name and his own in gilt letters on the spine. Gavin had been appointed his executor and presumably this was how these two volumes found their way into Buscot Park's library. Gavin's letter from Basque House to Robert after David's death reflects a sense of loss and perseverance:

"11.11.40.

My dear Robert,

Many thanks for writing. It is very sad about David – I heard of his death when I was in London last week (I was to be his executor and he asked the club for my address) but did not get the news until too late to attend the funeral. I rang Swan Walk & the servant gave me an account of the end – not in itself a bad end: but poor David would certainly have not welcomed any end – so perhaps it was as well that he had known nothing about it. Personally, I can't feel very sorry for anyone who gets out of the world at the moment. But in any case, it is rather for oneself than for the deceased that one is sorry – the loss is one's not his.

Do come down here soon – I have a spare room!

Yours

Gavin."

When war had broken out Robert Byron, bellicose by nature, had tried to enlist but was deemed *"too unfit for active service"*. Lord Beaverbrook, who had always admired the adventurous author's drive and resourcefulness, and had a close relationship with Winston Churchill, managed to pull a few strings on his behalf. The result was that Robert was appointed *"special political correspondent"* for Beaverbrook's patriotic newspaper the *Daily Express*. This meant that by November 1940, when David Fyffe died, Robert had become involved with covert wartime endeavours. This probably explains why it was announced that he had received orders to travel abroad under the guise of a *Times* correspondent. It emerged later that his mission was to make his way to Iran and then report back on oil supplies in Russia, as well as secret sales and supplies of pipes, valves and refinery machinery.

With this objective, Robert boarded the *SS Jonathan Holt* in Liverpool in early 1941. This small one-funnelled carrier went to Glasgow where she joined a convoy headed into the North Atlantic. Off the coast of Iceland, that convoy split into two, as they often did in order to confuse the Germans. Robert was aboard the same freighter, but it had turned around and was now heading south for Gibraltar, from where he planned to make his way via Greece to Persia, and afterwards on into Russia. At 2.00 am on 24th Feb 1941, two days before his 36th birthday, the *SS Jonathan Holt* was torpedoed by a German submarine. The logbook of Kriegsmarine U-97 recorded that it attacked from the surface in a snow-storm and the freighter sank fast. Three days later the lighthouse at Cape Wrath guided in a lifeboat bearing three survivors to Stornoway in the Outer Hebrides. Robert was not among them, nor were 40 crew and ten other passengers.

The power of Robert's personality was such that friends refused to accept that he had died. Rumours circulated that people had glimpsed him walking around some of his old haunts in London. His mother refused to believe that he had been lost at sea until she dreamt that he came to see her to say that he had drowned.

For security reasons, Robert's death was not officially announced until September 1941, and then only briefly in *The Times*. There was no obituary, but a private service was held for him at Westminster Abbey. Here his mourning family was joined by some of his friends. The congregation included Gavin, Lord Beaverbrook, Siegfried Sassoon, Sir Osbert Sitwell, Nancy Mitford, John Betjeman, Harold Acton, Brian Howard and others. Later a stone memorial plaque was erected on the south side of St. Katherine's church in his beloved Savernake Forest.

The war ground on and early in 1941 Sir Winston Churchill, then Prime Minister of the coalition government, praised volunteer fire-fighters as *"heroes with grimy faces"*. This was in order to counteract rumours that some fire-fighters were dodging proper wartime service. This resulted from the large numbers of pacifists and conscientious objectors in their ranks. But by and large, the public view of fire-fighters was that they were courageous and "doing their bit". An example of how much came when Gavin's friend John Betjeman wrote to him.

> *"I took a taxi in Swindon...the taxi driver said he had driven for you & that you were a very brave man – that you had gone up to London firefighting & become a hero in the thick of it".*

By the end of 1941, 22,176 tons of bombs had been dropped on the UK. The total had been greater in 1940 when 32,870 tons of bombs were dropped. The tonnage fell to 1,963 in 1944, and by March 1944 NFS units were being deployed in support of the Allied invasion forces. It was then that Gavin volunteered for the fire service in France and the Netherlands with the NFS column sent to assist the Allies advancing towards Germany – not the British forces, as they had the Army Fire Service (AFS). Gavin's NFS unit was attached to the US Army Ordnance Corps, who were assigned to protect rations, fuel and ammunition dumps, and consisted of black troops under white officers. They gradually moved into Holland, France, Belgium and Luxembourg. By March 1945, an NFS column had crossed over the Rhine into Germany. The American units did not embark on ships headed back to the USA until July 1945. By then, they and their allies had attended over 500 incidents on the continent. Gavin made friends during his time abroad and afterwards received letters from former colleagues in the Netherlands, Belgium and Germany. These offer eyewitness accounts of the complex clean-up and rehabilitation measures undertaken in the wake of the conflict. Many of the countries he passed through were on the point of famine. One of his former Faringdon NFS crew – who spoke several languages – joined the US occupation forces in Germany as an Intelligence Officer and wrote several long letters detailing the conditions in post-war northern Europe.

In July 1940, when the Battle of Britain was raging overhead, Gavin had received a somewhat subversive letter on House of Commons notepaper from the Liberal MP Richard Acland, who went on to found the populist Common Wealth Party with the author J.B. Priestley, Vernon Bartlett MP and Edward G. Hulton, the publisher of *Picture Post* magazine. At the time, these men were seen as the best morale-boosters beside Sir Winston Churchill. But the letter to Gavin shows that they opposed many of the Coalition government's policies and were seeking supporters for an alternative way forward.

> *"Dear Lord Faringdon,*
>
> *I wonder if you would help me with a project which I am told might be of some value, – I cannot tell you the names of the those who give me this advice, but they are qualified to know and you may guess their identity.*
>
> *It is proposed to send the enclosed letter and memorandum to Attlee and his four chief labour colleagues in the cabinet. The purpose of the letter sufficiency appears from its text. I am hoping to get it influentially signed by people outside the labour party.*

I write to ask whether you can advise me as to names and addresses of anyone, – particularly anyone in the world of business and commerce, – who might reasonably be asked to sign it?

Yours sincerely

Richard Acland."

This letter was attached to a four-page memorandum with headings on Peace Aims, Foreign Policy, Refugees, Social Justice, Public Opinion and Industrial Policy showing how their views differed with the Government Policy. For example:

"We appreciate that it must be one aim of our foreign policy to reduce the number of our potential enemies. But we believe it may be more important to increase the number of potential friends....While fully appreciating the need for taking every precaution against potential enemy agents, we must regard the indiscriminate internment of German, Austrians, and Italians whose whole lives had proclaimed hostility to Nazism, as a substantial victory for our opponents...It should be our aim to secure the most active vigorous and open co-operation of all anti-Nazis whatever their nationality... We cannot regard the Government's recent demand for Emergency Powers which will in fact make it possible for emergency courts to imprison anyone without any review. We would have thought the Government already had ample powers to deal promptly with any form of genuine sabotage or treachery..."

Whilst Gavin never joined the Common Wealth Party, the sentiments expressed here echoed many of his own which he had raised in debates within the Upper House. In a 40-minute speech a month later (6th August 1940) he challenged the Government's record on internment and transportation of aliens. Here he was able to detail a number of wrongful arrests of aliens who had been ant-fascists in their countries of origin. Many innocent refugees had been interned, as many were too poor to afford to purchase naturalisation certificates, or did not understand they were needed to permit residency. Gavin claimed that the Government's *"mistakes were not the result of malice"* but due to *"mismanagement and lack of foresight, forethought and consideration."* He then focused on the facts behind a horrific news story that had emerged in the past month:

> *"the sinking of the S.S. Arandora Star...I believe that this tragedy may even have served a useful, if a terrible, purpose, for it may have opened the eyes of those responsible and of members of the public and of His Majesty's Government to the conditions under which internees were being transported".*

This British passenger ship had been transporting 734 interned Italian men, 479 Germans and 86 German prisoners of war to Canada when it was sunk by a German U-boat. Over 800 passengers drowned including the ship's Captain, 12 officers, 42 crew and 37 military guards. Over 200 corpses had washed up on the Irish coast in the past few weeks. Some belonged to men who had fled Nazi persecution and hoped for new homes in Britain. The dead included Italians long domiciled in this country who were being transported to detention camps. Most of these perished as they refused to trust the crew and guards who were organising the evacuation of the stricken ship. Some of the survivors turned out to be Danish and Czech refugees who had been mistakenly interned as suspected Germans due to their surnames. A hero of the evacuation had been *"a good German"*, a former ship's Captain who had fled to England, but he went down with the *S.S. Arandora Star*, as there were too few lifeboats to get everyone off.

Gavin went on to say that he felt it important to acknowledge the deficiencies in the system. For example, Nazis and anti-Nazis had been detained in the same camps so that *"a Jewish girl of sixteen had for many weeks to share a bed with a Nazi girl".* Facing these facts, he felt, would make it less likely that

> *"…such treatment befall innocent people in our country*
> *again. Indeed, a good deal of the trouble probably arises*
> *from ignorance…Much can be excused owing to haste and to*
> *the difficulties of an emergency, but I hope the Government*
> *will be able to assure us to-day that that situation is being*
> *remedied immediately".*

He pointed out that at the moment the whereabouts of most of those interned were still unknown due to the lack of proper records; that letters from concerned parties were taking a minimum of eight weeks to be delivered; and that the fate of 18,000 internees were being handled by only three officials.

> *"Finally, I should like to mention one case, which came to my*
> *notice only this morning. All I received was a small printed*
> *formal card from a man I knew, from an internment camp*
> *near Liverpool. This man is not a German. He is not an*
> *enemy alien. He is a Czecho-Slovakian who was a member*
> *of the Czecho-Slovak Parliament. It is utterly incompre-*
> *hensible to me why we should give as one of our war aims the*
> *liberation of the Czech people, and yet intern a member of the*
> *Czech Parliament. For the internment of this man I can find*
> *no reason whatever. It must be a singularly bitter situation*
> *for him to escape from the secret police and the concentration*
> *camp in his own country and in Germany only to find himself*
> *interned on reaching the soil of his Ally, the country which is*
> *fighting for his national freedom. I do trust that this case at*
> *least may receive very speedy consideration and rectification".*

Gavin went on to provide a house in London as a home for exiled Czech refugees. The receipts show that he paid their utility and phone bills, but there was always someone ready to suspect that such humanitarian acts were following some hidden agenda. For example, in 1936 he had been invited to join the National Council for Civil Liberties (NCCL) – known as Liberty today, This was launched in response to the Government's draconian treatment of hunger marchers, and its avowed aim was to counter "the general and alarming tendency to encroachment on the liberty of the citizen". Its first president was the mild-mannered Cambridge don and novelist E.M. Forster. Other committee members were H.G. Wells, Havelock Ellis, Aldous Huxley, J.B. Priestley, Bertrand Russell, Clement Attlee and Aneurin Bevan.

Gavin was elected Hon. Treasurer of the NCCL and played a subordinate role politically. But in March 1940 his egalitarian principles were scrutinised in the press. This came about after several people he had worked with in the Spanish refugee camps were arrested by a newly elected French government anxious to appease its Nazi neighbours in Germany. Suddenly, being a member of the Communist Party in France became a criminal offence punishable by long-term imprisonment or execution. This resulted in thirty-five people who Gavin considered "former aid-workers" being arrested and taken to Paris where they were to face a military tribunal in camera. Some were to be charged with being in possession of communist literature. Gavin travelled to Paris with a barrister and spent several days testifying in court *to the character of the Communist deputies he met while engaged in humanitarian work for the Spanish Republicans"*. Afterwards, the *Manchester Guardian* reported the following statement by NCCL signed by the executive committee members E.M. Forster, H.G. Wells, J.B. Priestley, Aldous Huxley, and Lord Faringdon:

> *"We are convinced the world cannot be saved from Nazism and the barbarous oppression by the methods of that abhorred regime".*

Three well-known British communists co-signed this statement. They were the barrister D.N. Pritt, the physicist Professor J.B.S. Haldane, and the economist Professor Harold Laski. In the following year

D.N. Pritt was expelled from the Labour Party after defending the Red Army's invasion of Finland. George Orwell approved of this and called him *"perhaps the most effective pro-Soviet publicist in this country"*. Pritt continued to write books and pamphlets and during this period, and published one called *USSR Our Ally* in 1941. That summer Gavin was criticised at the Labour Party Conference by a delegate who claimed that the NCCL was controlled by communists. Gavin gathered a group of delegates to sign a letter refuting this, which was duly submitted to the Labour leadership. Nevertheless, for some in the Labour Party he and the NCCP remained guilty by association and were *" fellow-travellers."*

In truth, Gavin was fighting fires, literally and metaphorically, on many fronts. For example, he was keen to fight prejudice against aliens who might well have something to offer the country in wartime, and keen not to let someone's country of origin prescribe how they should be seen and treated. These concerns guided him in March 1942 when two Conservative peers moved the Enemy Aliens and Propaganda Bill. This sought to reduce the *"alarming"* number of foreigners working in Broadcasting House and proposed that more aggressive forms of propaganda be broadcast by the BBC. One of its proponents, Lord Vansittart, declared that as militaristic German leaders had been supported by the population of that country, so they should all *"be left in no doubt that the end of the conflict would mean dire retribution"*. Lord Elibank agreed enthusiastically, adding that *"Conscientious Objectors were little better than traitors"*. Gavin countered what he called their *"pernicious"* speeches:

> *"I should have thought that the noble Viscount, Lord Elibank, and the noble Lord, Lord Vansittart, when they put down this Motion, would have gone to the B.B.C. to ascertain exactly how much of this much-feared foreign influence there was in fact there. They do not seem to have done so. I myself did so…and as I am informed, there is no direct alien influence on propaganda at the B.B.C. All decisions are taken by Englishmen, and they are counter-checked by Englishmen.*

> *The only work done by Germans is the reading of the news,*
> *which I understand it is impossible for English people to do;*
> *it has to be done at very short notice and in good, intelligible*
> *German."*

Gavin said that they had exaggerated the extent of German influence in the B.B.C. and appeared to think that propaganda should solely consist of threats. He suggested that their proposals would lead to broadcasts as laughable and counter-productive as those by the notorious traitor *"Lord Haw-Haw"*. However, Lord Elibank replied contemptuously:

> *"The noble Lord's speech, in my opinion, was the most*
> *disastrous speech which could be made in this House at this*
> *time when we are fighting for our lives as nation and as an*
> *Empire, and when the enemy is almost at our gate. To uphold*
> *the German Army and the German nation, as the noble*
> *Lord did this afternoon, could be done only by one who is*
> *the greatest protagonist of the conscientious objector in your*
> *Lordships' House. I had differences of opinion with the noble*
> *Lord on a Bill some time ago on that subject. The noble Lord,*
> *who, as I say, is one of the greatest protagonists of the consci-*
> *entious objector in this House, has come here and held forth*
> *in a way which is to the detriment of the whole feeling in this*
> *country and of everyone who is fighting for this country."*

As usual, Lord Strabolgi, intervened to defend Gavin from their vitriolic attacks:

> *"Conscientious objection is the law of the land; it is*
> *recognized by Act of Parliament passed by your Lordships'*
> *House, including the noble Viscount himself... I hope that as*
> *long as Parliament exists in this realm Peers will be found*
> *who, when they are convinced that injustice is being done*
> *even to the most unpopular section of the community, the*
> *conscientious objectors, will have the courage and the honesty*

*to defend them in Parliament and to expose injustices. I
hope that Peers will always be found who will do that."*

Whilst Gavin won some support in the Upper House, and received
letters congratulating him on becoming the *"new Lord Haw-Haw"*,
he had made two more enemies in Parliament. By increments he was
becoming more likely to be opposed and attacked, and yet he seemed
careless by going on to castigate the Government. An example of this
came in February 1942 when *The Times* reported his contribution to
a debate on India:

> *"...he urged the announcement of a definite date when full
> self-government would be accorded and the sending of some
> person to negotiate with the Indian leaders....without the
> frequent choppings and changes that seem to indicate frivolity
> on the part of the government."*

Ministers in the wartime coalition government – many from the
Labour Party – resented the charge of *"frivolity"*. Later that year they
felt aggrieved when Gavin had accused them of a massive *"failure
of responsibility"* following the Japanese occupation of Burma, when
approximately a million people had died. Gavin's claim that this
was largely due to poor organisation seemed unfair to them. Since
then, further evidence of famine in India during WW2 have led to
accusations that Churchill had turned a blind eye to the crisis. But
the wartime coalition Government's infrastructure in the Empire was
newly patched together and stretched thin. Then natural disasters
had undermined everyone's best efforts as widespread flooding in
the sub-continent was followed by famine, due to poor communications and wartime shortages. Many in Britain thought these tragic
circumstances were beyond anyone's control. But Gavin took the
anti-colonialist's outlook, and saw the extent of the devastation as the
result of historic neglect and centralist policies.

Then, happily, he took on a more positive role amidst the destruction
on the home front. His experience as a fire-fighter gave him detailed

knowledge of the devastation caused by Nazi bombing raids, and he was asked to become President of the Friends of City Churches.

Whilst all this was going on, Gavin's interest in art and of finding ways to raise cash for the impoverished Spanish refugees continued unabated, as a letter from a friend shows. Sir Philip Hendy had begun his career as Assistant Keeper and lecturer at The Wallace Collection, London (where Gavin was to become a Trustee) in spite of having no training in art history. His entries for the *Burlington Magazine* so impressed the American philanthropist and patron of the arts, Isabella Stewart Gardner, that she funded a three-year study-stay in Italy. Hendy compiled the catalogue for the Gardner Museum before he went on to become curator of the Boston Museum of Fine Arts in 1930. Hendy returned to Britain and was appointed director of the Leeds City Art Gallery in 1934. During WW2 the threat of bombing led him to evacuate the gallery's works of art to Temple Newsam House. His work was so admired by the Director of the National Gallery, Kenneth Clark, that he appointed Hendy his successor in 1946. Four years before, this is what Hendy wrote to Gavin about trying to sell drawings by Diego Rivera to raise cash for Spanish Republican refugees:

"Temple Newsam, Leeds.

27.V.42.

My dear Gavin,

I got to London in the end. Most of Friday I spent with Calmann, seeing many things including your Riveras in the basement. He's not my Pidgeon (Rivera), but they seem to me fine ones, that would look good on a staircase.

It was nice of you to reappear in my existence. I loved my evening with you in your little house and my vision of your big one. You have indeed done wonders and justice by it. I hope one day I'll see it without schoolgirls or rain. But I hope before then you'll have me for a night again in your cottage. Perhaps one Wednesday early in October?

I shall be in Oxford only twice again this term.

I told Calmann he ought to show you a book he had compiled by an 18th Century English architect. Probably expensive but a most amusing mixture of architectural drawings, etc, superbly got up. Thank you for my bread and butter, dear Gavin, it was a very happy stay.

Yours,

Philip."

The three Diego Rivera drawings never sold and found their hanging place – as Philip Hendy had recommended – on a staircase in Buscot Park.

CHAPTER 13

A Handful of Friends

Gavin had a good many friends, women as well as men, who he outlived, but not all of his close friends fitted together like hand and glove. He mentioned an amusing example of this to his nephew. An embarrassing incident occurred when two dynamic women visited him at the same time. Jane Drew was one of the first women to be widely respected as an architect, and she arrived after Gandhi had praised her designs for social housing around New Delhi. She was sitting on a couch telling Gavin about it when she stopped and turned politely to ask the quiet and frail-looking woman sitting next to her, *"Have you ever been to India?"* The frail woman, Dame Alice Reading, smiled and answered,

> *"Oh yes my dear – I was the Vicereine".*

Dame Alice had been far more than that. She had been appointed Dame Grand Cross of the Order of the British Empire (GBE) in 1920 and Companion of the Order of the Crown of India (CI) in 1921. Her philanthropic work for women included schools, clinics and hospitals and led to her being awarded the Kaiser-i-Hind Medal in gold in 1924. She had returned to England in 1929 to be treated for cancer – that was why the 64-year-old woman looked so frail.

Five of Gavin's male friends deserve special mention. One was French, another a German-Jew, the other three were British: one each from the upper, middle and working classes.

Albert Forcinal

One night in the 1980s Lord and Lady Faringdon were enjoying a meal at a hotel in Moffatt when the owner approached their table. He apologised for disturbing them and asked if it was true that one of the diners was Lord Faringdon. When told that this was so he produced a large bottle of pear brandy with three glasses and said:

> *"I think you might need something to drink. You see, my father told me that your father, Lord Faringdon, freed my father, Albert Forcinal, from a Nazi concentration camp."*

Charles Faringdon explained that his uncle was the former Lord Faringdon – not his father; and that this was the first time he had heard of this. Intrigued, he asked for further information. The man explained that his father had been a socialist member of the French House of Deputies before WW2. He and Gavin Faringdon had met many times during the Spanish Civil War as they were both part of groups supporting the Republican side. After the fascists won, both men had worked to help evacuate refugees from the over-crowded camps in the south of France. After France fell to the Nazis, the man's father Albert Forcinal, had joined the French Resistance and gone underground for several years. Then he was captured by the Gestapo and sent to Buchenwald concentration camp. After the camp was liberated by the Allies his father was unable to be repatriated as the S.S. had destroyed his identification papers. This meant that he was "stateless" and had to remain in the camp until someone worked out what could be done with him and hundreds of others in the same position. When his father was interviewed by a British officer, he asked if he might try to get his superiors to contact Lord Faringdon to vouch for him. Then, a few weeks later, Gavin Faringdon arrived and identified him. His father was freed and able to return home. Lord and Lady Faringdon were touched by the tale and suspected that the hotel owner man could have added more; but he was anxious not to intrude any further. So, they drank some glasses of pear brandy and parted company with good wishes.

Then in 2014, a strange envelope with a letter inside was discovered in Gavin's papers. This had been posted during WW2, and rubber-stamps showed that it had passed through several censors. The sender's surname was Forcinal, and that surname popped up elsewhere in Gavin's papers. For example, there was a *passe-partout* (a document which translates as "free to pass everywhere") signed by Albert Forcinal. Clearly, he had personally authorised Lord Faringdon a free passage wherever he wished to visit *"for humanitarian purposes"* in 1939 at the end of the Spanish Civil War. Albert Forcinal was then the longest serving member of the French House of Deputies. He had won some of his country's highest honours during WW1; and he was to win even higher honours after WW2.

Albert and Gavin's friendship began in 1936 when they met in Barcelona after Gavin had driven his Rolls-Royce there to serve as a Republican ambulance. Forcinal had become a pacifist and been elected Mayor of Gisors (near Paris) three times after WWI. In 1935 he had joined the Socialist Party and became secretary of the French Chamber of Deputies. Like Gavin, he had supported the Republican side during the Spanish Civil War. Albert had urged his government to block recognition of General Franco's fascist regime. Gavin and Albert met many times since 1936. After the fall of Valencia in May 1939, Albert had arranged for a French warship to break the fascist naval blockade and help Gavin evacuate several hundred refugees and their families. Albert accompanied them by sea to Marseilles, where he met up with Gavin. Albert had authorised a *passe-partout* for Gavin, Peter Rodd, and Sir George Young – a Quaker from Scotland; as well as Donald Darling (an undercover British Intelligence agent working for the secretive "Z" force). They all operated together in the over-stocked and increasingly fetid refugee camps at Perpignan and Aigues Mortes.

According to a report sent by Donald Darling to his controller Claude Danzig in London, Albert Forcinal was the man in charge of *Le Comité de Placement Rural pour les Réfugi*. Darling described Forcinal as the man who

> *"organizes a network of support that encompasses all France*
> *and which all the authorities respect. It covers care for the*
> *sick, obtaining documentation, provisions for the concen-*
> *tration camps, visas for England and elsewhere; tickets*
> *for train and buses to enable movements to other regions*
> *of France, and the payment for passage abroad to other*
> *countries."*

In the following year Albert Forcinal risked life and limb by publicly refusing to vote Marshal Pétain into power as prime minister after the aged general signed an armistice agreeing:

> *"that the French Government will forbid its citizens to fight*
> *against Germany in the service of States with which the*
> *German Reich is still at war. That all French citizens who*
> *violate this are to be treated by German troops as insurgents."*

After publicly castigating Pétain as a traitor, Albert went into hiding and joined the Resistance. He was fifty-four years old and had managed to survive in hiding for two years when he wrote optimistically to Gavin from the "Free Zone" (unoccupied by German Troops but under Pétain's Vichy Government control) on 15th Oct 1942. Anyone examining it would have noticed that the stamp bearing an image of Marshall Pétain was stuck on upside-down – a gesture of disrespect. British censors' stamps show that it had been examined and not passed until two months later. His letter read:

> *"Having arrived in the zone they call "Free" it gives me great*
> *pleasure to send my best regards and high hopes that I will*
> *see you before long. This hope grows larger daily with the*
> *certainty that the real nature of these two zones will become*
> *apparent in the News over the next few weeks. I cannot be*
> *more precise about this due to censorship. What joy will*
> *be ours when our freedom has been resuscitated after its*
> *drowning!! If you have the chance, give my fondest regards*
> *to Sir George Young. In great friendship, I ask you my dear*
> *Lord, to speak out for the hopes we hold dear.*

*With waving hands and warmest regards, I hope that you
will reply with a few prudent words to this address: Monsieur
Senotier Pichot in Brinay, Cher. This man doesn't know me
but a friend will bring the messages."*

Brinay was a farming commune in a largely forested area of central
France within the Free Zone. Situated by the banks of the river Cher,
its pre-war population of 400 grew rapidly during the war years
as it became a haven for the Resistance fighters, escaped P.O.W.s,
downed allied pilots, as well as Gypsies and Jews hoping to dodge
Nazi persecution. However, all these newcomers were rounded up
after the Nazis abolished the "Free Zone" in 1943. Albert and his
wife were arrested in Paris where they moved to try to get French
youths to join the underground. He was arrested five months after
writing this letter. As a *Résistant* he was not entitled to protection
under the Geneva Convention as the French Government had signed
the Armistice in which they had promised to stop fighting. Albert
was sent to the notorious Gestapo prison of Fresnes, which had been
created for captured members of the French Resistance as well as
British SOE agents. Prisoners here were denied basic human rights,
held in harsh conditions, interrogated, and some were tortured
to death. After three months at Fresnes, Albert was deported to
Buchenwald, where he joined the throng of 25,000 French political
prisoners.

In the latter part of Forcinal's letter he asked Gavin to write to him
care of Monsieur Senotier Pichot and gave his address in a village
in the department of Cher in the centre region of France. Three
months after Forcinal's arrest a father and son named Léonce and
Gérard Pichot – members of *"Organisation Civile et Militaire"* (CMO)
network – were arrested at night by the Gestapo and Feldgendarmes
while gathering boxes dropped by parachute on a field near their
farm. The phrase "Monsieur Senotier" was code for underground
operatives. The boxes that were parachuted contained weapons sent
from London to equip resistance fighters. It was not the first time
Léonce and Gérard Pichot had collected and distributed such boxes.

The resistance had dubbed this the *"Pichot path"*. Father and son Pichot were sent to a prison in Poitiers, where they were interrogated and beaten before being sent to Buchenwald. There, like Albert Forcinal, they survived for almost a year as slave labourers until they were all liberated by the Allies.

On April 11th 1945 an advancing corps of American troops found Buchenwald camp, which no one had warned them lay on their path. The Americans soldiers were deeply shocked by what they saw and reported that

> *"The German guards had packed up and moved out about a*
> *few hours before leaving the crematorium going full blast and*
> *the chimney belching out black smoke."*

One of the first British servicemen to arrive was a special liaison officer Richard Crossman who had been assigned to work with this American advance unit. As luck would have it, in 1934, Crossman had been the leader of the Labour Party group on Oxford City Council's Labour Group. He was a socialist and a regular contributor to the left-wing *New Statesman* magazine. Naturally, Dick Crossman knew Gavin Henderson, and was such a personal friend that he was one of the Labour Cabinet Ministers who spoke at Gavin's funeral in 1977. At the outbreak of WW2, he joined the Political Warfare Executive, where he headed the German Section. He eventually became Assistant Chief of the Psychological Warfare Division of SHAEF (Supreme Headquarters Allied Expeditionary Force) as a special liaison officer, and was to be awarded an OBE for his wartime service. But in April 1945 Dick Crossman described the inmates that he saw at Buchenwald as

> *"pathetic, broken creatures – most of them homeless and*
> *stateless. When one had heard their story through, there*
> *always came the moment when one had to explain that we*
> *could not provide them with visas for England or the States:*
> *they must return to a Displaced Persons' Centre and wait."*

More British people who knew Gavin arrived a week after he did in a Parliamentary delegation. That included Lord Stanhope, Lord Addison (who Gavin had helped get elected in Swindon by ferrying voters to the polls in his Rolls -Royce) and Tom Driberg (a friend and contemporary at Christ Church, Oxford). Stanhope's speech in Hansard described what they saw in graphic detail. Here is a brief extract:

> *"Much the most painful thing that I saw was the condition of those who were still alive. The corpses we saw were merely skeletons covered with skin. They did not look like human beings. But living people who were lying on mattresses, and being carefully tended by the United States' medical authorities, had thighs that were not so thick as my wrist... At the time when the United States Army reached the camp, deaths were taking place at the rate of a hundred a day."*

Besides being an S.S. "Death Camp" Buchenwald had a factory where slave labourers – many of whom were captured French Resistance – had been forced to assemble V2 rockets. The R.A.F. had bombed this twice before the Americans arrived, and Dick Crossman had been sent to de-brief the survivors, amongst those he met and interviewed was Albert Forcinal. Somehow, Dick managed to contact Gavin, who was then serving with a fire brigade unit in Holland. Soon after Gavin was notified, he drove the 250 miles to Buchenwald. Albert had survived in Buchenwald for 11 months. Photographs of him in his in black-and-white, striped concentration camp uniform show that he looked like *"a walking skeleton"*. He weighed only 40 kilos. Apparently, his face was barely recognisable – but Gavin looked into his eyes and promptly identified his old comrade-in-arms.

Albert was repatriated in May 1945 on a special flight. In Gisors he discovered that his wife had been captured by the Gestapo and sent to Ravensbrück concentration camp for women. Shortly after his return to Gisors, Albert was made a Commander of the Legion of

Honour for the role he had paid in helping to organise the Resistance. A year later, having regained some of his former strength, he played a key role in the creation of the National Federation of Deportees, Internees, and Patriots, which assisted those who had been made stateless during WW2. In 1947 he was made Secretary of State for War Veterans and Victims of War. However, when Gavin wrote to the Home Office in the late 1940s asking if his daughter might come to England to find work, she was refused a work permit. Presumably, her father's socialist past was seen as a threat in cold war Britain. Today a street in Gisors bears his name.

The National Library of France records Albert Forcinal as follows:

> "A Councilman of Gisors (1925) – and member of the Eure
> (1928-1942, 1945-1955). After the fall of France he refused to
> grant constitutional powers to Pétain on 11th June 1940 and at
> the start of the occupation, launched himself with a 'careless
> temerity' into the resistance movement. Throwing caution
> to the wind, he set up meeting points around the Gare St.
> Lazaire in Paris at the Hotel Terminus and the Fox-Bar in
> the Rue Amsterdam, where he encountered young Frenchmen
> on their way to forced service in Germany and persuaded
> them not to go, but to join the maquisards. Forcinal's covert
> activities passed unnoticed until he was arrested by the
> Gestapo on May 11th 1943 (his 56th birthday) in the Fox Bar
> and transported to Fresnes Prison. After interrogation under
> torture he was transported in a cattle truck to Buchenwald
> over four days during which many perished from cold, hunger
> and for lack of water after the first day. In Buchenwald
> Albert joined its clandestine political committee, and many
> prisoners testified to his courage in helping them to survive.
> After they were freed he returned to Gisors in May 1945
> and helped create the National Federation of deportees and
> interned by the resistance. In 1947, he became Secretary of
> State for veterans and victims of war. Albert Forcinal died on
> November 1, 1976."

"Prod"

Readers of biographies of Nancy Mitford may well have a preconceived idea of her husband the Hon. Peter Rennell Rodd (1904–68). He is often portrayed as a handsome, virile, philanderer; a self-centred wild-child who never grew up. However, another side emerges in his letters to Gavin. Here he reveals a lively mind mingled with a robust sense of humour and a rebellious attitude to authority. The latter was possibly the bedrock of a friendship that lasted for half a century. They met at Oxford ten years before Peter married Nancy. What also emerges from his letters to Gavin shows that it is fair to say that Peter made a far better friend than husband.

Peter had what used to be called "a good war". After becoming a lieutenant in the Welsh Guards, he rose rapidly to the rank of Lt. Colonel due to the heavy casualties sustained by his regiment in Europe and North Africa. He soon proved useful due to his experience of dealing with displaced persons in France at the end of the Spanish Civil War, his facility with languages, and knowledge of the furthest flung corners of the British Empire. He served his country well, but sometimes in idiosyncratic style – towards the end of hostilities he was said by Nancy to have commandeered a boat (on which he flew his own flag) and swept through Italian ports seizing Axis petrol supplies on his own initiative. This piratical episode may be true but remains uncorroborated. People, especially his ex-wife, liked to report such scurrilous tales. In fact, in a letter to Evelyn Waugh she admitted that they had both made good money by writing about his escapades.

Peter was the second son of Sir Rennell Rodd (later Baron Rennell) the British Ambassador to Italy during WW1, who later served as a delegate to the League of Nations and as a Unionist MP. Sir Rennell had been so popular in Italy that the Government had presented him with a beautiful villa and property near Naples. Peter was a precocious youth, a brilliant linguist, and gained a coveted place at Balliol College. According his Oxford contemporary Harold Acton, he possessed *"boundless promise"* and *"abundant qualifications for success in any profession he deigned to choose"*. But Acton also found him *"pompous and pretentious…a bore…frequently spilling out all he knew on a subject without getting to the point"*. The Mitford sisters nicknamed Peter *"the old Tollgater"* after he lectured their father Lord Redesdale for two hours non-stop on that antiquated system.

Handsome, raffish, and with an aura of adventurousness, Peter made many female conquests. In July 1933, a month after Nancy Mitford ended her five-year-long on-off engagement with her brother's gay friend Hamish St. Clair-Erskine, she received a facetious proposal of marriage from an inebriated Peter at a party. He freely admitted that he had proposed to several other women there that evening and was pleased but astonished to find that she accepted him. In fact, he wrote her a note the next day to check that she hadn't changed her mind. The 29-year-old Nancy (who referred to herself as a virgin in letters to her sisters) had accepted him, and was happy to report to her sisters that Peter was *"extremely heterosexual"*. Nancy's nickname for Peter Rodd became *"Prod"*. At first this reflected his virility, later on that and his promiscuity. Nancy longed for children. The eccentric Welsh poet Evan Morgan, Lord Tredegar, must have heard of this and sent Gavin this unkind doggerel about the couple:

> *"To her husband remarked Mrs Rodd*
> *It really is increasingly odd*
> *That in spite of that feat*
> *During last Holy week*
> *There is no sign of a pea in my pod"*

In the summer of 1938 Nancy was pregnant and hoping for a girl. But she confessed in a letter to Robert Byron, *"2 Peter Rodds in 1 house is unthinkable"*. Sadly, she miscarried, by which time Peter had begun an affair with her cousin Adelaide Lubbock. That was to last for 12 years and Peter referred to her as *"almost a second wife"*. In spite of his indifference to her feelings, Peter devoted himself to helping refugees in Perpignan. Like Christian, the doctrinaire communist character she based on him in her novel *The Pursuit of Love*, Peter was selfless when it came to helping the masses. She arrived to find that he was having an affair with another aid-worker. He largely ignored her but nevertheless, she admired his efforts and wrote to her mother:

> *"Peter has two helpers, one called Donald Darling is a young*
> *man who owned a travel agency in Barcelona and is now*
> *of course ruined. He only thinks of the refugees although*
> *his own future is as much of a mess as theirs. The other is*
> *Humphrey Hare, a writer who lives in the South of France,*
> *came over to see the camps and stayed on. They both, like*
> *Peter, work 14 hours a day and seem done up."*

Nancy did not know that both men had been S.I.S. agents in Spain who continued to serve undercover as humanitarian aid workers. After the outbreak of WW2. Hare joined the Foreign Office and Darling was recruited by M19 and sent to Lisbon, where he helped thousands of British civilians and allied serviceman who had fled France to pass through neutral Portugal and Spain. Donald Darling wrote to Harold Acton that Peter at Perpignan was

> *"...very practical though his language and approach to the*
> *French dignitaries horrified some of the Quakers and the*
> *Duchess of Atholl in particular."*

Writing to Gavin from the Consulate General, Lisbon, 2nd July 1942, Darling referred to Peter's convivial side:

> *"I didn't see Peter Rodd when he was here. Rather a*
> *disappointment as he is very good after a Pernod or two."*

A letter Peter sent to Gavin on 8th August 1940 afterwards typifies Peter's roguish charm. This was handwritten on thick cream paper headed *"Guards Club, Brook Street W.1"*. However, these printed words were crossed through with a line from Peter's pen – for he was not actually staying there. The Guards Club was an elite club in

Mayfair and Peter, who had recently joined the Welsh Guards, would not have been treated as a member until they changed their rules in the mid-1960s. In other words, he had been taken there as a guest and helped himself to some of its headed writing paper. During the war, he appears to have spent much of his leave in London clubs – not letting on to his wife Nancy that he was in the country. For example, Gavin received another letter from him headed *"The Travellers' Club, 106 Pall Mall, W.1"*. However, few of his letters were as amusing as this apparently sincere letter, which contains enough slurred grammar and mis-spellings to suggest that Peter was *"half-cut"* when he wrote it.

"8ᵗʰ August 1940.

My dear Gavin

Do let me know when you are in London; then I will be. I am worried about some of my friends, but not as worried as I am about those who aren't. You seem to be battling and will surely help. If there are any survivors among the belligerents, I hope to be one, and to be back in that business because I know it. There are a lot of diry (sic) and suifical (superficial?) cracks, one can make, but if, as I am determined to do, I fight your war, I wish that you would keep my peace. I haven't ever seriously quarrelled with you about its implications and I think that you are most likely to be the bravest if most incompetent custodian of it.

Peter."

Peter was stationed overseas from 1941. He saw action with the Welsh Guards and proved himself to be a valuable liaison officer. This was due to his knowledge of languages and knowledge of how to repatriate or re-settle displaced persons and refugees. This letter of January 1944 to Gavin regarding his humanitarian work in North Africa shows an impressive grasp of facts and none of the *"Old Tollgater"* style the Mitfords had complained of previously.

"Senia Evacuation Office, Asmania, Eritrea.

My Dear Gavin,

As you probably know, I have been spending the last two years, population shifting, first in Ethiopia and then here. The difficulties of course are greater because of the huge distances and lack of resources and the fact that there is an enemy population which at times had to be held under pretty tight control, though I am bound to say that most of the time they were a pretty docile lot. The main difficulty was keeping them clean as I have never been a believer in the English institutional standard of cleanliness. It makes people unhappy. Apart from the chaps sent to East Africa about 20000 women and children have been sent to Italy and I have another 10000 to ship in a few weeks time. Then I think I shall be finished with this part of the world as the remainder can be allowed to stay here for the time being as there is work and a livelihood for them. One day I think I will have to go to as it is asking for trouble to leave any Italians on this bit of Africa on the Ethiopian border. Who will administer this place then, God knows. It is a pretty beastly country. The absurdly big Italian community existed only by taking in each other's and the army washing. There is no economic basis for it at all. They lived sort of Italian provincial life. The natives practically did not exist for them as they hardly administered them. There must be places like it in India. Buildings and institutions are in the flashy fascist bombastic style but the plumbing does not work. I am not sure where I shall go when I have finished here. I am supposed to be the great authority on population shifting now and have been warned that I shall probably spend the rest of my life taking Greeks back to Greece and Poles to Poland and minority swapping. I don't mind as I

said I like the work even though I am and suppose always
shall be chronically under staffed. The small team I have got
here and trained are good but they will have to be expanded.
I should like to get the Perpignan chaps back. I have just had
an order from the War Office to do a complete report on all
the various evacuation movements we have done here, which
will probably take me about a month to write. I am flying
to Nairobi for a fortnight next week to make notes from the
records there and then I shall try and get down to it. I'll look
up your friend Wolf when I am there. I have not been there
since May 41 when I was on my way through to Addis Ababa
though last year I got a short leave in Cairo where I saw
Patrick (Balfour, the latter word was crossed out) and a lot
of types I know. Patrick was rather gloomy and not liking his
job very much. I don't know where he is now probably in the
West. Materially life is agreeable in Egypt and East Africa.
One can get anything one wants but it is all very expensive.
I wish you would keep your eyes open for likely chaps, and
women, to give me a hand when this war is over. There is
going to be an awful lot to do. ...I think when I get back I
should like to have a crack at a constituency. My side of the
reconstruction business will need representation. But it will be
difficult after the long military sterilization from politics and
two years of exile. Write to me at the address at the top or
better c/o Political Branch, G.H.Q. Middle East Forces.

Yrs

Peter."

By March 1944 Peter had left Eritrea and moved into his family's villa
near Naples. According to his estranged wife Nancy, Peter had no cash
to buy fuel to heat the place so he burnt the furniture to keep warm.
Rather than face a squalid future in these luxurious surroundings,
Peter returned to London and applied for a Labour Party constituency
in the Attlee government. Peter claimed that he was a long-standing

socialist; but again, he stayed at a succession of clubs in St. James'. Perhaps this fact, or his reputation as a *"wild card"*, stood against him and his application to be adopted as a Labour MP was unsuccessful. Then in November 1944 an article he wrote entitled "The Psychology of Refugees" was published in Cyril Connolly's prestigious *Encounter* magazine. Here he described refugees as feckless, lacking initiative, depraved, lawless, unable to reconcile fact with fantasy, unable to accept routine, with a tendency to defy or cheat authority given a chance. Many who knew Peter thought this ironic as it was self-descriptive. In December 1944 he came to stay with Gavin at Buscot Park. Then he returned to Italy where he worked with the UNRRA (United Nations Relief and Rehabilitation Administration).

In 1954 Lord Stanley of Alderley devoted a chapter to him in a book about sailing called *Sea Peace*. Here he claims that he lent Peter his car in France, only to learn that he abandoned it in Paris. When police contacted Peter, he claimed that the vehicle was his and had been stolen by a man calling himself *"Lord Stanley"*. Peter claimed to have been told by friends at Scotland Yard that this *"Lord Stanley"*. was a notorious car-thief wanted in Belgium and the UK. When Evelyn Waugh reviewed the book, he appeared to want to land a knockout blow to Peter's reputation by referring to him as *"an ageing Bulldog Drummond"*, someone who *"rejoiced, always, in the spectacle of women at a disadvantage"* and had a system of *"push, appeasement and blackmail conducted for his own amusement"*. Peter had lawyers threaten to sue. Waugh had to apologise and pay compensation. Alderley's yachting memoir sunk almost without trace as it was not republished. His chapter on Peter said prophetically:

> *"As I write this, Prod has had another moment of prosperity and has bought his own yacht in the Mediterranean. I can only hope that when he loses his ship, as he surely will, she will be insured, that he himself will escape damage."*

Peter had received a bequest from his mother which he spent on that yacht. According to Nancy, he sailed this merrily around the Gulf de

Juan with a Spanish deckhand. There he roamed with the wind, made new sexual conquests; told tall stories; and ate and drank to excess whenever possible. He remained a popular guest with well-heeled friends in the Mediterranean and spent much of his last decade visiting them at their villas in Spain, on the Balearic Islands, the French Cote d'Azur and Italian Riviera.

Eventually, Peter's yacht broke its moorings in a storm and sank (uninsured). He was left homeless. By then years of convivial drinking and casual affairs had taken their toll. *"Feeling seedy"* he went to Malta where Gavin's friend Dom Mintoff had introduced a National Health system. Peter was broke but, as he had spent some time in uniform on the island during WW2, was able to get free hospital treatment. Aged 63, he been suffering for some time from a duodenal ulcer and heart problems. Soon after he got comfortable in hospital he died of an embolism. His brother and sister were at his bedside. He passed away while reading a letter from his former wife Nancy. She had divorced him nine years before and was to pass away five years later. In spite of a long period of separation before their 14 years apart her gravestone was inscribed *"Nancy Mitford, Author and wife of Peter Rodd"*. His elder brother Lord Rennell, who had inherited his father's title, and Peter's brother-in-law Simon Elwes R.A., had been stationed on the island during WW2 and both had been made Knights of Malta. They were able to get him buried an impressive plot in the British Military cemetery at Ta Braxia where his gravestone reads:

"Peter Murray Rennell Rodd b.16 April 1904 d.1968.

Second son of Lord Rennell of Rodd, GCB, GCMG, GCVO.

Lieutenant-Colonel, Welsh Guards, British Army.

2nd Lieutenant 1939 and 1941. Served in the 1939-45 War

In East Africa, North Africa, Sicily, Italy, Normandy."

"Ciggie"

Gavin's close friendship with an army driver in the R.A.S.C. (Royal Army Service Corps) resulted in 10 wartime letters, which he kept. Cyril Hughes (serial number T/140230) was a former chauffeur. Entries in the 1936–7 Buscot Park accounts show that a man of that nickname regularly received expenses for trips to London, Hythe and Folkestone, and on March 4th 1937 an entry appears for *"Cyril for petrol for 2nd Rolls-Royce. £1"*. Cyril William Hughes entered military service in 1942 and became a motorcycle dispatch rider and then a troop carrier driver. Wounded in North Africa he was promoted to Corporal, and went on to serve in Italy. He was an affable person and his letters express an unusual friendship between an aristocratic employer and his employee. For example, a brief undated one sent from an unspecified transit camp reads:

> *"Dear Gavin,*
>
> *Have arrived on shore – glorious trip, good food. For my sins I have been made Entertainments Officer on the way so that I had a busy time. Do not know how long I shall be here…We are not allowed to say much so I will close saying how much I miss you.*
>
> *Ciggie"*

Cyril always signs his letters *"Ciggie"* and Gavin regularly sent him blank airmail stationery to reply with, even though *"Ciggie"* wrote that they were allocated five per month. Still, he says that they were *"scarce or unobtainable"* in the desert posts. Gavin clearly relished the replies and complained to the G.P.O. Headquarters and War Office when lengthy delays took place between replies. He received several written apologies and explanations, and went on to raise the issue of the issue of low morale caused by poor postal service between soldiers and their families in the Upper House. In an early letter, dated February 1943, Ciggie touched on this problem, which was never entirely resolved due to his transfers between units and desert camps:

> "Its ages since I last heard from you. Are you writing? Already I have written you three letters…
>
> Are you still putting out fires? We have plenty every night, big ones. It's a damn fine show. It beats Blackpool in peacetime. However, apart from a little 'flame & bangs' there is little I can say. I have discovered, out here, in 'Africa', a dirty place with bad smells. You must have been in some other part of 'Africa' during your visit. I'm afraid I left England rather in a hurry, not being able to let you know anything. I'm sorry, but it was quite unavoidable."

The nickname *"Ciggie"* seems to have been earned from his smoking habit, and Gavin regularly sent him cigarettes. In one letter dated 11th April 1943 he thanked Gavin for one such present and mentions how he had been wounded in action:

> "During my short stay at the camp, which is in the second line, I received from you, a parcel in which there were tons of cigarettes. I do thank you so much, they were a very useful gift and quite sufficient to last the duration of this campaign…I had a short spell in this latest battle, coming out of the first round with a gun wound in the wrist, which has since been made perfect by our very efficient hospitals… I was delivering a dispatch, on a two-wheeler, when I met my man. He had all the advantage as it takes all one's time to dodge potholes on these bad roads, which makes it doubly difficult to defend oneself, in the circumstances. "

Wartime censorship meant that Ciggie was unable to mention his exact whereabouts – hence all country names were in quotation marks – but he was able to say that large numbers of Axis prisoners were being transferred to Libya and Algeria, and that the Germans were invariably *"well-groomed"* while the British in their Khaki shorts resembled *"an army of boy scouts"*. Ciggie was not politically minded. The most contentious sentence he wrote was the following, which sums up the feelings in the 8th Army at the time:

> *"I am glad to say this is a very different show from 'France',*
> *except for our leadership, which always seems to lag on."*

The context of this letter appears to have been before January 1943, when Montgomery took over from a series of other generals whom Churchill dismissed for being too slow to respond to the British Army breaking the Axis lines at El Alamein in November 1942. Elsewhere *"Ciggie"* mentions that the war in North Africa is going better than in "France", which presumably refers to German and Italian invasion of previously unoccupied Vichy France in November 1942. He subsequently mentions taking *"another long voyage"*, which may refer to the invasion of Sicily or the Italian mainland. Another letter mentions Gavin sending even more cigarettes and his appreciation of his former employer's friendship:

> *"July 28th 1943*
>
> *Gavin my dear,*
>
> *I have just received 1,000 cigarettes from you. How kind you are, it is impossible for me to find words to thank you enough for all you have done for me. My only words are these: I am overjoyed to be a friend of such a special person.*
>
> *Yours as ever,*
>
> *Ciggie."*

One undated and censored letter suggests a close friendship with Gavin as early as 1934 when he had a temporary home in Maidenhead while Buscot Park was being renovated.

"My dear Gavin,

I ask your forgiveness. I hadn't meant to take so long in answering your letter I have had a few days ago. I have completed another long voyage…Having got my feet firmly fixed on 'African-soil' we are now going to be extremely busy. I promise I will write as often as is possible. Please do the same. I am simply long to hear from you. How easy it is going to be to live in England after all these terrible places. I think I have <u>had</u> foreign lands. Well Gavin, I hope that you are fit and well. I am feeling the advantage of feeling the same, at the moment it is much a great asset. Do you go to 'Maidenhead', very often? The thought of that place always brings back memories of marvellous days spent there and the slow drive back to 'London', not be able to decide exactly how we wanted to spend the latter part of the day."

On April 3rd 1944, Ciggie wrote from Italy. This was the first of two letters that month, which evoke a sense of war-weariness. However, he took time to provide a vivid description of a natural disaster he witnessed, which displays a sense of compassion for the local peasants.

"Life has been hectic recently with Vesuvius playing us up. I had a lot to do as I had a stock of U.X. bombs right in the flow of the lava…. The general situation was ghastly – the lava which looked likes huge streams of coke – bursting into flames, was piled anything from 10 to 20ft: high, travelling at one time at about 300 yards per hour. Old substantial buildings such as churches, etc., were gradually surrounded, but modern buildings were crushed and then collapsed. The roads were full of people, looking very harassed, dragging along cows, sheep, pigs. Their personal belongings piled on trucks, carts; handcarts: anything they could get hold of. The land was covered in thick grey dust, choking all the plants, trees and vegetables; spoiling months of work, much money

*and hopes of returns in the spring. The people were wretched,
as when War passes you can return to your land, but when
lava smothers everything, well, there is nothing to go back to.
A.M.G. did a really good job with evacuation and feeding the
people they really proved worthwhile. Apart from all this the
sight was amazing, smoke rising to a tremendous height, and
after a fall of snow during the second or third night, the snow
coloured the smoke to a wonderful rose pink. Later, the smoke
could not rise on account of the damp clouds, and it poured
over everything, and with the horrible dust it was worse than
the desert."*

Ciggie's second letter from Italy, sent 10 days later, shows him prevaricating over Gavin's generous offers of help to get him settled in a new life after the War:

"Dear Gavin,

*I received your letter this morning, which was posted on the
13ᵗʰ of last month. I express to you my profound gratitude, for
the plans you are considering for me, in the future. Decidedly,
I am most interested in all you say, especially when it points
to fact, that all is being done in my interests. I would be a fool
not to try my damdest, concerning any one of your proposals
to get on. I am most delighted with the thought that you take
such great interest in my future. It is such a nice feeling to be
considered so specially, as one out of the many millions. Upon
my word, when this beastly job is finished and done with I
will be only too willing to coincide. In a later correspondence
I will endeavour to explain, more clearly, my views of your
very kind proposals. In the meantime, I have unfortunately
promised to go out for a drink with a pal of mine. Not being
gifted with a lot of pleasure these days, one has to grasp any
given opportunity when it comes. The question of being in
love out here, is certainly one of my greatest improbabilities
since I am as fond of the people out here as a soldier is of*

*doing guard duty on Easter Sunday. Oh no, the place could
never be my happy hunting ground...*

*As life goes on, I feel despite the fact that I have had little
interest in promotion (or anything that may alter my
appearance of driver in my address) it has undoubtedly
taught me to be a little more responsible for myself, and is
gradually chipping off my rough edges. I am not terribly
changed in appearance, but admittedly, do feel older...*

*In your letter of 13/3/44 you suggested a six-month holiday
in the West Indies, which sounds delightful. Nothing could
be more pleasing and satisfying to the brain after a dull
existence...*

*It won't be long now – roll on the finish. And now, I trust my
letter will explain sufficient for the moment, once again, I am
truly thankful. Do accept my apologies for not writing sooner,
the reasons for which I have yet to explain.*

As ever,

Ciggie."

For some reason, Gavin did not receive or keep the promised letter
explaining Ciggie's post-war plans; and Gavin's passports show that
he never travelled to the West Indies shortly after the war. However,
"Ciggie" was a beneficiary of £1,000 (£9,882.50 in today's money) in
Gavin's will.

"Mr Wolff"

In 1968 a letter arrived from the son of a Jewish friend who had
emigrated to Kenya.

"Dear Gavin,

Forgive this typed letter. I have some sad news for you. I should write by hand, but my hand will not obey. Fritz passed away – yesterday evening and although I have to write scores of letters, I want to write to you first. It was through you that Fritz came to Kenya in 1937 when you helped him so generously, and only through your kindness and understanding, that his mother and brother escaped Germany in 1939. So, we all owe our lives to you really, and now two have now gone. Toni my mother died in 1946 and Fritz yesterday. This sounds so dramatic – yet, I must tell you, I shall never forget what you did for us…

Frantz Wolff."

Gavin and Fritz met while they were both serving as stretcher bearers on the Aragonese front in the Spanish Civil War. Fritz Wolff-Auerbach was a German-Jewish pacifist who had come out to assist the International Brigade. The Buscot Park accounts book shows that he was destitute when he arrived in England. He had to be collected from Oxford station where his train fare was paid by "Ciggie", the chauffeur. Mrs Wildman, the housekeeper at Buscot Park, gave Fritz some cash to buy clothing, cigarettes, letter-writing paper and postage stamps. Some of her entries in the cashbook read:

"Given to Mr Wolff-Auerbach £2. 0s.0d. April 12th Mr Wolff's laundry 3rd and 11th 4s. 4½d. Oct: Mr Wolff's ticket balance to Reading to Swindon and 6d tip to porter at Swindon. 5s. 9d. Mr Wolff's luggage Oxford to London £1. 3s. 3d."

Over the following year Mrs Wildman came to refer to him simply as *"Mr Wolff"*.

Fritz had not returned to Germany from Spain as he was certain to be arrested as a dissident. His father and grandfather had been prominent Rabbis in Germany, and soon after the Nazis came to power most of the men in his family had been rounded up and detained in concentration camps. Fritz's brother spent six years in one before being released in 1939. Then he accompanied Fritz's mother abroad when they managed to flee Germany. They had hoped to able to join Fritz in England, and to move together to settle in Palestine, but they were told they would not be allowed into that British protectorate. It was then that Gavin helped Fritz and what was left of the family to settle in Kenya, where they purchased a farm in the remote highlands. It looks like Gavin gave them the money to do this, as in July 1937 a cheque for £75 (£5,142.00 today) was made out for Fritz Wolff-Auerbach.

Gavin probably recommended this move as there was a small but industrious colony of German immigrants in the area, whose presence Gavin's grandfather had supported after WW1 when their holdings had been confiscated. From Kenya, Wolff wrote many letters to Gavin, always taking time to share his news with pathos and humour. His command of English was superb and so he described the beauty of the remote mountainous area evocatively. Fritz seems to have been an easy man to like, and indeed someone who people loved. His life in exile had eventful phases – for example, he was arrested on suspicion of being an "enemy alien" after war was declared. Both Gavin and Jack, the Earl of Huntingdon, wrote to get him released. Fritz eventually married a British colonial woman and they raised a son who made his career in the famous Kenco Coffee company. Gavin sent Fritz money from time to time, but always relatively small sums as presents. Wolff never asked for any financial help. He was proud of the fact that he could source and repair antique furniture in a remote part of Africa, and so live in some style on a colonial hill farm. Interestingly, he made several trips to Palestine where he sold the antiques he had managed to acquire and restore in Kenya.

In their 30 years correspondence, Fritz and Gavin discussed many of the major political changes in colonial Africa. Wolff was able to give Gavin some background information on several topics that interested him. These were humanitarian issues such as discrimination against non-British immigrants to East Africa, and the way that native soldiers were routinely flogged for indiscipline. Fritz claimed that these floggings generally arose after native troops felt it necessary to return to their tribal areas in time to plant or harvest crops. Gavin was to take these matters up with the Colonial Office and mention them in the House of Lords with some successful outcomes. Colonial bureaucrats often queried where he was getting such detailed information. The other aspect of Fritz's letters which is worth noting is how often he asks about events in Spain; and about "Frank" and his hens. This must have been Frank Bourne, Gavin's secretary and poultry farm manager. Wolff was aware that he had accompanied Gavin to the refugee camps in France, and was standing as the Labour candidate for the West Berkshire. He also knew that Gavin had travelled to Mexico.

Here are some extracts from some of Fritz's 24 letters, each redolent of life on a remote African hill-farm during WW2.

"*Feb 1939:*

Herr Hitler has given me breathing time before the family arrives by making it difficult for them to leave. They need to settle all their property before they leaving, i.e. they need a certificate from the Finance Authorities about having paid all taxes, debts, fines, and therefore have to sell out houses, shares and whatnot. Not that they are allowed to take it out, No, it just has to be settled. They have to pay the state 70% of the value of quite useless furniture. All this this takes a lot of time..."

"*March 1939*

Last week for the first time they have been able to give an approximate date of departure, the end of April...

Tell me your news. Is Frank still mothering Jimmy and Josephine, if you still have your priceless stage butler, who will be using the swimming pool and if the al fresco between

*the theatre and the squash court has been finished, how
the terraces in front of the house are, and have you got
an air raid shelter in the kitchen garden? Have you still
got your garconniere in Brixton, and does Frank stand a
chance of becoming an MP after the next election? And still
outstanding, how was Mexico?*

*A lot of things I want to know, and waiting for vos Nouvelles
I am*

Toujours le votre,

Fritz."

"1st June 1939.

*I just have to unburden my soul, and I hope you will accept it
as proof of my friendship that you are the victim of the
unburdening.*

*It is MAMA….it all started this way. The train came in, and
out of the window she passed me her hand-bag, and then
expressed her joy at seeing me again, leaving me all the while
holding her hand-bag…*

*She has aged horribly since I saw her last. Her circumference
is elephantine, she can't sit down in a chair or get out of
one…She can easily digest lobster mayonnaise but is sick for
three days after fried potatoes – so terribly oily! She revels in
fruit which costs 3 bob for a tin but can't digest pineapples
that cost sixpence each – as they are far too sour for her…
She can't live in my house because the floors have been built
on what she calls the funnel principle, all inclined towards
the middle of the room, and can only live in a stone house
with inside sanitation, which I can't afford. She can't fit into
my kitchen but stands in the doorway and gives me constant
advice on how to cut onions, salt, pepper and spice the food.*

Motherly thoughtfulness is unsurpassed. She acts and looks like the Jewish edition of the Grand duchess Olga....

Please tell me your news! I naturally never heard a word about Casado here, and your expedition to Valencia came to my knowledge only after you sent me too short a word about it... Tell me lots more."

"14ᵗʰ *July 1939:*

Drop me a line if you feel like it. You don't say a word about Frank, how is he? Are the weekends at your house as amusing as they used to be? Lots of things I want to know."

"Dec 12ᵗʰ *1940.*

Dear Gavin,

In my last letter I began describing the beauties of rural life... I do not believe that one should wait to put down the impressions collected over the course of years – when by then everything one wants to say will have lost its lost freshness and become routine...I should like to tell you what this part of the world looks like – I seem to have forgotten to say a word about it, taking landscape for granted as everyone in Africa does. Well, the house lies at the foot of the Mt Elgon massive, which gives a rugged silhouette against the evening sky, but it is not all rock – as far as one can discern with the naked eye it had grass and clusters of thorn and other bush trees, which make the greater part of this area look like an orchard gone wild for lack of care. In front of the house are 30 miles of plain, all farmed and looking civilized with little groups of gum trees, dark green patches of coffee fields, and the curved lines the little rivers take. Then on the far horizon, a range of mountains – they are at their best just before the sun rises, or under the full moon. Three uninterrupted lines of hills, growing higher in the distance show different shades of blue...No one lives between here and the Sudan – there are only more mountain peaks, each rising separately above the horizon'.

The farm, or Shamba, as they call it in Swahili, has 5000 acres, which seems an immense amount of land, but naturally not all of it is, even if arable, is broken up. The crops are maize, wheat, barley, coffee, minor quantities of pyrethrum, beans, peas and sundry experiments. The livestock offers a great choice of imported cattle, for crossbreeding purposes, countless pigs bred for the local market. There are even some Danish type pig houses, but as many pigs sleep and propagate out of doors no one knows how many there are on the farm. I estimate, cautiously, 300. The monkeys who live in the thicket on the birds of the river do not come under livestock, but are most pleasant...

Enough! You haven't even acknowledged my marriage. Months ago, and here I am drivelling away. Let me know if your windowpanes are still intact, and what you do, and Frank."

Jimmy

A postcard in Gavin's file of wartime correspondence shows the famous Classical Greek statue of a satyr in the Athens Archaeological Museum. This is a sculpture of a half-man, half-goat, with one hand on his hip and the other raised palm upward. The satyr smiles while looking down at an erect penis that reaches halfway up his chest. The reverse of this postcard reads:

"Dear Pal,
Love and Kisses,
Jimmy. HMS Kelly."

HMS Kelly was a K-Class destroyer of the Royal Navy – the flotilla leader commanded by Lord Louis Mountbatten during the Battle of Crete. It became famous as the inspiration for Noel Coward's film *In Which We Serve*. In April 1941 she was attacked by a Stuka dive-bomber and capsized in around one minute, trapping many of the crew below decks. Survivors reported that the ship's propellers were still turning as the hull floated upside-down for nearly half an hour; and that the Luftwaffe returned to strafe the life rafts. A total of 131 men were lost, and Jimmy appears to have been one of them.

CHAPTER 14

"Conchies", Aliens and Agents

During WW2 Gavin made repeated efforts in the House of Lords to counter prejudice against conscientious objectors and foreign nationals; especially some who had sought to *"do their bit"* in the wars against fascism. One of his most important speeches on human rights was in March 1941 during a debate on charges of ill treatment of conscientious objectors detained in British Military prisons. He passed on detailed allegations of false charges; detention without trial; bread-and-water diets; solitary confinement in cells; forced parades of naked prisoners at night; head shavings; beatings; hard labour until physical and or mental collapse; menial and mindlessly repetitive tasks; disrupted sleep; unexplained punishments; denial of court martial, etc. There seemed to be a belief amongst prison officers that conscientious objectors were really traitors who deserved to be shamed and punished. His report in the Lords was lengthy, even though he had been advised that the War Office was making inquiries. In the meantime, the urbane Anthony Eden, who had become Home Secretary, felt that it was *"undesirable to wash our dirty linen in public"*. Gavin's answer was uncompromising:

> *"I think that on the whole it is better to wash one's dirty linen in public. It shows that when one's linen is dirty one is prepared to wash it, and that seems to me really the important thing. It is all the difference between a democratic country and the totalitarian countries. Under the veil of secrecy much can be done and is done which, were it known, could not be done."*

This produced an anonymous note in pencil which Gavin kept:

*"Your speech was very good & I found the conclusion a high
flight of oratory."*

A month later he addressed the issue of conscientious objectors again
when he rose to speak on the National Service Bill:

*"This Bill does provide opportunity for alternative and useful
service... and I oppose it because it contains in my view the
immoral principle of conscription – I am speaking for myself
and not for my Party; but I believe that if it were possible
for His Majesty's Government to accept the suggestions I
have made... and as to the possibility of transferring to the
Civil Defence Services men who find their position spiritually
uncomfortable and disagreeable in the Armed Forces, they
would, so far from hindering, actually help the country in its
present situation."*

On 3rd April 1941 Gavin spoke out against conscription in the Lords
debate on the National Service Bill. His opening remarks show that
he was aware of his reputation as a pacifist/conscientious objector,
and wanted to add that in his case *"the terms were interchangeable"*.
He therefore felt qualified to offer some practical suggestions about:

*"Your Lordships, will perhaps have expected me to say a
word of protest against this Bill. I do not speak in any way
for my Party, I suggest to His Majesty's Government that in
the case of these people whose consciences have caused them
a great deal of trouble, and who are at present in positions
which they find spiritually painful and uncomfortable, they
should be given the opportunity of rendering, willingly, freely,
and wholeheartedly, the service which they would like to
give to their country... the possibility of transferring to the
Civil Defence Services men who find their position spiritually
uncomfortable and disagreeable in the Armed Forces, they*

> *would, so far from hindering, actually help the country in its*
> *present situation."*

In parliament, prejudice against *"conchies"* persisted – even after the war from people who should have known better. For example, during a debate in June 1947, Lord Croft accused Gavin of having been

> *"not wholly on the side of the sailors and soldiers on every*
> *occasion."*

Gavin responded indignantly:

> *"The noble Lord has absolutely no right to make that*
> *statement – I take great exception to it."*

But Croft persisted:

> *"The noble Lord, during the war, was a conscientious*
> *objector."*

To which Gavin replied:

> *"I was a member of the National Fire Service."*

Then Lord Croft asked sarcastically,

> *"I hope the noble Lord did not get injured, in pursuit of that*
> *great duty."*

With dignified reserve Gavin answered:

> *"The noble Lord is now making a reflection on the National*
> *Fire Service. I think the National Fire Service did quite*
> *creditably, all things considered."*

Then the Labour peer Lord Strabolgi, a naval veteran, intervened:

"I have sat with Lord Faringdon for thirteen years and have been pretty closely associated with him... He served during the recent war in the National Fire Service, which is a perfectly honourable service. There is no dispute about that, and no one suggests that people serving in the National Fire Service were not helping the country... Conscientious objection is perfectly legal."

Objective as ever, the *Daily Mail* reported this exchange the next day under the headline

"Peer calls Peer 'Conchie'".

By 1941 Gavin's visitors' book showed that a good many aliens were coming to stay with Gavin in wartime. To make matters seem worse for xenophobes, many of these aliens were Jewish. Solly Zukerman came often and was contributing a great deal to the war effort. "Solly" was Solomon, Baron Zuckerman, OM, KCB, and FRS. He had been a zoologist who lectured at Oxford University from 1934 and designed the Civil Defence's "Zukerman Helmet", before serving as an operational research pioneer and advisor to the allies on bombing. Given an honorary commission as a wing commander in the RAF, he was later promoted to honorary group captain. Perhaps he discussed some military matters with Gavin, who appeared to have inside knowledge when he wrote a series of letters to the Air Ministry. Two other alien guests who made valuable contributions to Britain were Marian Mahler from Austria – the niece of the composer Gustav Mahler – who became an influential textile designer at Glasgow School of Art. But perhaps Paul Eisner had the greatest impact of any wartime immigrant, for he invented a favourite of British cuisine – the fish finger. He also dreamt up the printed circuit board, airborne instrument electronics, electrical under-floor heating, and car window heating elements.

However, on purely artistic grounds, the most remarkable of Gavin's alien friends was Alphonse Kann, who came to stay at Buscot in

July 1940, and returned to spend Christmas at the Basque House, which Gavin had just moved into in that autumn. Alphonse was a world-famous art collector. He had been a childhood friend of the writer Marcel Proust (author of the seven volume *À la Recherché du Temps Perdu*) who was said to have partially modelled his character Charles Swann on Kann. Well known for his discerning taste and shrewd collecting instincts, Kann shocked many in 1927 when he sold his old master works by Brueghel, Cimabue, Fragonard, Rubens, and Tintoretto. His collection still included significant paintings by Watteau, Chardin and Millet when he started to acquire works by Gauguin, Van Gogh, Matisse, Cézanne, Van Gogh, Monet, Degas, Renoir, Seurat, Picasso, Braque, Rousseau, Leger and Gris. His close friend Georges Salles, curator of the Louvre, called him the *"Prince of collectors"*. Passionate about all forms of expression, from Chinese ceramics to Gothic carvings, his home was a treasure trove with important paintings hung alongside tapestries, statues and antique furniture. Kann's 17th-century Hotel de Petites Ecuries du Roy in St. Germain de-Laye, was frequented by connoisseurs and other collectors, as well as modern artists such as Picasso, Braque and Matisse. He went further than most collectors by financially supporting struggling artists that he admired – such as Marie Laurencin, Jacques Lipchitz, Chaïm Soutine, Albert Gleizes and Kees Van Dongen.

At the age of 70 Kann was naturalised as a British citizen, and settled in London. He moved into a flat in the exclusive Albany in Piccadilly, next door to the Royal Academy. After the occupation of Paris in 1940 the Nazis began to systematically loot his collection and the closely typed inventory of what they had "confiscated" came to sixty pages. All in all, this amounted to 1,400 paintings as well as precious manuscripts, ceramics and statues. Some of the earliest paintings were reserved for what was intended to become Hitler's own museum of Art. Many of the Baroque and Romantic period paintings were taken by Reichsmarschall Hermann Göring for his personal collection. The modern paintings were seen as *"decadent"* and sold off cheaply to Swiss dealers in order to raise foreign currency. Many

Gavin Henderson, 2nd Baron Faringdon. When photographed here by Howard Coster in 1936, he was well known as a controversial Labour politician, pacifist and philanthropist.

Left: Lord Faringdon opening Buscot for a "Save Spain" fundraiser in 1937.
Right: Robert Byron, the close friend who motored with him across Europe and India before trekking to Tibet and Sikkim. In 1941 Robert was on a ship sunk by a Nazi U-boat off the coast of Iceland. His body was never recovered.

Below: In the 1950s Lord Faringdon commissioned the artist Roy Hobdell to decorate his London home with amusing *trompe l'oeil* murals. Dinner guests were overlooked by an image of the Roman senator Quintus Fabius, famous for his strategy of waiting for the right time to attack – the motto of the left-leaning Fabian Society. The image is topped with his crest, a reminder that Lord Faringdon was Chairman of the Fabian Labour party in parliament.

of these paintings were sold on many times to other dealers, possibly to obscure their origins before they were exported to the USA. In exile Kann escaped the fate of 76,000 other Jews who were rounded up and deported from France to Nazi death camps; but he was only able to recover a fraction of his collection before he died in London in 1948. The provenance of some paintings in American museums continues to be disputed to this day.

A handwritten letter from Alphonse concerns two oil paintings on canvas, which Gavin was to purchase from Agnews. The first, very much Kann's favourite, was Jordaens' *Portrait of an Unknown Woman* (59 x 45"). The second Sir Peter Paul Rubens's *Portrait of the Marchesa Veronica Spinola-Doria* (52 x 41½").

"Stanmore Court, 29 St. James St, W.1

18*th* March 1942

Dear Gavin

Jordaens is the finest portrait by that painter I have ever seen & as beautiful as any portrait I know: such dignity, such quality of paint, the head & hands & everything, including the dress & accessories, splendid.

One would wish to have a place palatial enough to hang it. What a fine thing a great painting of that size can be! The condition of it is remarkable.

The Rubens, though early & evidently painted in Italy, is extremely pleasing & also extremely decorative, though he did later some more delicate portraits: still it is a very good picture; the "matiere" of it is nice and rich, as also the colouring. I was most agreeably impressed with both & they would be the right size for your palace. If I had to choose between the two, I would take the Jordaens, which is as fine as anything can be; in his compositions he is not as great, but there he surpasses most painters & it is almost equal to Rembrandt, perhaps as good.

Ever yours,

Alphonse"

(Note: "Matiere" is a connoisseur's phrase for paint quality and aesthetic appeal, which the Rubens certainly has. It is interesting to see that Alphonse and Gavin visited York Minster, which has some of the finest examples of Early English, Decorated and Perpendicular style Gothic architecture as well as the largest expanse of medieval stained glass in the world. Kann's collection included illuminated medieval manuscripts. He also had paintings by the Jewish Ukrainian émigrés Emmanuel Mané-Katz and Abraham Mintchine. Gavin bought two paintings by the former artist and one by the latter after WW2. Both of these artists had been supported by Alphonse Kann. Gavin bought the Rubens (FC 28) and Jordaens (FC 22) from Thomas Agnew & Sons soon after he received Kann's letter.

Whilst some suspected *"Reds under the beds"* at Buscot Park, there were "spooks" or spies, but of a more home-grown variety. A seemingly innocuous letter from 1941 in Gavin's files was sent by a Military Intelligence (MI9) agent. It came from Donald Darling, who had originally been recruited by "Z" Organization which was set up in 1936 by Special Intelligence Services (S.I.S.) under the leadership of Lt Col Claude Dansey. Dansey, whose codename was "Colonel Z", became the spymaster of around 200 undercover operatives across Europe. These pre-war agents were not allowed to take extreme risks, meddle in politics, write anything down, take photographs, or carry equipment that might reveal they were involved in espionage. Darling was part of what was termed the "Observer Corps" in Spain, where he worked undercover as a travel courier in Barcelona.

When the Spanish Civil War made work in the travel business impossible, he moved to France. A capable administrator with an affable manner, he became Secretary of the National Joint Committee for Spanish Relief from 1937–40. This was how he met Gavin, who was closely involved with that organisation as well as another where Darling played an administrative role, Spanish Medical Aid. Darling and Humphrey Hare, a translator who became Donald Darling's assistant in the Spanish Republican refugee camps at Perpignan, came to stay at Buscot Park on two separate occasions in May 1938. A year later all three met up in France, where they worked with Peter and Nancy (née Mitford) Rodd to evacuate Spanish Republican refugees. Events from this episode were later included as fact-based fiction in Nancy's novel *The Pursuit of Love*. A clipping of an article about her in Gavin's files gives a flavour of the times:

> *"The Londoner's Log, Evening Standard, Friday June 16, 1939.*
>
> *From a refugee camp.*
>
> *Mrs Peter Rodd, dark, witty and cultured daughter-in-law of Lord Rennell, has returned to London from Perpignan, in the South of France, where she had been working for some time in the Spanish refugee camps. Her husband is one of three young Englishmen who have made themselves responsible for the moral well-being of the refugees in the camps, now numbering over 400,000. His associates are Mr Humphrey Hare, an author,*
>
> *and Mr Donald Darling.*
>
> *Mr Darling is following a tradition of good Samaritanism inherent in his family. He boasts kinship with Grace Darling, of lifeboat fame, and he has an intimate knowledge of Spain, where he lived for twelve years. He is a dark, attractive young man whose nickname, Donald Duck, parodies his name rather than his manner.*

Mrs Rodd intends returning to France in a few weeks time,
to rejoin her husband. She tells me that the refugees are
still pouring across the frontier at a rate of 180 a day, with
disquieting tales of the activities of the German Gestapo."

Donald Darling came to stay at Buscot Park for another weekend in July 1940. The letter below – written in the following year – reveals that by then he knew many of Gavin's friends, and that he had been a keen observer of life at Buscot Park. Soon after the fall of France he went to neutral Portugal, which had become a hotbed of espionage. Here he was responsible for escape and repatriation routes under the cover of being a Consulate official attached to the British Embassy. He had to keep escape routes open between Nazi occupied areas, Portugal, Spain, and London. For fairly obvious reasons he came to be codenamed "Di-Di" in Lisbon, while the French underground dubbed him *"Cheri"*. In Lisbon he met and worked with Ian Fleming, the future author of the James Bond books, who was posted there as a Naval Intelligence Division officer. After several years there both men were transferred to Gibraltar, where Darling's codename became agent "Sunday". Here he was joined by Airey Neave who became "Monday" after his daring escape from Colditz Castle in Germany.

In Portugal and Gibraltar Darling ministered to the needs of thousands of Allied military personnel and escaped POWs. All were debriefed and helped home or to join units stationed in North Africa. His letter below was written when neutral Portugal was thronged with people waiting to be repatriated, and contains a number of in-jokes and references, all of which will be explained later in this chapter.

"Consulate General, Lisbon, 2nd July 1941

Dear Gavin,

I received your telegram about Anne Cameron, who is at the

Hotel Paris and is not at all well, it appears. I had met her amongst a host of people some weeks ago. La Curzon Herrick is with her. I telephoned them yesterday and hope to get down to see them tonight or tomorrow. I have so much to do that often it is difficult to get away from the office before 8pm, so that Estoril is sometimes not feasible. They are both part of the panzer division that is taking part in the great battle for air priority, and appear to have penetrated the first defences of the Unimaginot Line. Isabel Jeans managed to get through it after a titanic hand-to-hand struggle as will no doubt describe, should you see her. The situation is understandable, of course owing to priority passengers on war business having first claim, and others not vitally concerned with the war effort have to be unloaded.

Also at Estoril is the handsome Listowel, whom I found very attractive. She appears to be waiting too. 9 weeks seems to be about the average time and that with luck. The throng at Estoril is quite incredible. I have never seen so many people. Rather like the Coronation. Lisbon is crammed with the poorer victims who are unable to get anywhere. About four "Queen Maries" might clear it up a bit, together with ten Clippers per day for six months. And that is not likely to happen.

How are you faring? I feel that the rose beds needs further attention and the lily pond its annual de-scumming. I wish I could do it for you, but the chances, I am afraid. Did you ever finish with the red peat in the chicken houses? I enjoyed the creosote fest.

I am rather amused at the latest Harry Pollittics and do wish they would get our American brothers into line as they are working with the loggerheads. The whole situation seems farcical. I should like to hear Isabel's version and explanation.

*Poppy writes to me regularly and, as usual, is extremely
funny and often indecent. She is a remarkable girl, and
a humourist, is of great value to the Nation. Can't you
recommend her to Duff Cooper, to put on the air once a
week? Just let her talk. We're tired of Bebe Danielle. My
listening is confined usually to the Pacific Programme at
breakfast and Ankara at midnight.*

*What happened to A.M. Kali, etc? Where is she? If you like
to give her my love, please do so. She would do rather well
here, I should have thought.*

*Do you know Portugal well? I am crazy about it and have
jilted Spain forever. I admit my knowledge of the country is
limited to glimpses from a car, but it has a charm I find hard
to describe. It is very clean and amazingly fertile.*

*There is nothing much one can say, without mentioning
unmentionable subjects, so I won't bore you further with
chit-chat. Are the Berners still with you? Regards if they are.
And love to Frank, if he is there.*

As ever,

Donald."

At least nine people who Gavin knew well are mentioned here. In
order of appearance, they are: Anne Cameron who was Gavin's
friend Jack Huntingdon's youngest sister, Lady Marian (nicknamed
Anne) who since 1933 had been the widow of a Captain Cameron.
She appears in the Buscot Park frescoes and was part of Gavin's inner
circle and mentioned in a 1929 letter to Gavin in India from Peter
Rodd. A strikingly beautiful woman whose marriage to a WW1 hero
had proved unhappy, she was rumoured to have had an affair with
Peter Rodd (*"after hours"* as he put it). Later these two women became
friends and both were house guests at Buscot Park on the weekend
when the news that Germany had invaded Poland was broadcast on

the B.B.C. *"La Curzon Herrick"*, was Anne's elder sister, Lady Maud Kathleen Cairnes Plantagenet Hastings, who had married William Curzon-Herrick. She was reputed to be somewhat haughty and this probably explains why Darling refers to her as *"La Curzon Herrick"*. Lady Maud had written a novel in 1939 called *The Disappearing Duchess* under her pseudonym "Cairnes". Like Anne Cameron, Lady Maud and her husband had visited Buscot Park several times in the run-up to WW2. Clearly, Gavin had written to Donald to find out how the sisters were. Darling's response sums up their predicament:

> *"both part of the panzer division that is taking part in the great battle for air priority, and appear to have penetrated the first defences of the Unimaginot Line."*

Many who knew him mentioned Darling's quips. This ironic reference to the 450-mile (720 KM) long fortifications, which failed to protect France from the German Blitzkrieg, is probably a good example.

Isabel Jeans was an English actress who had appeared in Alfred Hitchcock's film *Suspicion* that year with Cary Grant and Joan Fontaine. She went on to play a number of *Grandes dames* in Hollywood films for decades afterwards. However, she was not as impressive as *"the handsome Listowel, whom I found very attractive"*. Here Donald Darling is referring to Judith, Countess of Listowel, the British-Hungarian journalist and author who had married "Billy" Hare, 5th Earl of Listowel. She had been photographed by Cecil Beaton and included in his *Book of Beauty*. According to the author Nigel West – who is generally acknowledged as the best unofficial historian of the wartime intelligence services – Judith Hare *"acted occasionally as an MI5 source"*. Her presence in Lisbon resulted from having gone to see her kinsman the Hungarian Prime Minister Paul Telekom, as well as Count Ciano, Mussolini's son-in-law, to try to persuade them not to side with Hitler. Gavin knew her husband "Billy" Hare, 5th Earl of Listowel, very well as he was Vice-Chairman of the National Joint Committee for Spanish Relief as well as the Labour Party whip in the House of Lords.

Donald Darling's mention of *"Harry Pollitics"* is another in-joke relating to the political turmoil surrounding Harry Pollitt, General Secretary of the British Communist party. He had been forced to resign this position only a month before – a few days after Germany invaded the Soviet Union. Pollitt was a firm supporter of Stalin and had written to Gavin in 1937 attempting to persuade him that the Moscow *"show trials"* during the Great Purge were completely justified. Gavin does not appear to have accepted this party line, as within two years he had contacted the exiled Leon Trotsky – who Stalin had declared a traitor. Darling is also referring to the conflict between communist party members in the USA as *"the loggerheads"*, due to the loss of faith in Stalin on one side, and those who they saw as *"appeasers"* on the other, which had led to much public head-butting. He adds *"I should like to hear Isobel's version and explanation"*.

Isobel Brown was a communist fund-raiser who had helped establish the Spanish Medical Aid Committee. She had since become the National Women's Organizer for the British Communist Party. Darling clearly felt at ease poking fun at communists when writing to Gavin. This suggests that neither of them had a strong affiliation with the party. In a letter to Harold Acton after the war (quoted in his biography of Nancy Mitford) Darling mentioned how a communist cadre at Perpignan had insisted on evacuating a printing press with the Spanish refugees so that they might, as Darling put it, *"bore everyone on the voyage"*.

"Poppy" is the optimistic Basque Children's Committee organizer – Poppy Vulliamy – who had helped Gavin set up Basque House at Buscot Park. Darling clearly preferred her *"extremely funny and often indecent"* jokes to those of the American actress Bebe Daniels. The latter had retired from Hollywood and moved to London with her film actor husband Ben Lyon. Bebe Daniels wrote the scripts for their situation comedy *Life with the Lyons* on the BBC's Light programme. This was pure escapism and ran for years afterwards, but Darling suggests that Duff Cooper (then head of the Ministry of Information, hence in overall charge of BBC broadcasting) should replace her with Poppy. She was convivial company and came to stay with Gavin on a dozen occasions after the colony of refugees had moved out of Basque House. However, another mutual friend remains a mystery. Nigel West has been kind enough to offer the following explanation of Darling's reference to A.J. Kali: *"She is not mentioned in any wartime MI5 file, so presumably she was an Indian of some interest to SIS"*. This is plausible as Gavin had many contacts with Indian radicals especially during the war years when famine loomed in parts of the sub-continent.

Darling went on to mention that he was listening to Radio Ankara. This is probably not as offhand as it sounds today as the station was then reporting the effects of the Turkish-German Friendship Treaty. This agreement allowed German troops to cross its territory to invade British allies and had led to a military *coup d'état* in Iraq. That prompted a swiftly organised raid by British forces in order to restore the regency government, which favoured them. And so, even in apparently slight remarks, Darling reveals that his eyes were on current events elsewhere. His final remark, however, shows he was equally keen to know about matters closer to home.

> *"Are the Berners still with you? Regards if they are."*

This, of course, refers to Gerald, Lord Berners, Gavin's friend and neighbour, and his partner Robert Heber-Percy. Both had left Faringdon House soon after the outbreak of the war. Heber-Percy had tried his hand as an intelligence agent in Arabia and Gerald had moved into Oxford. But Heber-Percy's career as a spy was short lived and, after a sojourn as a private in the British Army, he and Gerald Berners returned to live in a few rooms of Faringdon House not occupied by the officers of the U.S. Army Quartermaster Corps.

The following sentence earlier on in the letter appears to be a reference to spring garden tasks at Buscot Park, with no cryptic meaning. *"How are you faring? I feel that the rose beds need further attention and the lily pond its annual de-scumming. I wish I could do it for you, but the chances, I am afraid".* The letter ends with, *"Love to Frank, if he is there",* which relates to Frank W. Bourne, Gavin's secretary, who Donald had met in Perpignan as well as at Buscot Park. He was a poultry farmer who Gavin had sponsored as the Labour Party candidate for West Berkshire in 1937. Frank's influence at Buscot Park was certainly felt for in April 1940 Gavin raised questions in the Upper House on the Poultry Industry and proposed widespread battery farming methods. So, the sentence *"Did you ever finish with the red peat in the chicken houses? I enjoyed the creosote fest"* suggests that Darling had seen the battery hen houses being constructed at Buscot Park when he visited.

More information about Donald Darling, showing how effective he was under cover, emerged two years before he wrote this letter. Nancy Mitford wrote to her mother quoting her husband Peter Rodd's comment that at the refugee camps in Perpignan he had met *"two chaps here who talk the New Statesman English, always a comfort abroad I find".*

Six years later, Donald Darling appeared as a genial character called Robert Parker in Nancy's autobiographical novel *The Pursuit of Love.* Humphrey Hare, who does not appear in the novel, translated half a dozen novels from French after WW2. Nancy does not seem to have ever been aware of their roles as undercover British agents. Perhaps this was due to their ability to melt into the shadows. As the author Nigel West put it in *The A to Z of British Intelligence:*

> *"Donald Darling had worked for Z organization of the Secret Intelligence Service (SIS) in France before the war, so it was no surprise in July 1940 when Claude Dansey, the assistant chief of SIS, asked him to act as repatriation officer in the Iberian peninsula, shepherding British military personnel home. His connections with SIS actually predated the war, for he had occasionally undertaken small jobs for them when he was operating as a travel courier in France and Spain during the Spanish Civil War. Once formally of SIS's books, Darling*

was attached to the British Embassy in Portugal in the guise
of a consular official handling refugee affairs... and spent
the next two years in Lisbon enabling Allied evaders to make
the arduous journey from Northern Europe across enemy
occupied zones and over the Pyrenees. One of the many
agents Darling dispatched into France was the Armenian oil
magnate Nubar Gulbenkian, who described his controller as
'a very cheerful, intelligent and dedicated man who lived for
his job. When one met him alone he was very witty and an
excellent raconteur. In company he sat like a clam'".

Gavin's meetings with Donald Darling, before and after the outbreak of WWII, suggest he may have had an involvement with British Intelligence's most pacifistic branch *"Z Organization"*. In contrast to that at least a dozen men working for other branches of British Intelligence either wrote to Gavin or came to stay at Buscot Park. This might simply have been due to the fact that they were part of the section of society from which the Special Intelligence Services (S.I.S.) tended to recruit. So perhaps there is nothing to be made of the fact that the following signatures appear in Buscot Park visitors' book: Sir Francis Rodd, who served with the S.I.A. in the Levant during WW1; Hugh Dalton, Minister in charge of Economic Warfare – charged by Churchill to set up Special Operations Executive in 1940; John Betjeman, who while working as a Press Attaché in Ireland asked Gavin to send him information on British T.U.C. members to the Dominions Office *"for security reasons"*; Anthony Powell, who gathered intelligence on Czech and French nationals in the UK during WW2 for S.I.S.; the *"camp"* Brian Howard – an MI5 agent until expelled in 1942 after calling his commanding officer *"Colonel Cutie"*; Guy Burgess, the MI5/KGB double agent, who came to stay in June 1940 with Richard Hare of the Foreign Office; and Angus Wilson, who worked at the code-breaking establishment Bletchley Park. What all this this adds up to is anyone's guess. It may simply be the result of the Intelligence services recruiting graduates from Oxford and Cambridge as they did. One thing is certain; while they came and went Gavin's younger brother Lt.-Col. Hon. Michael

Henderson was training Churchill's secret army of *"Auxiliary Units"* a few miles away at Coleshill.

Perhaps the most questionable character who came to Buscot Park during the war years and afterwards was Tom Driberg MP. Somehow, he embodied many of the contradictions of the decades in which he lived. At Oxford in the 20s, he was friendly with left-wingers like Auden and Gaitskell as well as with the right-wingers Waugh and Boothby. Afterwards, he found work as a gossip-writer for the *Daily Express* and then, as a socialite and socialist, he became a bosom pal of the Soviet spies Burgess and Maclean. He served as Labour MP for Maldon in 1942, Chairman of the Labour N.E.C. from 1957–58 and a confidant of Harold Wilson, Nye Bevan and Richard Crossman. He went on to become MP for Barking for 15 years until he was made a life peer Baron Bradwell in 1975.

Driberg had a record of promiscuous homosexuality in public places. In 1935 he was acquitted of *"gross indecency"* with two strangers. He was cautioned for the same act with a Norwegian sailor in 1943; arrested for indecency in 1951 – but not charged. A former MI5 agent claimed that this habitual behaviour led him into a *"honey-trap"* after which he was blackmailed into becoming a K.G.B. spy codenamed Lepage. Others alleged that he was a double-agent for S.I.S. but as his biographer pointed out, that seems unlikely as he was far too indiscreet.

In 1964 two Conservative back-benchers reported seeing Tom Driberg and Bob Boothby importuning boys at a dog track; and later these two friends, from opposite sides of the political divide, were reported by the press to have attended sex parties with male prostitutes and underworld figures – including the notorious Kray Twins. Both men managed to dodge the potential scandals that crossed their paths. Eventually, Driberg became better known as Lord Bardwell, a socialist with a charming wife at home in a Georgian mansion. After his death it was reported that he had provided information to a communist Czech controller for cash. This would have inevitably led to suspicion being cast on Gavin – who had provided a safe house for Czech refugees in London.

One of the most enigmatic guests was Baroness Moura Budberg. She was widely suspected of being a double agent for both the Soviet Union and British intelligence and had been called the *"Mata Hari of Russia"*. Before the October Revolution, Moura worked in the Russian Embassy in Berlin. She was arrested on suspicion of spying in 1918. Two years later she met the writer H.G. Wells and became his mistress. A close relationship with Wells continued until his death. The Soviet spy Guy Burgess, was a regular at Moura Budberg's bibulous parties in London.

Chapter 15

Executions. Part 1:
Another Greek Tragedy

While Allied troops were advancing towards Germany, shortly after Paris had been liberated, a contingent of Greek sailors seconded to the Royal Navy mutinied in Cairo. This was meant to be a protest against what the Allies had agreed for their country after the war ended. The British announced that they would reinstate the exiled Greek king and his government and the monarchists were ready to regain control. Communist freedom fighters, who had formed the backbone of the resistance against the Nazis and Italians, pledged to eject them. The British and Americans vowed to stamp out the communists. And thus, fresh conflict loomed over that half-starved country just as everyone was hoping to go home. An explosion was inevitable and the flashpoint was in Egypt, as this newspaper clipping from Gavin's files tells:

"GREEK SEAMEN MUTINY

Our Special Representative CAIRO, April 24, 1944 – AAP.

It is officially stated that three Greek warships, the Apostolis, the Ierax, and the Sachtouris, which for three weeks had refused to obey orders, were boarded on Saturday night by Greek officers and ratings under orders from Vice-Adml. Voulgaris, the Greek C-in-C. There was an exchange of machine-gun and rifle fire, resulting in a few casualties. The ships were recovered and the flag of Vice-Adml. Voulgaris was hoisted on the Sachtouris. It is understood that the crews demanded the formation of a new Greek Government. Vice-Adml. Voulgaris took the view that the men's action constituted mutiny, and for that reason they would be punished.

Greek sailors who were on shore in a Middle East port supported the mutineers on the three ships – a destroyer and two corvettes – demanding the formation of a new Greek Government, says Reuter's Cairo correspondent. The first signs of mutiny began on April 6 shortly after the resignation of V. Tsouderos from the Greek Premiership. A British liaison officer boarding the destroyer found it in the charge of a committee of men who said that they would not obey orders to put to sea unless a new Government was formed.

Trouble On Shore

Trouble, continues the correspondent, also developed on shore, where 200 Greek sailors barricaded themselves inside detention barracks. The Cairo correspondent of the National Broadcasting Company says it is stated in Cairo that it would have been dangerous to allow the mutiny to continue since it might spread to other units of the Greek Navy, which is now larger than at the time of the German occupation of Greece. The Cairo correspondent of the Times says that the Greek crews still insist that their action was not mutiny because it was due to political causes. They appear not to understand the seriousness of their offence, and in one instance offered to lay down their arms and return to duty if bygones were considered bygones. The fact remains that on the instigation of agitators, some of whom were possibly German agents, the Greek ships refused to sail as convoy escorts, necessitating British destroyers being hastily brought in from elsewhere to fill their places.

On 11th August 1944 the story continued in the *Times*:

> *"GREEK NAVY MUTINEERS TO DIE.*
>
> *Sentence of death was passed today on 12 members of the Greek Navy including one officer, when the court martial dealing with the mutiny on board the Greek destroyer Pindos concluded, says the Alexandria message. Eight other accused were sentenced to life imprisonment, two 20 years each, one to 10 years, two to three years and one acquitted.*
>
> *One further officer and a warrant officer were sentenced to 15 months each for perjury. During the hearing the Court ordered the arrest of three officers on charges of being concerned in the mutiny."*

Gavin had begun writing letters to the highest officials about these matters soon after news of the events reached him. The earliest replies came in three letters from A.W. Alexander, First Lord of the Admiralty. Whilst these were respectful of the humanitarian issues Gavin raised, it was clear that Lord Alexander's over-riding aim was to maintain discipline. Mutiny in the Royal Navy had always been punished and would continue to be. However, Gavin argued that the Greek seamen had been seconded to service in the R.N. and were therefore *"a special case"*. These sailors, he maintained, were unaware of British Naval traditions – they had their own more anarchic ones and most Greek sailors were volunteers. They had no idea that what they intended as their *"political protest"* would result in court martial.

Surprisingly, perhaps, a diplomatic solution was reached, intended to suppress further unrest. This was that six of the most politically naive of mutineers would be sent to prison for long periods, whilst the members of the Communist Party, seen as the hard-line organisers, would be executed in Egypt. Acknowledging the difficulty, the First Sea Lord wrote to Gavin:

"The case has been under my personal consideration and I hope that the Greek government may be prevailed upon to reduce the sentences. You will appreciate however that as the court martial was conducted by one of the allies this is a delicate matter. For this reason I must ask you to treat this paragraph a strictly confidential and for your personal information only.

As to the report which you have heard that the men were not allowed legal defence nor to call witnesses, I have found on enquiry that this was not the case: a Greek lawyer was present in Court ready to undertake their defence, but they refuse his services.

As to the calling of witnesses, I understand that the men <u>were</u> allowed to call witnesses, and that a few of them did so, although the majority did not.

Yours sincerely,

A.V. Alexander"

The legal position was that under the Allied Forces Act 1940 all disciplinary matters were to be conducted according to the laws of each country. The Admiralty, therefore, had no right to intervene. However, the severity of the sentences awarded to the eighteen Greek ratings was such that the Foreign Office made unofficial representations in the matter. The Greek authorities reviewed the cases again and decided that it was too early yet to make further reductions in the sentences. They intimated, however, that they might re-consider the position at a later date of the men are meanwhile of good conduct. A month later Lord Alexander responded to another letter from Gavin:

"The Foreign Secretary is therefore unable to intervene further in a matter in which an Allied Government is exercising authority given to it by its Parliament. You mentioned in your letter of 25th February the case on

Constantinidis. You will no doubt have heard that the King of Greece, to mark the occasion of Greek Independence Day, decided as an act of grace to reduce or remit the sentences of a number of the prisoners. One of the men whose sentences were thus remitted, was S.N. Constantinidis who is, I imagine, the same man as the Constantinidis referred to by you.

Yours sincerely,

A.V. Alexander."

It was the same Major Constantinidis, who was mentioned in reports from SOE British liaison officers operating in Greece 1943–44. These expressed the views of British officers liaising with the guerrilla bands in occupied areas under the jurisdiction of German, Albanian and Bulgarian forces. Constantinidis was one of the resistance leaders opposed to those supporting the return of the discredited monarchy and its proposed government made up of former fascists in the Metaxas regime. Funded more by the Russians than the British, he was accused of executing members of rival bands. He was captured and tried and sentenced to be executed. Then King George of Greece pardoned him in an effort to appease opponents of his return after the cessation of hostilities.

Gavin demanded a civil trial and his correspondence with the admiralty was followed by handwritten letters – boldly headed CONFIDENTIAL – from the Earl of Perth – a distinguished diplomat who had been the first Secretary General of the League of Nations. In an effort to get Gavin to re-consider, Perth passed on a letter from the Greek Ambassador to London:

"Confidential

Oakley Manor, Basingstoke,

July 4th 1944.

Dear Faringdon,

After our conversation in the House of Lords the other day, I wrote to the Greek Ambassador on the subject discussed. I have now heard from him and do not think I can do better than send you his letter, which you will note is non-official, for your confidential information.

You told me that you had mentioned the matter to Addison & therefore he may also like to see Aghnides' letter.

Yours sincerely,

Perth.

In writing to the ambassador, I made the various points you mentioned.

P"

"Ambassade Royale de Grece, 51, Upper Brook St., W.1. July 1st 1944.

My dear Lord Perth,

I have thought a good deal over the two letters you sent me on June 28ᵗʰ. It is only natural that I should give serious consideration to any hints coming from you.

My Government have not yet informed me of any death sentences passed on the ringleaders in the recent mutiny in the Greek Naval forces in the Middle East though I did hear this over the wireless.

Pending the receipt of further information on the question I can only bring to your knowledge some of the circumstances of the case.

(a) Last year trouble had broken out in the Greek destroyer 'Ierax' and two of the ringleaders were condemned to death. On grounds of clemency and in order to bring about reconciliation amongst the various Greek parties the sentence as not carried out.

(b) This has not prevented the recent new outbreak last March, in the same Ierax. It is even contended that had the sentence been carried out last year we would have been spared last spring's mutiny which was a much more serious affair, since the mutineers (1) refused to obey orders to join a convoy which in consequence suffered from enemy action and (2) killed officers and men of the Loyalist elements.

(c) The Lebanon Charter which was signed by all the parties – including the EAM (the Communist controlled Liberation Army Organization) – insists on the necessity of meting out condign punishment to the chief authors of those treasonable acts which in view of their seriousness it qualifies as 'high treason'.

(d) As the enquiry into the causes of the mutiny is still continuing it would not be fair on my part to prejudge the issue by telling you here what I consider to have been the political objectives of the ringleaders although several important witnesses, though differing in other respects, seem to agree on that point.

(e) If it is proven in the end that the real motive was to instore communism in Greece & to overthrow the present regime & government in the midst of a devastating war, notwithstanding the fact that military orders of the highest importance were ignored on the eve of the campaign in Italy and that not only those orders were directly connected with the campaign but also that the refusal of some of the units of the Greek fleet to protect a convoy transporting food to the

starving Greek people resulted for some units of the convoy
to be torpedoed by enemy action, the Government may be
assuming a heavy responsibility before the Greek nation
if they do not handle with the greatest care and political
fairness and firmness a matter of such importance.

(f) It will interest you to know that Counsel for the Defence
of the accused men have expressed their appreciation &
thanks to the President of the Court for all the facilities
accorded to the mutineers for the fairest possible treatment of
their case.

I shall not fail to communicate to you any views my
Government may send me on the issues raised by your letter
of the 28th June. Would you, in the meantime, consider the
present as a non-official interim reply?

Believe me, my dear Lord Perth,

Yours ever,

Tn. Aghnides."

After months of legalistic and diplomatic discussions, violent protests
had erupted on the streets of Athens and British troops had to be used
to suppress them. Gavin's friend the cartoonist Osbert Lancaster was
with the British Legation in Athens at the time and predicted a civil
war. Gavin felt that the British government were deeply involved
and behaved like an ostrich burying its head in the sand. His moral
indignation was seen as admirable but exacerbated. A report in *The
Times* (22nd December 1944) showed how isolated he was:

"Lord Faringdon, who explained that he was not speaking on
behalf of the Labour Party, moved that the House regretted
the policy of His Majesty's Government in Greece, which had
had the shameful result of military action against our Greek
allies."

Gavin's use of the word *"shameful"* excited indignation and a furious backlash in the Lords. Viscount Cranbourne, the Conservative Leader of the House, tore into him:

> *"My Lords, we are always accustomed to use so far as we can extremely temperate language in your Lordships' House, but I feel bound to say in all due seriousness, and with all due deference to the noble Lord, Lord Faringdon, who is responsible for this Motion, that in the form in which it is put before your Lordships and in the wording which is placed before the House it is ill-judged, ill-timed and ill-drafted…. the noble Lord has chosen to table a Motion in a form which, I am bound to say, is not merely offensive in itself, as I think it is, but which amounts to a censure on a Government containing all the main leaders of the three Parties; and this he has done at a moment of very great delicacy, when it is essential that everyone should weigh his words with the greatest care. I can imagine nothing more irresponsible than that… The noble Lord, if he will forgive my saying so, is always irresponsible, and here in this House we do not take him too seriously… Indeed, his speech was such a tissue of misstatements that I cannot attempt, however long I speak to your Lordships, to answer them all."*

This was devastating. Even Gavin's most stalwart supporter Jack Huntingdon left the chamber unable to witness his humiliation. The debate was covered in the *Daily Mail* which noted that the Labour Whip in the Lords intervened to disassociate his Party from Lord Faringdon. Gavin had gone too far. But a few days later the following letter of support arrived:

> *"Dear Gavin,*
>
> *I am glad you forced the Greek question! I see from the Times that you certainly made Cranbourne furious. So I suppose you must have spoken well. Though as usual it is*

hard to gather what you said. I really must see Hansard &
I also infer you must have got quite a good vote because the
numbers aren't given. It is a horrible business.

All my best wishes – I hope you will have a pleasant
Christmas.

Yours,

A.S.L."

The writer was his old friend, Susan Lawrence, the first woman to sit in a Labour Party cabinet, going blind but still a stalwart left-winger. Then another letter arrived, handwritten on notepaper with the House of Commons seal embossed on it:

"23/12/44:

I was annoyed to see the intervention when you spoke on
Greece in the Lords. It seemed to me to be a perfectly proper
thing for you to say. I admire your courage.

The King has sent a telegram to his Prime Minister, M.
Papandreou, refusing the setting up of a Regency. I submit
that in those circumstances His Majesty's Government should
bring their influence to bear'

Yours ever,

A. Creech-Jones."

More support was apparent in a brief note from Tom Driberg MP:

"When I asked Eden yesterday to restrain the king from
sending these un-conciliatory messages to Greece, he said
that it would be unreasonable to do so."

Sir Anthony Eden was the Foreign Secretary who had been instrumental in proposing this post-war policy on the Greece – which many Greeks resented. Eden may well have thought this was inevitable in a country that had always been politically fractured. Britain's policy was the result of Churchill's agreement with Stalin at the secret Yalta talks, where it had been agreed that Greece would be in Britain's *"sphere of influence"*. But the bone of contention for many Greeks was that Eden planned to reinstate an unpopular King, who had fled into exile in Egypt in 1941, along with some of his quisling ministers. Some of these had openly supported fascism before and during the conflict, even using the Greek police as an arm of state. In Greece this seemed an undemocratic reward for the long and costly support of Britain during the war years. Churchill and Eden were aware that militant communists were already fanning the sparks of that resentment into flames. This had led Jack Hastings to propose a compromise he must have discussed with Gavin. This was that a Greek National Army should be formed with:

> *"enough strength enough to maintain peace…British Forces would support the selected Government, whether of the Right or of the Left. I suggest that terms on that sort of basis would be acceptable to all Parties in Greece. In any case, it is worthwhile to attempt to get out of this terrible fighting between Allies, which might well turn into an ideological war which would blaze from one end of Europe to the other in the liberated countries. No nation has fought more heroically against the fascists and Nazis than the Greeks, no nation has suffered more. Do not let our country add to their injury and their suffering."*

However, chaotic events on the ground soon made this unfeasible. While Allied troops were pouring into northern Europe and an end to the war seemed imminent, Parliament supported Churchill and Gavin received this bald response from Eden:

> *"Foreign Office. SW1. 6th July 1944.*

Dear Faringdon,

*Thank you for your letter of June 30ᵗʰ about the sentences
passed by the Greek Courts Martial in Egypt.*

*I understand from Cranborne that he has since spoken to
Lord Southwood on the same subject and explained the
position.*

Sincerely,

Anthony Eden."

Lord Southwood was Labour Party Chief Whip in the House of
Lords, having replaced Lord Snell, Gavin's mentor who had died
eight months earlier. Southwood intervened to make it clear that
Gavin was acting against Labour Party wishes. The result was that
after a three-hour debate Viscount Cranborne, Conservative Leader
of the House of Lords and Secretary of State for the Dominions,
gained the complete support of the Upper House. Gavin was seen, at
best, as having spoken from his heart not his head. Others accused
him of trying to mislead the House. For someone who aimed to serve
the highest humanitarian ideals, this was humiliating. The debate
ended with this speech – indicating a battered and bowed retreat:

> *"I have detained your Lordships for too long. I thank you for
> your patience, and I should like to say a word of apology for
> having offended your Lordships. In your Lordships' House
> I have always spoken as I have felt, and I believe that your
> Lordships respect other people's convictions as you expect
> your own to be respected. I have stated what I conceive to be
> the truth and what I think are the possibilities, and if what
> I said gave offence I am sorry, particularly because it may
> have covered up more important points which arose in the
> debate. However, that may be, I always regret to call down
> on myself the condemnation of your Lordships' House, and
> in particular of the noble Viscount, the Leader of the House.*

*I regret that he should have described my Motion as being
in bad taste. I think that that was perhaps a little unfair. He
seemed to think that I ought to put down a Motion which
would fall in perfectly with Government policy, but as my
Motion was a complaint against Government policy I think
that he was asking too much. We have had an interesting
debate. While the noble Viscount, the Leader of the House,
has made a very good case from his material, and while I
agree that the situation is very difficult, I do not feel that it
has been dealt with as it should have been."*

The Greek Civil War broke out in 1945 and raged for three years
between the Greek army – backed by Great Britain and the USA – and
the Greek Democratic Army (DSE) and the Greek Communist Party
(KKE), backed by the USSR, Albania, Yugoslavia, and Bulgaria. As
such, it was a proxy military conflict at the start of the Cold War. The
fighting was particularly bitter as many of the insurgents were former
partisans who had fought against the fascist forces during WW2;
and on the other side, many had felt forced to collaborate during the
Italian and German occupation in order to survive. After three years
both sides were exhausted and the Government forces prevailed. But
the war simmered away underground for decades afterwards. Some
claimed that the embers were fanned to flames during the harsh rule
of a military junta popularly known as *"The Colonels"* in the 1960s.

Part Two: Black Executions at Midnight

Whilst Gavin was still involved with the Greek tragedy, an African-
American one grabbed his attention on the home front. Again, this
occurred shortly before Operation Overlord, the Allied invasion of
Normandy. Before the war Bishop's Cleeve, a rural village on the
outskirts of Cheltenham, had a population of 400. On March 4th 1944,
it had untold thousands due to the arrival of two camps of American
soldiers preparing for "D-Day". One of these camps consisted of
black American soldiers and the other white American soldiers. On
a snowy night, Dorothy Homes, a 16-year-old local girl, left a dance

at the village hall with her new boyfriend, 18-year-old American Pvt Edward J. Heffernan. They were both white. As Edward walked Dorothy home through the village the couple were set upon. Edward was knocked out and did not see his attackers. When he regained consciousness and could not find Dorothy, he ran back to the village hall for help. Some of the villagers and soldiers there turned out to search for her. Tracks in the snow led them to find her at the bottom of a lane where she had been dragged and assaulted by a brook. Shaking and too shocked to speak, she was escorted home. The next day two local policemen assisted by an U.S. Army Sergeant traced footprints in the snow to the black Americans' camp. Here they arrested two soldiers in the barracks, both of whom claimed to be innocent and offered alibis. Seven weeks later, on April 28th 1944, both men, Privates Eliga Brinson and Willie Smith (aged 25 and 21 respectively) of the 4090th Quartermaster Service Company were convicted of rape and sentenced. According to the United States military tribunal, they were to be hung simultaneously at midnight.

Race relations had become such a serious concern for American Army that censorship ensured that this case would not be reported until seven weeks later – and then with no mention of the soldiers' colour the following appeared:

> "*Syracuse Herald-American, April 30, 1944. 2 Soldiers Condemned.*
>
> *Somewhere in England. April 29 (INS).*
>
> *Two American soldiers Pvt. Willie Smith, 21, and Pvt. Eliga Brinson, 25,*
> *were sentenced to death by hanging today after being convicted by a court*
> *martial of rape. U.S. Army headquarters refused to further identify the soldiers."*

The authorities were aware that black troops had proved popular with British women. This had caused violent reactions from some white American servicemen who were shocked and angered by a phenomenon they had never encountered in their segregated communities back home. Black men were still being lynched in some American states for merely fraternising with white women. To British people, concerned with civil rights, it seemed deeply wrong that black American soldiers could be convicted of rape in Britain with no details of their defence ever released. This made some NCCL members wonder if their trials and sentencing had been unaffected by the racial discrimination endemic in American society. Rape was not a capital offence in the UK, but black American soldiers were sentenced to death for that crime here. Gavin knew that under the Visiting Forces Act of 1942, foreign servicemen were to be tried and sentenced by their own military tribunals for crimes committed in the UK, irrespective of British law. NCCL committee members wanted to challenge the rulings and Gavin was ready and willing to do that. He started by collecting newspaper clippings and placing them in a file with relevant correspondence.

On Saturday April 29th 1944, the *Derby Evening Telegraph* headlined the bombing of Berlin by the USAF and of Oslo by the RAF together with this article on its front page:

"DEATH SENTENCE ON TWO U.S. SOLDIERS.

After a trial lasting 16 hours, two American soldiers, Private Willie Smith (21) and Private Eliga Brinson (25), were sentenced to death by hanging at a court-martial, which concluded to-day in the West Country, for the forcible rape of a 16-years-old girl at Bishop's Cleeve, near Cheltenham, after a dance on March 4.

DRAGGED INTO A LANE

One of them struck her companion on the head with

something shiny and then dragged her down a lane and committed the assault. Edward J. Heffernan said he was stuck with something made of glass. He was in a dazed condition when he got up and went to the Police station for help.

FOOTPRINTS

Police Constable W.G. Hale, Detective-Constable E.W. Slade and other witnesses gave evidence of footprints in the snow, of which plaster casts were made. A search among soldiers' huts was instituted, and a pair of shoes belonging to Smith was found to bear a close resemblance to the pattern of footmarks in the snow.

ALIBI PLEADED

Both accused pleaded an alibi in defence. When they were found 'Guilty' evidence of three previous convictions in the case of Brinson and two in the case of Smith was given by the Judge Advocate.

The court was closed for two hours before the board decided on the death penalty. The verdict of the court was unanimous."

This article was the first and only time that previous convictions of the accused was mentioned. That begged the question of how could they have been tried, convicted and survived in their home states of Florida and Alabama where rape was a capital offence? How could men with criminal convictions had been allowed to serve in the U.S. Forces? Was this false evidence? The result was that dozens of British citizens wrote letters of protest to General Eisenhower, the Commander in Chief of Allied Forces in Europe. The NCCL encouraged people to write expressing their misgivings with the arrest and to ask him to commute the death sentences to periods of imprisonment. It appalled people that the prisoners were to be hung simultaneously at midnight using a double trapdoor specially built for the purpose. Some complained to the Home Office that H.M. Prison Shepton Mallet was used for such a *"barbaric"* procedure – one entirely alien to the legal system. On May 15th 1944, the Labour party activist and left-wing author Ethel Mannin wrote to Gavin,

> *"The sentence awaits confirmation by General Eisenhower, and it occurred to my husband Reginald Reynolds, and me that if various well-known people wrote to Eisenhower on the lines that if the sentence is carried out it will deeply offend progressive English thought, his clemency might be invoked. It is not a colour, as officially at least, the same law applies to black and white alike in the State in which it operates – though, of course, whether so barbarous a sentence would have been passed had the men been white is open to conjecture."*

Ethel Mannin and her husband – a Quaker, anti-colonialist and conscientious objector who worked in hospital units during the Blitz, wrote letters of protest, along with the members of the NCCL she mentioned in her letter. Dr Eustace Chesser, was a Scottish psychiatrist, social reformer and writer. In 1940 he published a sex manual *Love Without Fear* which sold 5,000 copies before it was withdrawn and Dr Chesser arrested for obscenity. Rather than pleading guilty and accepting a fine, he chose trial by jury and won. Julian Huxley, an ardent pacifist, wrote another letter. He was Secretary of the Zoological Society of London, and destined to become the first Director of UNESCO, and a founding member of the World Wildlife Fund. Others letters were written by the playwright and author Lawrence Housman (a committed socialist and pacifist), Ruth Fry (Quaker, pacifist and peace activist), Augustus John (official war artist who had turned pacifist), Dame Sybil Thorndike (actress and pacifist), Claire Sheridan (pacifist, sculptress and cousin of Winston Churchill) and Beatrix Lehmann (pacifist, actress, theatre director and author).

Eisenhower's reply to Lord Faringdon at Buscot Park is a typed letter headed:

> *"Supreme Headquarters*
>
> *Allied Expeditionary Force*
> *Office of the Supreme Commander*
> *28th May 1944*
>
> *Dear Lord Faringdon,*
>
> *Thank you for your letter. I will have the case of the two soldiers you mentioned investigated fully and will write you further in due course.*
>
> *Sincerely,*
>
> *(signed) Dwight D. Eisenhower*
> *Lord Faringdon*
> *House of Lords*
> *London."*

While he waited to hear more, Gavin, like everyone else, would have been aware that on 6th June 1944, 155,000 Allied troops landed in Normandy, and that a week later the first V-1 rocket landed on London. In spite of this, questions were asked in parliament and newspaper articles by NCCP members such as the barristers Ronald Kidd and D.N. Pritt; protests that millions of the same size and make of shoes said to have left footprints in the snow were being worn by American troops; nearly a thousand letters of protest to British newspapers. Privates Eliga Brinson and Willie Smith were hung on 11th August 1944.

The Gloucestershire Echo carried news of the joint execution on 12th August. The story appeared less prominently the next day in *The Western Daily Press and Bristol Mirror.* It had a widespread coverage outside the UK, and was reported in Australia and the USA. Eight days after the executions, the weekly *Cheltenham Chronicle and*

Gloucestershire Echo reported it – with the first passing mention of race – the fact that a pair of *"negroes"* had assaulted a *"white"* soldier. Given that General Eisenhower's priority was the advance of Allied troops across Western Europe, he had a reasonable excuse for not writing again. But his legal advisor promised to have had the case *"investigated fully"*, as the next letter to Gavin from his Headquarters states.

> *"Judge Advocate Section.*
> *Headquarters,*
> *European Theatre of Operations,*
> *United States Army.*
>
> *17th August 1944.*
>
> *Dear Lord Faringdon,*
>
> *Your letter of 28th May 1944 addressed to General Eisenhower respecting the case of Privates Eliga Brinson and Willie Smith, sentenced to death for the crime of rape committed against a British civilian, has been referred by him to me for further reply on his behalf.*
>
> *Each of the soldiers was found guilty of rape by a United States Court-martial; and under the law applicable to all ranks in all components of the United States Army no matter where stationed the prescribed punishment is either death or imprisonment for life. These measures are regarded by our government as requisite and appropriate. To insure not only penalties adequate to punishing the individual for such heinous crimes, but also to deter others from the commission of acts of violence.*
>
> *In keeping with desire that justice be done, General Eisenhower repeatedly reconsidered his action in this case; and, you may be assured that in carrying out the grave responsibilities which devolve to him by law, he gave full consideration to the matter of clemency as petitioned by you.*

It is regretted that in view of all the facts, not the least being the bestiality of the crime itself, execution of the sentence of court-martial was deemed requisite to justice.

Sincerely,

(signed) Ed. C. Betts.
Brigadier General, U.S.A.,
Theatre Judge Advocate."

Then a second, more strongly worded, letter from Brigadier-General Betts arrived:

"2 October 1944.

The Rt. Hon. Lord Faringdon,
The Basque House,
Buscot Park,
Faringdon, Berks.

Dear Lord Faringdon,

Your letter of September 2 acknowledging my letter of 17 August has just come to hand – having been forwarded to me upon the continent, whence General Eisenhower's Headquarters have been transferred.

General Eisenhower appreciates your considerate thought-fulness in acquainting him with your views upon his action in the cases of Brinson and Smith, to whom your letters of May 28 and September 2 refer. He is anxious that you know of the genuineness of his regret for the necessity of action by him in these cases at variance with the English penal code and exceeding in severity of punishment considered adequate by you and English opinion. He is hopeful that you and members of Parliament who may raise his action in these premises will regard the fact that it was taken in the performance of duty and in keeping with his sole responsibility for the proper discipline of the American forces under his command.

Sincerely,

(signed) Ed. C. Betts.
Brigadier General, U.S.A.,
Theatre Judge Advocate."

Under the provisions of the Visiting Forces Act 1942, eighteen American servicemen were executed in HM Prison Shepton Mallet by 1945. The executioner Albert Pierrepoint described these wartime hangings as the worst experiences of his career. This was due to the length of time that condemned American soldiers had to stand blindfolded on the scaffold while their sentences were read to them. Nine were convicted of murder, six of rape, and three of both crimes. Although the American army was 90% white, ten of the 18 men hanged were black and three were Mexican-Americans. After the war all their remains were exhumed from the prison graveyard and interred in the *"Dishonored Dead"* section of the WW1 Oise-Aisne WW1 cemetery, France, where their grave markers flush with the mown grass bear no names but only serial numbers.

This had a deep effect on Gavin, who began a campaign for the end of corporal punishment in British colonial regiments. A decade later in 1955 he was a signatory to a letter published in the *Daily Mail* demanding an end to capital punishment in the wake of the Ruth Ellis case – the last woman to be hanged in Britain. In 1961 *The Times* listed Gavin as a committee member of the National Campaign for the Abolition of Capital Punishment. In 1965 *The Times* reported that he had spoken and voted in favour of the abolition of the death penalty.

CHAPTER 16

Rumours and Reputation

A quote attributed to Gavin, been repeated so often that it became legendary, may just be myth. He was said to have addressed the Upper House as *"My dears"* – and to have quickly corrected this slip of the tongue to *"My Lords"*. Hansard did not record this, and so in 2014 I wrote to the editor to ask why and received the following reply:

> *"House of Lords Hansard (the Official Report) is the edited verbatim report of proceedings of the House of Lords. Members' words are recorded by Hansard reporters and then edited to remove repetitions and obvious mistakes but without taking away from the meaning. Hansard will publish Members' speeches as beginning with 'My Lords', regardless of how a Member addresses the Chamber, so Lord Farringdon's mistake would almost certainly have been edited out of the official report."*

One has to conclude that Gavin may have said it. If so, why? Was it because he was under tremendous pressure in the Lords after a series of defeats which led to him being publicly humiliated? His career was certainly undergoing an eclipse at the time. Or was it simply a careless slip of the tongue from someone who was a camp homosexual?

The earliest mention of this verbal slip came in a diary entry by Sir Alan Lascelles, the private secretary to King George VI, and dates from April 1945. He wrote that during a lunch, the newly appointed Parliamentary Under Secretary for Air, Quintin Hogg confided that:

> *"Lord Faringdon, a notorious pansy, had recently thrown*
> *the House of Lords into consternation by addressing their*
> *Lordships as 'My Dears'."*

Referring to Gavin as *"a notorious pansy"* revealed quite a lot about the speaker. Gavin did not strike everyone as a *"pansy"* – the slang word at the time for an effeminate gay man – nor was he *"notorious"* for being one. He was not an outrageously camp character such as Quentin Crisp or Steven Tennant. Workers on Gavin's estate at the time recalled that while he was always nattily dressed, they were aware of a steely determination under the surface. People who knew he was homosexual said that he was a discreet, private one – they never saw him behave ostentatiously. Also, when one considers the privates lives of some noble Lords at the time – when many were bisexual or *"closet"* homosexuals and had friends who were too – it is hard to believe that any would have been disconcerted by the phrase *"My Dears"*. However, others, like Quintin Hogg, would have howled with delight at having found a stick to beat the *"faggot"* with after some of Gavin's speeches had angered peers.

An example of the way that Quintin Hogg spread his "gay" insinu-ations can be found in a diary entry by the distinguished historian A.L. Rowse. *"Lesley"* was a friend of Gavin's who came to stay with him at Buscot Park a few months before the incriminating words *"My dears"* were said to have been used in the House of Lords. Soon afterwards, the following conversation took place in this history don's rooms when Lionel Curtis C.H. and Quintin Hogg (styled Hailsham) came to tea:

> *"Why am I mixed up between Lord Faringdon and Lord*
> *Berners?*
> *Quintin Hailsham, wickedly:*
> *Ask Leslie (Rowse): he knows.*

Lionel: But I don't know. Which is which? Why do I confuse
the two?
Quintin (with a meaningful look at me):
Ask Leslie. He knows.
Lionel, thinking this over, raised his voice:
Do you mean that he is an Enemy of the Family?
The butler, appearing round the screen, announced
Lord Faringdon to see you, sir."

Hogg had salaciously disclosed that the two neighbours – Lord
Berners at Faringdon House, Faringdon, and Gavin, Lord Faringdon
at Buscot Park – were homosexual. Lionel Curtis, a Fellow of All
Souls College, tactfully employed a euphemism, probably because
he was aware that his host Leslie Rowse was homosexual as well.
No one there was thrown into *"a state of consternation"* by the mere
notion of what the law of the land then deemed deviant sexuality.
On the contrary, they savoured the sophisticated way the subject
was dealt with.

Amongst this erudite and sophisticated group, only Quintin Hogg
detested homosexuals. In 1957 details of his homophobic prejudices
were published in "The Report of the Departmental Committee
on Homosexual Offences and Prostitution" (better known as
the Wolfenden Report, after Sir John Wolfenden, the chairman of
the committee). The historian Patrick Higgins noted that Hogg used
the occasion as *"an opportunity to express his disgust"* stating that
"the instinct to describe homosexual acts as 'unnatural' is not based
on mere prejudice" – as it is *"a proselytizing religion"* that aimed to
corrupt society. Not many people would have agreed with this, apart
from bigots prone to pre-digested strong opinions. Seven years later
in 1964 the satirical magazine *Private Eye* published a "Special Spring
Number". This showed a corpulent Quintin Hogg dressed in an
unflattering toga. Musical notes sprout from his mouth as he frolics
among lambs and tosses daisies into the air. In a vignette beside this
image a man is writing a letter. The caption reads:

"Dear Sir, I have just heard the first cuckoo."

Quintin Hogg made his derogatory comments about Gavin shortly after he got a junior post at the Air Ministry. This was one of the departments in Whitehall where Gavin had made himself unpopular. If he was *"notorious"* there it was due to his persistent letters of criticism during WW2. Hogg's superiors had been forced to reply in a series of carefully worded letters relating to questions Gavin had raised in the Upper House. Many of these letters still exist, all headed Air Ministry, Whitehall, and bearing the Secretary of State for Air logo (an eagle flying with outstretched wings below an Imperial crown). They all have the words PERSONAL AND CONDIDENTIAL emblazoned in red ink on them. Each was addressed *"Dear Faringdon"*, and personally signed. One came from Sir Archibald Sinclair, Secretary of State for Air, who sat in Churchill's cabinet; and others from his subordinate Lord Sherwood, Parliamentary Under Secretary of State for Air (Lords). Gavin's questions in the Lords had forced them to take time to explain, for example, that the high losses of pilots and crews were not due to *"ineffective"* and *"obsolete aircraft"* as Gavin suggested. Raising such a sensitive subject in wartime was certain to get the questioner disliked in Whitehall. Moreover, it was galling for military supremos to have to explain themselves to a pacifist. Especially as many in wartime thought pacifists unpatriotic, unmanly and conflated the word *pacifist* with cowards and *"Pansies"*.

Gavin had first begun to raise questions about RAF Coastal Command soon after the War artist Eric Ravilious was lost at sea off the coast of Iceland in September 1942. In this case a Lockheed Hudson had failed to return from a patrol. The next morning three other Hudsons were sent out to search for the first. Eric Ravilious, who had come to stay and paint at Buscot Park a year earlier, was now an official war artist and chose to join one of the crews. Then the Hudson that Ravilious boarded failed to return. After a four-day search, the RAF declared the war artist and the aircraft's four-man crew *"lost in action"*. This amounted to a total of nine men lost in a week. Hudsons had been acquired by the RAF as a temporary solution to the shortage of aircraft. They were American-made cargo aircraft that had been adapted for coastal defence as submarine hunters and destroyers. Gavin had been informed that the Lockheed Hudson was designed long before the war and better alternatives were around. But the Air Ministry claimed that these alternatives were not available to the RAF. Gavin argued that they should be as many pilots thought Hudsons were *"inadequate and obsolete"*. This had to be refuted by the Air Chiefs, whose letters to Gavin made it clear that they wished he would let the matter lie for the sake of wartime morale. The Air Ministry tried to remedy the deficiencies in *"range, radios and radar"*, but further Hudsons and their crews were lost. The fact was that Coastal Defence was not the top priority. That was for the RAF to extend fighter cover over mainland Britain with Spitfires and Hurricanes during the Battle of Britain.

In addition to complaining about Lockheed Hudsons in Iceland, Gavin made himself unpopular at the Air Ministry by raising the issue of Gloster Gladiator biplanes in Malta. Having served as a fire-fighter in the Blitz there, he heard that these *"obsolete aircraft"* were all that the RAF had to fly against modern Italian and German single-wing fighters. The Gloster Gladiator biplanes were slower and less manoeuvrable. There were only three of them and with grim humour they had been nicknamed *"Faith"*, *"Hope"* and *"Charity"*. Again, the problem was due to wartime shortages. Eventually enough Spitfires were sent to Malta. But Gavin had cemented his unpopularity at the Air Ministry by raising other issues: overdue pay and leave. Yet again, the Air chiefs, had to explain that they were doing as best they could in difficult wartime conditions. Resentment was discernible in some of the Air Ministry replies. For example, in 1942 he had written in great detail about a man who came from an adjacent county (presumably someone he had met). Gavin suggested that this man, who had served during the siege of Malta, was suffering from combat exhaustion, and that this was conflated with cowardice by his superior officers. Matters came to a head with a series of replies from Lord Sherwood, Under Secretary of State for the Air Ministry.

"Private and Confidential.
Air Ministry.
King Charles St.
Whitehall S.W.1.
9th January 1943.

Dear Faringdon,

The Secretary of State has asked me to reply to your letter
of 5th January about the Air Ministry's procedure in dealing
with airmen who have, for various reasons, been taken off
flying duties. The question is a complicated one and there are
so many different types of case that I have thought it best to
send you the enclosed memorandum (Two densely typed
foolscap pages followed, labelled CONFIDENTIAL).

I can assure you from personal knowledge of many cases
which come to my notice that each and every one of them is
examined with the greatest care before the decision is reached
by the Squadron Commander, the Station Commander, the
Group Commander and finally, by the Air Ministry. A full
statement is prepared and every aspect of the individual's
career is fully weighed. His flying history, together with his
medical history, is reviewed, and the individual is permitted
to make any statement, written or oral, in his own defence
and, if he requires it, he is given an interview with the Air
Ministry. Equal weight is given to the man's own defence
as to reports on him by the Service authorities. Every case
which involves consideration for removal from flying duties
is never the subject of a hasty decision, and always, because
of the separate treatment involved as set out in the attached
memorandum, we are searching in our analysis of the case as
to whether it properly falls to be dealt with as a 'medical' case
or as a case of forfeiture of confidence If there is any element
of doubt the benefit is always given to the airman.

Yours ever,
Sherwood."

Nevertheless, Gavin was not satisfied. The man concerned had transferred from the Army to the RAF and had lost his nerve after a couple of air crashes during training. The switch from one arm of the service to another had not helped as he felt himself side-lined. Lord Sherwood assured Gavin that the case was being looked into. But he had to write again in April 1943. This time a three-page letter mentions Sergeant Allison, whose case Gavin suggested had been *"wrongly handled"* as he was obliged to continue flying after he had repeatedly asked to be given ground duties.

> *"Dear Faringdon,*
>
> *Many thanks for your letter of 24th March about the treatment of airmen who have to be removed from flying duties. I would make the following points in reply... A man who is suffering from genuine operational stress would not be forced to continue flying to the danger of himself or his friends...As you say, it would take some very strong cause to make a man, who has volunteered for flying duties, put himself apart from his fellows by saying that he is not prepared to carry on flying. In such cases, the cause is sometimes a lack of 'guts', and it is in these cases that man is reduced. The need for a 'deterrent' may perhaps be best explained in this way:*
>
> *A flight over Germany is a very frightening experience and the airman who makes it, if he is a normal person, will be afraid. He does, however, find from somewhere that extra bit of determination, which pulls him through. It would be much harder for him to find this extra determination if he knew all the time that whatever happened there would be a comfortable job waiting for him on the ground with no loss of rank or prestige. I have enquired into the case of Sergeant Allison but found no indication that it has been wrongly handled. The R.C.A.F. Authorities have concurred in his treatment has been in accordance with the procedure*

*explained in the Memorandum I sent you with my letter of
9th January. I should perhaps mention the following specific
points. Allison has not done any operational flying. In the
opinion of his Commanding Officer, the two crashes in which
he has been involved (no-one was hurt in either of them)
did not constitute exceptional flying stress. In none of the
reports on his case, including that of the Medical Board, is
mention of concussion, nor does Allison mention it in his
own statement. I might add that concussion is treated very
seriously indeed in considering this type of case. Allison has
not said he is willing to continue as an Air Gunner. He has,
however, asked to be re-mustered as an Airfield Controller,
which is a ground job.*

Yours ever,

Sherwood."

Tragically, this correspondence became redundant a month later.
Sergeant Allison died after bailing out of a Halifax bomber in panic
soon after it was hit by enemy anti-aircraft fire while on a raid into
Germany. Sgt Allison's parachute failed to open in time to arrest
his fall. The rest of the crew survived after the pilot flew on and
crash-landed.

Lord Sherwood had to write a third letter to Gavin in 1943, again
on behalf of Sir Archibald Sinclair, Secretary of State for Air. In this
reply one gets a sense of his frustration with having to deal with
continued criticism:

> *"the process of re-equipping our squadrons with the latest
> aircraft cannot be accomplished in a moment…the older
> types of aircraft which are in the process of being replaced, are
> employed on the less difficult operations…*

*I should like to refute most categorically the suggestion that
we 'expose our airmen to great risks by the use of obsolete
aircraft when modern machines are available'. This is not and
has never been the case."*

By this time Quintin Hogg had arrived at the Air Ministry and it is
likely that he overheard unflattering comments about Gavin, whose
humanitarian instincts would have been seen as unreasonable; and
his pacifism as unpatriotic.

For Gavin this was a period when he had to endure a personal
eclipse. In spite of the fact that few had campaigned for the Labour
Party as hard as he since he joined more than a decade earlier,
he was *persona non grata*. Few had attended or organised as many
fund-raising events, driven to speak in support of candidates across
the country; faced personal criticism in the press as a *"class traitor"*.
In spite of all this he was side-lined when Labour won the general
election in 1945. He had been snubbed by the new Prime Minister,
Clement Attlee.

In spite of his disappointment, Gavin wrote to his parliamentary
colleague, and to a certain extent his chief rival, "Billy" Hare, the Earl
of Listowel, to congratulate him on becoming Postmaster-General in
the new cabinet. Listowel replied

*"I heard from someone who had been at one of your election
meetings that you had made a big impression, and feel that
the party owes you a great deal for your immensely hard
work."*

Gavin's Fabian Society colleague Arthur Creech-Jones expressed
dismay:

*"After all your work and service Attlee had nothing to say to
you."*

Susan Lawrence wrote:

> *"I am disappointed with the new ministers – such old crones*
> *most of them. I did think Creech-Jones should have had*
> *Colonies, and Ellen is not a very good choice for poor old*
> *Education…I am <u>convinced</u> that there is nothing against you.*
> *The very worst comment I heard was that you had not done*
> *'party-work' until the election. Otherwise, everyone spoke of*
> *you in the most handsome terms. And of course with Listowel*
> *and Huntingdon in there wasn't room for another Lord.*
> *And your election services were considered splendid…But it*
> *is a horrid disappointment and very wrong & absurd from*
> *the point of view of the real interests of the Party. For I am*
> *certain that you have the capacity for big things and there is*
> *time enough before you, this is only a check.*
>
> *Affectionately yours,*
>
> *Susan Lawrence."*

Clearly, the new Labour leadership saw Gavin as beyond the pale – ungovernable, maverick. Part of the reason for this was probably Gavin's track record of putting his personal interests above the party agenda. "Billy" Listowel, one the other hand, was a team player who had Clem Attlee's full confidence. Listowel went on to become Minister of Information, Deputy Leader of the House of Lords, as well as Under-Secretary of State for India and Burma. In fact, this Anglo-Irish peer won all glittering prizes Gavin had set his sights on when Listowel became the last Secretary of State for India as well as the last Governor-General of Ghana.

Whilst Attlee never commented on his reasons for bypassing Gavin, a remark by Lord Winster quoted by Hugh Dalton (Chancellor of the Exchequer from 1945–57) may offer an explanation. In Dalton's diaries of 1942 he recorded Winster – who was seriously ill at the time – had complained that his fellow Labour peers were *"quite impossible"*. Lord

Winster described Lord Listowel as *"always white with stage fright"*; Lord Snell as *"very old indeed and deafer still"*; and Lord Faringdon as *"a pansy pacifist of whose private tendencies it might be slander to speak freely"*. This slur was sloppily attributed to Hugh Dalton in the *National Dictionary of Biography*, and that error has continued to be recycled in print and on the internet. Contrary to the false impression this has created, the sentiments were not Dalton's but Winster's; and after his illness he revised his views of Lord Faringdon and was to work well with him. As for Hugh Dalton, his signature appeared in the Buscot Park visitors' book ten times during the post-war years, and he always wrote effusive thank you letters, so he does not appear to have suffered from any *"slanderous"* events there, and never mentioned any impropriety in connection with his host. Many other Labour luminaries and their wives or partners found no problem accepting Gavin's hospitality: Hugh Gaitskell, Harold Wilson, James Callaghan, Roy Jenkins, Margery Fry and Wilfred Roberts. None of these passed on any ribald tales. The only *"corridor creeping"* involved was extra-marital and heterosexual. Nye Bevan and Jennie Lee came while having an affair; and Mrs Barbara Castle, Minister of Transport, had a *"very warm"* relationship with the Rt Hon. Dennis Healey, Chancellor of the Exchequer. The sexual climate at Buscot Park was not quite *"tropical"*.

Gavin's sense of righteous causes may have been justified, but as Voltaire once warned: *"It can be dangerous to be right when your government is wrong"*. He had always been resented in some circles, but now he was losing public respect in spite of working harder than ever on humanitarian issues. The *"My Dears"* slip (which some claimed was intentional) was repeated so often that it became an indelible stain on his reputation – marking him out as effete dilettante, undermining his sincerity and altruism. It affected his ability to be taken seriously. For example, in 1951 the Labour MP Tom Driberg (who was arrested for an indecent act in a public place that very year) wrote: *"His political career was not advanced by an accidental prefacing a speech not by 'My Lords' but by 'My dears'"*. And later in the same book Driberg recounted a time when Gavin came to speak on his behalf during the general election campaign and *"whinnied: The rain, My dears, it poured"*. Was Gavin's voice so high pitched and equine? Or was that line an irresistible caricature one for a journalist? Others contradicted this impression of Gavin's vocal delivery. For example, a letter sent after a Labour Party conference debate on India in 1941 from the delegate G.M. Pulimond:

> *"I was sitting with friends at the back of the hall and your voice, having an unusual carrying power, came through forcibly to us in the back seats. I heard someone say 'Lord Faringdon did it very well'."*

Nevertheless, mud sticks, and in 1968 another friend, Alan Pryce-Jones, the former editor of the *Times Literary Supplement* wrote in the *The Bonus of Laughter*:

> *"Gavin's famous mistake of prefacing a speech with 'My Dears' not 'My Lords' in the Upper House."*

And on Wikipedia one finds that Gavin,

> *"known for his effeminate demeanour, once opened a speech in the House of Lords with the words 'My dears' instead of 'My Lords'".*

More recently, Andrew Lownie, a literary agent turned author, circulated a rumour of a Communist Party cell at Buscot Park. This was based on a paragraph in the unpublished memoirs of Kenneth Sinclair-Loutit's, *Very Little Luggage* which Lownie cited in his book *Stalin's Englishman: The Lives of Guy Burgess*. As it happens, Kenneth Sinclair-Loutit had never been to Buscot Park and what he wrote was hearsay or fiction with very little weight:

> *"It seems that his butler had become convener of the Party cell and had the responsibility for the agenda of its meetings, which took place in the library of Buscot Park. Legend had it*

that the butler would say at the end of dinner, 'May I draw
his Lordship's attention that this evening there is a meeting in
the library', but once the meeting started the forms of speech
became more appropriate. The butler would ask Comrade
Henderson to read the minutes of the last meeting. I am not
clear about the membership of this Party branch; the butler
chaired the meetings, and Comrade Henderson was the
branch secretary."

Gavin's butler during this period was Mr Buck, known elsewhere
for being self-effacing and apolitical. Indeed. Buck was affectionately
referred to as *"your priceless stage butler"* by the Jewish refugee Fritz
Wolff-Auerbach. Apart from this distorted view of him, it is unlikely
that any political meetings would have been held in the library (on the
ground floor) as those invariably took place in the sitting room on the
piano nobile above. Here political portraits on the walls set the tone.
One over a fireplace is of Gavin's relative Lord Shaftesbury, holding
a copy of the Mining Act that ended the employment of juveniles
underground. Another by Joshua Reynolds shows the Countess of
Coventry, a philanthropist who set up soup kitchens for the destitute
poor in cities; another formerly thought to be of William Wilberforce,
the anti-slavery campaigner hangs nearby. The theme on the walls
here was meant to encourage social conscience and this is where
Trade Union leaders and Labour politicians tried to forge an alliance
called "In Place of Strife". In contrast, Sinclair-Loutit's anecdote seems
gossip with no basis in fact. It was passed on by Andrew Lownie with
the claim that the spy Guy Burgess *"often spent weekends"* at Buscot.
However, the visitors' book shows that Burgess only came only once,
and he was accompanied then by several S.I.S. operatives. Andrew
Lownie did not try to verify the facts by contacting someone at Buscot
Park. He didn't and as a result his assertions are misleading, especially
when he claims that Gavin was:

"an effete Old Etonian homosexual Marxist…who would
preface his remarks in the House of Lords with 'My dears',
rather than 'Mr Lords'".

A critical but more balanced view of Gavin came in a letter written by another gay man – Alan Bennett – to his tutor the Jewish refugee Karl Leyser, who had become Fellow in History at Magdalene College, Oxford. This was dated 26th August 1945 – "V-J Day" when the future playwright saw him as:

> *"an extremely young 45 who looked about 30 with all the aristocratic delicacy of feature and figure that you often find in the third generation parvenu. He is a labour peer and strikingly got up in a sort of grey uniform, trousers, and wind-jacket and shirt. He and I rather hit it off. Some would say he is rather cissy; certainly not clever, but cultivated and animated."*

Alan Bennett and the historian Prof. A.J.P. Taylor visited Kelmscott Manor and then had lunch with Lord Berners at Faringdon House. Alan Taylor was a Labour-voting pacifist and socialist but could barely contain his dislike of the red peer:

> *"At the gate we were caught up by Gavin F. in his ancient family Rolls-Royce. He said that we must come and see his house…and he would drive us to Oxford himself. He and Alan didn't like each other and there was an embarrassing pause before I accepted. So off we went to Buscot Park. F. Inherited it half a dozen years or more ago from a grandfather who built many railways in Spain and South America – the first peer. F. doesn't live there now but alone in the keeper's lodge at the gate while a girls' school has been there all the war and just gone. …the lodge beside the lake where he lives with alone with three or four charming cats and a collection of modern paintings – Duncan Grants chiefly. And after he had changed into his Fire Guard uniform we set off on the Rolls for Oxford. Alan and I sat behind and we had one of those difficult conversations in which one of the party has his back to the other two.*

Alan was awfully bored by F.'s views on international affairs
(Note A.J.P. Taylor was notorious at the time for his
firmness of his opinions on Russia – many of which he
altered afterwards) *and by his inability to hold forth himself.*
He said afterwards, he thought F. a 'very stupid man and
so boring', and the thought was quite obvious throughout.
But I, as I said, liked him. He was sympathetic to me – and
we parted with every intention expressed of meeting again. I
hope we do."

CHAPTER 17

The Expatriate Brother

Gavin's youngest brother Roderic lived abroad for most of his life. In 1945 he passed through England on his way to Sweden when he was 36 years old and had spent the previous seven years in South America. His mother, sister Peggy and sister-in-law Oonagh met with "Roddy", but his brothers Michael and Gavin avoided him. Afterwards, while staying at the grandest hotel in Stockholm, he wrote a 12-page letter to Gavin in which he mentioned several criticisms of his conduct by someone outside the family that Roddy believed had led to his brothers to shun him. These had come from the Rt Hon, Brendon Bracken MP who had served as Minister of Information for four years during the time Roddy was abroad:

> *"Peggy had put me on the track a week ago, but by wishing to spare my feelings she had not convinced me that I was the victim of a brotherly boycott. Oonagh told me that Bracken had told Mike that I had hurriedly joined the British Legation as Hon. Attaché in order to avoid the war & to have money sent to me from England."*

Bracken had been Gavin's neighbour in North St., Westminster, and as mentioned in an earlier chapter, had tried to help Lady Violet launch her son's political career as a Conservative in the late 1920s. Their plans collapsed when Gavin unexpectedly joined the Labour Party. Since then, "B.B.", as he often signed himself, had risen to become a powerful politician whose opinions some regarded as infallible. But the left-wing author George Orwell, who had worked under "B.B." in Whitehall, thought of him very differently. In 1945, the year that Roddy wrote his letter to Gavin, Orwell had caricatured "B.B." as *"Big Brother"*, the despotic ruler of the Ministry of Truth, in his novel *1984*. So it might be that Bracken had been mistaken about Roddy. However, his brother Michael was a Staff Officer attached to the War Office, which was being run by the Prime Minister Sir Winston Churchill himself, during WW2; and "B.B." was one of his chief advisors. Criticism of Roddy had come from the highest echelon of power, within the chain of command governing Michael, from his boss. Such disapproval would have struck Michael, Peggy and Lady Violet like a blow from Thor's hammer. Only one family member would be expected to challenge the establishment view, and so Roddy had written to Gavin hoping to exonerate himself:

> *"Six months before war was declared the F.O. wrote to me*
> *asking me to come back to the Communications Dept (where*
> *as an 'Honorary Attaché' I had obtained rudimentary*
> *training in ciphering before being sent abroad). Naturally, I*
> *had no choice, even if I wanted to, to what in effect amounted*
> *to a mobilisation order."*

Unfortunately for Roddy, Gavin knew this was misleading. Roddy had trained in cipher work from 1932–33 after which he had lived well abroad on the income from his inheritance, invested and managed by a wiser head appointed by his grandfather, the first Lord Faringdon. After five years not having to work for a living, the Foreign Office had offered him a job based on his cipher training in London. But Roddy demurred as he was hoping for something more. He claimed to have *"reached a compromise with the F.O. before going to Argentina for the winter"*, but perhaps this was in his own mind, as the F.O. were already doing him a favour by offering him an unpaid position. In January 1938 Roddy arrived in Buenos Aires, and he was still there in June 1939 when he was offered an unpaid post in Montevideo 120 miles away. The offer came from a celebrated diplomat Sir Eugen Middleton-Drake, Minister in charge of the small but influential British Legation in Uruguay. Again, Roddy demurred:

*"I was flattered by his wish to include me on his staff & by
his importunity over the long distance wire. He brushed my
reasons for not joining aside, by immediately telegraphing the
F.O. explaining that I was desperately needed etc. He received
a telegram from the F.O. agreeing that I could join his staff
on condition that in the event of National Emergency I
should immediately occupy the post of Cipher Officer & carry
out the duties in Montevideo which I should otherwise carry
out in London."*

Up until now, Roddy had lived a "gay" life in both senses of that
word. Playful, flamboyant and vain, he saw the Minister's job offer as
a seduction. This was just a fanciful way of describing negotiations
with Sir Eugen Middleton-Drake who, with war looming, offered
Roddy the position of Honorary Attaché because Roddy had been
trained in cipher work and was living only 120 miles away. This
would be an unpaid internship from which he could expect to rise
in the diplomatic service if he proved useful. But Roddy was angling
for a more prestigious role, such as the salaried position he was given
four years later – Civil Attaché and Private Secretary to the British
Ambassador in Argentina. As nothing of the kind was on offer Roddy
prevaricated until Sir Eugen confirmed by telegram to London that
Roddy was *"desperately needed"* and the F.O. agreed he might be
promoted after war broke out. However, when that happened just
over a month later Roddy was disappointed to find that he was
expected to do the job he had been trained for five years previously:

*"My chief was his own Press, Cultural & every other kind
of attaché & what he needed was an elegant 'Yes' man. The
position was farcical. The outgoing attaché had taken the
line of least resistance and become a stooge. What line I
should eventually have taken was decided for me. War was
declared and I joyfully shed my attachéship to glue my nose
to ciphers."*

Roddy went on to claim that during *"the first two and half years of the war"* – when he assisted the Legation's cipher officer and his *"geriatric clerk"* – that he had personally done *"the work of four men"*. That was a histrionic exaggeration. It was followed by a false comparison of F.O. staff wages with his private income, but here he admitted one of Bracken's criticisms – that he had had broken wartime exchange control rules:

> *"The income I was meanwhile drawing from England, was, with the fall on the exchange, fairly approximately that of a cipher officer, so that I was not even depriving my country of sterling."*

Foreign exchange was something "B.B." knew a great deal about. He had founded *The Financial Times* as well as *The Economist*, and went on to use his influence in parliament to create laws limiting movements of sterling out of the country. One of the few ways that could happen legally was if you were employed by the Foreign Office. But as Roddy did not appear on their official staff lists until 1942, he had to find another way of bypassing the wartime restrictions, and in his own words, did so:

> *"Luckily, before the war I had brought some money to Uruguay, at the old rate of exchange, I had paid my house rent for a whole term of the contract in advance, had built and paid for a little seaside house which I could easily rent, a motorcar, furniture, etc. so that my position was far more favourable than a salaried cipher officer."*

Roddy had taken a large amount of cash abroad. In addition, three years before war had been declared, he had transferred a financial portfolio to the USA thus allowing him to receive dividends in dollars. He did not hint at this here. It was not illegal and would not have made him guilty of tax evasion. In fact, it could be argued that it had been a shrewd move. But when the war came some in Whitehall, and the patriotic public at large, would have deplored his benefiting from the dollar's rise against the pound. Many people, his brothers included, had sacrificed throughout the war and now feared bankruptcy in its aftermath. In 1945 Gavin was about to lose much of his inheritance to the newly elected Labour government's wealth tax. Michael's army pay as a Lt.-Col was insufficient to support his wife and three children, and he would have to retire and forge a new career. Roddy had no financial problems – but his vanity caused him to suffer from how others saw him. Still, he was tactless and sought to restore Gavin's faith in him with this disingenuous remark:

> *"Incidentally, for no apparent reason the treasury released grandpa's final settlement money which considerably relieved my financial position, made it possible for me to add to my Buscot & pay for the more expensive life of B.A."*

The first Lord Faringdon had died eleven years before and the executors had settled probate within two years. Roddy had not received his *"final settlement money"* then (in 1936) as he was domiciled abroad. By 1945 when Roddy did get the money, it was because exchange controls on funds from the UK to Uruguay had been lifted as a favour to the former ally. Whilst Roddy claimed that this *"considerably relieved my financial position"*, his letters to his mother show that he had not been short of funds in South America. On the contrary, he had taken holidays in Argentina, Chile, Uruguay and Brazil; purchased and furnished a town house in Montevideo (not simply rented one as he claimed in his letter to Gavin). When he wrote that he could now *"add to my Buscot"* he meant that he could expand the beach house he had built for himself in fashionable Punta del Este.

Roddy never admitted any wrongs and so he never showed any remorse. He was invariably smug and patronising. His letter offered only condescension and hostility to his brothers. This emotional detachment had become characteristic over the years. The brothers had always been very different. Gavin was now an idealistic socialist – a dangerous fool in Roddy's eyes. He saw Michael, the army officer, as a conventional martinet. His brothers, on the other hand, both saw Roddy as a social butterfly who in spite of having lived abroad for years had never quite *"flown the nest"*. In this they were correct, for Roddy was more emotionally attached to his mother than most people would consider normal.

Family bonds had loosened after his father's death in 1922 when Roddy was 13. Gavin moved out of Buscot Park and married in 1927. Michael had moved away and married in 1929 as did Peggy in 1932. Gavin visited his mother regularly but continued to disappoint her. Roddy witnessed her frustration and came to see himself as the more loyal and deserving son. After he left Britain in 1932, he wrote frequently, and sometimes returned to stay with her for a month at a time. A recurrent feature of his letters was their fear that Gavin, the socialist, might give away heirlooms they felt should stay in the family. There was more to this relationship. Normally, the third son in a titled family would go off to make his way in the military, clergy or colonial administration service. Or his mother might have steered an heiress his way, as Lady Violet had done with Gavin. But none of this happened. The reasons were that Roddy's financial resources were sufficient for him to live well without working; and he was so close to his mother that there was never any space for another woman in his life. On top of this, Roddy was homosexual. This meant that he could be prosecuted and imprisoned for committing a criminal offence; or worse, blackmailed. So, it was pragmatic for a hedonistic extrovert like Roddy to live abroad.

A letter in Lady Violet's files shows that by the age of eighteen Roddy had misbehaved repeatedly and thrown her into a kind of maternal despair. This was spoken of so openly that in January 1927, Gavin's friend Robert Boothby MP took it upon himself to counsel Roddy. This urbane young politician was to serve as the best man at Gavin's wedding six months later. His letter was written as a family friend and was both critical and affectionate. He gave a list of Roddy's misdeeds and offered achievable advice on how he could improve his behaviour. Boothby was uniquely equipped to do this being a noted debonair *"man about town"*, as well as a rising star in Conservative political circles. He was also someone who knew how to misbehave and get away with it. After all, he managed to hide the fact that he was a promiscuous bisexual for years. Any young man hoping to get on in public life might well have been flattered to receive Boothby's attention. Roddy, who was vain by nature, must have shown and discussed the letter with his mother. She kept it, and so here is Bob Boothby's view of the Hon. Roderick Dalzell Henderson:

> *"Beechwood, Murrayfield, Midlothian.*
>
> *Jan. 2. 1927.*
>
> *I wonder what you have been up to lately. However it doesn't much matter because now you have a chance to turn over a new leaf. Perhaps you will become such a jolly fellow in 1927 that Gavin won't know you when he comes back from Australia, and I'm sure you would appreciate that.*
>
> *Now that I have become Parliamentary Secretary to the Chancellor of the Exchequer with a large room in the Treasury all of my own, you will have to treat me with great reverence.*
>
> *Read the enclosed New Year Message. It will help you in the fight for the right. Perhaps I shall see you at Buscot, in which case I shall have a splendid opportunity of carrying on the work of Reform which has been so sadly interrupted.*
>
> *Yrs ever*
>
> *Bob*
>
> *RESOLUTIONS FOR THE YEAR 1927*
>
> *By Roderick Henderson.*

———————————————

1. *I will never tell a lie in 1927.*
2. *I will be sweet and kind always to everyone, but especially to my enchanting mother, to whom I have caused enough trouble in the past to do for six.*
3. *I will not pretend to be more of an outsider than I am.*
4. *I will attend to the advice given to me by my elders and betters.*
5. *I will think kindly of my brother Gavin, whatever he may think of me.*
6. *I will not hire expensive motor-cars to take me for trips in France, and send in the account to other people's mothers.*
7. *I will be industrious, and humble.*
8. *I will go to Cambridge.*
9. *I will not go to Oxford, because I know it would not be good for me.*
10. *When I feel a wave of wickedness coming over me, and that it is rather a good thing to be wicked, and great fun, I will remember that I was born with a White Angel and a Red Devil inside me, and if I only try a little bit to be good, the W.A. will beat the R.D., and Angels are better than Devils, and rarer."*

Roddy's *"White Angel "*spread its wings two years later in May 1930 when he was an undergraduate reading languages at Pembroke College, Cambridge writing to Gavin. This is the only written evidence that they had been close.

> *"My dear Gavin,*
>
> *Forgive this card but I have run out of paper. Yr gems arrived here safely, & are really stupendous. It was really very sweet of you to send them to me. They are the most fascinating peacock blue-green shade at night, but so magnificent that I am afraid everyone will think they are Burma gem & I shall feel a trifle ostentatious & Hohenzollern! Please come down anytime you like. I should love to see you, but let me know in advance at least a day because I should like to do more for*

you than the casual weekend guest. I have every hope you will
come.

Thank you so much again, bless you. Roddy."

Roddy liked to express himself extravagantly and his reference
to *"Hohenzollern"* was typical. They were the family of German
aristocrats who produced "Mad Ludwig of Bavaria", the prince who
lived in fantasy castles inspired by Teutonic legends and Wagnerian
opera. Roddy's note flutters with girlish delight, which suggests he
was a far more ostentatious gay than Gavin.

Four years later in 1934 Alexander, the 1st Lord Faringdon, passed
away and Gavin inherited the title, a substantial financial trust fund,
as well as the contents of Pomfret Castle, 18 Arlington Street, W.1.
His grandfather had left a fortune of the gross value of £1,021,696.
In today's values this would be nearly £74 million on which estate
duty of over £68 million has already been paid. Michael, Roderic and
Margaret (Peggy) were to receive one-ninth part of the net worth
after Gavin (who got a third). Three Sotheby's sales raised more than
enough to settle the death duties and let Gavin buy seven pictures at
probate value. This was the start of his lifelong quest to create the
Faringdon collection of fine art and antique furniture at Buscot Park.
Gavin's having the means and place to do this in was something that
Roddy would always resent.

In September 1934, six months after Lord Faringdon's death, Roddy
wrote to his mother from a fashionable seaside hotel in Biarritz where
he was staying with his partner, who was a Swedish interior decorator
nicknamed Babel. He was also the Baron Axel Thure-Gabriel
Rudbeck. Other aristocratic male friends had joined them there to
enjoy the thermal baths, casino and motoring along the Atlantic
coast or up into the Pyrenees.

"Morrogh Bernard and Arthur Duckworth here we had a
great time together, our two cars – Rolls and Sibley – being

very much in evidence, even here where Rolls and Hispanos
seem to flourish like the daisy."

(Note: The Sibley was an American cabriolet or "convertible").

Roddy invited his mother to come and stay at his new home in
Portugal. This was what the Portuguese register of historic buildings
refers to as *"an 18*th *C Prince's recreational farm"* which had three
neo-classical buildings, French-style terraced gardens, mature
orchards and vineyards, as well as acres of good pasture. The Paço de
Palmeira estate had belonged to Don José de Bragança, Archbishop
of Braga, and the King of Portugal's half-brother. Roddy and "Babel"
renovated one part as an up-market hotel called the Turismo.
Babel was an artist and interior decorator. His family seat was the
castle Edsberg, a Nordic style manor that resembled a large white
barracks set in parkland beside the Baltic Sea. Roddy had taken
to writing *"Edsberg, Tureberg, Stockholm, Sweden"* as his address in
his mother's visitors' book when he came to stay. In the meantime,
Babel redecorated Roddy's Paço de Palmeira with Baroque, Rococo,
Chinese and Turkish style bedrooms. In 1935 Roddy wrote to his
mother about his and Babel's life there:

> *"Our first calf, bull of course, arrived last night and we are*
> *in a whirl of almost paternal excitement from the humblest*
> *farm lad upwards. She was a model mother & did all the*
> *right things, & as the dairy is now in working order, we soon*
> *hope to have our own milk, cream & butter. In preparation*
> *for this Babel and I have been making our own butter for*
> *some time with bought milk. We have a tame seagull in the*
> *court which appears as a fixture now. It stalks about very*
> *pompously, & each time anyone picks her up she plunges into*
> *the tank and washes herself thoroughly and ostentatiously.*
> *Last night she walked into my bedroom & very affectionately*
> *expectorated half her dinner at my feet.*

*Next week I have to go to Lisbon for a dinner the
Ambassador is giving to the President of the Republic & the
Dictator & will stay a few days at the Embassy. I hope my
former attachéship may be of some use to them, as the
attaché has gone to Brussels."*

Roddy went to Lisbon and met the Portuguese president Antonio
de Olivera Salazar – who styled himself "The Dictator". He told his
mother that they got along well, and proof of that emerged a few
months later. In the meantime, Roddy wrote to his mother about his
plans to celebrate the silver jubilee of H.M. King George V & H.M.
Queen Mary with a banquet for twenty-five people. A subsequent
letter six months later mentioned that most of those guests had been
staff that he had *"let go"* due to the unexpectedly high running costs
of his estate. That letter followed one in which she expressed her
worries about how much Gavin was spending on renovations at
Buscot Park. Lady Violet felt that these were unnecessary as the 1st
Lord Faringdon had passed Buscot in excellent condition only twelve
years before. Roddy was keen to agree with her and find fault with
Gavin:

*"It seems tragic that G should spend so much money on
Buscot, since it is such good material, & after all, no one
could blame him for the architectural excrescences that exist,
and it would surely have been more fun to use one's wits in
modifying them by cheap methods than by employing an
architect to spend such a vast sum on it all. I am so afraid
when it is all finished he will have nothing left outside trust
funds, & will spend the rest of his life thinking how many
varied things he could have done with all that money."*

In 1940 Gavin's architect Geddes Hislop tendered accounts showing
that the renovations had cost £36,263. 14s. 4d. (equivalent to £1.86
million today). This was an unusually high sum. During the inter-war
years hundreds of English country houses suffered from neglect, fell
into disrepair, and were demolished. Save Britain's Heritage now

claims that over a thousand historic houses were lost due to the increased costs of maintenance and the diminished revenues of their owners. Roddy may have taken a more shrewd approach than Gavin at Buscot, but that seems unlikely as he proved himself to be a spendthrift at Paço de Palmeira. Here he appears to have sought to create an estate that rivalled Buscot Park, and this exacerbated his envy of brother's much larger inheritance. Roddy began to deal with Gavin at one step removed, using Lady Violet as a go-between. For example, after Gavin asked his siblings to let him know him if they wanted anything from Arlington St., Roddy wrote to his mother:

> *"When is the sale? Do you think Gavin remembers those chests?"*

And two months later on July 4th he asked again:

> *"If you ever locate those Italian chests I might bid up to 100 guineas the pair, since I have not become the possessor of anything else at Arlington St., & it would be nice to have something."*

The value of 100 guineas then was equivalent to £7,500.00 today. Roddy could probably have afforded that because a legacy from his father had been released to him that year when he reached the age of 25. This windfall might have helped him purchase his *"Prince's palace"* in Portugal, which was badly mismanaged. This occurred after he and Babel tried to run the farm for the first two years, milking their own cows, churning butter, making jam, restoring terraced gardens, and inviting a stream of friends to stay. Then Roddy hired a Swedish-Portuguese friend of Babel's called Donna Clotilde as his hotel manager. When she got hold of all the bills and tendered accounts, they showed that paying guests were only bringing in a fifth of the hotel's running costs. Roddy had also employed an Estate Manager called Senhor Macedo, to whom he had promised 30% of the profits. When it became clear that there were none, Senhor Macedo had simply added his percentage to the bills. Most of Senhor

Macedo's time was spent at his own rival hotel on the Algarve. Without permission, he booked costly advertising in Portuguese magazines and crammed a tennis court into a courtyard. Donna Clotilde wanted him sacked. He accused her of spreading malicious rumours about him. Roddy had to employ a firm of solicitors to mediate and avoided mentioning this when he wrote home to his mother:

> *"Something goes wrong every week, electric switches in the wrong places, too bulky radiators, wrong angled gateways & so on, small things, but all taking away from the convenience of the house unless corrected. I am very nervous of going away even for a few weeks…"*

Back in England Lady Violet had suffered her own housing problems. Four months after the first Lord Faringdon's death, she moved out of Buscot Park and into Shrivenham, nine miles away. From here she wrote to Gavin complaining about how he had managed the sales and dispersal of his grandfather's possessions. Gavin's scrawled reply on Savoy Hotel notepaper suggests he wrote after dinner there:

> *"30.12.34.*
>
> *Darling Mum,*
>
> *Many thanks for your nice letter. I'm awfully sorry almost the same and quite understand that you were unusually peeved. It was dense of me not to appreciate that. However on the matter of the house I don't quite understand your attitude. If you really feel you would be happier in a house of your own I should certainly not try to prevent you from having Buscot – you complain that I never made any sentimental appeal to you to remain with me. I am surprised that you should not understand that to make such an appeal in a matter in which obviously I was initially enmeshed seemed to me dishonest. After all, if you didn't know that it was*

more important for me to have you than the furniture in my house it was certainly hardly worthwhile mentioning it. In any case my complaint is not that you are having Buscot – I dislike influencing other people's movements – but really that before I left England, and before I sold the contents of Arlington St., you gave me to understand – and I can quote your words with time and place – that you would try a joint existence in the restored house. On that understanding I sold up the contents of Arlington St. which was obviously not worth storing for several years – or even as I hoped forever. My attitude about the pictures is different. It is not personal. I had considered the collection as a kind of trust to which I had hoped to add – to find that I must add almost nothing it is distressing to me.

Anyhow it is unfair, as I wrote you before, to reproach me that I made no comment on or had no interest in the 'perfect house' until you yourself wrote you presented me with a 'fait accompli'. I repeat as I wish then that I hoped you will be very happy in it. May I come down tomorrow night and say goodbye?

Gavin."

Gavin was apologetic and conciliatory – he always tried to lessen friction with his mother. Soon he was to give her a lot of help moving into Barnsley Park, an 18th-century ashlar house set within its own parkland three miles in circumference. With Grade 1 listed features such as an oak-panelled sitting room, library and orangery designed by John Nash, as well as Baroque plasterwork interiors, this was far more attractive than Buscot Park. But a future "bug-bear" reared its head in that letter. This was their different opinions of where and how the collection of family paintings should be housed. Gavin wanted the best at Buscot Park; Lady Violet felt that she and his siblings should have some to live with. Her family had passed down many heirlooms, including dozens of watercolours by the Victorian master Peter De Wint. She had also inherited a large quantity of antique furniture and silverware. Now she wanted her offspring to enjoy these heirlooms. Roddy was her most enthusiastic supporter. Michael and Peggy were happy to have a few token items to live with, but as they had children who might damage them, they preferred items that were not too precious. After prolonged discussions, Buscot Park ended up with all the major paintings, while Lady Violet retained some for herself Roddy, Michael and Peggy.

In late 1936 Roddy wrote an ecstatic letter to his mother about what he saw as his social success of his in Portugal:

> *"I am sitting very much on top of the world, since the Portuguese government have announced that I am to be created Commander of the Order of Benemerencia in recognition of all I have done for Portugal, & they have made Babel an official of the order as well, which I am very pleased about as I could have done nothing without him really. I was enchanted though the retiring Ambassador was not, to find I was better news value in the press than he was & the city of Braga are raising a public subscription to buy us the insignia.*
>
> *It will be very pleasant to have a Portuguese title, since I am addressed as 'Senhor Comendador', while the Benemercncia is a very exclusive order founded by the dictatorship for merit to the state. I am really delighted and have received masses of congratulations & invitations to stay from people I hardly know!"*

Roddy was to receive the "Order of Instruction and of Benevolence" to reward him for attracting tourists and foreign exchange to the country via his hotel Paço de Palmeira. The medal was to be awarded at a banquet funded by the most prominent citizens of the local town attended by President Antonio de Olivera Salazar. His "National Dictatorship" was run by right-wing military officers and was anti-democratic, opposed to colonial independence, and was sending troops to assist General Franco's forces fighting Republican militias in Spain. Roddy hoped to be offered a diplomatic post in Portugal, but was unaware that accepting a medal from "The Dictator" would make him appear a supporter of a regime that was everything people like Gavin deplored. The Foreign Office regarded Portugal as *"Britain's oldest ally"* and were keen to find subtle ways of countering the German and Italian fascist influences. Their approach paid dividends when Portugal declared itself neutral at the outset of WW2. In the meantime, the offer of a medal from Salazar did not lead to Roddy being offered the vacant post of Honorary Attaché at the British Embassy in Lisbon. Instead, he was offered a position in London.

A few weeks later a letter arrived from W.W. Brabner, the Managing Director of Henderson Administration Ltd. He had served the first Lord Faringdon for many years and was regarded as the family's financial guardian. Brabner pointed out that if Roddy moved to London, he would lose his *"claim as a foreign resident"*. That tax rebate was worth £80 (roughly £6,000 p.a. in today's values). W.W. Brabner mentioned that Henderson Administration Ltd had given Roddy a loan, which was now *"down to £2,373. 4. o., and I think it would be satisfactory if you could pay off a further £750 early in the New Year"*. He went on to offer him some Argentine and Uruguayan stock options, which suggests that Roddy was contemplating South America. Then another letter came from Roddy's solicitors who had offices in London and Lisbon. This showed that Paço de Palmeira had become a *"money-pit"*. The solicitors itemised the problems over several pages before suggesting the following exit strategy:

> *"The difficulty about disposing of the property to a local*
> *buyer is that Palmeira is not yet self-supporting and that,*
> *until it is and figures can be produced, there is no basis on*
> *which it can be offered as a going concern. However, I have*
> *noted your wish to be quit of any further responsibilities in*
> *Portugal, and, as I said in my last letter, I think it ought to*
> *be possible to find one or two reliable people who would be*

prepared to put up some money to keep the place going on the
footing of its being transferred to an English Company. The
Company would nurse the property and then either sell at the
opportune moment or alternatively make arrangements to
run Palmeira in conjunction with a hotel scheme."

He took their advice and left Portugal without selling Paço de Palmeira or accepting his medal from "The Dictator". His solicitor's letters, estate accounts, manager's reports, etc, were all sent to his mother's address at Barnsley Park where Lady Violet might have shown and discussed them with his siblings. Peggy visited fairly often, as did Gavin, and Michael lived with his family in a house on the estate. In December 1938 Roddy and Babel came to stay at Barnsley Park. Babel signed into the visitors' book, giving his father's castle *"Edsberg, Hygel, Tureburg, Sweden"* as his address. Roddy left the space for his address blank. Within a month, he was in Buenos Aires. From July 1939 he was addressing letters to his mother from Carrasco, Montevideo. In his first letter he told her that he found his work boring. His boss, was a fitness fanatic who expected staff to join him for early morning exercise on the Legation roof. Roddy did not fit in.

In December 1939, in the first great naval battle of WW2, the German battleship *Admiral Graf Spee* was badly damaged by Royal Navy warships and sought refuge in Montevideo. What followed came to be called the Battle of the River Plate in which the staff of the British Legation played a vital role behind the scenes. At the start of the war the Uruguayan government wanted to join the Allies until Sir Eugen Middleton-Blake pointed out that as the country depended on exports for its survival, and the Axis powers would sink or capture as much Allied shipping as they could, Uruguay would be better off if it declared itself neutral. This they did after Sir Eugen guaranteed that Britain would take the bulk of Uruguay's exports. The result was that it became a British ally in all but name. So, when the *Admiral Graf Spee* berthed in Montevideo, Middleton-Drake was able to use his influence to frustrate German interests.

The Nazi high command expected their damaged battleship would be repaired and refuelled in Montevideo. But Middleton-Drake reminded the Uruguayans that a convention signed by each party only a few months before stipulated that war ships were not permitted to *"remain in the ports, road steads or territorial waters for more than twenty-four hours"*. The German Ambassador argued that the convention allowed for a longer stay *"to repair damage"*. After consulting Middleton-Drake, the Uruguayans allowed them 72 hours. This gave the British Legation enough time to issue a stream of radio and telegraphic signals – some of it in codes known to have been cracked by the Nazis – which created the impression that a powerful Royal Naval fleet had gathered off the coast to sink the *Admiral Graf Spee* as soon it as entered international waters. As the German captain did not want his ship destroyed by overwhelming British firepower, he arranged to get his crew off the ship before scuttling her outside Montevideo harbour. Timed explosions ripped holes into the hull and the wreck sank onto a sandbank leaving her superstructure exposed above the waterline. Roddy sent his mother this personal account of what he saw the next day:

> *"December 1939. Carrasco, Uruguay.*
>
> *We have had the most hectic days with our own particular naval battle, starting off Punta del Este & more or less ending at Carrasco, in fact between my two residences!! Last night or rather at 2.AM. I jumped into the car after listening to the most thrilling broadcast commentary I have ever heard (for the thing that made it most thrilling was that no one knew until the last moment which was the injured ship) & rushed down to the harbour, where thousands of people had surrounded the ambulances which were bringing the German wounded ashore. But I thought it was rather ghoulish even if they are only modern day pirates so I went home & today paid my 50 cents & went out in a launch which cruised slowly round the great battleship, while we admired the results of British gunnery on her hull & conning tower, & the sailors*

carried the coffins around the decks or waved to us gaily,
as they felt inclined. When one saw all the brown healthy
smiling German sailors on the decks among the piles of coffins
the terrible waste of war seemed so particularly futile. The
Uruguayans never answered their cheery waves, but they
remained dignified & aloof, which considering it was the
proletariat with a capital P in my launch showed admirable
restraint, as they were wild with delight at our action, almost
to a man, as far as we could judge."

Roddy wrote highly subjective letters to his mother and this one revealed his snobbish side when he referred to the passengers on the launch as *"proletariat with a capital P"*. An intelligence attaché at the Legation took a launch around the battleship and noted that farmers of German extraction (part of the largest immigrant community in Uruguay) had come to see the battleship. Roddy typed a follow-up letter at work a few days later in which he complained of being *"constantly interrupted by things to be done"*. Presumably this referred to the surge in cipher traffic generated by Sir Eugen Middleton-Drake. Roddy went on to gripe that all would be well *"if only the Minister would dry up"*. All this suggests he was disaffected and not fully in touch with what was going on around him:

"We have been enormously busy with the Graf Spee business,
often working until four or five o'clock in the morning, in a
desperate effort to keep up with the spate of telegrams in and
out. It is all very disheartening when one takes into account
that a great art of the lengthy communications from this end
could have been compressed into about one third of the words
the Minister uses with such obvious disregard for the welfare
of his subordinates, the patience his superiors in London and
the National expenditure, one feels like walking out of the
Legation and never returning…. even if we cannot shorten
one of the minister's telegrams, we may be helping shorten the
war."

Roddy did not appear to know the volume of signals had risen again after the Germans had the wreck sold for scrap in order to try and prevent any of their secrets getting into British hands. Unfortunately, they sold it to a company owned by a Uruguayan businessman in touch with Sir Eugen. The bill went to the Admiralty and the following was recorded in dispatches:

> *"I have done this for love of the good cause which England*
> *is defending and out of personal friendship for the British*
> *Minister, Mr Millington-Drake."*

A Naval attaché photographed a strange device mounted on the *Admiral Graf Spee*'s conning tower. Soon after the Admiralty saw the photograph, they sent an expert on RDR (which was to become RADAR) to Montevideo. Middleton-Drake arranged for this agent and a retired R.N. officer to pose as scrap merchants and secure the device. This turned out to be advanced range-finding equipment that had enabled the Germans to locate and hit Royal Naval vessels. This discovery prompted the Admiralty to send a further nine undercover operatives.

Roddy does not appear to have been involved in these covert operations as his letters to his mother show he was self absorbed. Their relationship had always been unusually close, and he wrote as if he was feeling very much alone. An extract from a letter he wrote to her on New Year's day 1940 illustrates this:

> *"I have been waiting for a letter from you by every post and*
> *I am getting really worried about you as I have a feeling you*
> *must be ill. Darling please, get well quickly and get fat, really*
> *fat with middle aged spread, because though you don't look it*
> *you are middle-aged you know, or at least bordering on it and*
> *I want you to look matronly when I come back.*
>
> *The longer I am away from you the more dismal it seems,*
> *whereas as a rule one gets used to being without people as*

time goes on. I realise only too well now that I was a wretched
son always running away as soon as I got home, but as you
know, I felt acutely that feeling of impending disaster and
a sort of restlessness which made me think happiness was
something one found, whereas one creates it.

When I come back we shall run the farm together if you like
and you shall give me a piece of garden right away from your
own where I can make my own little plans and surprise you
when you get permission to come and see it. Or if you come
here, we shall have to plan your garden here. I am an awful
duffer in the garden really and you will probably have a lot
of criticisms to make when you come. It will be lovely to be
criticised and I shall get awfully angry inside and say 'That
woman thinks she knows more about gardens than I do just
because they name a hardy and prolific rose after her' and I
shall make all the same mistakes as before."

In the meantime, signals activity at the Legation grew again as MI6
began to broadcast misinformation about a Nazi coup in Uruguay.
Bogus reports were sent to American news agencies and in June
1940 the *New York Times* published several *"scoops"*. These claimed
an American Congressional Committee had uncovered a *"powerful*
military, political and economic Nazi network", and *"a plan for the*
military occupation with distribution of troops, placement of German
officials, division of land, repression of enemies, and the conversion of
Uruguay into a colony of German peasants". The *New York Times*
reported that the police in Montevideo had arrested Nazi leaders.
All of this was Allied propaganda intended to raise support in the
USA, which had still not entered the war. There was no planned Nazi
a coup in Uruguay, and few there believed it. But Roddy did – or
claimed to – in his letter to Gavin:

"My life would have been worth exactly nothing if the
abortive Nazi putsch had come off. It is quite ridiculous to

compare life in South America with the daily hazards and
dangers you incurred at home."

Ironically, it was *"quite ridiculous"* for him to compare his life in South America with conditions in wartime Britain. But that is precisely what he had done in a previous letter to his mother. On that occasion he had made some scornful remarks about his brothers in connection with something British Intelligence considered very "hush-hush". The chances are that the censors had reported this breach of security to their superiors.

"British Legation, Montevideo, Uruguay.

August 29. 1940

What a pity Gavin & Mike quarrelled, but I know from
experience that when one has been working like brother
Mike, one gets short-tempered with obstructionists. Of course,
I fully realise if one runs to the luxury of a secretary, it is
essential to use him, but I think Mike might have justifiably
expected a direct answer on such a question, which, in the
long run, concerns Gavin's comfort personally. I suppose
Gavin could always refer the parachute troops to Frank, too,
if the worst came to the worst, but the simple lads would
probably not appreciate this procedure. Actually though, I
think poor Mike was right, though I am sure he came out of it
the worst, while Gavin performed miracles of mental ju jitsu
for his benefit."

Whilst this was clearly meant to be jocular it was written when the slogan *"Careless Talk Costs Lives"* was everywhere. Discretion was of particular importance in this case as *"Mike"* was the General Staff Officer dealing with the invasion of Britain threat being countered by *"Churchill's Secret Army"*. After their London H.Q. was bombed, Michael had been asked to find a covert location in the countryside and came up with Coleshill, adjacent to Buscot Park. This had a large house designed with extensive cellars. It was surrounded by an estate with secluded copses and abandoned quarries – ideal for training men to use weapons and explosives. Here "Auxiliary Units" of five to six men learnt hand-to-hand combat techniques, how to take out strategic targets and to assassinate German officers or British collaborators. These auxiliaries had local knowledge (one was a Vicar) and were trained to live off the land. Roddy's letter mentioned *"Frank"*. This was Frank Bourne, Gavin's part-time secretary and the manager of his chicken farm. Frank had caught some auxiliaries stealing chickens and eggs, seen them off, and gone on to inform "Mike" and Gavin. One of them had told Lady Violet and she had passed it on, probably as an amusing anecdote. Roddy had made her security slip-up many times worse by referring to the auxiliaries as *"parachute troops"* and *"simple lads"*; and his gratuitous slurs about his brothers merited investigation. Roddy ended his letter with the following prediction:

> *"Only one month more now & the then the war is going to*
> *be on the ebb tide for the Nazis. I think that is a statement*
> *which the Germans can hardly fail to realise the truth of &*
> *once the German people get to realise it they will bite the*
> *hand that has fed them so assiduously with guns instead of*
> *butter."*

The war lasted for another five years. During that time he grew increasingly disaffected and political rants became a feature of Roddy's letters to his mother. The latter may have been due to too many glasses of local wine. He must have found it dispiriting to reflect that men from both sides of his family had come to South America and left their mark. Lady Violet's great uncle Simon Temple – Lord Palmerston's nephew – opened up trade between Britain and Chile. Roddy's uncle Frank had expanded Argentine exports to Britain during WW1. Frank's brother Brodie built railways financed by another brother, Alexander – the first Lord Faringdon. Amongst these were the Buenos Aires Great Southern, Central Argentine, the Antofasta in Bolivia, and the Transandine in Chile. Uncle Brodie had designed and overseen the construction of new docks for Buenos Aires, and there was even a district of that city called Henderson. Some of Roddy's cousins owned farms and vineyards in Uruguay and Argentina. On Sept 1st 1940, Roddy wrote to Lady Violet about his proposed visit to one:

> "I must go up to Snaviyu soon, as I have promised to build some workmen's cottages. This sounds like a big order, but of course they are very simple structures. It is tragic how the people live there, in mud huts, while we all live in comfort in the great city, which the poor peasants really pay for. It is even more disgraceful in Argentina…"

This excursion was at odds with Roddy having to do *"the work of four"* at the Legation. Whilst it was an escape he needed, three weeks later he was back in Montevideo feeling dejected and wrote:

> "I am trying to come to a decision in my own mind whether I am really pulling my weight here. Life is altogether too easy to let my conscience rest & I am going to try either to get more work, or else go to Canada to work in a war industry factory if they want workers now."

Roddy had lived in Canada when his father was the Chief Military Officer. Now, two decades later, he contemplated returning there to do war work. Perhaps he was tipsy when he wrote it. Not long afterwards, in December 1940, he wrote a sarcastic comment about Michael that was ill-considered and unnecessary.

> "I hope you got your Xmas present safely. It is at the chief doorkeeper's at the F.O. addressed to Mike…I was amused by your descriptions of his shoeing in wartime. The great trouble is that Mikes are desperately needed to win wars & are entirely unsuitable to make peace."

Like many people, Michael was finding it difficult to get new shoes in wartime. One of Uruguay's principal exports was leather, so Roddy might have sent some. Or he could have offered to get a pair of shoes made in Uruguay for him to send. But neither crossed his mind. His response was a pompous tirade against the military without pausing to consider what the censor would make of it.

> "With an entire lack of logic, derived from the importance
> they feel in being entrusted with our safety & destruction by
> the enemy, they try to continue their wholly unsocial labours
> in time of peace... I wish Mike the best of everything at this
> time, but I feel he will be a very disgruntled person one day,
> unless he keeps a sense of proportion."

The irony was that Roddy's prediction of what Mike might face in the future was what had happened to Roddy himself. He was disgruntled and had lost his sense of proportion. He may have been showing signs of this mental stress at work, for in January 1941, he was released from the cipher office:

> "I am going on my vacation today, flying over to Chile... this
> will be the first real vacation I've had since I came here 18
> months ago. One feels very guilty taking it in these times, but
> the Ambassador in Buenos Aires is insisting on my having a
> month, so it seems allright. "

Someone on high in the F.O. must have arranged for this to happen as the British Ambassador in Argentina was not Roddy's boss – that was still Sir Eugen Middleton-Drake in Uruguay. This benign change occurred soon after "B.B." took over as Minister of Information. It is possible that Lady Violet had asked him, in his capacity as her friend, to keep an eye on his wellbeing. It was probable that some of Roddy's indiscreet comments had been reported, which would have made him seem a security risk. From 1941 all of Roddy's letters went via the diplomatic bag from Buenos Aires to the F.O. in Whitehall. After returning from his holiday Roddy wrote the last letter to his mother that reached her by the standard post. It was also the last letter of his that she kept.

> "I may be selling the house in Carrasco, as there are people
> after it & I always meant to sell it anytime someone wants
> to pay the price, now that you are not coming out. I suppose
> Hitler's war of nerves is more on us out here than at home
> since we see all the angles. So far I can see crux of the
> situation will be shipping when all is said and done...."

He was wrong to claim that *"Hitler's war of nerves is more on us here than at home".* In Britain the Nazis had unleashed the "Blitz" on towns and cities that had eight more months of bombing to endure. Fighting was to peak that year in North Africa, Yugoslavia, Albania and Greece. Germany would invade Russia, declare war on the USA, and the Japanese attack Pearl Harbour. Roddy's notion that he had it worse was a self-pitying fantasy. But then, all of a sudden, his outlook brightened as Sir Eugen Middleton-Drake was replaced by Sir Ralph Stevenson:

> "When Ralph Stevenson became minister in Montevideo, he
> felt my talents, such as they were, were not fully developed
> in the cipher room, & he made my life more colourful, &
> incidentally far more hectic, by letting me write some of
> his speeches, give lectures, radio talks, write book reviews,
> be legation member of British Red Cross, Anglo-American
> Committee, etc."

Stevenson had chaired the Joint Intelligence Committee, which consisted of the chiefs of the Defence Staff, as well as the permanent undersecretaries from the Home Office, Foreign Office, Ministry of Defence, and the Treasury. This committee set the requirements for the Secret Intelligence Service and GCHQ. Stevenson had moved to Montevideo during the height of the secret investigations into the *Graf Spee*. One of the first changes he made at the Legation was to move Roddy from the cipher office. He wisely gave him a public relations role and the result was that Roddy felt useful at last. His petulance vanished and he described Sir Ralph as *"the finest chief anyone could have"*. Stevenson was only there for a year, but he won Roddy's adulation by recommending him for a post as a Civil Attaché and Private Secretary to the British Ambassador in Argentina. This was what Roddy had always wanted and he proved successful there from 1942 to 1946. During this time he was able to develop a market garden enterprise in Argentina and take holidays, such as when he visited Britain and Sweden in 1945.

After the war the brothers saw little of each other. In a way, a cold war of resentment and suspicion continued between them. Their sister Peggy acted as mediator from time to time. Their mother Lady Violet was in a slightly more difficult position than her offspring, as Roddy remained more emotionally attached to her than the others. From 1946–57 – when he lived in South and then North America – he returned to stay with her 14 times. Perhaps this was a measure of his love for her. Certainly he had no love for Gavin. Roddy's last letter to him came in 1957, shortly after Lady Violet passed away. In it he waived his right to choose any of the three paintings from her collection that her will entitled him to, claiming that he was certain they could only be ones that Gavin had rejected. He ended with venomous sarcasm:

> *"the wine was as I remember one of Mummy's happiest little triumphs when she secured it from Buscot under threat of having it valued for probate in Grandpapa's estate. A cheery little repeat of history which must gladden all lovers of the fighting Dazell spirit. Naturally, I stand squarely with Peggy on this issue & I look forward to the day that we shall be able to drink some really good blood curdling toasts in our slightly corked & oft moved booty...*
>
> *So far as I know, we have the same forbears & collaterals even if my conception was so inconveniently delayed in that*

topsy turvy land where socialist ideals can be so happily wed
to the principle of primogeniture."

In spite of this bitterness, Roddy managed to live in enviable comfort for the rest of his days. Having sold his properties in Uruguay and Portugal, he spent his last 40 years in the USA moving from one beautiful home to another in Vermont, New York, Illinois, Rhode Island and Florida. He put together a fine art collection, which he exhibited publicly with a printed catalogue that listed 105 paintings, including oils by Courbet, Derain, Dufy, Landseer, Lavery, Sargent; and with watercolours and drawings by Guardi, Prout, Orpen, Richmond, Utrillo, Lear and Wilkie. In the 1960s he gave two 19th-century romantic paintings of the American West to Colby College Museum in Maine; and donated six historic oil paintings of western scenes to the Smithsonian Institute in Washington (the cultural equivalent of the British Museum).

His last written words on his brother came in a letter to his nephew shortly after Gavin's death:

"206 Caribbean Road,
Palm Beach,
Florida 33480

Jan 29/77

My dear Charles,

It was most kind and thoughtful of you to phone me this
morning advising me of Gavin's death.

Although seven years difference in age is a formidable barrier
to intimacy when one is young, in recent years he had been
most kind & affectionate on my visits to England, & although
it is easy to say that we all mellow with age, I did sense a real
affection & a certain sentimentality which he would probably

have repudiated if charged with it. But which nevertheless I feel was there.

He had some of the disconcerting qualities of your grandmother, which engendered a love-hate relationship there which curiously enough brought them closer together than I could ever be with Mummy, although when we went to dinner with him, she would always as a fellow-conspirator with me plan to get away early!

It is a sobering thought to realise I am the last of the four & sometimes the homing instinct becomes very strong. Memories are too often poignant & certainly my memories of Gavin in recent years have only been of a brother for whom I have real affection, I feel was mutual. My love to you and all & please keep in touch.

Roddy."

In 1995, at the age of 86, he passed away. His obituary in the *West Palm Beach Daily News* read:

"Roderick Harold Dezell Henderson dies Thursday March 30 1995, at Good Samaritan Medical Centre after a short illness. He was 86.

Born at Buscot Park, England, Mr Henderson was educated at Eton and Cambridge. He was a member of the British diplomatic service for many years, serving as first secretary in Stockholm Sweden: Buenos Aires, Argentina, Montevideo, Uruguay; and Rome, Italy. He made his home in Newport, R.I. and Palm Beach for the past 30 years. Mr Henderson is survived by his nephew Lord Faringdon and his nieces, Lady Tennant and Mrs Richard Nicholson, and many grandnephews and grandnieces. Memorial services will be held at Buscot Park, England, at a later date."

Roddy would probably have been annoyed that the newspaper misspelled his middle name "Dazell" derived from his beloved mother's surname. But he might not have minded that the newspaper was wrong to claim that he had been a *"first secretary in Stockholm Sweden: Buenos Aires, Argentina, Montevideo, Uruguay; and Rome, Italy"*. That was an archaic title used in diplomatic circles to describe the Minister or Ambassador. The truth was that he was a far humbler Honorary Attaché to Stockholm between 1932 and 1933; Civil Attaché and Private Secretary to Buenos Aires between 1943 and 1946; Civil Attaché and Private Secretary to Rome in 1946; and finally, Civil Attaché and Private Secretary to Stockholm in 1947. A total of six years of diplomatic service. His obituary made no mention of his connoisseurship, art collection, and generous donations of historic paintings. That was a pity, as these were things he had achieved thanks to his own eye and personal drive.

CHAPTER 18

Political Snakes & Ladders

In spite of being left out of the post-war Labour Party cabinet, Gavin prospered in the parliamentary Fabian Society. Their odd-sounding name was chosen to remind members of the Roman general Quintus Fabius whose successful strategy for defeating Hannibal was waiting patiently for the right moment. Two hundred and twenty-eight Fabians were elected in the 1945 Labour landslide. Many of them saw Gavin's connections with independence movements in the colonies to be of great value. Like Gavin, Fabians were passionate about social justice and the progressive improvement of society. They were socialists who had rejected communist ideology. They did not want revolutions or seek violent upheavals that led to democratic change. Fabians preferred steady improvements in local government and trade union democracy. They already had an agenda mapped out for change in the empire. This was the Colonial Bureau of the Fabian Society, to which Gavin became attached. This aimed to reform the colonial administration and ultimately dispense with British imperialism. Over the next few decades Gavin was to work closely with Fabians such as Tony Crosland, Richard Crossman, Denis Healey, Barbara Castle, Roy Jenkins and others to try to redress social inequalities. Their signatures are to be found repeatedly in the Buscot Park visitors' book, as the place became a think-tank to rival the Conservative Party's court at Cliveden.

Whilst Fabians saw Gavin as a passionate advocate of social change in the colonies, others resented his *"sticking his nose in where it isn't wanted"*. An example of this is a vituperative letter from a tea planter's wife in Kenya inspired by his speeches in the Lords. Gavin's facts had come from Foreign Office and Colonial government reports on drought, plagues of locusts, the shortage of labour, etc. He had compared and contrasted these with the findings published in pre-war books and official publications. On top of these sources, he was guided by his friend the German refugee Fritz Wolff-Auerbach, who was farming in the Kenyan highlands. A few months after his lengthy and detailed speech in the Upper House, a report of it appeared in a Kenyan newspaper. That produced this *"stinker of a letter"* which, characteristically, Gavin kept.

> *"Kaisuya Kericho, Kenya.*
> *16.7.44*
> *Lord Faringdon.*
> *Sir/.*
>
> *I take great exception to your untruthful statements with regard to Conscription of Africans, made in the House of Lords. You should verify your facts before you give rein to vivid imagination in this unseemly, & distressingly dishonest manner. Whoever gave you the facts quoted in your speech is <u>lying</u>. I say this most vehemently.*
>
> *I have laboured in Kenya since 1931, helping my husband to grow tea. We have not a single conscript on our estate, nor have we ever had. With a population greatly increased by the influx of the Army & the Navy. With refugees from Poland, Germany, France & Malaya, with prisoners of War also, to say nothing of the several thousand schoolchildren from Malta, Malaya, Tanganyika and Zanzibar who cannot just go home to England for their education! These children are still supported by Kenyan efforts. With all our young men away fighting, & most of our Labour in Services, this work of Production rests mainly upon the women. I'll thank your lordship to mind his own business. By the extreme stupidity you exhibit when minding other people's, I gather you will find this difficult…"*

The letter went on in the same manner for several pages. However, back in Westminster, Fabian ministers and the younger input of Fabian MPs were admiring what they saw as Gavin's far-seeing views and commitment. Amongst these was Tony Crosland who became an MP in 1950, contributed to the *New Fabian Essays* in 1952, and wrote *"The Future of Socialism"* in 1956 – two of the most inspirational books in left-wing politics of the era. He became a member of the Fabian executive committee for many years, and chairman from 1961-2. Tony Crosland went on to serve as a cabinet minister under Harold Wilson and James Callaghan as Education Secretary, President of the Board of Trade, Environment Secretary and Foreign Secretary. The following brief and light-hearted letter shows his appreciation of what Gavin brought to the party in those years:

> *"House of Commons,*
> *London W1*
>
> *Dear Gavin,*
>
> *You shot off in the green Rolls on Sunday deserting our dull session for (I hope) something more (here he drew a flaming sun) -y and glamorous. You had not returned by the time I had to leave so I was not able to say goodbye & thank you.*
>
> *How you manage to put up with all those interminable discussions is quite beyond me; as they are infinitely more boring through being at Buscot.*
>
> *Even Fabians are capable of gratitude, so thank you for your courtesy and hospitality.*
>
> *Yours,*
>
> *Tony Crossland."*

An example of Gavin's unusual influence came when a Ugandan dignitary wrote to say that he was studying at Magdalene College,

Cambridge and wondered if he could come to see Buscot Park. The result was that the 21-year-old Mutesa II, the 35th Kabaka of Buganda, came to stay from 29th December to Jan 1st 1945. Popularly known as King Freddie, he was to become the first President of Uganda in 1963. As soon as Tom Driberg MP heard that the Kabaka of Buganda was coming he wrote to ask if he could be there as a fellow guest on New Year's Eve. Driberg was a genial man but genuine *"wild card"* and one wonders if he behaved himself that night. He wrote afterwards to say how much he *"enjoyed meeting your Black King"*. Anyone aware of Driberg's libido and promiscuity might speculate he could have offered a homosexual dalliance. However, a brief look at King Freddie's private life suggests this might not have been his cup of tea. Several of his fellow women students at Cambridge recalled King Freddie as a *"lion rampant"*. When he died at the age of forty-five in 1969 the Kabaka had 13 wives and had officially fathered 12 sons and nine daughters.

If there were sober moments that New Year's weekend one of the topics under discussion would have been something on Gavin's mind: the flogging of troops in the Ugandan Rifles. This was the foremost African regiment, with troops based in Nyasaland, Kenya, Uganda, Somaliland and the Sudan. Ten years earlier Gavin had written to the Foreign Secretary Anthony Eden to ask *"in what circumstances the flogging of natives in the Sudan is permitted"*. Eden's Foreign Office officials had written to the High Commissioner for Egypt, who replied several months later that the following sections of the penal code applied:

> *"Penal Code 76: not exceeding twenty-five lashes on an adult male offender in lieu of imprisonment.*
>
> *Penal Code 77: whipping not exceeding 25 strokes on any male offender less than 16 years old in lieu of punishment for any offence he may be punishable for*
>
> *Penal Code 270: the sentence shall be inflicted at a time and*

place chosen by the court official and inflicted in their or a
Magistrate's presence."

The letter went on in great detail to cover three sheets of closely typed foolscap paper. Basically, humanitarian concerns were addressed only in that floggings or whippings had to be administered all in one go with approved implements. There was no mention of women or girls receiving either punishment, but that did not mean they were spared; the instances were simply never deemed important enough to be recorded. Nor was there any sensitivity to the implications of racial discrimination until the last paragraph:

> *"Power to inflict lashes is delegated to British Officers, and*
> *Native*
>
> *Officers have no authority to inflict lashes."*

Corporal punishment had been considered by a Colonial Office Committee in 1938. As far as Gavin was concerned, this committee had proposed reforms which had stalled during the war years. Now Gavin refused to let the matter be put to one side any longer. Armed with fresh evidence from planters he had met in East Africa (Fritz Wolff-Auerbach amongst them), he wrote to the War Office early in 1946 to ask for details of flogging of native troops in Kenya and the Sudan. Within a month a reply came from Hector McNeill, Parliamentary Under-Secretary of State at the Foreign Office to say that they were still looking into the matter of floggings in the Sudan Defence Force. The War Office was then run by a Fabian, Lord Nathan of Churt, who did not reply until Nov 20th, but when he did Gavin was assured:

> *"The order to permit corporal punishment for desertion of*
> *men in the King's African Rifles was introduced because*
> *of the large number of desertions occurring. Commanding*
> *officers were swamped by Courts of Enquiry and Courts*
> *Martial and had decided, therefore, to declare desertion and*

absence without leave liable to punishment by caning, in an
effort to control the number of desertions. A new leave system
was introduced which made desertion less possible and as
soon as this system was working well corporal punishment
for desertion was discontinued. General Anderson has been
instructed that corporal punishment by summary award (i.e.,
without a full trial) can on no account be permitted, and the
while question of corporal punishment by court-martial is to
be re-considered in the light of the ending of the war."

Boiling with indignation, Gavin immediately wrote to another
Fabian, Arthur Creech-Jones – who had recently been installed
as Secretary of State at the Colonial Office. Again, he received a
frustrating response that the post-war situation had rendered the
subject:

"...far from satisfactory. Whilst, our policy will be directed
to eventual abolition, we are obliged to give Colonial
governments a little longer time to build up again their
establishments, which have become sadly depleted as a
result of the war, but it is certainly our intention to make
further moves for a reduction of this form of punishment and
substantially to contribute to its abolition."

Creech-Jones explained that Corporal Punishment could be imposed
by an order of a Court for crimes of violence or sexual offences.
Unfortunately, a clear overview of the situation was unavailable at
present because records compiled during the war years had made
no distinction between the numbers of adults and juveniles that had
received floggings or lashings. The Colonial Office's statistics showed
merely that *"corporal punishment had been imposed"* on 8 adults in
Ceylon, 33 in Uganda, 38 on the Gold Coast, 14 in Nyasaland and
12 in Northern Rhodesia. Whilst those for Tanganyika and Kenya
were much higher at 138 and 166. There were no recorded instances
of corporal punishment in Barbados, British Honduras, the Gambia,
Malta and Sierra Leone. In many colonies it was standard practice for

juvenile offenders to be whipped for theft as there were no alternative punishments available, such as probation or Approved Schools.

The Foreign Office wrote with reference to Gavin's letter to acknowledge that his motion regarding the flogging of members of the Sudan Defence Force was scheduled for 23rd January, adding

> "I have asked the Governor-General of the Sudan to furnish
> additional information for which you asked in your letter
> of 28th December, but I am afraid that I shall not have it
> available by then."

Then, in total contrast, a detailed letter arrived from J.V. Rob, the Private Secretary. This gave the total number of men flogged for the past three years as 2,178 and the number of boys whipped over the past three years was 828. This letter stated that the Government had considered the abolition of flogging as a punishment in the Sudan Defence Force, but, as it was still under active service conditions, it deemed it inadvisable to make changes which might affect its discipline.

> "While occasional cases of excessive use of this punishment
> did occur in the early part of the war, the General Officer
> Commanding has tightened up the regulations, and
> sentences of flogging and whipping can only be passed by
> courts-martial and by officers commanding units. Finally, in
> scattered posts where facilities for detention are non-existent
> and fining is no immediate deterrent, urgent disciplinary
> action has in the opinion of the Governor General sometimes
> to be taken.
>
> I am sorry that it had taken so long to procure this
> information."

It was clear that Gavin had won a significant victory by getting the Foreign Office to admit to the extent of the punishments. Also, that there had been misuse of the system; and that it was now on the way to being abandoned. However, Gavin kept up the pressure with a series of letters. Four months later they wrote again to say that *"having compiled more information, due to an unfortunate understanding"* they had neglected to send it. This looked as though there were opposing factions at work within the Foreign Office. Whilst the letter had regretted that it was not possible to answer all Gavin's questions regarding the Sudan Defence Force, which was stated to have been due to staff shortages as a result of *"the large-scale demobilisation now in progress"*, the letter was a model of prevarication. It outlined what *"indiscipline"*, *"insubordination"* and *"insolence"* meant (refusing to obey orders, striking a superior, creating a disturbance); and gave the punishments decreed under the Sudan, and Egyptian Civil codes. Then it went on to answer Gavin's questions generally:

> *"Flogging is used as a summary award when speedy justice is essential... It can be awarded by a Commanding Officer for any offence within his jurisdiction; by Courts Martial for any offence against military law. In special circumstances authority can be delegated to Company or Detachment Commanders distant from Headquarters, but only on the recommendation of Area, Brigade, or Corps Commanders... When these powers are given to Company Officers it is comparable with the Civil powers of a second-class magistrate who may award "flogging up to twenty-five lashes" as an alternative punishment in all cases where imprisonment is the main award....*
>
> *It is possible that during the earlier years of the war these powers were delegated to officers who may not in some cases have used them with due care and discretion. The continuance of flogging is coming up for reconsideration as soon as the Force reverts to peacetime status."*

By this time Gavin had become an important influence on the Government's colonial policy. Creech-Jones was Permanent Under

Secretary of State and made Gavin Chair of the Parliamentary Labour Party's Colonial Subjects group. When Creech-Jones was promoted in 1946, Gavin moved up a peg to join the Colonial Development Council, which led to his assuming the Chair of the Party's Imperial Advisory Committee – the body that prepared papers for the National Executive Committee. It was in this context that he received a letter from Frank Horrabin (the lover of Ellen Wilkinson, the Education Minister) where the topic of racial tension arose:

"16 Endersleigh Gardens, Hendon, NW4. Feb 23rd 1946.

Dear Faringdon,

I believe there's a meeting of the Party Advisory Committee on Imperial Affairs next week, & do hope that it will be possible to bring up again for discussion the question of Kenyan Land Settlement policy.

I don't know if you heard a report of our (Bureau)) delegation to Creech at the C.O. – when Arthur Lewis* forgot his Downing St. manners & really did let fly superbly about the failure to break the White Monopoly in the Highlands, & said things which we all badly wanted to say. In reply to him Creech more or less promised to make certain modifications when he spoke in the house 2 or 3 days later. But his speech then was, as before, a defence of the more conservative proposals, on the grounds that 'one couldn't do anything drastic in the present critical world situation'. That excuse is going to hold good for some time, whenever a test case between conservative & socialist policy comes up: & I do feel strongly that (however full of 'home priorities' the Govt's timetable may be) We must go on pressing in every possible way that Empire problems shan't be shirked.

Yours sincerely,

Frank Horrabin."

It is worth noting that Arthur Lewis was a black West Indian Nobel laureate, who became economic advisor to Gavin's friend Kwame Nkrumah of Ghana. J.F. Horrabin was another friend in the political sphere that Gavin was now moving in. Briefly Labour Party MP for Peterborough, he was a radical writer and cartoonist and a close friend of David Low and George Orwell. He co-founded the Fabian Colonial Bureau (later the Fabian Commonwealth Bureau) with Rita Hinden and Arthur Creech-Jones, and edited its journal, *Empire*. Horrabin was chairman of the Fabian Commonwealth Bureau from 1945 to 1950 and wrote a regular column for the *Socialist Commentator*.

Gavin's important colonial work continued after he was appointed as a member of the Colonial Services Welfare Advisory Committee in 1947. This had an extraordinarily wide spectrum of concerns including *"clubs and associations for adult and adolescent men and women, rural welfare, training in agriculture and home-making; juvenile delinquency, approved schools, Borstals and after-care, training for welfare-workers, the sociological aspects of housing, etc, etc."* After this, he was regularly acknowledged in *The Times* for his services. For example, it reported his contributions to the debates on overseas development such as a speech to the United Nations Association on *"Trusteeship and the Colonies"*; and that he had hosted a week-long event at Buscot Park for socialist administrators and economists from seven western European countries. Without encouragement from the Labour leadership, he had found his *metier*. Whilst parliamentary faction-fighting meant that his work in Westminster was *"snakes and ladders"*, whenever he applied himself to foreign affairs he did well for everyone. But in March 1948 *The Times* reported he had cancelled all his engagements. This was because he had been infected with jaundice on a visit to Africa. A month later he had recovered and raised the United Nations Trusteeship Council's report on Tanganyika in the Upper House. His delivery of this earned high praise from Sir Thomas Drummond Shiels MC MB ChB – a successful former Parliamentary Under-Secretary of State for the Colonies, who had recently been knighted for his service as the Chairman of the Joint Standing Committee for Educational work of the Non-political Empire Societies. He was now Deputy-Secretary of the Commonwealth Parliamentary Association and on 15th June 1949 wrote the following complimentary letter

> *"Confidential:*
>
> *Dear Lord Faringdon,*
>
> *I have just read your speech in the Lords on the U.N. Commissions Report on Tanganyika and I would like to congratulate you on it. It was finely balanced comment – moderate in statement and yet courageous and outspoken on important points.*
>
> *I am particularly pleased that you spoke as you did about communal representation which has been the curse of India. We abolished it in Ceylon in the Donoughmore Constitution, in spite of much prophecy of oppression and discrimination. and we see the result today in a united Ceylon becoming a dominion... There is no doubt that the C.O. are dabbling a bit in this dangerous region and we shall have to keep watch. Another danger is the giving of unofficial majorities without corresponding responsibility and calling it constitutional progress and a concession to indigenous peoples*
>
> *Drummond Shiels."*

Shiels was probably right to suspect that the Colonial Office were *"dabbling a bit"*, as the issues raised by racial tension were complex. An indication of this came in a pusillanimous response to Gavin's practical proposals to avert racism, from Lord Listowel, the Minister of State for Colonial Affairs.

> *"Colonial Office, The Church House, Great Smith Street, SW1.*
> *23rd September 1949.*

Dear Gavin,

We have now had time to study your letter of the 24ᵗʰ April proposing legislation against discrimination on account of race and colour. As you know, all of us in the office have the greatest sympathy with the objects of your proposal. We are greatly concerned at the incidents of discrimination which arise from time to time, particularly over accommodation, and the reluctance of some employers to employ coloured peoples. We always take up any individual cases when we think that injustice is done to colonial subjects on the grounds of their race and we usually have a good measure of success when we do so.

Nevertheless after very careful consideration and consultation with other Government departments we have regretfully conclude that any legislation to prevent colour discrimination would be unenforceable and wholly ineffective....

Yours ever,

Billy Listowel."

This typewritten letter went on for three pages detailing why the Attlee Government found none of Gavin's proposals practical. A hand-written postscript suggested that, in future, Gavin should come to the Colonial Office to discuss any matters privately. It appeared that he was being given the brush off, but was not about to pull in his horns. On 22ⁿᵈ March 1950 *The Times*, always eager in those days to report what Gavin was up to, described a deputation he led on behalf of the Fabian Colonial Research Bureau to Patrick Gordon Walker, Secretary of State at the Commonwealth Relations Office, expressing

"their regret that the decision of the Bamangwato tribe to accept Seretse Khama as their chief had not been recognized by the British Government."

This heir to the throne of the British protectorate of Bechuanaland, had been excluded because he had married Ruth Ellis, a white English woman, and this inter-racial marriage was deplored by apartheid South Africa. Gordon Walker prevented Seretse Khama from returning to his homeland for the next five years. Gavin was incensed but at that moment he appeared to have suffered a mild stroke. This led to his not being able to climb stairs and so he was confined to the lower floor at home. For some reason, he received and kept a copy of a medical report that his consultant (Dr E.M. Buzzard) in Oxford had written and sent to his general practitioner Dr Morgan in Lechlade:

> *"Re: Lord Faringdon, aged 48, Buscot Park, Faringdon, Berks.*
>
> *Since I saw him last, he has had some five weeks more or less in bed, with a gradual increase in activities since, but I gather he is living on the ground floor, and doing comparatively little still.*
>
> *A week ago he went to London for two days, rather unwisely I should have thought, and had some definite angina symptoms when he was tired and when walking or standing for too long. He felt rather exhausted, and admits that it was all too much for him.*
>
> *He has been all right since he came home: he does, however, find himself a little dyspnoeic (breathless) on exertion, and this is quite marked when he came up stairs to my room.*
>
> *Examining him, there was remarkably little to find; as you know, there has never been very much. There is no anaemia, his pulse is steady at 80, there is no gallop rhythm, arteries are soft, blood pressure 105/70 and there is no failure. Retinal vessels are normal, lungs and other systems likewise normal.*
>
> *I had a further series of E.C.G.'s done, and they show a*

remarkable improvement. The T wave in lead I is now positive, whereas it was negative, likewise the T wave in C.R.4. Altogether it shows very satisfactory progress in the right direction.

I also got him along to the hospital, and got Kemp to screen him, and x-ray him, to see if we could make out any enlargement of the aorta, or the heart itself. It is a difficult one to assess radiologically, because the depressed sternum produces some definite displacement, but we can definitely say that there is no gross abnormality, and certainly no aneurine dilation or anything like that. I think one can reasonably pass it as normal.

I thought he was generally much better, and certainly temperamentally more amenable and sensible. I think he ought to continue on his mercury and iodine mixture for a long time yet, preferably about 12 months in all. I would very much hesitate to give him any more potent anti-specific treatment, such as penicillin, anyhow at the moment, for fear of causing acute obstruction in the mouth of the coronary arteries.

He ought to continue living on the ground floor, and certainly ought to potter about for the next three months, and he should be dissuaded from going to London or doing any trips for as long as it is possible to impose one's will on him. I cannot believe it is wise for him to drive that damn great car himself, not because of any question of black-outs or anything, but purely because it must be very heavy to drive, and throw unnecessary strain on the heart. It is another matter whether he will agree to have someone drive it for him!

I don't think we need x-ray him again, unless things are adverse in the future, but a further E.C.G. in two months' time, would certainly be advisable.

Kind regards,

Yours sincerely,

E.M. Buzzard."

Gavin took their advice and remained living on the bottom floor of Buscot house for some months. However, he had this "basement" redecorated in order to make his time there more agreeable, and the result is still enjoyable today. While he was confined there, he engaged an extraordinary young artist to redecorate his temporary prison – a word that seems apt because every window on the lower floor of Buscot House was protected by wrought iron bars. The artist was Leslie Roy Hobdell, who Gavin described as *"a wayward genius"*, and he was to transform this rooms with his elegant mixture of style and humour. Using the magic of painted *trompe l'oeil* imagery, Hobdell transformed the Breakfast Room into an imaginary theatre. Muscular giants lean against the painted neo-classical entrances. A scarlet macaw has perched on one and a kingfisher flies over the other. One wall shows a languid scene of Venice and its lagoon. Next to it a group of naked fauns are gathered at a ruined temple beside a bubbling spring in an Arcadian wood. Opposite this, a mural shows the gardener flirting with a maid carrying a basket; a black boy dressed in a gold and red medieval jerkin lingers beside a pool hidden behind high hedges; nearby flowers bloom, fruit hangs, tall trees line hills topped with castles, waterfalls tumble and statues seem about to come alive. In the hall above this room, Hobdell painted a neo-classical frieze, armorial shields, and his *pièce de résistance* – a niche where a painted shadow falls from a real 18th-century Italian alabaster statue of Apollo. Below this the artist's signature appears on a painted scrap of paper that seems to have just fallen there.

These paintings are exquisite, great fun, and highly personalised if you look closely. For example, one of the male figures in the Breakfast Room is a portrait of Kenneth Samuel Harris, Lord Faringdon's partner and friend for many years. His appearance here is almost identical to how he was depicted in another portrait Hobdell painted of him as Prometheus ("the fire-bringer") on a wall between windows in the dining room at 28 Brompton Sq., London. Both images show a glimpse of him naked below the waist. Another amusing side-line is that Hobdell painted a portrait of Gavin as Quintus Fabius, the Roman senator, on the wall of his dining room in London. This *trompe l'oeil* image in grisaille shows him as a bust on a plinth – as it were half sculpture, half alive. Here he wears a senatorial toga round his shoulders and a laurel crown on his head. This "bust" sits in a roundel with a keystone on top where the Faringdon crest – an "F" topped with a baronial coronet appears. The account books show that Roy was paid £200 in 1950; £50 in 1951; and £25 in 1953. (£9,450.00 in today's values). These sums seem to have been to cover his work at Buscot Park, where he also did four life-size *trompe l'oeil* paintings outside the theatre. Thereafter, he undertook further commissions for Gavin at 28 Brompton Sq. in London and at Barnsley Park in Gloucestershire. In 1958 Roy received £250 (£9,000). There are two accounts of Roy's death at the age of 50 three years later. The first came from the housekeeper at Barnsley Park, who said he died after falling from a high ladder while working (his paints and pallet are still there). The second came from his nephew and niece who were told that he took his own life after his first love affair with a woman failed. Either way, Britain lost a special talent with a great sense of humour. It is still possible these days to pick up a *trompe l'oeil* painting by him signed as either Giles or Miles Farqueson, the names of his pet cats.

At some time after Gavin recovered, an intriguing man named Gerald Green came to stay twice in 1950 – three nights each time – and again in 1957. This was a very British ex-pat Major-General Gerald Green, who was then serving as private secretary to the Emir of Bahrain. They may have met there, as Green always dealt with distinguished visitors; or they may have crossed paths earlier, as Green served in the Sudan and Malta during WW2, and then in Greece during its civil war. In 1945 he was awarded the War Cross for Valour in Greece, was twice mentioned in dispatches, and appointed

Commander of the Order of the Redeemer (Greece). Whenever they met, they would have had much to discuss, for Green would have been better informed than most about Greece, as well as on corporal punishment in the defence forces of colonial Egypt and Sudan. Green worked in a country where a thief could have a hand cut off, but Gerald Green respected traditional justice because it made Bahrain virtually crime free. At some point he gave Gavin a file of 10" x 8" photographs of Bahrain as well as detailed geographical data and maps. These included a fine portrait of the colonel in full Arab dress. Green was a close friend of Prince Philip's mother, who he met in Greece, and she visited him in Bahrain. In 1963 he became private secretary to the Emir, after whose death he was awarded a CBE. Green then became councillor to the new Emir, Sheikh Hamed bin Eissa Al Khalifa and in 2001 was awarded the Order of Sheikh Eissa Bin Sulman Al-Khalifa, the only foreigner to have ever received this high honour.

In March 1951, Jim Griffiths, the Labour Party's new Secretary of State at the Colonial Office, wrote to Gavin asking him to serve a further three years on the Colonial Economic and Development Council. But eight months later, after the Conservative Alan Lennox-Boyd took over, the latter wrote to thank Gavin for his service and to inform him that the council was being disbanded immediately. Three years later in December 1951, Alan Lennox-Boyd wrote again, this time to thank him for agreeing to continue serving as a member of the Advisory Committee on the Treatment of Offenders in the Colonies. Clearly, both sides of the parliamentary divide thought that Lord Faringdon was fulfilling a valuable role in this regard, but neither quite knew how to proceed. It was a time when the Foreign Office tended to be involved with arranging magnificent Independence Day celebrations on behalf of former colonies. Three years later, the nation and commonwealth received the sad news of the death of a much-loved King – and a tonic when his eldest daughter was crowned Queen Elizabeth II in June 1953.

This was the first state occasion to which Lord Faringdon had been invited and was expected to wear his baronial robes. This offered Gavin the opportunity to wear that ermine collar which had been a gift from Joseph Stalin eight years earlier. Such an important occasion meant that he had to be chauffeured. But, as he no longer had a regular one, the task of driving his green Rolls-Royce fell to Alfons Gaffka. He was a Polish man who had fled to England after the Nazi invasion and found work as Gavin's cook, handyman and general factotum. The Home Office granted him permission to stay in the country after he married Buscot Park's housekeeper, Nora Reynolds. Alfons' driving that day was memorable. As Gavin's nephew recalled:

> "Driving Gavin to the Coronation in the open-topped light-green Rolls-Royce Alfons was decked out in livery. He was unused to the Rolls on which the accelerator was in the middle and the brake pedal on the right. He got to the port of the House of Lords when an Austin Princess conveying an Ambassador suddenly turned out. Forgetting the unusual layout of the pedals, Alfons pressed what he thought was the brake – the accelerator – and the car mounted the back of the Austin Princess."

Some years later there was another problem with this vehicle – or rather the driver. A decade after Gavin's medical consultant Dr Buzzard advised that he stop driving, the following occurred. Dr Dick Squires and his wife Pat were leaving the golf course at Frilford Heath, Oxfordshire, when they noticed that a green Rolls-Royce had come off the road and a man in his sixties was sitting on the ground beside it. He looked badly shaken so they stopped to offer help. Dr Squires asked the driver's name and where he lived, and thought he was concussed when the man kept mumbling *"Faringdon, Faringdon"*. The Squires knew that town was about half an hour's drive away and invited him to get in so that could take him home. When they reached Faringdon's market square the man said *"No, no, not here… Buscot, Buscot"*. Luckily, Dr Squires knew where that was and drove on another four miles to the gated lodges outside Buscot Park. He was directed to go up the tree-lined drive and park in front of the

Georgian mansion. Then some servants emerged to take their shaken employer inside. Dr Squires advised them to call the man's doctor and left. A few weeks later a letter arrived asking them to come to lunch at Buscot Park. After Dick and Pat Squires arrived, they discovered that their host was a close friend of neighbours in Wantage – John and Penelope Betjeman. Gavin learnt a lesson from his car accident, for in April 1961 *The Times* reported that his contribution to a debate on the Road Traffic Bill was to suggest that drivers over the age of 60 should have to retake their driving test every five years.

Over the next decade Gavin remained involved with social developments in Africa as many former colonies were becoming independent. In January 1960 *The Times* reported that he attended an Independence Day reception at the Savoy, hosted by the Ambassador for the Sudan. And a few months later he contributed to a debate on Kenya in the Upper House:

> *"Kenya is the scene of possibly the most difficult problem in*
> *Africa, that of a multi-racial community. This can be a source*
> *of appalling trouble. Many troubles have already arisen from*
> *this source. It can also be a source of strength. It can be a*
> *source from which all the many races can draw inspiration.*
> *By their inter-relationship and their contacts they can bring*
> *forth something new, something fresh, something good. I*
> *hope that the necessary co-operation will be forthcoming,*
> *that this transitional period will be got through safely, that*
> *the Constitution will work successfully and that independence*
> *will be attained very quickly."*

In February 1961 *The Times* reported that he had demanded funds for the former colonies during a parliamentary debate on Overseas Aid; and in November 1961 he was re-elected to the Executive Committee of the Fabian Society. Closer to home than Africa – but still a colony – was the island of Malta. Gavin had served as a fire-fighter there during its "Blitz" when Malta was one of the most bombed places in Europe. Afterwards, the entire population of Malta was granted the

George Cross in recognition of their endurance and bravery. Then
the British government promised the Maltese their independence
and in 1946 Gavin told the Upper House:

> "...the time when we were able to treat Malta as a military
> station, and to more or less ignore the inhabitants, their
> views and their wishes, has passed. suggest that a good
> many troubles have been due to that tendency to treat Malta
> as a Colony... inhabited by backward people...not by an
> extremely lively European people."

In 1947 the island was granted self-government in everything but
the key elements of defence, foreign affairs and security. Gavin's
friend Dom Mintoff- leader of Malta's Labour party – had been
elected P.M. on the platform of integrating the island with the UK.
This aim had been welcomed by Anthony Eden, the Conservative
prime minister, and by the Labour leader, Clement Attlee. But three
years later there had been little progress and Mintoff resigned and
vowed to fight for Malta's complete independence. From that time
onwards Dom Mintoff managed to alienate every elected British
politician who tried to deal with him. The Conservative colonial
secretary, Alan Lennox-Boyd and Labour's James Callaghan found
him *"untrustworthy"* and *"exasperating"*. The lack of goodwill on
both sides led to the planned changes in island's constitution being
suspended for a decade. During this period the Roman Catholic
archbishop of Malta excommunicated anyone who voted for
Mintoff – an avowed atheist and socialist – and his clergy refused
to bury Labour party officials in consecrated ground. Still, Gavin
remained Mintoff's friend and ally which led Dom Mintoff to write
over forty letters to him. The early letters were handwritten and
one dangled the prospect of Gavin playing a key role in a proposed
Round Table Conference on Maltese Independence. As time went
on, Mintoff's letters became more controversial and were typed.
Gavin received carbon copies of letters to the Labour leaders Clem
Attlee and Harold Wilson, as well as to the left-wing journalist
Paul Foot at the *New Statesman*. It must have been gratifying for

Gavin, so often reviled at home, to have the confidence of this foreign politician. However, at one point the Foreign Secretary James Callaghan wrote to ask with some asperity if he could tell them what Mintoff was *"up to"*. Gavin's reputation at home was not enhanced by his association with this *"maverick"*.

Mintoff's letters show that he tried to involve Gavin in local *"schemes"* – projects that often seemed self-serving. For example, in 1955 he asked Gavin for £500 (£13,500 today) to lease the Inquisitor's Palace in Valetta. Locals called this imposing building the *Castellania*. This historic landmark had been built by the Knights of St. John between 1530 and 1570. It looked like what it was – a cross between a castle and a palace. Mintoff wanted to convert it into the Maltese Labour Party's offices, and promised that a portion would be reserved as a holiday home for Gavin. However, this would have been costly and difficult as the Inquisitor's Palace had long been a courthouse with prison cells on its lower floors. During WW1 it had been adapted for use as a vast military mess hall before it became a hospital. During WW2 its use changed again after the convent and church of the Dominican Friars was destroyed by bombing. When Mintoff managed to move them on and began holding Labour Party meetings inside there were near riots outside. These were organised by Roman Catholics, the largest and most conservative faction on the island. Mintoff's letters to Gavin described how the protestors made it impossible to be heard inside. The police were called but, as they were predominantly Roman Catholic, they did nothing to supress the rioters. The result was that Labour Party members feared to attend, especially as they had to run the gauntlet of angry Maltese in the street. Mintoff's plan had to be abandoned and the *Castellania* eventually became Malta's National Museum of Ethnography with an up-market hotel on one side. The next scheme was when Mintoff tried to get Gavin to purchase the oldest theatre on the island for the price over £2 million today. Gavin thought well of the intention, but pleaded poverty and backed out.

Finally, Dom Mintoff managed to persuade him to commit funds to restore an old fortress known as *"the Red Tower"* because of the colour of its stone walls. The *Torri l'Almar* (St. Agatha's Tower) had been built by the Knights of St. John in 1647 to strengthen coastal defences against Barbary pirates and other invaders. A marble plaque over its entrance shows it was dedicated to St. Agatha, venerated as a symbol of strength against invasion and the plague. Gavin's files show receipts for work done there. In 1960 he paid £333 for general repairs which included new windows and stairs, as well as £313 for plumbing, sanitation, solar and underfloor heating. This came to a total of £645 (£15,000 today). In addition, insurance cost £1,000 (£23,000). So altogether he spent £38,000 on it – but why he wanted to do so remains a mystery. He must have had something in mind for this renovated fortress. It consisted of a square central tower with four more towers at each corner. Cannon ports in each tower were designed to defend it with interlocking fields of fire. The walls were four metres thick at the base and there was a barrel-vaulted chapel in the main tower. It remained a fortress perched on a commanding coastal position on the north west end of Malta, overlooking the natural harbour. It had been one of the Knights of Malta's strongholds, manned by a garrison of 30 men who, supplied with ammunition and supplies, could withstand a siege of 40 days. Unsurprisingly, it had been garrisoned by British troops during both World Wars. It was just as well that his connection with it was short-lived. Political satirists would have had a field day with the fact that *"The Red Tower"* was in the hands of a *"Red Peer"* – a pacifist, socialist., and Labour Party activist. Luckily, no news leaked out after his contribution to the Parliamentary debate on Malta in June 1961, which included a suggestion for Maltese independence based on his:

> *"...personal acquaintance with the Maltese, and with Dom Mintoff in particular, and nearly all the leaders of the Maltese Labour Party, with whom I have been in fairly close touch over a number of years... Malta is not only an island with a population of some 300,000 souls but also a naval base*

*quite valueless for modern warfare... if these people ask for
independence... I believe that this is the attitude which all of
us in this country who are democrats should support.*

*I have never in my life – and this is why I live in Malta –
been to any other country where I have been made to feel so
fundamentally welcome as I have been in Malta. There is an
immense amount of goodwill in Malta which could be used
to make a permanent settlement which would be creditable
and satisfactory to all concerned. I hope we may draw upon
that...*

*I know of others who were as distressed and depressed as
I was by the failure of the integration movement. But that
is past history and, I submit, no longer possible. But what
is possible is that the Maltese people could be given the
independence that they want and, as an independent country,
live in terms of the closest amity with ourselves."*

Gavin's claim to *"live in Malta"* was exaggerated. True, he had spent
a small fortune on *"The Red Tower"*. He had worked there as a
fire-fighter during the Blitz and stayed fairly often after the war at a
rural property called "The Olives" loaned to him by Dom Mintoff.
But in truth, Gavin had spent more time in Corsica in the 1930s
and never claimed to have lived there. In Malta's case, it might be
truer to say he intended to live there. Gavin's last known contact
with Dom Mintoff came three years after he paid for the repairs
to The Red Tower. Mintoff lost the election of 1964 and Malta was
granted independence. It was given a British Governor-General who
signed a new defence agreement under which the island became a
NATO base. But when Mintoff and his Labour Party were returned
to power in 1971 he dismissed the British Governor-General, sacked
Malta's Chief of Police, and got rid all military bases. Russian and
American naval vessels were refused access to Malta's harbours, and
Mintoff demanded payment for any continued Royal Navy presence.
Malta had been part of the British Empire for 150 years when the

British refused and closed their military bases. The island became detached from the Western world's sphere of influence as Mintoff sought alliances with Mao Zedong of China; Kim IL-sung of North Korea; Nicolae Ceaușescu of Rumania; and Colonel Gaddafi of Libya. Mintoff became a political pariah and Gavin never returned to Malta.

Chapter 19

The Garden

"We must cultivate our own garden. When man was put in the garden of Eden he was put there so that he should work, which proves that man was not born to rest." Voltaire.

The last decades of Gavin's life were eventful, productive and enjoyable when his health permitted. But soon after he passed the milestone of his fiftieth year, he suffered two tragic losses. The first was when his nephew, Alexander Henderson (his brother Michael's eldest son), a boy on whom he had doted after his parent's divorce three years earlier, died following a motor-cycle crash. This occurred only a week before Alexander's 19th birthday in 1951. Gavin attended the funeral at Buscot Church where his nephew's remains were interred in the Henderson family's sarcophagus. Gavin's friend the artist Felix Kelly had just finished a painting in which James featured. This was a view of Buscot House from the east with Alexander and his younger brother Charles on the lawn. They had often come to stay during their school holidays as their father was in the Army and, after their mother remarried, she had gone to live in Greece. The painting shows the mansion's façade between the stone piers on either side of the old carriage drive entrance. The brothers stand together side-lit by a path of sunlight, which falls theatrically across them and onto the house. Over their heads is a patch of blue, beyond them black and grey clouds streak away. This was one of the most evocative of the five images Kelly painted of Buscot.

Almost three years to the day after James's death, Gavin's closest sibling (and heir presumptive) Lt.-Col Michael Thomas Henderson, passed away. Michael had always been a popular figure in the family and elsewhere. Soldiers who served with him in the covert army camp at Coleshill said he was genial and unpretentious. Even as a schoolboy, Michael seems to have been likeable. His father Harold mentioned him warmly in his letters home as someone who it was always fun to be with. Michael never showed any competitiveness with Gavin, unlike their younger brother Roddy. Losing Michael probably made Gavin reflect on his own mortality. Early death had been a feature of the family ever since the first Lady Faringdon passed away at the age of 46. Her eldest son Harold died at the same age. Both of these had died when they were a year younger than Michael – who passed away at the age of 47, as had their uncle Frank. Two other uncles Alec and Arnold, lived slightly longer to 55 and 50 years respectively. Gavin must have wondered what was left in his allotted span. Psalm 90 famously gives a man's lifespan as *"three score and ten"* i.e. 70. Gavin was to pass that milestone and pack in more than most others might have in his remaining years.

In spite of playing useful roles during the war Gavin had been left out of the Attlee government. In 1942 he had chaired a committee that considered the appearance of local authority housing estates for the National Buildings Record. Eventually, similar socially conscious roles eventually came his way. In 1946 he was elected to serve on the Central Housing Advisory Committee and became president of the Theatres Advisory Council. Then he was elected to serve as member of the Colonial Economic and Development Council from 1948–51; and from 1957–60 was a Lords member of the Parliamentary Labour Party's executive. He proved himself popular as a London County Councillor from 1958–61, and went on to become an alderman from 1961–65. After the creation of the Greater London Council, he served on its Historic Buildings Council from 1961–73. During the war he had served on the executive committee of the Fire Service Association, and was to become its chairman from 1960 to 1969.

Gavin's experience with, and deep concern for, fine art and cultural heritage came to fruition in the later part of his life. For fourteen years he was to serve as a Trustee of the Wallace Collection – a non-departmental public body which safeguards some of the finest works of art in the country. Most of this had been purchased by the first four Marquesses of Hertford, passed on to Sir Richard Wallace, the 4th Marquess's illegitimate son, and bequeathed to the British nation by his widow in 1897. This outstanding collection of fine and decorative art remains displayed in one of that family's former London homes, Hertford House in Manchester Square. It is one of the cultural highlights of London, with paintings such as *The Laughing Cavalier* by Frans Hals, views of Venice by Canaletto, and Rembrandt's portrait of his son Titus. These and collections of porcelain, furniture, and other decorative arts and crafts are displayed with great charm in over 30 galleries. The style and grace of this collection affected the way in which Buscot Park came to be arranged as a home where art is lived with as it was meant to be, not as antiques in a museum. Gavin was a trustee of the Wallace Collection from 1946–53 and later from 1966–73.

In the late 1940s and early 1950s Gavin's concern with the issues raised by pacifism, conscientious objection and conscription led him to contribute enthusiastically to debates on those subjects. Then his seasoned interest in the country's artistic heritage came to the fore when he joined his old friend "Jack", the Earl of Huntingdon, to appeal in the House of Lords against the Government's decision to discharge half the staff employed to do restoration and maintenance work for government and royal art collections. Somewhat surprisingly, his contribution to a debate on historic buildings was to claim that the maintenance costs were so great that it was impossible for anyone to continue to live in them. He proposed that it would be prudent for them to be acquired by some authorised body and for uses to be found for them that would benefit society at large. Then in July 1949 the following appeared in *The Times*:

> *"The National Trust announces that Buscot Park House and*
> *grounds, Berkshire, has*
> *been given to the trust by the purchaser of the Buscot estate,*
> *who has recently acquired*
> *the estate from Lord Faringdon."*

The purchaser was Ernest Cook, the philanthropist grandson of Thomas Cook, the Victorian travel entrepreneur. After a successful career as a banker, he spent his fortune acquiring country estates and collections of art with the intention of setting up an educational charity dedicated to the conservation and management of the countryside. This was to actively encourage the younger generation to learn traditional and new skills. Cook was keen to preserve not only buildings and landscape, but the social, economic, architectural and environmental aspects of rural life nationwide. This was very much what Gavin had dreamt of – something almost socialistic and utopian. After Cook's death in 1955, over 100 museums and art galleries benefited from the dispersal of his art collection, and many of the buildings and estates he acquired found a new lease of life. His other interests around Buscot Park included the Buscot Manor Estate and the Coleshill Estate, which were all to be given to the National Trust.

The Buscot Estate consisted of 3,863 acres, the Mansion House and grounds, a number of secondary houses (leased) numerous cottages, woods, and areas where fishing and shooting were available. On 12ᵗʰ April 1949 the Executive Committee of the National Trust:

> *"...resolved that on completion of the gift of Buscot Estate,*
> *the NT, with the object of preserving the estate, together with*
> *the House and its important collection, will hold the Estate*
> *inalienably except for such land as may be required by Public*
> *Authority."*

Subsequently, an agreement took place between them and Mr Cook, Lord Faringdon and the 1920 Trustees; and there were further negotiations over details such as water supply, leasing of woods to the Forestry Commission, cottage and farm tenancy agreements, etc. Ernest Cook's agents Whatley, Hill and Co. wrote in June 1955 saying that they would *"be grateful to know if you would kindly confirm that you are willing to surrender your lease…provided you are relieved of all obligations for repairs"*…and that they *"understood from the National Trust that they were going to try and get you to modify the terms by making you pay something towards the dilapidations, that is the repair to the roof, etc."* The latter turned out to be a standard clause. Gavin pointed out that as the house was virtually rebuilt 15 years earlier this was not something he was inclined to do. Such attention to details turned out to be necessary as many were to have far-reaching effects.

The freehold of the lease was assigned to the National Trust, whilst the rest of the estate was kept by Mr Cook until his death. During that period Gavin entered into a Deed of Covenant with the NT in which, together with the entrance fees and grounds he voluntarily renounced in their favour, until his death in 1977. The Buscot estate was run in conjunction with the neighbouring Coleshill estate which Cook planned to leave to the National Trust, when historic Coleshill House (designed by Inigo Jones) burnt down in 1953. As neither estate included a mansion house, the National Trust labelled them as *"Investment properties"*. Unfortunately, this created a bone of contention in years to come, as all surplus income was passed to the central office rather than recycled into the estates as originally intended. Under the lease, the National Trust took responsibility for the upkeep and repair of roofs, main timbers and walls. The Trust also agreed the repayment to the lessee of two indoor staff and two gardeners; to pay an agreed sum towards heating the show rooms; the water supply to all properties, to insure the property and to pay the general rates. The lessee would be responsible for internal and external maintenance (other than roofs, main timbers and walls) and for the upkeep of the grounds; to open the *Piano Nobile* to the public two days a week, and keep the show rooms heated.

This arrangement allowed Gavin time to be involved with his multiple interests in London and the colonies. His relationship with the National Trust's secretary of the Country House Committee, James Lees-Milne, never mended. Milne resigned in 1950 and luckily, Gavin was on very friendly terms with the new Deputy Director-General, Robin Fedden. But it dawned on Gavin and many others that the Trust had taken on too many historic houses to fund them as they would like. By 1963 he was receiving letters from former tenants and others elsewhere with grievances. Several came from Lord Bristol, who invited Gavin to join a National Trust Tenants' Association. This peer's sentiments must have appealed to the old civil rights campaigner in Gavin, as Bristol put it:

> "By far the largest group of all National Trust tenants are the cottage tenants who, around here, appear to be getting pushed around very badly. In fact, the National Trust are known by the working people in the village as the 'National Mistrust', which is a very poor state of affairs indeed...I am afraid that the National trust has got too large and lost its grip on reality. Another bad thing is that they will not pay decent salaries to their employees, and so they cannot expect the best persons!!"

However, whilst these complaints may have been justified, Gavin did not join. Perhaps, this was because Victor Hervey, 6th Marquess of Bristol (imprisoned for jewellery theft in 1939) had recently inherited his title after his father's death. Lord Bristol had a sizeable inheritance which he enlarged by his business acumen to make it worth his while registering as a tax exile in Monaco. Whilst this was legal and prudent it was the opposite of what Gavin had done with his inheritance. In addition, Lord Bristol had recommended the Conservative M.P, Sir Jocelyn Lucas KBE, MC, as chairman of the Tenant's Association with the accolade *"there could be no one better"*. But whilst it was true that Major Lucas had a distinguished war record, he had been Portsmouth's District Officer for Sir Oswald Mosley's British Union of Fascists. So, unsurprisingly, Gavin did not join. In fact, he was probably preoccupied with London County Council politics as he won and held the seat of Woolwich West for Labour from 1958–61.

This led to his holding the position of Postmaster General in Harold Wilson's Shadow Cabinet from 1959–62. However, when Labour got back into government in 1964 the position went to Tony Benn MP.

In May 1961 three writers contributing to a new satirical magazine called *Private Eye* came to Buscot Park. These were Auberon Waugh – son of Evelyn – along with John Betjeman and his daughter Candida. The Betjemans had started a column called *"Nooks and Corners of New Barbarism"* which was concerned with how modern developers were vandalising old towns and cities – something John and his friend Gavin had already been campaigning about. By then Gavin was chair of the GLC's Historic Buildings sub-committee and had asked borough councils to forward copies of applications for planning permission on *"buildings of merit"*. He was also in contact with another *Private Eye* contributor, the journalist Paul Foot, at the *New Statesman*; and Gavin knew that Tom Driberg, the Labour MP for Maldon in Essex, was secretly compiling *Private Eye*'s hilariously obscene crossword puzzles. Three years into the life of the magazine Gavin was appointed a member of the Historic Buildings Council for England at the same time that *Private Eye* was facing bankruptcy. This was because the magazine had been started with only £350 and was under capitalised. Basically, it needed more money to be able to increase its circulation, improve sales and survive. Sadly, potential investors did not think that a magazine known as the *"scourge of the establishment"* had a secure future, so funding was proving hard to find. With so many friends at work there Gavin decided to step in and today the magazine's website mentions *"Saved from bankruptcy by Lord Farringdon"*. It hardly matters that the name is misspelt. According to Patrick Marnham who was working there at the time, *"Lord Faringdon strolled in off the street to hand over a cheque"*, but no one could remember how much this was for. Gavin on the other hand, was less vague. He told his executor that he and the actor Dirk Bogarde had made sure the magazine survived by covering the staff's wages for a month or two. For this they were both issued shares in Pressdram. At the time it was quite a good percentage, but after Peter

Cook recapitalised the business, their shareholding was very much reduced. When asked why he invested in *Private Eye* Gavin replied:

> *"It is better to have safety valves in society rather than explosions."*

Today, the magazine's list of owners with inherited shares includes *"executors of the estate of Lord Faringdon"* and *"Brock van den Bogaerde (a nephew of Bogarde)"*.

The context was that Sir Compton Mackenzie, a prolific author as well as the literary critic of the *Daily Mail*, had become a near neighbour after he moved into Denchworth Manor, by Wantage, in 1950. He came to dinner in 1952 and contacted Gavin in 1955 while researching his book *Thin Ice* – not one as well known today as some of his others such as *Monarch of the Glen* or *Whiskey Galore* – but socially far more important. Mackenzie visited Gavin while writing his novel *Thin Ice*, which concerns the fall from office of a homosexual politician. The book detailed the dangers facing many of Gavin's friends at a time when over 2,500 men were being arrested for *"homosexual offences"* every year – about seven a day. According to Mackenzie, *"three-quarters of the male suicides in England were due to blackmail for homosexual offences"*. In other words, the law was both ineffective and inappropriate as it promoted the criminal offence of blackmail. A few years later, Dirk Bogarde, another *"closet"* homosexual, was brave enough to appear in *Victi"*, a film based on *Thin Ice*. Here a married man discovers that his former lover has hanged himself in police custody, and that the blackmailers are threatening to expose him. This was the sort of dilemma that had been brought to light in the Wolfenden Report, which advocated homosexual law reform. At the time, *Private Eye* consistently supported changes in the law.

Arthur Gore, the 8th Earl of Arran, was a Conservative whip in the Upper House known affectionately as *"Boofy"*. His elder brother was said to have committed suicide after being persecuted for being gay,

which impelled the Earl to introduce a Sexual Offences Reform Bill
to the Upper House. He wrote to Gavin on House of Lords paper.

"15ᵗʰ June 1965.

HOMOSEXUAL LAW REFORM

Dear Lord Faringdon,

Thank you for voting for my bill on the second reading.

*I now write to ask whether you can again support me in the
Committee stage, which is Monday, June 21ˢᵗ, or better still
by speaking should you feel like doing so. Though it is not
possible to present a bill to the other place this session, it
will be useful, I think to know, if we can at least get through
Committee in our House before Parliament rises, so that
when we reassemble we can quickly offer the Commons an as
it were signed and sealed statement, though we ourselves will
first have to go through the whole business again.*

*I believe that we may have a fairly rough ride in Committee.
Amendments have been put down, which though not
seemingly wrecking amendments, could go for weakening
the main purposes and recommendations of the Wolfenden
Committee: and some will need to be firmly opposed. Others
which I hope will be put down by more authoritative peers
and which are, in effect, straight Wolfenden, may receive
general support through of course there is no currency for this.*

*Put briefly, the issue is I believe by no means decided in
our House, and I deeply hope you may be able to come on
Monday, June 21ˢᵗ, so that we see this thing through. I am
sorry to bother you with it: my hope had been that we could
have waited until the Autumn and then started again. But
it has been borne in on me that not to proceed straight away*

might be to seem to withdraw – which I have no intention of doing.

Yours sincerely,

Boofy Arran."

In June 1966 Gavin's contribution to the third reading of the Sexual Offences Bill was a crucial one at the final stage. This was to ensure that provision was made so that as soon as the bill was passed – and homosexual acts between consenting adults were no longer a criminal offence – all prosecutions and pending trails would be dropped. One amusing side line of this serious subject was a comment by "Boofy" Arran. In his private life he was devoted to badgers, and even had several living in his house with him. So, it was natural that he sponsored a bill for the protection of badgers in the wild. But this failed to get enough support soon after his homosexual reform bill was passed. When a journalist asked "Boofy" why he thought this happened he answered: *"Not enough badgers in the House of Lords".*

Living proof of prejudice, blackmail, arrest, trial by media, imprisonment and exile could be found in the life of Gavin's friend Rupert Croft-Cooke. A successful author and playwright, he spent 15 years abroad after spending six months in Brixton prison for an alleged homosexual act in 1953. He had been prosecuted on the evidence of two sailors detained for burglary. They had been released after they supplied the police with evidence against Croft-Crooke. Rupert returned to Britain after the Sexual Reform Bill was passed in 1965 and wrote a glowing account of Gavin in his autobiography *The Ghost of June*, which was published three years later.

The last words of Voltaire's Candide are an injunction to *"cultivate our gardens".* These words are often interpreted metaphorically. Gavin went further, as he arranged to have his mortal remains lodged in his garden at Buscot Park. Its "Pleasure Grounds" were begun in the late 18th century to complement the Palladian house. The first

Lord Faringdon commissioned Harold Peto to design a water garden, which Peto began in 1904 and, after Lord Faringdon decided it to be extended, returned to finish in 1911. This was an elegant series of stone-lined pools and canals with paved walks on either side that took visitors down to an ornamental lake. Part of Peto's original design was a long rose pergola running from the steps near the top midway down to a fountain. This might have worked well in the sort of garden Peto had designed in the Mediterranean, but it had not proved a great success here. The reason was that the water garden occupied an area that had been clear-felled through dense woodland. On either side, rows of tall mature trees stood blocking out the light. Not even the best gardeners could make roses thrive in what was essentially a narrow woodland glade, especially one that seldom got direct sunlight. The first Lady Faringdon had planted species of roses that *"did not do"*. Gavin's mother, Lady Violet Henderson, replanted with fresh varieties. Still, the roses suffered from mildew in the gloomy, damp conditions. Then, after two generations, Gavin had the pergola removed. This had the wonderful effect of opening up the view across the lake. The current Lord Faringdon fondly recalls the artist Felix Kelly visiting and admiring the view to the *faux* temple on the far shore. Then he told his uncle that he thought it a shame that the lake was so small. Gavin indignantly replied *"This is our Big Lake!"* Then Kelly explained that if the roof of the temple were lowered it would make the lake appear larger and the temple further away. That persuaded Gavin, who sent for a carpenter and got him to lower the height of the temple's pillars.

Each generation of the Faringdon family has added to the plantings and prospects with the pleasure gardens. A *patte d'oie* is the 18th-century French garden designer's term for a set of avenues or *"rides"* fanning out into a landscape garden. This was Gavin's contribution to Buscot Park. Peto's Water Gardens were the first toe of the *"goose-foot"* and Gavin designed four more toes – or rather avenues. The second toe was a tree-lined avenue punctuated by a circular garden where all the flowers would be white or blue. This was designed to be a quiet place to pause before advancing to the Big Lake past a marble vase on a plinth. The third goose's toe was an avenue lined with fastigiate and weeping oaks, leading to a sunken garden with prostrate roses and a recycled Venetian well-head, and from there on between he added a pair of life size Coade-stone statues of Osiris/Antinous – a God created after the Emperor Hadrian's favourite page drowned in the Nile River. This avenue then continued up through Lombardy poplars to a circle of wild roses on top of the hill. It starts at the steps below the theatre which are flanked with two sphinxes on plinths with inscriptions in Latin and Greek. Translated these read *"Who can unravel the enigma of the Sphinx. Men of Power assume Ownership. True or False?"* This seems to suggest the philosophy that would have suited Gavin. That no one could actually own Buscot Park – the privileged few who lived here were only ever its temporary custodians. The Sphinx and the two Osiris/Antinous statues resulted in this central ride being called the Egyptian Avenue. The third ride, or avenue, was planted with fastigiate and weeping beech trees that led to a bronze statue of a Sun God at the end. The fourth avenue was incomplete when he died. It led past a crescent pool where a stone sculpture of a naked man stands among bulrushes. This is said to be a sculpture of Adam, a gift from the man who carved it, Arthur Mackenzie, who used the surname Kennethson as his professional moniker. He was a friend and neighbour of John Betjeman's, who lived in Uffingham. Gavin had planned to take this avenue up further to terminate with a bust of Antinous under a Wellingtonia, but he died before this was done. The fifth avenue, completing Gavin's grand design of the goose's foot, was the original carriage drive which he planted with lime and London plane trees, leading to a statue of Ruth on the top of a high point known as Canon Hill.

In 1913 the *Architectural Review* published an illustrated feature on Harold Peto's Water Gardens and mentioned *"two fine terminal figures which stand facing each other at the top of the staircase are of Cipollino, and were bought by Mr Peto in Naples"*. These monumental grotesque heads on baroque-style spiral columns were similar to the pagan sculptures added to some 18th-century Italian gardens. These monstrous figures were meant to create a sense of fantasy. Gavin had them moved to frame a view of the lake at the end of his third avenue. Here they are less visible but come into their own as a pair of primordial water gods. He added some steps into the lake beneath them, as though this was a landing or departure point. This is just beyond where the marble vase on a plinth stood. And in this he intended that his ashes were to be placed after his death. He asked for no ceremony or flowers, and this seems a suitably peaceful and poetic end for one who had led such a hurly-burly existence.

Elsewhere in his garden at Buscot, things were busy but more pragmatic. He kept up the four-acre walled garden as best he could. Here there was almost a quarter of a mile of glasshouses, some of which required a boiler and coal bunker to heat. He tried to run things along the lines set by his grandfather from whom he inherited in 1934, but those were the days when a country house garden had a dozen or more gardeners and was like a food factory. There were glasshouses devoted to carnations, cattleyas, dahlias, pelargoniums, as well as others for avocados, melons, cucumbers and grapes. Gavin tried to keep as many of these going as possible but most of the glasshouses had become dilapidated during WW2. However, guests recalled that the gardeners grew exotics impossible to get elsewhere – yellow tomatoes, supposed to be the original stock called *Pommo d'Oro* or Golden Apples – as well as black tomatoes – in preference to the usual red varieties. Gavin's nephew remembers his uncle keeping some glasshouses very hot in order to able to germinate seeds and cultivate tropical plants sent by President Nkruma of Ghana. And that Gavin, who deplored the fact that his nephew had been sent to Eton, instructed Mr Chapman, the head gardener, to cut carnations, wrap them in tissue, pack them inside wooden pencil cases, so that they could be sent to him. Three carnations came each Tuesday and four every Friday so that there was always a fresh button-hole. Charles Faringdon wrote that he still retains *"fond memories of the glorious white warm peaches grown against a heated back wall, the rows of avocados in nets and heaving melons in their sunken beds. Then the orchid houses and the vegetables all went"*. The reason they *"went"* was that most of the glasshouses were demolished by the National Trust after it was agreed they were too costly to maintain.

A close woman friend who visited often in those years was Lady Ashton, better known as Madge Garland. She had edited English Vogue from 1933–40 and founded the Royal College of Arts Fashion School in the 1950s. Married (briefly) and divorced twice, she came to stay with different lesbian partners – always discreetly with few if any other guests. Her circle of friends included the couturier Paul Poiret and the sculptor Constantin Brancusi. Elegant and gazelle-like, her portrait had been painted by Marie Laurencin and she was one of Beaton's earliest photographic subjects in his *Book of Beauty*. In the 1960s she wrote several books on gardening under the name Madge Garland. She obviously meant a lot to Gavin as he left Lady Madge Ashton £1,000 in his will. Another interesting visitor to Buscot Park during the post-war period was Russell Page, one of the "greats" of modern architectural garden design. This follower of Harold Peto worked mainly for wealthy clients in southern France and Italy.

Whilst they were on either side of the political divide for forty years Gavin's former best man – Lord Boothby – who had failed to get Gavin to the church on time for his wedding in 1927 – was attentive when he learned that Gavin's health was failing. He wrote with evident concern and the woman who he mentioned was his second wife, Wanda Sanna, thirty-three years his junior who he had married five years earlier. In spite of his louche reputation, Queen Elizabeth, the Queen Mother, confided to Ludovic Kennedy that she was very fond of *"Bob Boothby"*, adding that he was *"a bounder but not a cad"*. This letter, hand-written on note paper embossed with the House of Lords logo in red, shows that the Queen mother probably had the true measure of the man.

"1 Eaton Square, SW1
January 25, 1972.

Dear Gavin,

*Wanda told me of your talk with her. I cannot urge you too
strongly to go and see Dr. Denis Williams or Dr. Christopher
Earl – both equally good – at the National Hospital, Queen's
Square. My doctor sent me there, and they cured me in
a fortnight, and I was <u>much</u> worse than you. All you are
suffering from is nerves; and in this field they are pre-eminent.
I beg of you to do this, and let us know the result.*

Yours ever,

Bob.

(Telephone not in the book – 235. 5171)"

Unfortunately, Gavin turned out to be suffering from more than a
case of nerves. No one seemed to be able to pin down the problem
until he went to a consulting surgeon in Harley St. who had served
in Malta during WW2. Colonel Ronald William Raven had gone on
to become senior surgeon at the Royal Marsden Hospital. He had
just retired, but took on Gavin's case, by writing to Dr Macdonald
Critchley CBE, the most prominent British neurologist:

"29 Harley Street, W1

Dear Dr Macdonald Critchley,

*May I introduce Lord Faringdon, I excised his carcinoma
of the anus (followed by radiotherapy). He used to be a
good orator but his speech has slowed…this has become
more marked as his mobility grew somewhat difficult, and
now he forgets words. The circulation of his blood seems
fine but his left hand has a tremor…I would be grateful for
your opinion and help for this special patient. I wondered
if there is Parkinson's disease here or brain change from the
arteriosclerosis.*

Ronald W. Raven."

Raven had successfully operated on a haemorrhoid a few years earlier. Gavin had recovered after fearing cancer and undergoing a strict diet regime. That worry may well have been misplaced as his ailments could have been reasonably attributed to age until now. But the letter above indicates that he had developed the first three classic symptoms of Parkinson's Disease: a tremor in a hand, slowed movement and changes in speech. Parkinson's is a progressive disease and soon the other classic symptoms developed – loss of balance and incapacity. He appears to have had a fall as the nurse's note below starts by mentioning a replacement prosthesis for intracapsular femoral neck fracture. His other notes outline how much he had declined:

> *"Lord Faringdon*
> *Aged 74.*
> *Femur Austin Moore Prothesis.*
>
> *Walked at 8 am before night nurse goes off. Breakfast at 9*
> *am & sat out of bed for I hr around 10-11am.Lunch taken*
> *at 1.pm glass Complan, usually sits out of bed for an hour*
> *in the afternoon. Back and heels rubbed ever 3-4 hours or*
> *more frequently if bed is wet. Bottle in situ at all times as he*
> *is incontinent of urine at times. Bowels open daily sometimes*
> *faecal incontinence due to ca bowel – small amount has been*
> *resealed) usually has a jam sandwich around 3.00 pm. Leg*
> *exercises encouraged as much as possible. Dressing to wound*
> *changed as required. Supper take at 7 -7.30 pm & sometimes*
> *he will sit in the chair for this."*

In careful and considerate hands such as these, Gavin had a quiet and peaceful end to his eventful life. Lord Faringdon died on 29th January 1977. His death certificate gave the cause as acute myocardial failure, atherosclerosis of Coronary arteries, and Parkinson's disease. According to his previously stated wishes, he was to be *"cremated without religious ceremony"* and his ashes placed in *"unconsecrated ground"*; a place he had arranged to be put in Buscot Park's pleasure grounds. Sir John Betjeman attended along with some prominent Fabian socialists. It was introduced by the Rt. Hon. Michael Stewart,

MP, who had served twice as Foreign Secretary in Harold Wilson's cabinet. The author and educationalist Dame Margaret Cole was there. Like Gavin she had been a pacifist during WW2 and gone on to serve as an alderman on the London County Council. There was a reading from E.M. Forster's *Two Cheers for Democracy* by the Rt. Hon. Dame Shirley Williams MP. And there was a second reading by the Rt. Hon. William Rodgers, MP from the *New Fabian Colonial Essays*. John Parker MP (the Father of the House of Commons) attended and wrote a touching obituary for *The Times*. Here is an extract:

> *"He was a kindly man …When a boy in the Fabian*
> *Bookshop got married to one of its office girls Gavin learnt*
> *that they could not afford a honeymoon. He promptly invited*
> *them to spend a week in his absence at Buscot, gave them*
> *first-class railway tickets and sent his Rolls to fetch them*
> *from the station. He arrived back to drink their health in*
> *champagne and wish them luck."*

A similar story was told by his nephew who recalled a retired cleaning lady who came to stay at Buscot Park. Gavin had met her one day while she was on her knees scrubbing the white brick front steps of a house in Brompton Square with Vim. When he complimented her on her work, she had thanked him and replied that this was her last day on the job, and that the steps would probably never gleam like this again. Gavin immediately gave her his card and invited her to come and stay at Buscot Park. A few weeks later she arrived with her husband at Challow station, where Alfons Gaffka was waiting to collect them in Gavin's green Rolls-Royce. Lord Faringdon sat her on his right at dinner, in spite of the fact that a lady was present who, according to etiquette, should have been accorded that privileged position.

Amongst those who wrote letters of condolence to his nephew Charles was one from Robert Heber-Percy, Lord Berners' former partner known as *"The Mad Boy"*.

"Dear Charles,

I want to write and say how much I shall miss Gavin - I first knew him when I came in 1930, forty-seven years. I won't say we never had a cross word but they were soon forgotten.

We had a lot of jolly jokes, I even got him on a horse, and we surprised your grandmother in the shrubberies.

He had a sterling character he was brave and strong in all the illness that beset him. He never broadcast his generosity but there were many who he helped.

Through not country minded he was much liked and respected

I am sure that you will miss him very much and I send you all my sympathy

Yours,

Robert."

A second letter from Hugh Cruddas, who resided with Heber-Percy at Faringdon House between 1950 and 1970, an ebullient character who worked for Gavin for a time:

"Of course, it was not unexpected. One cannot wish for him to have gone on living with that disability and humiliating disease. His courage and determination in fighting it over the last 2 years, have filled me with admiration.

I shall miss him very much as an employee, as a good neighbour and above all as a very good friend."

CHAPTER 20

Epilogue

In January 1778 *The Daily Telegraph* published the following pinched but revealing epitaph:

> *"LABOUR PEER LEAVES £214,445*
>
> *By our Estates Correspondent.*
>
> *Lord Faringdon, reputed as one of the richest socialists, who died in February, aged 74, left £214,445 net (£282,385 gross) it was revealed today.*
>
> *His family interests make a sizable fortune but they are on trust, in which he had no interest. The wealth stems from his grandfather, whom he succeeded as second baron in 1934. He was one of the 'railway' barons of the 19th century.*
>
> *The late peer was a philanthropist; most of his gifts were made anonymously. He was active in many Labour causes and was once Labour leader in the Lords. He lived as National Trust tenant at Buscot Park near Faringdon, Berks."*

During the latter phase of his life Gavin put considerable thought and time into who might benefit in his will. There were many changes over the years, mainly due to people passing away before he did. Finally, he made generous provisions for family members, close friends, employees at Buscot Park and Brompton Square, and his Trustees.

One beneficiary, Kenneth. S. Harris, owned Taskey's Antiques in Chicago. In 1944, after James Lees-Milne visited Buscot Park, his diary entry mentioned *"A young American with a baby face was staying"*. A year later Felix Kelly painted *Buscot Park from the south, with two figures*, which probably shows Kenneth and Gavin standing side by side. In 1950 John Betjeman, writing to John and Myfanwy Piper, described Kenneth as *"Gavin's little American friend"*. Two portraits of a short, baby-faced man appear in murals by Roy Hobdell painted in the 1950s, and in 1955 he painted a *trompe l'oeil* called *Ken's Blotter*. Kenneth Harris was a permanent fixture in Gavin's household between 1944 and 1964. But they drifted apart after 20 years and Philip Edwards replaced him in the mid-1960s. Gavin left them joint ownership of 28 Brompton Square in his will which led to problems after Gavin died. As his nephew recalled:

> *"Kenneth came scooting over from Chicago and popped receipts from Christies and Sotheby's in front of Philip who could not prove that these purchases he claimed to have made on Gavin's behalf had been re-reimbursed. This led to the exodus of much of the furniture to Chicago and Philip made do with what remained."*

After Kenneth's death his collection of antiques was auctioned by Sotheby's. Lord Faringdon bought back a number but, *"unfortunately, he had sold other items on (like the dining room chairs)"*.

Other beneficiaries were Judah Cohen of Batty St., London, a Jewish Labour Party activist from Whitechapel; Cyril Millard of Mortlake, Surrey (this was "Ciggie" his former chauffeur, with whom Gavin had a lively correspondence after Cyril joined the army during WW2). Henry Smith, the caretaker of 28 Brompton Square; Ilsa Barea, widow of the Spanish writer and broadcaster who had lived at Middle Lodge on the Buscot estate; and Alfons and Nora Gaffka, Gavin's handyman and general factotum who married his housekeeper at Buscot Park. In addition, his estate employees received £200 each. Sadly, Gavin's trustees were unable to locate *"Jean Giudicelli of Lumio, Corsica"*. This may have been due to variations in Corsican spelling. A Mademoiselle Eugenie Guidicelli had been paid an annuity and additional sums from 1938–48. However, since then there appeared to be no one with either surname living in Lumio.

By and large, something unusual was to be expected in the 2nd Lord Faringdon's personal life; and it was sometimes amusing. The following extract was taken from a monograph on Buscot Park gardens written by his nephew and heir, the 3rd Lord Faringdon, in 2013.

"When my uncle died, in his Letter of Wishes was a simple touching request to put his ashes in the open 'stone' vase overlooking the Big Lake, and a stopper be made to keep them dry. I scraped a bit of lichen off the pot – it was marble but nonetheless we had an elegant stopper designed incorporating the floral motif found on the vase. We could find no one in this country to carve it for us – the design was sent to Siena and we were told we would have the object with us in six months. The executors were alerted, the scaffolding put up, but no sign of the stopper even though we had been assured it had been despatched by rail some weeks previously. We were in a dilemma, as it would have been difficult to postpone or cancel the arrangements at short notice. Alfons Gaffka, who by then had become our Maintenance man, came to the rescue by suggesting he cut up my cork bathmat and attached a rather fetching door knob he found in the workshop to give it a finial and some style. The rather macabre ceremony came and went and Alfons grouted in my bathmat – as a temporary measure, we thought it passed muster. What we had not taken on board was the unintelligible Italian labelling on the sack containing the stopper, or the likelihood of it being left in a British Rail goods van which

stood in an Edinburgh siding for two years. By the time we had retrieved our stopper and pulled the cork, to our horror, we found my Uncle had been swimming – somehow water had seeped in. Another visit to my bathroom unwrapped a huge new sponge I had just brought back from Crete, and with it the water was delicately absorbed and the top left open, allowing the hot summer sun to dry it out, before the much-travelled stopper was introduced to hermetically seal the vase for good.

If that had been the end of the story, it would have been an unfortunate episode in what was a more exacting task than my Uncle had envisaged. What he had not prepared us for was the Letter of Wishes of his great friend, Philip Edwards, who asked if his ashes could be co-mingled in the vase. As he had been enormously generous to our family, it seemed churlish to put any obstacle in the way of his request and, sure enough, the stopper was prized off, the scaffolding erected and his Executors marched to the site carrying a huge casket. Someone had forgotten to bring the key, and of course, the casket was itself too big to fit in the vase. I suggested that the casket be buried beneath the plinth much to the approbation of the Head Gardener who started to dig the hole, and in no time the casket was all covered up and the stopper replaced. That might have seemed a perfect ending, but over the course of the ensuing years first his chef and then his housekeeper asked if their ashes might go there too – luckily, we had a precedent, and placed them on either sides of the plinth, and gave all four Maltese Crosses with their initials on them. I hope my Uncle will forgive me for allowing him to get wet as he is now surrounded by his friend, his chef, his housekeeper, and he is dry – he should be in Heaven."

Bibliography

Harold Acton. *Memories of an Aesthete.*

Harold Acton. *More Memories of an Aesthete.*

Harold Acton. *Biography of Nancy Mitford.*

Rosemary Bailey: *Love and War in the Pyrenees.*

Patrick Balfour. *Society Racket. A Critical Survey of Modern Social Life.*

Alan Bennett: *London Review of Books.* Vol. 19 No. 17. 4th September 1997.

John Betjeman. *Collected Letters.*

Robert Boothby. *Recollections of a Rebel; My Yesterday, Your Tomorrow.*

Robert Byron. *Europe in the Looking-Glass.*

Robert Byron. *The Road to Oxiana.*

Robert Byron. *First Russia, Then Tibet.*

Robert Byron. *Letters Home.*

Humphrey Carpenter. *The Brideshead Generation.*

Cyril Connolly. *The Rock Pool.*

Joseph E. Davies. *Mission to Moscow.* (1943 Propaganda Film)

Hugh Dalton. *Political Diaries: 1918–40 & 1945–60*

Tom Driberg. *Ruling Passions.*

Selina Hastings. *The Red Earl.*

Selina Hastings. *Biography of Nancy Mitford.*

Hansard. Proceedings and Debates of the House of Lords. 1934-77.

Ankaret Howard. *The Quarryman.*

George F. Keenan. *Memoirs 1925–50.*

James Knox. *A Biography of Robert Byron.*

James Lees-Milne. *Fourteen Friends.*

Guy de Maupassant. *A Parisian Affair and Other Stories.*

Guy de Maupassant. *A Life.*

Compton Mackenzie. *Thin Ice.*

Compton Mackenzie. *On Moral Courage.*

Diana Mitford. *A Life of Contrasts.*

Nancy Mitford. *The Pursuit of Love.*

Nancy Mitford. *Wigs on the Green.*

Nancy Mitford. *Pigeon Pie.*

Nancy Mitford. *Highland Fling.*

Nancy Mitford. *Letters to Evelyn Waugh.*

Beverley Nichols. *All I Could Never Be.*

Beverley Nichols. *Cry Havoc!*

Beverley Nichols. *The Sweet and Twenties.*

George Orwell. *Homage to Catalonia.*

Anthony Powell. *A Dance to the Music of Time.*

Paul Preston. *The Spanish Holocaust.*

Alan Pryce-Jones. *The Bonus of Laughter.*

Joseph Stalin. *On the Great Patriotic War of the Soviet Union.*

Lord Stanley of Alderley. *Sea Peace.*

D.J. Taylor. *The Bright Young People.*

Leon Trotsky. *The Lessons of October 1917 and other essays.*

Evelyn Waugh. *Decline and Fall.*

Evelyn Waugh. *Vile Bodies.*

Evelyn Waugh. *A Little Learning.*

Evelyn Waugh. *Diaries* edited by Michael Davie.

Evelyn Waugh. *Letters* edited by Mark Amory.

H.G. Wells. *The Outline of History.*

H.G. Wells. *The Science of Life.*

H.G. Wells. *The Work, Wealth, and Happiness of Mankind.*

Francis Wheen. *Tom Driberg His Life and Indiscretions.*

A.N. Wilson. *Betjeman.*

Glossary

Anarchist: Member of a political party aiming to abolish the established state.

Army & Navy Stores: A department store in London started in the 19th century as a co-operative society for military officers and their families in the colonies.

Basque Children's Committee: Set up after the Conservative government agreed to allow Spanish child refugees to come to Britain on the condition that they found homes within 30 days. Failing that, the *Niños de la Guerra* (Children of the War) were to be repatriated.

B.B: Brendan Bracken, the Minister for Information during WW2, signed memos with his initials "B.B." George Orwell, who worked at The India desk, felt that he suppressed truth and free speech. In his novel *1984* Orwell created a dictator called "Big Brother" or "B.B." who crushed individuals via "newspeak" and the "thought police" of his "Ministry of Truth".

BCRS: British Committee for Refugees from Spain, provided material aid and advice to individuals in Britain and France. The BCRS contributed to the establishment of a central organisation in Perpignan for the issuing of food and clothes to refugees in transit; establishing a home for 100 refugees in Narbonne. They also helped refugees to emigrate to South America; co-chartering the

S.S. Sinaia to transport 1,800 refugees to Mexico, and publicised living conditions in camps.

Blitz: Colloquial word for *Blitzkrieg*, German for "Lightning war". During WW2 the word Blitz referred to the intense aerial bombing of cities.

Bolshevik: Member of the radical social-democratic party founded by Lenin that seized power in the Russian Revolution of October 1917.

British Raj: Also called "Crown rule in India", or "Colonial India". Refers to the native states in the Asian subcontinent ruled by the British Crown from 1858 to 1947.

BYP: "Bright Young People" or **BYT** "Bright Young Things". Upper-class jokers in the late 1920s and early 1930s who organised events such as a "Chloroform Party" in the Royal Hospital Road, a "Fancy Undress" party, etc. They were both celebrated and reviled in the press.

Capital: In economic theories, capital consists of monetary wealth for investments, as well as the assets used for the production of goods and services, such as the machinery used in factories.

Capitalist: A person, or state, using their wealth to invest in trade and industry for profit.

Cavendish Hotel: Rosa Lewis's establishment at the junction of Jermyn and Duke Streets, Piccadilly, W.1. Rosa, sometimes called "The Duchess of Duke St." was a survivor from the Edwardian age who knew, or thought she knew, everyone. A likeable eccentric who appeared in novels by Evelyn Waugh and Anthony Powell.

CGA: Country Gentlemen's Association, was established in 1893 to provide a wide range of professional services to rural landowners.

It offered everything from seeds and farm equipment to horse tack, livestock, ploughs, fencing and legal advice.

Communist: Believer in the economic ideology and political movement aiming for common ownership of all capital and assets and the absence of social classes, money, and the state.

Confirmed Bachelor: In normal usage a phrase to describe a man who has been a bachelor for a long time and who shows no interest in marrying. However, it was also used as a euphemism in the 1920s and 1930s to describe a homosexual or gay man.

Conservative & Unionist Party: The "Tory" or Conservative Party allied with Liberal Unionists in 1886 and held office for all but three of the following twenty years. Lord Salisbury's and Arthur Balfour's governments between 1895 and 1906 were "Unionist". In 1909, the Conservatives became Conservative Unionists.

Dravidian: An ethnic and linguistic group of peoples from South India whose ancient temples were wonderfully decorated with stone carvings.

Fabian Society: A British political group dedicated to advancing socialism in democracies. It was named after the Roman Senator Quintus Fabius – famous for patient waiting.

Foreign Office: A branch of the British government since the 18th century, this department evolved to include the Commonwealth and the Department for International Development.

Gandhi-Irwin Pact: Was signed in March 1931 leading to the 2nd Round Table Conference.

Labour Party: A British political party that has been described as an alliance of social democrats, democratic socialists and trade unionists; the centre-left of the political spectrum.

League of Nations: The first worldwide intergovernmental organisation whose mission was to maintain world peace. Founded on 10th January 1920 following the Paris Peace Conference that ended the First World War, it ceased operations on 20th April 1946.

Marxist: Follower of Karl Marx's theory that bourgeois oppression of the workers under capitalism should be replaced by a dictatorship and a classless society.

Mobil-Shell: A subsidiary of the American and Royal Dutch oil companies pioneering the sales of kerosene, oil and petrol in the Asian subcontinent during the 1930s.

Molotov-Ribbentrop Pact: A non-aggression treaty signed in 1939 that enabled the Soviet Union and Nazi Germany to invade, partition and govern Poland.

MI5: The United Kingdom's domestic counter-intelligence and security agency, which works alongside the Secret Intelligence Service (SIS), Government Communications Headquarters (GCHQ), and Defence Intelligence (MI6).

MI6: Originated as Military Intelligence, Section 6 during WW2. The abbreviation MI6 is still used today.

MI9: Was a section of the British Directorate of Military Intelligence, part of the War Office. During WW2 it was responsible for assisting allied personnel to escape from occupied territories and obtaining information from enemy prisoners of war.

Nawab: A king, viceroy, prince or male ruler of an Asian state. The female equivalent is called a *Begum* or *Nawab Begum*. Their primary duty was to uphold the sovereignty of the Mughal emperor in a province.

NCAS: National Committee for Aid to Spain, a food aid organisation with Communist links.

NCCL: National Council for Civil Liberties (now called Liberty). An advocacy group set up in 1934 to challenge unjust legislation and promote human rights. Mainly composed of liberal social-minded reformers, its chairman was the novelist E.M. Forster, and the committee members included H.G. Wells, Clement Attlee, Augustus John, Vera Brittain and Professor Julian Huxley, with Lord Faringdon as its Treasurer.

New Statesman: The leading progressive political and cultural magazine in the *United Kingdom since 1913.*

NJCSR: National Joint Committee for Spanish Relief (often abbreviated to the **National Joint Committee** or **NJC**). Chaired by The Duchess of Atholl. Vice-Chairmen: The Earl of Listowel and Eleanor Rathbone MP the NJC provided aid to Spain transporting medical supplies, including ambulances & hospital equipment, food & clothing, as well as providing assistance for refugees from Franco's Spain to emigrate, including the co-chartering of the *S.S. Sinaia* to transport 1,800 refugees from France to Mexico. Intended to be purely humanitarian and non-sectarian, the NJC raised funds through a wide variety of means, including concerts, lectures, exhibitions (including an exhibition of Picasso's *Guernica* at the New Burlington Galleries, London, in October 1938), cinema screenings, house to house collections, and appeals to local and national newspapers. Co-operating societies included the **BCRS** British Committee for Refugees from Spain, and **SMAC** Spanish Medical Aid Committee.

Oxford Railway Club: An undergraduate society for upper-class men at Oxford University. Members donned evening dress, drank to excess, and rode trains giving impromptu speeches.

Pansy: Contemptuous slang term for a gay, conflated to mean a weak, effeminate or cowardly man. Less derogatory euphemisms of the day were "not as other men" or "confirmed bachelor". The novelist Nancy Mitford, who had many gay and transvestite friends in common with her brother, accepted them as natural and used the words "pansy" or "queer" to describe – not criticise – them.

Pomfret Castle: The 1st Lord Faringdon's house at 18 Arlington St., sold and demolished soon after his death. This 18th-century Gothic-style town house in London was commissioned by the Countess of Pomfret, a wealthy widow keen to stand out from the crowd.

Prod: The novelist Nancy Mitford's nickname for her husband, the Hon. Peter Rodd hinting at his virility and promiscuity.

Pukka: A colloquial term of Indian origin meaning "proper" or "very good".

Residency: Official home of the highest ranked Army officer in a British colony.

Round Table Talks: Three peace conferences organized by HM Government and Indian political leaders to discuss constitutional reforms, dominion status and future independence for India. These started in November 1930 and ended in December 1932.

Shell-shock: Combat-related post-traumatic stress disorder. The WW1 poet Siegfried Sassoon described Army medics urging affected soldiers to repress their memories, shake themselves out of depression, and carry on manfully.

SIS: The Secret Intelligence Service is the foreign intelligence service of the United Kingdom. Whilst it incorporates MI6, it is tasked mainly with the covert overseas collection and analysis of human intelligence in support of the UK's national security.

SMAC: Spanish Medical Aid Committee. Within weeks of

the outbreak of the Spanish Civil War, the Spanish Medical Aid Committee was formed to provide practical medical aid and to act as a demonstration of international solidarity with the Spanish Republican government.

Socialist: Believer in state ownership and democratic control of the means of production.

SOE: Special Operations Executive was a secret British World War II organisation formed in July 1940 under Minister of Economic Warfare Hugh Dalton MP and dissolved in 1947.

Spanish Civil War: Fought from 1936–1939. Republicans loyal to the left-wing "popular front" fought in alliance with anarchists, communists and local militias against an insurrection by the right-wing Nationalists allied with the Falangists, Monarchists and Conservatives. The latter were led by a military group under General Franco, and supported by German and Italian Fascists. It was seen as a struggle between peasants and landowners, dictatorship and democracy, fascism and communism. It was also a rehearsal for mass aerial bombing of cities during WW2.

Stalinist: Believer in the dictatorial government and policies implemented by Joseph Stalin in the Soviet Union from 1927 to 1953.

Trotskyite: Believer in the political ideology and branch of Marxism developed by Ukrainian-Russian revolutionary Leon Trotsky. His criticism of Stalin's excessive control of the Russian state was fatal. It led to his followers being persecuted, and his own assassination in exile by agents of his political rival Joseph Stalin.

TUC: Trades Union Congress is the national federation of trade unions in England and Wales, representing the majority of trade unions in the UK. The TUC disapproved of autonomous local committees and preferred centralised control. During the Spanish Civil War, it refused to support the NJCSR as it was a "united front" organisation, including the BCRS (British Committee for Refugees from Spain) and the SMAC (Spanish Medical Aid Committee) both of which had some Communist Party members.

WW1: World War One. Global war starting in Europe, lasting from 1914–18.

WW2: World War Two. Global war starting in Europe, lasting from 1939–45.

Yeomanry Regiments: Local regiments that formed the British Army reserve Territorial Force. At the start of WW1 in 1914 there were fifty-seven regiments and fourteen mounted brigades.

Author Biography

Roger Vlitos was born in New York to a French mother and Greek-American father. Educated in the USA, West Indies and UK he studied Fine Art, History of Art, and Photography in London, and English at Bristol University. Now naturalised as a British citizen, Roger has worked in marketing and has published illustrated non-fiction titles. A freelance writer and photographer for periodicals as diverse as *The Smithsonian Institute Magazine* and *Gardens Illustrated*, he has researched and written materials for The British Museum and Natural History Museum, London. In addition, he has undertaken teaching and part-time lecturing at the University of Bath and was curator of the Lord Berners Collection at Faringdon House. For the past seven years Roger has been curator and archivist at Buscot Park.

Index